SHELLEY'S MIRRORS OF LOVE

D1564578

SUNY Series in Psychoanalysis and Culture
Henry Sussman, Editor

SHELLEY'S MIRRORS OF LOVE

Narcissism, Sacrifice, and Sorority

TEDDI CHICHESTER BONCA

State University of New York Press

The publishers have generously given permission to quote from the following copyrighted work: *The Palm at the End of the Mind: Selected Poems and a Play* by Wallace Stevens, ed. Holly Stevens. Copyright © 1967, 1969, 1971 by Holly Stevens. Reprinted by permission of Alfred A. Knopf, Inc. and Faber and Faber Limited.

Published by
State University of New York Press, Albany

© 1999 State University of New York

Printed in the United States of America

For information, address State University of New York Press,
State University Plaza, Albany, N.Y. 12246

Production by M. R. Mulholland
Marketing by Dana E. Yanulavich

Library of Congress Cataloging-in-Publication Data

Bonca, Teddi Chichester, 1960–
    Shelley's mirrors of love : narcissism, sacrifice, and sorority /
Teddi Chichester Bonca.
        p.   cm. — (SUNY series in psychoanalysis and culture)
    Includes bibliographical references (p. 295) and index.
    ISBN 0-7914-3977-1 (hc : acid-free paper). — ISBN 0-7914-3978-X
(pb : acid-free paper)
    1. Shelley, Percy Bysshe, 1792–1822—Knowledge—Psychology.
2. Psychoanalysis and literature—England—History—19th century.
3. Shelley, Percy Bysshe, 1792–1822—Psychology. 4. Poets,
English—19th century—Psychology. 5. Gender identity in
literature. 6. Poetry—Psychological aspects. 7. Self-sacrifice in
literature. 8. Narcissism in literature. 9. Sisters in literature.
10. Love in literature. I. Title. II. Series.
PR5442.P74B66 1999
821'.7—dc21   98-6222
                                                                            CIP

10 9 8 7 6 5 4 3 2 1

For Cornel

Light of Life

CONTENTS

PREFACE

In his essay "On Love," Percy Shelley writes of an "ideal prototype" within us, a miniature being within our being that allows us to discover, or at least to search out, a corresponding being who will love and be loved. At one point in the essay, Shelley calls the prototype "a mirror whose surface reflects only the forms of purity and brightness." The metaphor of a mirror was a favorite of Shelley, and in this essay, as elsewhere in the poet's writing, it shimmers with multiple images, multiple meanings. The mirror's position *within* us initially suggests the kind of self-adverting gaze associated with the narcissist, and "On Love" has certainly been read as an endorsement of, and an exercise in, self-love. Yet Shelley maintains that only "forms of purity and brightness" appear on this mirror's surface. With its emphasis on sympathy, connection, relation, the essay implicitly denies that the self-enclosed, isolated narcissist will be, *could* be one of those splendid forms. This Shelleyan mirror will show us the face of Love, not the visage of Self.

"On Love" was written in 1818, yet its concerns and tensions, as well as its imagery, pervade even the earliest of Shelley's writings. These writings take us back to the poet's boyhood home, Field Place, perhaps glimpsed in "On Love" as that "Paradise which pain and sorrow and evil dare not overleap." The letters, novels, and poems that Shelley wrote before his final expulsion from his Eden reveal how essential, even primal the battle between Selfhood—confining, contaminating, destructive—and Love—sympathetic, self-sacrificing, redemptive—was for the poet. Communion with a beloved circle of sisters, first love and first loss, and an initiation into the worlds of intellect and imagination—these experiences from the Field Place period all shaped the ways that Shelley would view the irreconcilable demands of Love and the Self.

The face of Love that Shelley most cherished belonged to a beautiful sister-spirit, purified of all Selfhood, glowing with sweetest sympathy. It was in the mirror of her eyes that Shelley hoped to see himself—transformed by her loving presence and kindled by her radiant femininity. Though the Shelleyan sister-spirit is in many ways a mythic creature, we can discern beneath her luminous veil the contours of some very real young women: Shelley's own sisters and the beautiful cousin, Harriet Grove, to whom the young poet was engaged. These women emerge from the study at hand as compelling figures, both in their own right and as they illuminate the actual and textual presences of women who later entered Shelley's life, most important, Harriet Westbrook Shelley and Mary Wollstonecraft Shelley. Thus Field Place, its sororal ambience and the texts it inspired, will be the center but not the confines of the book.

Because they emanate directly from the critical period of Shelley's adolescence, when Shelley lost his place within his sororal paradise, lesser-known works such as *Zastrozzi*, *The Wandering Jew*, and poems from the *Victor and Cazire* volume receive particular attention. Another neglected volume, *The Esdaile Notebook*, written in the aftermath of this crisis, is also key. These early texts shed new light on the ways that Shelley grapples with the problems of the Self and the complexities of Love in the works of his maturity. *Laon and Cythna* and *Prometheus Unbound* will be the central poems in this respect.

As this book is organized thematically rather than strictly chronologically, it at times circles back to certain biographical episodes and literary texts. Each chapter examines several texts through the prism of a specific theme, so I revisit a number of works—and biographical incidents—as the study unfolds. Shelleyan love is truly a many-sided mirror, and I hope to peer into both its brightest and its most obscure surfaces.

It is a pleasure finally to thank those people who have helped me write this book. As an undergraduate at the University of California, Santa Barbara, I was lucky to have a number of superb professors whose voices I still hear as I read great passages of literature—and as I attempt to do these texts justice in the classroom and in my own writing. Patrick McCarthy, Lee Bliss, and Garrett Stewart were especially inspiring, and particularly kind to me. To Donald Pearce I owe my introduction to the romantic writers. His teaching was enthusiastic in the truest and best sense; in his classroom, we were all lifted into the heady regions of Blake's prophesies and Keats's dream visions, and it was sometimes hard to return to our sole selves and mundane concerns.

At the University of California, Los Angeles, I was equally fortunate. Frederick Burwick and Paul Sheats, wonderful teachers and scholars, were invaluable guides as I steered toward this project in my early years of graduate school. I thank them, as well as Janet Hadda and Kathleen Komar, for serving as dissertation advisors.

I owe special thanks to Anne Mellor, who generously served as chair of my dissertation committee and even more generously read this book in its various stages thereafter. My ideas about Percy Shelley first took shape in her classroom and in conversations with her. Our views of this poet were often quite different, yet she always encouraged me to pursue my own vision. Her advice, her support, and her friendship mean a great deal to me.

My colleagues at UCLA Writing Programs have also been gracious in their interest and encouragement. Cheryl Giuliano, Jennifer Westbay, and

Bruce Beiderwell deserve special mention. Offering practical and moral support, they, along with Jennifer Michel, Mitzi Myers, and Patricia Gilmore, were especially good to me during the final hectic weeks of the project.

The advice and insights of Kathleen Lundeen, Anthony Harding, Beth Lau, and Victoria Myers have also found their way into the book. I could not have asked for a more attentive, sensitive, and shrewd audience than the anonymous readers at State University of New York Press. I feel very lucky indeed to have worked with James Peltz, my editor at State University of New York Press. His professional acuity and personal warmth are both extraordinary. I am also grateful to Megeen Mulholland, the Press's production editor, for her ingenuity and hard work, as well as to Camille Hale, who meticulously copyedited my manuscript, as well as created the index.

I thank the *Keats-Shelley Journal* and its editor, Steven Jones, for allowing me to reprint as part of chapter 3 "Shelley's Imaginative Transsexualism," *KSJ* 45 (1996): 77–101.

This book was completed only because I had friends and family who gave me the confidence to go on with the work—and who gave me the *opportunity* to do so. My parents, Ben and Nadine Chichester, continue to exemplify selfless love—for each other and for their family. I thank my sister, Lauri Chichester-Taylor, for her humor, patience, and affection. Good friends such as Lisa Maynord, Jennie Welsh, Julie Giese, Kimberly Monda, Robert Metzger, Jodi Johnson, Laurence Roth, Suzanne Greenberg, and Michael Smith helped keep me focused—and helped me look away from the work and enjoy the pleasures of conversation and companionship. Yvette Flaherty and Fern Rouintree provided secure and loving child care as I wrote. Two dear women, Alice Johnson and Jean Luce Lee, gave me solace and perspective when I most needed them.

To my sons, Alexey and Nicolai, I owe joys I never could have imagined. Daily you give me, as Shelley writes in *The Sensitive-Plant*, "love, and beauty, and delight." I save my most heartfelt thanks for last. To my husband, Cornel Bonca, I dedicate this book. Your love and your light more than anything else inspired this project and allowed it to be written. In many ways acknowledgments are also apologies. If I may presume to quote again from Shelley, "The toil which stole from thee so many an hour / Is ended." I look forward to recompensing you in full.

TEXTS AND ABBREVIATIONS

Unless otherwise indicated, my text for Shelley's works will be the Norton Critical Edition, *Shelley's Poetry and Prose*, ed. Donald H. Reiman and Sharon B. Powers (New York: Norton, 1977). I will occasionally abbreviate this text as *NCE*. Other essential editions used and their abbreviations appear below.

Bodleian I   *The Bodleian Shelley Manuscripts—Vol. I. Peter Bell the Third* and *The Triumph of Life*. Ed. Donald H. Reiman. New York and London: Garland Publishing, Inc., 1986.

CW   *The Complete Works of Percy Bysshe Shelley*. Ed. Roger Ingpen and Walter E. Peck. 10 vols. London: Ernest Benn; New York: Scribner's, 1926–1932 (Julian Edition).

Esdaile   *The Esdaile Notebook: A Volume of Early Poems*. By P. B. Shelley. Ed. Kenneth Neill Cameron. New York: Knopf, 1964.

JMS   *The Journals of Mary Shelley 1814–1844*. Ed. Paula R. Feldman and Diana Scott-Kilvert. 2 vols. Oxford: Clarendon Press, 1987.

LMWS   *The Letters of Mary Wollstonecraft Shelley*. Ed. Betty T. Bennett. 3 vols. Baltimore: Johns Hopkins University Press, 1980–1988.

L   *The Letters of Percy Bysshe Shelley*. Ed. Frederick L. Jones. 2 vols. Oxford: Clarendon Press, 1964.

Notopoulos   Notopoulos, James A. *The Platonism of Shelley: A Study of Platonism and the Poetic Mind*. Durham, N.C.: Duke University Press, 1949.

PS   *The Poems of Shelley*. Vol I. Ed. Geoffrey Matthews and Kelvin Everest. New York: Longman, 1989.

Prose   *The Prose Works of Percy Bysshe Shelley*. Vol. I. Ed. E. B. Murray. Oxford: Clarendon Press, 1993.

SC   *Shelley and His Circle, 1773–1822*. Ed. Kenneth Neill Cameron (vols. I–IV) and Donald H. Reiman (vols. V–VIII). Cambridge: Harvard University Press, 1961–1986.

Clark   *Shelley's Prose: The Trumpet of a Prophecy*. Ed. David Lee Clark. London: Fourth Estate, 1988.

Individual Works

Defence	*A Defence of Poetry*
Epi.	*Epipsychidion*
"Hymn"	"Hymn to Intellectual Beauty"
JM	*Julian and Maddalo*
LC	*Laon and Cythna; or, The Revolution of the Golden City*
PU	*Prometheus Unbound*
QM	*Queen Mab*
RH	*Rosalind and Helen: A Modern Eclogue*
SI	*St. Irvyne; or, The Rosicrucian: A Romance*
S-P	*The Sensitive-Plant*
TL	*The Triumph of Life*
Witch	*The Witch of Atlas*
WJ	*The Wandering Jew; or the Victim of the Eternal Avenger*
"WW"	"Ode to the West Wind"

INTRODUCTION:
THE PRINCIPLE OF SELF AND
LOVE'S TRANSFORMING PRESENCE

The partaker partakes of that which changes him.
The child that touches takes character from the thing,
The body, it touches. The captain and his men

Are one and the sailor and the sea are one.
Follow after, O my companion, my fellow, my self,
Sister and solace, brother and delight.

—Wallace Stevens

At the structural and spiritual center of Stevens's *Notes Toward a Supreme Fiction* we find these "romantic intoning[s]," this superb vision of mutuality, unity, and love that harks back to the fluid, intermingling worlds and selves of another supreme fiction-maker, P. B. Shelley, whose sublimely egotistical command in "Ode to the West Wind" Stevens parodies a bit later in his poem:

Bethou me, said sparrow, to the crackled blade,
And you, and you, bethou me as you blow,
When in my coppice you behold me be.

(219, 214, 220)

A loving and exacting critic of his precursor, Stevens knew how easily partaker becomes merely a taker when otherness and selfhood become almost indistinguishable, when fellow and self, sister and brother become one in the way Shelley so often longed for them to do. As Harold Bloom, working with Martin Buber's model of I-Thou relation, points out, psychic fusion—as opposed to interchange—may in fact become "communion of an I with an I . . . selfhood-communion" that simply leaps over rather than respects "the gap between I and Thou" (*Shelley's Mythmaking* 211, 219). Such a self-contemplating singer is Stevens's static, aggressively absorbing sparrow. Embracing and imposing being disguised as becoming, uniformity disguised as unity, this "tireless chorister" is "a bird / Of stone, that never changes," though it poses as an evangelist of commingling selves, a role that Shelley himself relished (*Notes* 220–21).

Those Shelleyan imaginings that correspond to, and perhaps inspired, the Stevens passage that I have quoted as my epigraph include the "mutual atmosphere" created within the "garden sweet" of *The Sensitive-Plant* (I. 69; Conclusion, l. 17), the dynamically interpenetrating cosmos of *Prometheus Unbound* IV, and the interacting self and "surrounding universe" celebrated in the essay "On Life" (477). However, the "granite monotony" of the sparrow's "bethous" comments on the outbreaks of solipsism in the guise of communion that mar some of Shelley's most potentially expansive visions (*Notes* 220). But as both poets knew, these seemingly opposed conceptions of selfhood (as partaking and as simply taking) in reality form a kind of continuum that may prevent us—that is, both poet and reader—from distinguishing between genuinely sympathetic exchange and what Shelley calls in an early letter "delirious egotism" (*L*, I, 34).

Percy Shelley, the man and the poet, has undergone countless transformations as, every few years, a new group of readers, including professional critics, grapples with his personal and artistic legacy. Yet one of Shelley's countless incarnations has demonstrated tremendous staying power. Denounced by the poet's own contemporaries, Shelley the delirious egotist, or "narcissist," has become especially conspicuous in recent years, as feminist critics in particular began scrutinizing the poet and his romantic brethren. Sexist as well as self-involved, the Shelley who emerged during the last decade or so often seems as blithely, and blindly, egotistical as Stevens's obnoxious sparrow.[1]

The debate over whether Shelley practiced and preached sublime (or ridiculous) egotism and sexism or unselfishness and feminism still rages, both in the classroom and in scholarship.[2] I do not claim that the present study will settle the matter, but I do want to assert that Shelley had much more self-awareness regarding these conflicting stances than either his defenders or detractors acknowledge. In fact, the narcissistic Shelley is largely a creature of the poet's own invention, a sometimes hideous progeny of his own pressing need to examine, to indulge, and, most important, to eradicate "the dark idolatry of self" (*CW*, I, 362: *LC*, VIII. 192).

While gender-based criticism continues to help us see how entangled Shelley's so-called narcissism and his attitudes toward women really are, I want to put the latter issue on hold and look more closely at what he calls in *A Defence of Poetry* "the principle of Self." Despite the rather abstract nature of this phrase, the problem of Self remained a deeply personal one for the poet, who struggled since boyhood not simply to understand the Self's various manifestations but also to purge it from his own consciousness, his own experience.

It is appropriate, therefore, that the earliest extant version of this key phrase appears in an emotional, starkly confessional letter. Written to his bosom friend Thomas Jefferson Hogg on New Year's Day 1811, this is the same letter that refers to "delirious egotism," or rather, to "*my* delirious egotism" (*L*, I, 34, emphasis mine). This and other letters of the same period allow us to witness Shelley engaging in what will become his greatest and most artistically fruitful psychomachia, a battle whose contestants are, to cite from the January 1 letter, "that *hateful* principle . . . *self*" and "Love! dear love," be it philanthropic, erotic, spiritual, familial, or, so often for the poet, a compound of them all (*L*, I, 34, italics Shelley's). While the eighteen-year-old Shelley, "sick to Death at the name of *self*," attempts to bid "adieu to egotism," the spectre of (his own) Selfhood continued to captivate, even obsess him for the rest of his life.

Influenced by the Christian tradition of self-denial and by moral philosophers such as Shaftesbury, Hutcheson, Hume, Smith, and Godwin, Shelley regarded self-transcendence, with its concomitant power of sympathy, as man's highest good.[3] As he asserted in the journal that he shared with Mary Godwin during their early years together, "the most exalted philosophy, the truest virtue consists in an habitual contempt of self" (*JMS* 36). The primary obstacle to social, political, and personal reform, the Self as Shelley perceived it was the cornerstone of oppressive regimes, religious intolerance, and familial/marital tyranny. In the *Defence* and throughout his poems, essays, and letters, the baneful principle of Self, the Mammon of the world, stands opposed to the divine power of poetry and to the "transforming presence" of Love (*PU*, I. 832).[4] Both a psychological "drive"—or *demon*—and an external spiritual force, the Shelleyan principle of Self emerges as a kind of primeval power bent on infecting the human imagination as well as spreading "the contagion of the world's slow stain" (*Adonais*, l. 356).

Except for rare instances, such as the "Self-esteem" bestowed by Intellectual Beauty, the word *self* (often capitalized) holds a dishonorable place in the Shelleyan lexicon ("Hymn," l. 37). Throughout his writings, beginning with his earliest letters, the poet uses this term to invoke a whole host of ills. For Shelley, aggression, acquisitiveness, revenge, and lust were among the most grotesque offspring of the Self; while vanity, egotism, jealousy, and "mere" selfishness proved to be the Self's ostensibly innocuous, and thus more insidious, spawn. Finally, so pressing was the poet's desire to annihilate (his own) Selfhood, that even personal identity, individuality often became suspect.[5]

I would like to return for a moment to Bloom and his Buberian analysis of Shelley before sketching the contours of my own argument. While Bloom rightly distinguishes between (self-other/I-Thou) relationship and coalescence, his somewhat rigid adherence to Buber's undeniably compelling paradigm prevents him from considering Shelley's artistic representations of merger—in *Epipsychidion*, for instance—as part of the poet's mythmaking enterprise. In devaluing Shelley's depictions of fusion in favor of those suggesting relation, he implies that the self's merger with its other necessarily entails "selfhood-communion." Thus he, and many other readers with very different critical agendas, disregards the possibility of, and profound wish for, loss of self in the other, loss of the "I" altogether that dwells within Shelley's writings. The poet's psychic and artistic strategies for achieving such a loss, whether through empathic and/or erotic mingling or through more radical, violently imaginative means, will be the focus of this study.

In an omnibus review of recent Shelley scholarship, Richard Holmes identifies a critical approach to the poet's life and work that closely resembles my own. Holmes calls this new way of reading Shelley "microbiography," which he defines as "the examination in detail of a fragment of life, which bears a significant relation to the whole" ("He Doth Not Sleep" 20).[6] The "fragment of life" that I have found most fascinating and most crucial occurs during the poet's late adolescence, when Shelley suffered a devastating rejection—at the hands of his beautiful and slightly older cousin, Harriet Grove, to whom he had been informally engaged. Though the problem of Self had concerned the young poet well before Harriet's final break with him, it was from the wreck of his first love affair that Shelley first struggled to create a doctrine of love that absolutely precludes egocentrism. He also began at this time to fashion—or, rather, to attempt to fashion—for himself and for his fictive surrogates what can only be called a "selfless identity," complete with a martyr-like devotion to the "Spirit of love" (*S-P*, I. 6).

A number of quintessentially Shelleyan figures emerged from this emotional crisis and its aftermath, figures that would play prominent roles both in the poet's best known and in his more obscure writings. Villains, protagonists, and personae, these children of his fertile (or fevered) imagination allowed Shelley, sometimes within the same work, to plunge into "the little world of self," to cleanse himself of its "dull vapours," and even to become the radiant exemplar of self-abnegating Love (*Defence* 497). This last achievement is particularly important to a poet who not only wrestled with his own private demons but who also, in Stephen Behrendt's words, "envisioned a public career of conversion" (*Shelley and His Audiences* 55).

The "missionary zeal" that Behrendt highlights in his excellent study brings us to the most compelling and complex figure in Shelley's psychic and evangelistic battle against tyrannous Self: the "love-devoted" martyr (*Shelley and His Audiences* 3; *JM*, l. 373). Paradoxically selfless and self-advertising, the Shelleyan martyr generates, I believe, from the poet's profound—and profoundly vexed—relationship with the radically self-sacrificing Christ. This relationship, or, more accurately, identification, with the martyred Christ greatly illuminates Shelley's (and his protagonists') notoriously narcissistic tendencies.

Even at an early age, as Bryan Shelley has shown, the poet was steeped in Scripture. And he took very seriously Jesus' admonition, "If any man will come after me, let him deny himself, and take up his cross, and follow me" (Matthew 16:24). From boyhood, Shelley largely modeled his own struggle for self-renunciation on the Passion of Christ. And though his mission and message were anything but conventionally Christian, Shelley also patterned the "career of conversion" that Behrendt examines after that of the charismatic prophet-teacher who gathered about him a band of loyal disciples. For the young Shelley, this vital group consisted of his four younger sisters and his beloved cousin Harriet, "sister-spirits" whom he "Deistif[ied]" and dosed with radical philosophy—that is, until Harriet's parents in late 1810 put a stop both to Percy's proselytizing and to the cousins' engagement (*CW*, II, 382: "Fragments Connected with *Epipsychidion*," l. 173; *L*, I, 42). Perhaps most galling to Shelley was the fact that it was Harriet herself, alarmed by her fiancé's increasingly bold impieties, who informed on him and then willingly withdrew from his intimate circle. The circle dissolved altogether when Percy's best-loved sister Elizabeth also retreated from him—and back into orthodoxy—during the spring of 1811.

As Holmes points out, Shelley's letters, including the impassioned New Year's letter quoted earlier, became "almost pathologically unhinged" during this tumultuous time ("He Doth Not Sleep" 22). Breathless and chaotic, these letters, written to his primary confidant Thomas Hogg, are full of hurt, despair, avowals of self-abnegation (sometimes coupled with threats of suicide), maudlin verse, and, most conspicuously, rage. Remarkably, this rage is not directed at Harriet Grove or even at her family, nor does it target Shelley's sister Elizabeth, though her abandonment of him was at least as painful as Harriet's. Instead, the spurned lover (and brother) reserves his ire for Christ himself, once the highest embodiment of Love and Self-conquest and now "this horrid Galilean," a hated rival who has lured the young poet's beloved women (back) into his fold (*L*, I, 66). My first chapter employs psychoanalyst Heinz Kohut's theory of narcissistic wounds and his concept of the self's merger with idealized others as it examines the ways that Shelley's ardent relationship with Christ swings wildly between extravagant hatred and intense love/identification in the wake of what we might call "the Harriet Grove crisis." This chapter explores how the poet's thwarted and distorted connection with Jesus seems to have resulted in the strident self-concern or "unmodified narcissism"—Shelley's own or that of his martyr-heroes—which Kohut links with the unavailability of the idealized figure to the aspiring, developing self ("Narcissism and Narcissistic Rage" 364).

From the Shelleyan martyr, who at least *claims* to be Love- rather than Self-devoted, we turn to a more straightforward incarnation of Selfhood within the Shelley canon. Chapter 2 focuses on the figure of the dark double, whose initial fascination for the poet coincided with his impending and then his actual loss of Harriet (and of Elizabeth). Like Blake, Shelley knew the temptations and dangers of becoming a "self-closed," "self-contemplating shadow," and his various fictive *Doppelgänger* allowed him both to indulge and to discipline those deadly Self-engendered impulses that he first confronts in the correspondence and creative works of 1810 and 1811. The Gothic villain Zastrozzi and his better-known heirs, Othman, from *Laon and Cythna*, and *Prometheus Unbound*'s Jupiter, served in part as conduits through which Shelley could discharge (his own) aggression, bile, and self-pity, while at the same time distancing himself and his more respectable surrogates from such tendencies by punishing the transgressive shadow figure.

Freud's comments on doubling in "The 'Uncanny'" help illuminate how displacement and discipline govern the gloomy world of the Shelleyan *Doppelgänger*. Consulting and elaborating on Otto Rank's *Der Doppelgänger*, Freud first looks at the double as "an insurance against the destruction of the ego, an 'energetic denial of the power of death,' as Rank says." He then continues:

> Such ideas, however, have sprung from the soil of unbounded self-love, from the primary narcissism which dominates the mind of the child and of primitive man. But when this stage has been left behind, the "double" reverses its different aspect. From having been an assurance of immortality, it becomes the uncanny harbinger of death.
>
> The idea of the "double" does not necessarily disappear with the passing of primary narcissism, for it can receive fresh meaning from the later stages of the ego's development. A special agency is slowly formed there, which is able to stand over against the rest of the ego, which has the function of observing and criticizing the self and of exercising a censorship within the mind, and which we become aware of as our "conscience." (*SE*, XVII, 235)

Certainly such figures as Zastrozzi, Jupiter, and Shelley's own visionary double bending over Mary's bed and strangling her serve as "uncanny harbinger[s]"—and agents—of death.[7] They also signal another kind of psychic division in Shelley and his fictional heroes, the kind which Freud identifies with the formation of the conscience. Thus these *Doppelgänger* allow the poet both to imaginatively enact and to censor the most destructive of Self-created scenarios.

However, it is when we turn to the notion of "primary narcissism" that we discover what is perhaps the central function of the *Doppelgänger* in Shelley's thought: the pledge of good faith in his problematic commitment to the paradigm of a fluid, sympathetically bonded universe, a universe in which the borders between self and other, I and Thou remain blurred or disappear altogether. While Freud, in *Civilization and Its Discontents*, links primary narcissism with the maligned "oceanic feeling" in religious, romantically involved, and/or deluded individuals, psychologist-sociologist Nancy Chodorow sees primary narcissism—or "primary identification"—in more positive terms as the infant's state of undifferentiation "between the 'I' and the 'not-I,'" a state that serves as a crucial precursor to love and empathy (*Reproduction of Mothering* 61).[8] The conviction of unity upon which Freud and Chodorow, in very different ways, comment pervades Shelley's remarks on childhood sensations and adult reverie in his 1819 essay "On Life." As children, Shelley writes, "we less habitually distinguished all that we saw and felt from ourselves. They seemed as it were to constitute one mass" (477). He then goes on to describe the sense of utter continuity with the world that those subject, like himself, "to the state called reverie" enjoy: they "feel as if their nature were dissolved into the surrounding universe, or as if the surrounding universe were absorbed into their being. They are conscious of no distinction" (477). Here we find the Shelleyan loss of self and sublime egotism in a rare, perfectly balanced marriage: his highest, elusive ideal of "unremitting interchange" between self and other ("Mont Blanc," l. 39).

But the notion of a primal unity within "one mind" of "*I, you, they*" that Shelley sets forth in this essay in fact presents him with a knotty problem: too many of the "you's" and "they's" with whom one might "commingle," to use a favorite Shelleyan term, seem to inspire loathsome rather than loving sympathy and to place the "I" in a psychically vulnerable position as a recipient of their noxious atmosphere ("On Life" 477–78).[9] Moreover, if we harbor within ourselves such deadly, Self-spawned vipers as hate, pride, and lust, we exude—according to the model of mutually interpenetrating beings—a "killing air" that literally influences those around us (*Epi.*, l. 263). This thrusts us into the role of agent rather than victim of the contamination, invasion, and infection which compromise the underside of the process, the transference or "becoming-other," in Jerrold E. Hogle's terminology, that Shelley depicts throughout his writings (*Shelley's Process* 18). While Hogle's Shelley emerges as an exemplar and celebrant of radically "relational thinking" and being (27), I see real suspicion, and even terror, on the poet's part that this process may be a dangerously promiscuous one. In order truly to embrace the egalitarian concept of an interconnected world, Shelley had to confront the darker shadings of his vision. This involved confronting his own kinship with even the most repulsive of beings, and thus, like Prospero, to declare of a Caliban, a Jupiter, even a Count Cenci, "[T]his thing of darkness I / Acknowledge mine" (Shakespeare, *The Tempest*, V. i. 278–79), or more radically, "I acknowledge *me*." The poet's demonic doubles—icons of Selfhood, purveyors of contagion—thus compel him to identify not only with the beautiful but also with the grotesque "which exists in thought, action, or person, not [his] own"—as well as to face his own complicity in such corruption (*Defence* 487).

The problem of gender, touched on earlier, is central to my analysis of Shelleyan *Doppelgänger* and of another, very different sort of double that haunted the poet's imagination. The malevolent *Doppelgänger* examined in chapter 2 and the loving "second self," focus of my third chapter, reveal how the poet saw both Selfhood and Love in gendered terms. For Shelley, the principle of Self was a masculine one, allied with patriarchal tyranny and rapacity and with male aggression and violence, particularly the sexual violence inflicted by the poet's most famous fictive *Doppelgänger*: Jupiter and Count Cenci. Shelley's ideal embodiments of Love, on the other hand, were always feminine, though not always female. In fact, Shelley's most important feminine archetype was arguably the suffering, compassionate, and maternal Christ. Introduced in chapter 1 and emerging at various points throughout the book, the feminized Christ, a shadowy figure in scriptural texts, came into sharp focus during the eighteenth- and nineteenth-century "feminization of religion" (Barker-Benfield xxvii).

Chapter 3, centering on the idealized second self, investigates how Shelley exploited the rather well-worn notion of feminine love and self-abnegation to create a variety of compelling heroines. These vibrant sister-spirits not only exemplify sympathy and loving self-sacrifice but also infuse their brother-lovers with their own womanly essence. Based on the poet's original band of sister-spirits, his Field Place coterie of cousin and sisters, these radiant figures help Shelley's heroes to defuse (their own) masculine, Self-serving impulses and, most important, to achieve a rather dramatic sexual crossover. Through a process of radical transsexualism, Shelley's male protagonists re-enter the feminine Eden that the poet himself lost during the eventful winter and spring of 1811.

Shelley's penchant for feminine second selves, both real and imaginary, has attracted quite a bit of (negative) critical attention in recent years. In fact, it is on his obsession with mirroring females that charges of narcissism have most often been based.[10] Just as the disturbing presence of the masculine *Doppelgänger* at times suggests the poet's imaginative capitulation to what in *Queen Mab* is termed "the sordid lust of self," his invocation of the sister-twin may signal a retreat from the world's chaos and contagion into the protective haven of narcissistic self-communion (*QM*, V. 90). But these readings of Shelley's doubles seem to me to be somewhat simplistic. If, in his most subtle and efficacious role, the baneful *Doppelgänger* allows (or forces) the poet into the sometimes muddied "streams of sympathy," the idealized second self lures him, and his heroes, away from Self and toward Love and sympathy in quite a different way (*Prose* 233: *On the Death of Princess Charlotte*). Ostensibly a shadow figure or flattering mirror, the Shelleyan sister-spirit in fact teaches her mate to overcome masculine Self-possession and to reflect her own feminine—and Christlike—virtues, including compassion, selflessness, and, of course, sympathy.

The power of sympathy is also central to my final two chapters, which explore what Shelley calls in his 1816 poem "The Sunset" "the unreserve of mingled being" (*PS*, I, 511). For Shelley, mingled being was the ultimate communion between self and other; it was a privileged state wherein lovers literally shared one another's "electric life," the sexual and sympathetic energy that, according to the science of the day, they exuded as a kind of electro-magnetic fluid (*Defence* 508). Shelley's 1819 lyric "Love's Philosophy" lightly and elegantly invokes the complete interfusion—physical, emotional, and spiritual—that this erotic union involves:

> The fountains mingle with the river,
>   And the rivers with the ocean;
> The winds of Heaven mix for ever
>   With a sweet emotion;
> Nothing in the world is single;
>   All things by a law divine
> In another's being mingle—
>   Why not I with thine?
>
> (*CW*, III, 299)

Couched in the language of courtly invitation, this charming lyric asks a crucial question in the guise of playful seduction, a question which the poet, not the coy mistress must answer. Shelley began to formulate his answer quite early on, in his adolescent fiction and poetry and in his remarkable correspondence with Hogg during the winter and spring of 1811. In these writings Shelley consistently, if regretfully, links sexual desire with the principle of Self—"I am afraid there is selfishness in the passion of Love"—and found it increasingly difficult to dissociate the two (*L*, I, 36). While, as a poem such as "Love's Philosophy" suggests, the natural world sets the standard for the kind of loving mutuality that Shelley idealized, genuine "commingling," the poet suspected, might prove too intimate, too "unreserved" for humanity to imitate.

Chapters 4 and 5 look into the kinds of obstacles and conditions Shelley creates in his own personal and artistic quest for the unreserve of mingled being. These chapters also uncover his strategies for excluding Self from the magic circles of (sexual) Love that he envisioned and experienced. First, chapter 4 takes us back to the Field Place of the poet's boyhood, where young Percy harnessed the wondrous power of electricity to create and join a scintillating band of sister-spirits, an archetypal circle which the poet constantly strove to recreate and whose erotic, sympathetic, and feminine energy the poet hoped to imbibe. These final chapters then move through three of Shelley's passionate attachments—to Harriet Grove, to Harriet Westbrook, and to Mary Godwin—as they explore how Shelleyan sex and sympathy pulse through various texts that clustered around these crucial relationships.

Through his imaginative identification with the various martyr-heroes, *Doppelgänger*, and sisterly second selves who people his poetic universe and who, for better or for worse, interpenetrate one another, Shelley enacts a moral drama that was both personal and universal. No struggle was more central to his life or to his work than that which pitted the demands of the Self against the claims of Love, and no vision was as passionately—if ambivalently—embraced as that of a world in which the streams of sympathy flowed unimpeded. His political opinions, his social theories, and his attitudes toward gender, sexuality, and sentimental love were all shaped and re-shaped by the ongoing dialectic that the powerful forces of Love and the Self created. As we look back to the seminal period of romantic despondency and artistic fruition that comprised the poet's nineteenth year, we can see the seeds of his mature thoughts on Love's dominion and the Self's dark idolatry spring forth. And as we watch the "busy phantoms" of mortal Selfhood perform their "ghastly dance" in Shelley's last great work, *The Triumph of Life* (ll. 534, 540), we can only guess whether they would encounter Love's transforming presence as they continue on their way.

1

SHELLEY, CHRIST, AND NARCISSUS

It has long been a commonplace among Shelley's readers that he hated the Christian religion but loved its originator. It has more recently become a critical commonplace that Shelley's life and writings betray a strong element of narcissism, a particularly insidious brand of narcissism which undervalues, appropriates, or altogether eliminates any (feminine) other whom the poet or his protagonist encounters. David Lee Clark's essay introduction to his collection of Shelley's prose, along with his introductions to many of the texts themselves, epitomizes the former stance: that Shelley easily and consistently made a neat distinction between the Christian doctrine, institution, and so-called practitioners on the one hand, and Jesus Christ himself on the other. Clark in fact repeatedly insists on this unproblematic separation between Church and Son as it supposedly existed within Shelley's own mind and writings.[1] Barbara A. Schapiro's chapter on Shelley in her study of "narcissistic patterns in Romantic poetry," *The Romantic Mother*, exemplifies the more recent trend in Shelley criticism: locate and denounce evidence of narcissism in the Shelley canon.[2]

The charge of narcissism, like that of sexism or racism, is often easy to make and even easier to resist examining—somehow the label seems enough. Yet it is crucial that we understand and not simply identify those undeniably narcissistic tendencies in Shelley's psyche, for, as Shelley himself knew, self-concern, if not self-love per se, continually prevented him from realizing what is arguably his most cherished artistic and personal goal: conceptualizing, representing, and participating in what he calls "consentaneous love" (*QM*, VIII. 108). I believe that the only way to get at the roots of Shelley's complex kinship with Narcissus is to recognize the poet's even more troublesome kinship with Narcissus' polar opposite, Christ, the great exemplar of selfless love who did not escape but in fact provoked and received much of the wrath that Shelley ostensibly reserved for the Christian church.

Shelley's obsession with Christ and his preoccupation with the clash between selfishness and love burst simultaneously onto the pages of his 1810 and 1811 letters to Thomas Hogg, letters that chronicle the most momentous rejection of the poet's life: the loss of his beautiful cousin Harriet Grove, with whom he was informally engaged.[3] Although, as her diary reveals, Harriet was in many ways an ordinary young woman transformed by her cousin's needs and desires into his muse and soul mate—a pattern he would repeat many more times—Shelley's love for her was obviously genuine. Moreover, the circumstances under which the engagement broke off and the fact that Harriet bore a remarkable resemblance to him converted this romantic disappointment into something of far greater impact on Shelley's theories of love and selfhood as well as on his actual relationships.

Neither Shelley's "narcissism" nor his vehement anti-Christianity is the product of a kind of spontaneous generation in the wake of lost love. But the fact that Harriet pulled away from him because of his alarming "speculations" seems both to have heightened his susceptibility to the temptations of Self and to have inflamed his budding skepticism about orthodox Christianity.[4] To begin with the former issue, the most notorious manifestation of Shelley's self-involvement is his penchant for his own (feminine) "twins," beginning with his look-alike sister Elizabeth and continuing with Harriet Grove and even Beatrice Cenci.[5] This emotional dynamic might have taken hold during early childhood as a mild form of narcissism, which was then exacerbated by his exile from the maternal and sororal circle when he was sent away to Syon House Academy in 1802. Kenneth Neill Cameron speaks of "a partial rejection of the boy by his mother," which perhaps helped create the poet's "phobia of the withdrawal of love (e.g. in *Alastor*)"—and, I would add, his need to create a series of self-imaging lovers, a pattern evident in the poem that Cameron cites (*Young Shelley* 4). Holmes pursues Cameron's line of thought, locating this "rejection" in the Syon House period: "From a few stray remarks in letters from Oxford, and from passing references by his cousin Tom Medwin and his undergraduate friend T. J. Hogg, we can gather that the feelings between mother and son were exceptionally close and warm up to the time that Shelley went to school. After this Shelley seems to have found his mother increasingly distant and unresponsive, and there are indications that he felt deeply rejected" (*Pursuit* 11).

However, Barbara Charlesworth Gelpi finds that the "mother-son alliance" (*Shelley's Goddess* 105) survived the Syon House "banishment," though she recognizes both Percy's sense of maternal "betrayal" in this matter and the deep ambivalences that permeated this intense relationship (101).[6] Both Christine Gallant's Jungian (and Kleinian) reading of the Mother-archetype in Shelley's work[7] and Gelpi's psychobiographical account of the Shelleys' actual mother-son bond emphasize maternal power and the fear—as well as the love—it inspires. Shelley's turning back toward the self and his proclivity for what Freud terms "narcissistic object-choice"[8] may have been the poet's response to the (perceived) withdrawal of his beautiful, vibrant mother, incarnation of the mythic Mother Goddess at the center of Gelpi's illuminating study. And Shelley's ethereal sisters of the soul, real and imagined, may be less threatening, less forbidden, so to speak, versions of the omnipotent and elusive mother.

To return to the period of the poet's late adolescence, Shelley's incipient tendency to replace his ambivalently loved mother with a sister-twin would receive a powerful catalyst in his adolescent losses of his closest female companions, Harriet and Elizabeth, whom he almost compulsively attempts to re-create in the idealized sister-lovers of his post-1810 writings. (Elizabeth retreated from Percy and his "deistifying" in the spring of 1811, if not earlier.) This mother-sister-cousin constellation crystallized not just within Percy's mind, for Harriet, daughter of Elizabeth Pilfold Shelley's *own* sister, had always been close to her "Aunt Shelley" and became an intimate friend and correspondent of young Elizabeth in the summer of 1809. The second poem in *Original Poetry by Victor and Cazire* is in fact a chatty and affectionate verse epistle from Elizabeth to her cousin, dated 30 April 1810 (*CW*, I, 7–9).

While the sources of Shelley's narcissistic tendencies remain somewhat obscure, it is much easier to pinpoint the beginnings of his anti-Christian views. The poet's questioning of Christianity began at least as early as his years at Syon House Academy (1802–1804), where a "choleric divine" and exposure to scientific thought "alienated him further from religious views" that were already fragile due to the superficial orthodoxy observed at Field Place, the Shelley home (Cameron, *Young Shelley*, 71). Percy's personal vendetta against Christ himself, though, seemed to begin only when his and Harriet's parents started interfering with the cousins' relationship in September 1809,[9] and it gained momentum after Harriet showed some of Shelley's impious letters to her father in the fall of 1810. Harriet, writes her brother Charles, "became uneasy at the tone of his letters on speculative subjects, at first consulting my mother, and subsequently my father also on the subject. This led at last . . . to the dissolution of an engagement between Bysshe and my sister, which had previously been permitted, both by his father and mine" (Hogg, II, 155). Thus such poems as "To Death" (1810) and particularly *The Wandering Jew* (1810), though written before the final break with Harriet early in 1811,[10] evince an increasing fascination with and hostility toward the person of Christ, whom Shelley will energetically curse for tearing "the dearest the tenderest of [his] ties" (*L*, I, 35: 3 January 1811).

It is in his remarkable, explosive series of letters written to his best friend, Hogg, between December 1810 and the summer of 1811, when Shelley eloped with Harriet Westbrook, that we can witness Shelley reviling Christ in one breath and taking up his cross in the next (and I would like that final pronoun to remain ambiguous). The venom with which the young poet lashes out at the "adversary" who, in Percy's mind, robbed him first of Harriet and then of Elizabeth, betrays his own intense emotional investment in and identification with this most despised and most exalted of men, the archetype of that selfless love that Percy himself so desperately wanted to embody (*L*, I, 29: 20 December 1810).[11] As early as his boyhood "conversion" to the "Spirit of BEAUTY," an epiphanic experience that both the "Hymn to Intellectual Beauty" and the dedication to *Laon and Cythna* commemorate, Shelley was actively cultivating his messianic impulses ("Hymn," l. 13). Declaring war against the world's "dark slavery," he apparently saw himself even then in overtly Christlike terms, as a "meek and bold" victim who is also a savior ("Hymn," l. 70; *CW*, I, 252: *LC*, Dedication, l. 36).[12]

More than just a role model, a Bloomian precursor, or a surrogate for his "Christian" father, Jesus comes closest for Shelley to what the twentieth-century psychoanalyst Heinz Kohut would designate a "selfobject" or what the nineteenth-century philosopher Søren Kierkegaard would call a "para-digm." Although, as Jane Rubin has pointed out, Kohut's "selfobject" and Kierkegaard's "paradigm" differ in some important ways[13]—as do their notions of identity—both terms imply a person with whom the self psychi-cally merges as it *becomes* that self.[14] For Kierkegaard, Christ is "*the* para-digm," he who "help[s] every man to become himself" when he "draw[s] all unto [Him]self" (111, 159).[15] For Kohut,[16] Christ embodies one version of the "idealized" selfobject of whose "omnipotence" the self can partake as it grat-ifies and, in turn, modifies "the grandiose self," the potential source of two quite different offspring: realistic self-esteem and excessive self-involvement, both of which became central concerns for Shelley during the Harriet Grove crisis.[17]

According to Kohut, the latter may emerge when the grandiose self is repressed or somehow denied access to the idealized selfobject. In effect, Shelley cut *himself* off from his own omnipotent selfobject, Christ. The Kohutian narrative would suggest that the poet thus "suppress[ed] the aspira-tions of the grandiose self"[18] which then turned inward and developed into immoderate narcissism. Actually, "narcissism" is a rather misleading term, especially when we consider Shelley's evident lack of authentic self-love or "self-devotion."[19] And Shelley certainly does not exude the kind of "bloated self-esteem" that, as Peter Gay points out, has become loosely synonymous with this word (340).

Freud's concept of "secondary narcissism" perhaps best approximates Shelley's own psychological pattern *and* the kind of egocentrism that he con-demned under the heading "principle of Self." To begin with, Freud posited a "primary narcissism," the "original libidinal cathexis of the ego" that defines the infant's state of fusion with the world, a kind of innocent egotism that precedes true object relations ("On Narcissism: An Introduction," *SE*, XIV, 75). We might think of Freud's second type as "fallen" narcissism, a retreat back into the self after the world of objects has been recognized and entered: "the narcissism which arises through the drawing in of object-cathexes [is] a secondary one, superimposed upon a primary narcissism" ("On Narcissism," *SE*, XIV, 75).[20] Freud's image of "the drawing in" of energy from the world, from others, provides a nice contrast with Shelley's own definition of Love in the *Defence* as "a going out of our own nature, and an identification of ourselves with the beautiful which exists in thought, action, or person, not our own" (487). For both Freud and Shelley, the coiling back into the self that characterizes (secondary) narcissism signals a lost connection with an "object-world" that is sometimes beautiful and sometimes bruising.

Kohut's model of a developing self-in-relation illuminates how a series of narcissistic injuries, which in Shelley's mind revolved around a complex configuration of loved ones (his mother, his favorite sister, his cousin, and Christ), culminated at a critical time in Shelley's emotional and intellectual development.[21] Freud and Kohut both trace what the latter calls "narcissistic vulnerability" to early childhood trauma, with Freud emphasizing the oedipal period and Kohut the preoedipal stage of the inchoate self.[22] According to Kohut, it is the (preoedipal) infant's harmonious interaction with "archaic selfobjects" (the parents themselves) that determines later selfobject relations—and that in effect *creates* the child's self, his or her sense of stability and cohesion. "Empathic failures" on the part of the parent(s)—or, more neutrally, a lack of "empathic resonance" between parent and child—can prevent such self-development and make the child particularly susceptible to severe narcissistic wounds in later life. Kohut's comments in his seminal essay "Thoughts on Narcissism and Narcissistic Rage" illuminate the psychological patterns that Shelley himself exemplifies:

> the vicissitudes of the early formation of the self determine the form and course of later psychological events which are analogous to the crucial early phase . . . certain periods of transition which demand from us a reshuffling of the self, its change and its rebuilding, constitute emotional situations which reactivate the period of the formation of the self.

Kohut then turns to one of these transitional phases:

> The psychopathological events of late adolescence . . . —I would call them the vicissitudes of self-cohesion in the transitional period between adolescence and adulthood—should neither be considered as occupying a uniquely significant developmental position, nor should they be explained primarily as due to the demands of this particular period. But an adolescent's crumbling self experience should in each individual instance be investigated in depth . . . What traumatic interplay between

parent and child (when the child began to construct a grandiose-exhibi-
tionistic self and an omnipotent self-object) is now being repeated?
(367, 368)²³

It is such "traumatic interplay"—missed connections, failures in empathy and
mirroring—that Shelley seems to have reexperienced (or reenacted, as
Freud's repetition-compulsion would suggest²⁴) during his own late-adoles-
cent crisis, a crisis which certainly inspired its share of narcissistic rage and
retreat.
    The narcissistic wounds—or "scars," as Freud calls them²⁵—that Shel-
ley received during the winter and spring of 1810–1811 would have been
unusually severe in that Shelley's mirroring sister and cousin, surrogates for
the original, maternal source of love, in essence threw him over for his own
idealized selfobject. Moreover, as former devotees of the young poet, Elizabeth Shelley and Harriet Grove not only had "mirrored" him in the more figurative (and psychoanalytic) sense of "confirming" or "approving," but had
become for Shelley "second selves"²⁶ who resembled him physically and, for
a time, ideologically.²⁷ Thus, their betrayal—and Shelley clearly regarded it as
such—took on the bizarre and particularly mortifying character of a self-
rejection. It is not surprising, then, that genuine "Self-esteem," the counterpart, not the obverse, of Love, would remain for Shelley an elusive gift, "for
some uncertain moments lent" by an "unseen" and "inconstant" Power, as he
would write in 1816 ("Hymn," ll. 37, 38, 1, 6).
    Moreover, though as Jerrold E. Hogle has argued, Shelley never con-
sidered personal identity as something stable or even desirable,²⁸ it is evident
that in the midst of the emotional upheaval that marked his nineteenth and
twentieth years, Shelley was engaged in his most self-conscious and strenuous struggle to "conceive" himself. At the core of his endeavor is his debate
with Hogg regarding the nature of love and self-sacrifice. While Kenneth
Neill Cameron has painstakingly demonstrated that Shelley's "genesis" as a
radical was a complex and gradual process, there is also something incredibly
Gatsby-like in the way that Shelley (re)invents himself during his late adolescence: if he did not quite "spring from the Platonic conception of himself," he
did become in his own mind "a son of God . . . [who] must be about His
Father's business," like Christ himself who renounced all blood ties as mean-
ingless (Fitzgerald 99).²⁹ To be more precise, as the self-styled "hapless victim of unmerited persecution,"³⁰ Shelley dispensed with Father—and father—
in order to confront directly the Son who embodied his greatest persecutor
and, as archetypal victim and incarnation of selfless love, provided him the
"pattern" for his own suffering, his own identity, *and* his own Self-abnegation.
    While dismissing a heavenly Father via a "systematic cudgel for Xian-
ity"³¹ seemed relatively easy for the young skeptic, bypassing "the 'pater'"

was another matter (*L*, I, 47); and Percy's oedipally tinged clashes with Timothy Shelley pervade the 1810 and 1811 letters and resonate throughout his writings, from *Zastrozzi* to *Adonais*. Moreover, his resentment of Christianity and of his father converge as Shelley metes out blame for his severance, first from Harriet Grove and later from his sister Elizabeth. Yet it would be a mistake to view Shelley's violent execrations of the "horrid Galilean" merely as displaced hatred of his father (*L*, I, 66: 24 April 1811). As Shelley's often high-spirited letters to Hogg reveal, Timothy Shelley and his "equine argument[s]" defending Christianity provoke in his son more satirical laughter than rage (*L*, I, 38). In a strange way during this chaotic period of late 1810 to early 1811, Shelley was attempting to wrest from his father not his mother, whom he had already in a sense "lost," nor his sisters, who were still in varying degrees under Shelley's spell, but rather Christ himself, victimized—like Shelley—by such "bigots" as the superficially Christian Timothy Shelley.

If Shelley sometimes seems to conflate his father, Christianity, and Christ in those "mad effusion[s]" to Hogg that lash out at his own "tormenters," he already has discerned in Christ a more worthy opponent and idealized selfobject, to return to Kohut's terminology, than the rather unimposing Timothy Shelley ever could be (*L*, I, 74). The volatile mix of rage and contempt that we observe in the poet's dealings with his father during and after the Harriet Grove crisis points to a much earlier—Kohut might say "preoedipal"—experience of massive disappointment in the parent who should in fact serve as an "omnipotent selfobject." (Shelley's creative and energetic attacks on his father—"old Killjoy"—throughout his 1811 correspondence resemble Kohut's notion "oedipal dramatizing" that masks deeper narcissistic disturbances ["Narcissism and Narcissistic Rage" 371].) Kohut speaks of "stand-ins for the archaic idealized figure," and for the young Shelley, the powerful, captivating figure of Christ may have emerged originally as a surrogate for an essentially "unidealizable" father ("Narcissism and Narcissistic Rage" 390).[32] The fact that Timothy Shelley promoted himself as an exemplary Christian certainly would have complicated matters; and it is intriguing to watch the young poet lecture his father on true "Christian forbearance & forgiveness," accusing Timothy of rank hypocrisy and presenting himself as the true Son (*L*, I, 140).[33]

It is difficult to discern the origins of Percy's intense identification with Jesus, but this hypocrisy, both on his father's part and in the wider social sphere, may give us a clue. As Bryan Shelley writes, "however little exposure Shelley may have had to an authentic form of Christianity at home, he would have had access to its main text" (21). The poet's "addiction to reading the Bible," as this critic accurately puts it (22), seems to have begun early on, offering the boy memorable glimpses of the "extraordinary person" and "vivid poetry" of Christ, not "distorted" by the system that bears his name

(*Defence* 495). It was against the background of this system, doggedly preserved by perfunctory Christians such as Timothy Shelley,[34] that the morally earnest and keenly imaginative boy read vivid scriptural accounts of Jesus' life and words—and death. Moreover, the Church of England itself was in a particularly sad state during Shelley's time. The Anglican church that Shelley would have known was, in Robert Ryan's words, "intellectually becalmed, spiritually desiccated, and aesthetically impoverished . . . [its] official spokesmen . . . worldly, self-serving chaplains to the status quo in a repressive society" (20–21).[35] The profound hollowness and secularity of the contemporary English church may have made the young poet even more sensitive to and protective of the spiritual and "poetic" essence both of the Bible and of the figure who for Shelley was its supreme genius.

In continually recreating—and reenacting—Christ's Passion, the poet Even the most savage of the adolescent Shelley's later diatribes against Christ strike one as oddly possessive—Shelley longed for "that imposter, Christ"[36] to be *his* to emulate, *his* to crucify, *his* to purify, *his* to resurrect.[37] Embroiled in his own fervent *imitatio Christi*, with its insistent flavor of "emulation opposite," the young atheist at one point assigns himself the double role of Antichrist and Christ, while the latter, in Shelley's tangle of inversions, becomes his own "mighty opposite," Satan crushed by the true Christ, P. B. Shelley: "Oh how I wish I *were* the Antichrist, that it were *mine* to crush the Demon, to hurl him to his native Hell never to rise again" (*L*, I, 35: to Hogg, 3 January 1811). The final infinitive phrase, to complicate matters further, denies Christ his greatest triumph, the Resurrection, and establishes the Shelleyan pattern of "containing" Christ within the parameters of his human suffering.[38] Shelley's is the gospel not of Christ risen but of Christ crucified, the Christ who, in "present[ing] [his] bod[y] as a living sacrifice, holy, acceptable unto God" (Romans 12:1), provided his young disciple/adversary the "paradigm" of glorious and agonized passivity that Shelley embraced as early as 1809 when he created the character of Verezzi.[39]

In continually recreating—and reenacting—Christ's Passion, the poet can both "do" and "suffer," a favorite Shelleyan dialectic that at times seems a twisted version of the maxim offered by Milton's Christ: "who best / Can suffer, best can do" (*Paradise Regained*, III. 194–95).[40] Almost an objective correlative of the poet's lifelong ambivalence to Christ, this interplay between doing and suffering in Shelley's writing enables him to play the kind of double part exemplified in the previously cited letter. Thus Shelley can "guide the spear to the breast of [his] adversary" in order to "ensanguine it with the hearts blood of Xt's hated name," while receiving that same spear into his own breast as he imaginatively fuses with the persecutor who is also his victim (*L*, I, 29: 20 December 1810). As the crudeness and often amusing fury with which Shelley attacks Christ disappears with the passing of the Harriet Grove crisis and his elopement with Harriet Westbrook, he developed more subtle techniques for punishing and emulating his rival, the idealized selfobject whom the poet in his late adolescence began imperiously to absorb. He would lay claim to Christ's martyrdom by linking it directly to himself or to his protagonists, who would then heroically "suffer," at the hands of those who "do": the split off but still potent pole of the poet's extreme ambivalence to "the cold Christians' blood-stain'd King of Kings" (*Esdaile* 38: "A Sabbath Walk").[41]

The exaltation of passivity in Shelley's works—and this includes the sexual passivity embodied by male protagonists such as the *Alastor* Poet and Prometheus—seems, then, to have its roots in Shelley's early fascination and identification with Jesus' passive, selfless suffering on the Cross. The poignant image of "a youth / With patient looks nailed to a crucifix" would always hold deep attractions for Shelley (*PU*, I. 584–85). In part because of the poet's own temperamental and even physical affinities with the feminine gender—the latter of which were evident in his "delicate and fragile" build, his "frail, feminine, flexible" face, and his high-pitched voice[42]—Christ's "womanly" mildness, "amiability,"[43] and passivity strongly appealed to Shelley. Moreover, at the same time that his desire to embody such qualities himself escalates (in proportion to his fear that "there is selfishness in the passion of Love" [*L*, I, 36]), so does his need to project them onto others increase in intensity. Such others include Harriet Grove, all of his young sisters, and eventually Harriet Westbrook, whose soul the newly wed Shelley will ask yet another of his female votaries—Elizabeth Hitchener—to "assist [him] to mould" (*L*, I, 13, 163).

Perhaps most audacious, though, are Shelley's attempts to "mould" Christ into his own image and likeness even as he endeavors to "follow" his predecessor onto the thorny path of self-denial. In light of Bloom's work on the *agon* with the precursor in which the "strong poet" must engage, Shelley's early 1812 project, the *Biblical Extracts*, with a hubristic Shelley in the self-appointed role of Christ's "editor," may strike us as an oedipally tinged enterprise. However, the two "strong poets" we are concerned with here do not quite fit the Bloomian profile of virile combatants engaged in "the crucial warfare of fathers and sons" (Gilbert and Gubar 47)—despite Bloom's caveat that if Freud's "is to serve as model for the family romance between poets, it needs to be transformed, so as to place the emphasis less upon phallic fatherhood, and more upon *priority*" (*Anxiety* 64).[44] Although Shelley in 1810 and 1811 regarded his "precursor" as a kind of romantic rival who lured from him his cousin and sister(s), he never saw Christ simply as a father figure to be toppled or even as a threatening masculine presence.[45] If, as Bloom claims, "all Romanticisms whatsoever, are quests to re-beget one's own self, to become one's own Great Original," Shelley's adolescent efforts at self-creation involve coalescing with a "Great Original" who resembled not so much the penetrating Father as the (traditionally) receptive, self-abnegating Mother (*Anxiety* 64).

In seeing Jesus as a feminine figure, Shelley was responding to a rich theological tradition. First of all there is the key Biblical text in which Jesus presents himself as a feminine—and maternal—figure: "O Jerusalem, thou that killest the prophets, and stonest them which are sent unto thee, how often would I have gathered thy children together, even as a hen gathereth her chickens under her wings" (Matthew 23: 37). Perhaps the most dramatic flowering of this theme appeared in the medieval devotion to a graphically maternal Christ. Carolyn Bynum's fascinating study *Jesus as Mother* examines what she calls the "affective spirituality of the high Middle Ages," expressed most explicitly in images of a pregnant and lactating Christ (80).[46] While the young Shelley probably had no direct knowledge of the devotional literature in question, the notion of a feminized Christ would certainly have been familiar. The "affective spirituality" that Bynum discusses had again taken root— this time in the England of Shelley's boyhood. As G. J. Barker-Benfield writes, the eighteenth century saw a "movement for the softening of God's face and the elevation of the suffering Son over the grim Father" (267). And the Son's suffering, and his love, was presented throughout the hymns and sermons of the period in overtly feminine terms. In the hymns of Charles Wesley, for example, Christ the tender Shepherd provides his needy flock with nurturing, consoling breasts and a sheltering womb.[47] That this womb is actually a wound—"the cleft of [Christ's] side"[48] received during the Crucifixion—suggests how Christ and/as woman contributed to the poet's idea(l)s of sacrifice, selflessness, and suffering.

When Christ dwells in Shelley's consciousness not simply as "that which injured me" but also as "the victim" of his own "severe anguish," he exerts the greatest influence on Shelley's self-conception (*L*, I, 32, 36). In taking Christ as his paradigm in the dual enterprise of fashioning a self and a viable doctrine of love, Shelley in effect attempts to create a "selfless identity." As the 1810 and 1811 letters to Hogg and, later, to Elizabeth Hitchener, dramatically disclose, Shelley at that time was simultaneously engaging in self-conception and *Selbsttödtung*, the "Annihilation of Self" that Carlyle would later extol as the prelude to good works and "Blessedness."

However, in Shelley's case, his willful and premature efforts to achieve selflessness, heartbreakingly earnest though they were, often brought him closer to Narcissus than to Christ. By setting up the rigid dichotomy between Self and Love, he forced himself into the position of radical self-abnegation à la Christ and such feminine exemplars of disinterested love as Shelley's favorite heroine, Antigone, and Eloisa, "who sacrificed all *self* for another" (*L*, I, 81). This dichotomy will at times evolve into a more fruitful dialectic—as in parts of the "Hymn to Intellectual Beauty," *Prometheus Unbound*, and the

Defence—but Shelley never lost his conviction that only "αφιλαυτια [lack of self-love]," which often comes perilously close to the "self-contempt" that Cythna warns against, can open the path to sympathetic love for others (*L*, I, 77; *CW*, I, 360: *LC*, VIII. 183). As the young Shelley systematically severed familial (and class) ties and fashioned himself into a liberal reformer and atheist, his feverish efforts not only to cleanse himself of "selfishness or interested ambition" (*L*, I, 30) but also to "divest [him]self of individuality"[49] may have prevented him from attaining the "self-cohesion" that according to Kohut's model helps avert regressive, immoderate narcissism (Kohut, *Seminars*, 51).

Thus, it is the figure of the humble yet exalted martyr—with his "imperial crown of agony" (*CW*, III, 11: *Prologue to Hellas*, l. 89) or her "strange ruin" (*Cenci*, IV. i. 26)—rather than the (masculine) lover in search of his (feminine) "antitype" or "epipsyche" that comprises the archetypal image of the Shelleyan "narcissist," an icon, like the hermaphrodite, of an uneasy marriage of opposites.[50] By embracing the stance of the martyr, Shelley can both assert and deny the self, as well as emulate and crucify the idealized selfobject who "betrayed" him. Moreover, those aspirations for selflessness that began to flourish with his first disappointment in (romantic) love and that spawned his martyr-like postures also gave rise to those attendant facets of his strange breed of narcissism: the urge to project the forbidden, necessarily imperfect self onto "a mirror whose surface reflects only the forms of purity and brightness" ("On Love" 474) and the desire to incarnate "the Spirit of love" itself (*S-P*, I. 6).

My third chapter will address the former issue, which involves Shelley's need to create for himself and his surrogates "sisters of the soul" with little independent status. I do, though, want to emphasize here that this tendency emerges not so much from some vague, universalized "masculine" appetite to devour or, as Alan Richardson puts it, "colonize" the feminine as it does from a particular set of circumstances in Shelley's life that culminated in his violent renunciation both of Christ and of (him)self. Bereft first of Harriet Grove and then of his favorite sister Elizabeth, Shelley in 1810 and 1811 was nursing real grief compounded by deep narcissistic wounds when he rejected as "*hateful*" the "principle of *self*" (*L*, I, 34) and spurned his own idealized selfobject, Christ. Thus, Shelley seems to have been left with an internal void—his "*lack* of self-love" (emphasis mine)—as well as with a gap in his object relations which he would desperately fill with female *and* male "others" such as T. J. Hogg, Elizabeth Hitchener, and Harriet Westbrook and, later, with Mary Wollstonecraft Godwin and her famous father. Upon discovering that "there is selfishness in this passion of Love" when he continued to covet his cousin's affections (*L*, I, 36), it seems that Shelley became convinced that he must "fear himself" before he could love others, others who would allow him to cultivate "Self-esteem" indirectly by reflecting back to him his purest, most beautiful qualities ("Hymn" ll. 84, 37).

We can then, I believe, trace a direct lineage from Shelley's adolescent struggles to eradicate or "abstract" self (*L*, I, 173) to the "psyche/epipsyche strategy" which Richard Isomaki acclaims as Shelley's "mature version of love" (661) and which many have deplored as codified narcissism and sexism. While the latter judgement may be the more accurate, Isomaki's word *mature* is suggestive, for such later works as "On Love" (1818) and *Epipsychidion* (1821) reveal the ingenuity with which the older Shelley developed a conception of sympathetic love which would reinstate the self that he had continually and futilely tried to banish and/or punish since his earliest attachment to Christ.[51] Selfhood threatens to return with a vengeance in these works via the narcissistic configuration of prototype and antitype, but essentially as the victim of "repulse and disappointment" ("On Love" 473) or, along with the beloved, "annihilation" (*Epi.*, l. 587). From selflessness back to selflessness: this is the cycle that produces and chastens Narcissus as he lurks in Shelley's consciousness.

Yet the postadolescent Shelley, still pursuing his Christlike goal of perfect "self conquest" (*L*, I, 180), not only devised a poetic strategy for indulging and then subduing his own "egotizing variability" (*L*, I, 44) but he also found a way to escape "the little world of self" by instead imaginatively *becoming* a "world of love" (*Defence* 497; *Epi.*, l. 346). When, for example, he calls his surrogate in *Adonais* "a Love in desolation masked"—properly endowed with Christ's "ensanguined brow"—Shelley ostensibly eliminates Self, which he consistently represents as the antithesis of Love (ll. 281, 305).[52] In fact, though, such a stance effectively obviates the *object* (the "other" as well as the aim) of love and allows the self to embody and monopolize a kind of directionless or inward-directed love.

Roland Barthes has written, "No one wants to speak of love unless it is *for* someone" (74), but as Shelley learned when Harriet Grove disappeared from his life, or, even earlier, when his mother appeared to withdraw her affection, that "someone" can be elusive, hurtful, and even provoke in the lover the very selfishness which Shelley valiantly tried to sequester from "devotement and love" (*L*, I, 183). Shelley's hubristic desire, then, not simply to express but to incarnate love—as Christ himself did—emerges from his attempts to envision and advocate "love *infinite in extent*, eternal in duration" (*L*, I, 35), a love that is purged of "the dull vapours of the little world of self" as well as of an other who would tempt one toward this dangerous morass. Along with his penchant for martyrdom and his (ambivalent) embrace of a prototype/antitype model of interpersonal relations, Shelley's visions of himself *as* love offer us the most striking glimpses into the crucial battle between Christ and Narcissus as they struggle for ascendency over Shelley's soul—while he just as strenuously battles against them both.

Shelley's Gothic Gospel: *Zastrozzi*

Even in the realm of Shelley's juvenilia we never encounter the kind of
unadulterated love for Christ that would seem to warrant my use of the term
idealized selfobject to describe his role in Shelley's psychological development. We hunt in vain through Shelley's works for pious meditations in the
spirit of Thomas à Kempis (though like Thomas, whose language Shelley
often seems to echo, his "chief concern" was to become "completely dead to
self" [*Imitation of Christ* 31, 69]).[53] But when Shelley vows as a youth to
"walk forth to war among mankind," he is both adopting Christ's mission "to
set at liberty them that are bruised" (Luke 4: 18) and imitating his "meek" and
"mild" character (*CW*, I, 252: *LC*, Dedication, ll. 42, 36, 32) Moreover, the
fury with which the eighteen-year-old Shelley vilifies Christ and the concomitant desperation with which he attempts to emulate Jesus as a "conqueror
of self" (*Imitation of Christ* 71)—both triggered by the breakup with Harriet
Grove—reveal a pre-existing and deep-seated longing for merger with an
omnipotent selfobject such as Christ.

Such a merger, according to Kohut, offers "narcissistic fulfillment" to
the aspiring self as it gradually "assimilates" and "accommodates functions
and capacities" of the idealized selfobject, be it a parent or a cultural icon such
as Christ (Klein 318).[54] We cannot pinpoint a moment in Shelley's youth when
the beloved Master became "this horrid Galilean" (*L*, I, 66), for Shelley's
regard for Christ was probably always tinged with an ambivalence that would
grow with his increasing enmity toward the Christian religion. Yet ambivalence and idealization are not mutually exclusive, as Shelley's representations
of women and of sexuality remind us. Shelley would eventually come to
(re)acknowledge Christ as the highest ideal of moral excellence, but the poet's
sudden recoil from his loved selfobject in 1810, it seems, transformed gradual internalization (and healthy "narcissistic fulfillment") into aggressive
absorption: he rejected and appropriated simultaneously, now yoking himself
with Christ with the common appellation "wretch."[55]

"The wretched Verezzi" is the first being we encounter when we enter
the world of Shelley's first novel (*CW*, V, 5). Besides a handful of letters written between 1803 and 1808 and a few poems found in *The Esdaile Notebook*,
Shelley's initial foray into Gothic territory, *Zastrozzi: A Romance*, comprises
the earliest of his extant writings. If we accept Cameron's conjecture that Shelley composed this novel between March and August 1809—before he felt that
his cousin Harriet was slipping away from him—it appears that the fixation on
martyr-like suffering that pervades the 1810 and 1811 letters and much of the
later poetry grew out of an already established preoccupation with Christ's suffering, represented in pictures hanging in Timothy Shelley's library (Cameron,
Young Shelley, 124) as well as in Percy's own room (*L*, I, 102). Thus, it would

seem that when he finds himself prostrate "on the altar of [Harriet Grove's] perjured love," Shelley's radical appropriation of the Passion supersedes his early sympathetic identification with Christ as an "idealized selfobject" exemplifying self-transcendent love (*L*, I, 27). Although I believe that this is a largely accurate picture of Shelley's shifting attitude toward Christ, we must also take into account the fact that *Zastrozzi* did not appear until the spring of 1810. The clouds that began to gather over the cousins' engagement in September 1809—which while composing the novel Shelley must have anticipated and almost deliberately invited—may have affected Shelley's revisions, provoking him to heighten both his hero Verezzi's passivity and his suffering to reflect his own experience as an "outcast" (*L*, I, 27).[56]

In a May 1810 letter to his friend Edward Fergus Graham, Shelley remarks on a mutual acquaintance's interpretation of *Zastrozzi* as an autobiographical novel: "If he takes me for any one whose character I have drawn in Zastrozzi he is mistaken quite" (*L*, I, 11). A pastiche of Lewis, Radcliffe, Dacre, and Walpole, among others, *Zastrozzi* embodies what Shelley would later describe to Godwin as a "distempered altho' unoriginal vision" (*L*, I, 266). Yet in an earlier letter to Godwin, the former "votary of Romance"— now sheepishly repudiating his adolescent Gothics—admits that both *Zastrozzi* and *St. Irvyne* "serve to mark the state of my mind at the period of their composition" (*L*, I, 227: 10 January 1812).[57] Besides modifying Shelley's original disclaimer regarding the personal nature of his first novel, this important letter to Godwin suggests a fruitful way to approach *Zastrozzi*: as an exercise in audience manipulation.[58] For Shelley in 1809 and early 1810, the most important members of his audience were Harriet Grove and Elizabeth Shelley.

The January 1812 letter just referred to is only Shelley's second to Godwin, and it is the one in which Shelley narrates "the leading points of [his own] history," carefully chosen—and slightly distorted—to insinuate a teleology that seems providentially fulfilled when William Godwin enters Shelley's life, first as an author and then as a correspondent and friend (*L*, I, 229). Shelley closes the letter with a dramatic tribute that both flatters Godwin and implicates him—permanently, it turns out—in his young admirer's life: "To you as the regulator and former of my mind I must ever look with real respect and veneration" (*L*, I, 229).[59] As Stephen Behrendt has shown, Shelley demonstrates a keen awareness of audience in even his earliest writings, including his letters, and this letter beautifully exemplifies the nineteen-year-old Shelley's remarkable skills as a rhetorician and psychologist. But whereas in his initial letters to Godwin, he convincingly casts himself in the role of disciple, beginning with *Zastrozzi*, Shelley demonstrates that his natural talents and inclinations lie with cultivating his own disciples.

While the ostensible hero of the novel, "the hapless Verezzi," languishes in "torpid insensibility" or actual unconsciousness, his tormentors Zastrozzi and Matilda tirelessly plot and carry out their designs against their prey (*CW*, V, 37, 11). Because the fiercely passionate Matilda longs to possess Verezzi sexually, Zastrozzi can exploit her obsession in order to avenge, we finally learn, his mother's ruin at the hands of Verezzi's father.[60] Verezzi himself must be destroyed as part of Zastrozzi's mission to "revenge [his mother's] wrongs" on her seducer's "progeny for ever" (*CW*, V, 102). In the course of his exploits, Zastrozzi manages to "convert" Matilda to "the doctrines of atheism" (*CW*, V, 90). Although at this point in his life, Shelley probably would have called himself a deist rather than an atheist, like Zastrozzi, he considered orthodox Christianity "a false and injurious superstition" and was anxious to convince his (female) loved ones of this, especially his sister Elizabeth and cousin Harriet (*CW*, V, 100).

Judging from the fury with which he reacts to the two young women's eventual return to Christ's fold, Shelley enjoyed quite a bit of success in his proselytizing until late 1810 and early 1811, when first his cousin and then his sister retreated from him.[61] For Shelley, whose earliest audience was made up of a mother and young sisters who listened raptly as he spun his own tales or recited the poetry he learned at day school, his most coveted disciples would always be women.[62] Mary, Martha, and Mary Magdalene could help him recapture his halcyon days at Field Place much more effectively than could Peter, James, or John. According to Medwin, one of the first recipients of Shelley's anti-Christian evangelism was the young Felicia Hemans (née Browne), with whom Shelley evidently carried on a "skeptical" correspondence in 1808 and 1809 until her mother—like the Groves after her—put a stop to it (59).[63] Following this (briefly) disheartening episode and the eventual "apostasy" of his sister and cousin, Shelley attempted, with varying degrees of success, to "illuminate"[64] and cultivate as disciples his sister Hellen, the poet Janetta Phillips (*L*, I, 73–74), Elizabeth Hitchener, and Harriet Westbrook. It is not surprising that Shelley's first reference to the latter in his correspondence is a request that his publisher John Stockdale "send a copy of St Irvyne, to Miss Harriet Westbrook" (*L*, I, 40: 11 January 1811). Analogous to his earlier gifts to Harriet Grove of *Zastrozzi* and of Locke's *Essay*, this tactic involves what Cameron in an amusing phrase dubs "subversion by remote control" (*Young Shelley* 296).[65]

Shelley's first Gothic novel, which he sent to his cousin as soon as it was published, comprises one example of the "deistifying" that he engaged in from 1809 through 1811.[66] In this early novel, composed before Shelley had reason to excoriate Christ himself, neither Zastrozzi's condemnation of religion nor Verezzi's suffering strongly implicates Christ as a target for Shelley's own hostilities. Yet the readiness with which in late 1810 the bereft lover Shelley directed his wrath at Christ reveals that his own gathering of disciples not only imitated but challenged his precursor, to use the most apt term for the dynamic at work here. After all, when Percy attempts "to make a deistical coterie of all [his] little sisters" and of his cousin Harriet—an enterprise which he had initiated long before his mother suspected it in early 1811—he is plundering Christ's flock in order to augment his own (*L*, I, 38).

However, before the onslaught of parental interference begins to undermine the cousins' engagement in late 1809, this largely unconscious "competition" with Christ resembles the gradual demystification of the idealized self-object and the internalization of his of her qualities that Kohut regards as the key to a stable sense of self and its attendant self-esteem. But once the young Shelley almost intentionally sabotages his first engagement and then bewails its destruction, he overtly pits himself against Christ and perversely refuses to dissociate him from the trappings of Christianity, ascribing to "cold Prejudice & selfish fear" the "Love of God Xt or the H[oly] G[host] (all the same)" (*L*, I, 70: 26 April 1811). In Shelley's mind, Christ has despoiled him of his own best-loved disciples, the cousin and sister whom he himself had originally enticed away from Christianity: "Xt how I hate thy influence" (*L*, I, 45: 12 January 1811).[67]

Until Harriet and Elizabeth abandon him, though, Percy's deeply ingrained worship of selfless love and the Christlike mission he carved out for himself as an unhappy schoolboy suggest that he was heretofore careful not to identify Jesus himself with institutionalized Christianity. And not much later in his career, in works such as *Proposals for an Association of Philanthropists* and *A Letter to Lord Ellenborough*, both written in the spring of 1812, Shelley will perceive and portray himself as one of the few true disciples who struggle to salvage the Master from his own wreck and restore to him his rightful throne, if not as the Godhead then as "the most just, wise, and benevolent of men" (*CW*, III, 57: Note to *Hellas*, l. 1090). Yet between Shelley's relatively untroubled boyhood embrace of Christ and his often troubled attempts to return to him as an adult, lies the largely uncharted territory of the adolescent poet's violent break with this "man of pure life" and pure love (*PS*, I, 396: Note to *Queen Mab*, VII. 135).

To turn back to the Gothic world of *Zastrozzi*, this early work is particularly intriguing in that it contains glimmerings of the clash to come: Shelley's decisive battle with Christ and with his own family. Because it straddles the relatively undefiled paradise of the young cousins' love and the gloomier region of romance gone awry, *Zastrozzi* offers us a unique glimpse into a key moment of transition or "liminality" in Shelley's personal, philosophical, and artistic development.[68] Perusing the pages of this "terror novel," we meet a playful sixteen year old cheerfully trotting out his Gothic paraphernalia and parodying—via his narrator—the moral platitudes offered by religious conformists.[69] But we also see a serious young propagandist, planting "calculated subversions" in his melodramatic text and thus in the minds of his readers

(Behrendt, Introduction to *Zastrozzi and St. Irvyne*, xv). In a strange way *Zastrozzi* is a novel that records its own effects: it launches Shelley's controversial career as a romantic rebel and anticipates both its own reception and the impact of that reception (or rejection) on its author.

As mentioned earlier, Shelley seemed deliberately to court disaster when it came to his engagement to Harriet Grove. Although she was much more than a "convenient Muse" for the adolescent Shelley, those scholars such as Frederick L. Jones and Desmond Hawkins who underestimate Shelley's love for his lovely cousin do rightly remind us of something which Shelley himself must have realized on some level: that Harriet was an essentially conventional young woman, certainly not the soul mate and intellectual sophisticate that he would later discover in Mary Godwin (Holmes, *Pursuit*, 29). When he has Zastrozzi scorn the "false, foolish, and vulgar prejudices" of orthodox religion and characterizes Verezzi as an antimatrimonialist (*CW*, V, 48, 75), Shelley is equally intent on shocking as he is on "illuminating" his reader. Although it was not *Zastrozzi* itself that finally alarmed Harriet enough to consult her parents on Percy's suitability as a mate, this novel, with its barely disguised admiration of its villain, exemplifies the kind of ammunition with which Percy assailed not only his cousin's beliefs but eventually the relationship itself as well.

While Percy would never insult Harriet by explicitly likening her to the novel's villainess, as Zastrozzi's "student" in atheism, "the guilty Matilda" (*CW*, V, 26) functions as a kind of surrogate for the young preceptor's own most cherished pupil (and also as a stand-in for the general reader). Matilda is highly "susceptible"—a favorite Shelleyan word and a quality that Shelley hoped to and apparently did find in his "amiable" cousin/fiancée as well as in his eldest sister. Desperate to possess Verezzi—in body if not in soul—Matilda eagerly drinks in Zastrozzi's attacks on religion and on "the misguided multitude" (*CW*, V, 47). She accepts his challenge to "dare boldly, [to] strive to verge from the beaten path" in her quest: "Thus, by an artful appeal to her passions, did Zastrozzi extinguish the faint spark of religion which yet gleamed in Matilda's bosom" (*CW*, V, 48).[70] Zastrozzi's triumphant "conversion" of Matilda parallels Percy's own victories over his cousin's conventionality, victories that the novel itself could either augment or undo, depending on how "towering" Harriet's mind actually was (*CW*, V, 48).

The Matilda who embraces "the doctrines of atheism" exhibits astonishing passion, tenacity, and resourcefulness that easily eclipse and finally destroy her paramour's true love, the pallid Julia (*CW*, V, 90). Until the novel's penultimate chapter, Matilda represents one possibility in terms of the reader's (i.e., Harriet's) response to its impieties: a firm and daring "contempt of religion" (*CW*, V, 90). Yet Shelley also includes in *Zastrozzi* an alternate reaction to its "speculations" when Matilda herself, pierced by "the arrows of repentance," at the last minute rejects Zastrozzi's lessons (*CW*, V, 97). As his essentially conventional cousin was soon to do, Matilda (re)turns to "the shackles of prejudice, the errors of a false and injurious superstition," as Zastrozzi puts it (*CW*, V, 100). Simultaneously beckoning the young woman and pushing her away, then, this early work accurately forecasts Harriet's retreat into orthodoxy. Shelley would later write in a draft of his Preface to *Adonais* (1821), "As an author I have dared and invited censure";[71] and as early as 1809 he was inviting—at least unconsciously—not only his cousin/fiancée's "censure" but her abandonment of him as well.

Perhaps Percy himself at least vaguely realized what he had done by flaunting his "Deistical Principles" (*L*, I, 26), when in the winter of 1810, he rages over the loss of Harriet, his persecution at the hands of his family, and his father's meddlings into his friendship with Thomas Hogg (a suspected "bad influence" on Shelley). At this point, Shelley's earlier identification with Christ as an exemplar of generous self-sacrifice radically metamorphoses into the murderous and suicidal fury that allows the "delirious" Shelley to conflate himself with Christ in a new way when he threatens to "stab the wretch in secret" (*L*, I, 29, 27).[72] The dawning awareness that his own inflammatory compositions, such as *Henry and Louisa* (1809), *St. Irvyne* (1809–1810), and *Zastrozzi* itself, helped instigate the series of events that culminated in Shelley's break with Christ, with Harriet, and with his family could not have been of much comfort to the young author as he furiously scribbled that remarkable series of letters to Hogg between December 1810 and the spring of the following year.

Before turning away from *Zastrozzi* and toward works in which Shelley confronts Christ more directly, I would like to look at an even more intriguing aspect than this early novel's "containment" of its own primary audience: its adumbration of Shelley's own reaction to the reception/rejection with which that very audience would greet *Zastrozzi*, a text that is itself a kind of synecdoche for the subversive letters and literary works he was busily composing.[73] Read as a kind of dress rehearsal for the inevitable rupture with Harriet and with his own family, the novel carves out two divergent paths that Shelley could take once he dons the role of outcast that Verezzi and Zastrozzi share. Most important, it allows us to watch Shelley moving toward his quintessential role: that of the martyr.

Throughout the novel Shelley insistently opposes Zastrozzi's inexhaustible physical and mental energy and ceaseless activity with the torpidity of his prey. Whereas the Satanic Zastrozzi resolves "never to rest" until he accomplishes his vengeful purpose, we encounter the "hero" himself more often than not as "the unconscious Verezzi," more sinned against than sinning if only because of his utter inertia (*CW*, V, 16, 44). However, as Jerrold Hogle emphasizes, these antithetical characters in fact "melt into one another" as

Doppelgänger who are ruled by similar "propensities for self-damnation" ("Shelley's Fiction" 79, 85). Hogle's probing analysis focuses on structural aspects of Shelley's fiction, but his remarks illuminate the biographical parallels that I am exploring. If Shelley the budding revolutionary, poised to wage war against his family's religious, social, and political traditions, did not quite envision for himself the melodramatic descent into self-destruction and alienation that dooms his central male characters, he did project for himself the emotional and often physical isolation that torments both Zastrozzi and Verezzi. By the end of the novel, after imaginatively participating in Verezzi's ineffectual passivity and Zastrozzi's often frantic "energetical exertions," Shelley implicitly rejects both approaches to the role of outsider—and of the martyr—that he anticipated for himself (*CW*, V, 48). To do *and* to suffer will become Shelley's philanthropic ideal; though, as I stressed earlier, when it comes to Christ himself and Shelley's complex identification with him, the latter tends to take precedence.

Taken as a composite character, Shelley's first protagonist and his first villain incorporate the revolutionary spirit and capacity for suffering that the poet revered in Jesus and attributed to his own Christlike characters, particularly Cythna and Prometheus.[74] Unlike these later creations, though, Zastrozzi and Verezzi are merely victims and not—despite their "soul-illumined countenance[s]"—heroic martyrs who sacrifice self for a worthy ideal (*CW*, V, 86, 103). As Hogle points out, they both "die with the same 'bitter smile of exultation' (V, 88) on their grim and tormented faces" ("Shelley's Fiction" 85), but in fact they are sacrificed to the principle of vengeance—"the epitome of self-centredness"—and thus to the principle of Self that Shelley even in this earliest of his published works was attacking (Behrendt, Introduction to *Zastrozzi and St. Irvyne*, xvii).[75] It is, however, vengeance, and vengeance on "the Incarnate," that will soon dominate Shelley's own thoughts as he grapples first with his impending and then with his actual loss of Harriet Grove (*Queen Mab*, VII. 163). Until the narcissistic wounds he incurred during this tumultuous romance began to heal, or, rather, scarify, Shelley could not overtly acknowledge Christ as his prototype of the selfless martyr. And to understand the way that he "avenged" himself on Christ, his own ideal-turned-rival, we must turn to a figure who never ceased to fascinate, even obsess, Shelley: the Wandering Jew.

The *Via Crucis* of the Wandering Jew

Beginning with his appearances—in *propria persona* or slightly disguised—in *St. Irvyne*, "Ghasta; or The Avenging Demon!!!" (1810), and *The Wandering Jew*, Ahasuerus shows up so often in Shelley's works that Mary Shelley refers to him as "Shelley's old favourite, the Wandering Jew" (*CW*, V, ix).[76] When, as an unhappy schoolboy, the budding revolutionary resolves to "walk forth to war among mankind," he clothes himself in the "linked armour" of Christ, himself a valiant *and* "mild" opponent of "the selfish and strong" (*CW*, I, 252: *LC*, Dedication, ll. 42, 41, 32, 33).[77] But in the fall of 1809, when Harriet Grove's parents joined forces with his own mother and father in order to shield the young woman from Shelley's blasphemies, it seemed to the young anti-Christian (not yet the aspiring "Antichrist") that they were robbing him not only of Harriet but of Jesus as well, by claiming him as their own (*L*, I, 35). Rather than insisting at this juncture, as he will later, that Christianity has become Christless,[78] he perversely dissevers himself from Jesus, conceding him to the enemy camp and then lumping him in with family, religion, and convention itself as "that which injured me" (*L*, I, 32: 26 December 1810). Shelley never completely abandons Christ even during the years of his most venomous hatred of his "paradigm," to return to Kierkegaard's term, and he continues to pattern his own suffering and attempts at selflessness on Christ; but in the Wandering Jew, Shelley found an alternative to Christ as his model of the defiant outcast and martyr as well as a vehicle for his own aggression toward the "blood-stain'd King of Kings" (*Esdaile* 38: "A Sabbath Walk").

The poet's identification with Ahasuerus, however, does not simply emerge from that resentment of Christ which Shelley discharges in his 1810 and 1811 letters to Hogg. When Shelley invokes the Wandering Jew—as Queen Mab herself does in Canto VII—he is also summoning a number of other figures, such as Satan, St. Paul, and St. John, through whom he can explore his conflicting feelings toward Christ. George K. Anderson sums up the basic legend with which Shelley worked:

> [It] is the tale of a man in Jerusalem who, when Christ was carrying his Cross to Calvary and paused to rest for a moment on this man's doorstep, drove the Saviour away . . . crying aloud, "Walk faster!" And Christ replied, "I go but you will walk until I come again!" (*Legend of the Wandering Jew* 11)

Anderson and countless others have remarked upon Ahasuerus' almost unrivaled appeal to the romantic imagination, which seized upon and transformed him into an Ancient Mariner or a Childe Harold. As Crook and Guiton point out, the Wandering Jew "obsessed Shelley to a greater degree even than it did his contemporaries" (29), but most commentators, including those I have just cited, ignore the crucial confrontation between Christ and Ahasuerus that ignited Shelley's imagination at the same time that it troubled his conscience.[79]

By reenacting this confrontation and its aftermath, Shelley can both punish and be punished by Christ and even (obliquely) reunite with him by conflating these two adversaries as he does, for example, in *Hellas* where he assigns some of Christ's most famous words to Ahasuerus. Moreover, when he alludes to alternate versions of the Wandering Jew legends that seem to mitigate the Jew's crime, Shelley is not merely justifying and/or downplaying his own animosity toward Christ. He is instead embarking on a kind of *via negativa* that will effect the kind of reconciliation which he longs for almost as soon as he recoils from his most important "martyred prophetic forebear" (Behrendt, *Shelley and His Audiences*, 3).

It is likely that Shelley first met the Wandering Jew on the pages of his boyhood favorite *The Monk*, where the Jew appears as "the Great Mogul" with a flaming brow who exorcises the bleeding Nun for Don Raymond (Lewis 167).[80] Lewis derived his own portrait of the Wandering Jew in part from Christian Friedrich Daniel Schubart's "Der ewige Jude" (1783), "Eine lyrische Rhapsodie," that Shelley himself encountered in translation on the pages of *La Belle Assemblée* during 1809.[81] Schubart's work is a particularly important source for Shelley because it comprises, as Anderson notes, a "*complainte* of the Wandering Jew" and thus provided a model for the young poet's adoption of Ahasuerus as a persona with whom he could imaginatively coalesce (*Legend of the Wandering Jew* 172).

That Shelley strongly identified with Ahasuerus—especially in the midst of the Harriet Grove crisis—is evinced not only by his literary compositions centering on the Wandering Jew but even more strikingly by an impassioned letter to Hogg written from Field Place during the eventful Christmas vacation of 1810 and 1811.[82] With the lightning shifts in tone and theme that distinguish these remarkable letters, Shelley moves from God and immortality to suicide with brief, intense stops along the way to praise love, to pledge "lasting long revenge" on Christ, to bewail his loss of Harriet, and to repudiate selfishness (*L*, I, 35: 3 January 1811). Venting the full force of his pain and rage, Shelley not only implicitly links himself with the Wandering Jew when he sees himself scourging and scourged by Christ,[83] but he even quotes the Wandering Jew himself from the prose fragment that he derived from Schubart and later gave to Hogg: "For the immoral 'never to be able to die, never to escape from some shrine as chilling as the clay-formed dungeon which now it inhabits' is the future punishment which I believe in" (*L*, I, 35).

In terms of Shelley's own moral system, which he was then developing, he was himself currently indulging in "immorality" in that he was allowing "that *hateful* principle" of Self—wearing one of its most insidious guises, vengeance—to cancel out consecrated love (*L*, I, 34, 35). Although he longed to express and receive the "[l]ove, love *infinite in extent*, eternal in duration" that he saw as the "reward" for, and "First Cause" of, morality, he now found himself in Ahasuerus' position, hating Christ and imprisoned in mortal selfhood (*L*, I, 35).[84] The only avenue of escape seemed to lie in the "willed selflessness" that Curran notes in the Maniac of *Julian and Maddalo*.[85]

With its Christlike proclamations of love and self-abnegation careening into its Ahasuerus-like fixation on revenge, hatred, and the fetters of the physical body, it is appropriate that this tempestuous letter to Hogg culminates in a (tentative) embrace of the most extreme form of *Selbsttödtung*, the literal selflessness that only death can provide:

> I am afraid there is selfishness in the passion of Love for I cannot avoid feeling every instant as if my soul was bursting, but I *will* feel no more! it is selfish—I would feel for others, but for myself oh! how much rather would I expire in the struggle. Yet that were relief—Is suicide wrong? I slept with a loaded pistol & some poison last night but did not die. (*L*, I, 36)

When Christ and Ahasuerus collide in Shelley's consciousness, as they so dramatically do throughout this letter, the only way to reconcile them is to allow each his own proper martyrdom. By identifying with the former's willingness to "expire" in the struggle against "selfishness," Shelley can preserve a remnant of his love for Christ, whom he will continue to emulate and to resist. At the same time, he imaginatively participates in the very different martyrdom of his fellow scorner of Christ when he evokes Ahasuerus' yearning for death and his fruitless attempts at suicide.

Almost exactly four years later, Shelley will trace the steps of another wanderer, the Poet of *Alastor*, whom the misguided Narrator—redundantly— wants to resurrect as another Ahasuerus, "Lone as incarnate death" (l. 681). The Narrator's telling invocation of the Wandering Jew merely makes explicit the parallels between this "vessel of deathless wrath" and the poem's protagonist that Shelley weaves into the text (l. 678). In *Alastor*, Shelley brings together—within the person of the Poet—the Wandering Jew and Narcissus, the principle opponents of Jesus in Shelley's private mythology and thus the antitheses of genuinely disinterested love. Because of his acknowledged sympathy for the Poet, Shelley's conflation of him with these two notorious figures reminds us just how aware he was of his own affinities with such "self worshippers," to borrow a phrase from Keats. *Alastor* and, later, *Epipsychidion*, with their depictions of narcissistic love, or "object choice," to be more precise, display the ingenuity with which Shelley gratified and punished that self-involvement which began to flourish when he lost, in Kohut's terminology, his "mirroring selfobjects" (Harriet and Elizabeth) as well as his "idealized selfobject" (Christ).

However, long before he had conceived these two poems and even before he composed the 1811 letter to Hogg I have just examined, Shelley was exploring the "self-centred seclusion" that "blasted" both Narcissus and Ahasuerus (*Alastor*, Preface, 69). In the winter of 1809 and 1810, following the first wave of parental interference in the cousins' relationship, Percy wrote a number of gloomy poems addressed to or about Harriet as well as composed three works featuring Ahasuerus: *The Wandering Jew*, *St. Irvyne*, and "Ghasta." He had clearly found in the Wandering Jew a fitting emblem of his own rebellion against Jehovah and Christ as well as of the isolation—from Harriet and from his family—that this rebellion was beginning to impose on him.

Shelley's first representation of the Wandering Jew, in the *Monk*-inspired terror-poem, "Ghasta; or The Avenging Demon!!!," offers a much more conventional, less psychologically-oriented portrait of Ahasuerus than those found in *St. Irvyne* and *The Wandering Jew*. The longest poem in Percy and Elizabeth's *Original Poetry of Victor and Cazire* and dated January 1810,[86] "Ghasta" depicts Ahasuerus less as a victim of "God's eternal ire" than as a divine scourge who blasts others with his "cross of fire" (*PS*, I, 38). This poem tells us more about its author's interest in the Wandering Jew within the context of the volume as a whole than it does on its own.[87] Ahasuerus—who summons Ghasta, the spirit of vengeance—is but one of many "avenging demons" in the volume, most of whom populate its last four poems (although written earlier than most of the other pieces, "Ghasta" is the book's penultimate poem). Except for Elizabeth's lively verses, which open the volume, and a handful of heroic ballads, *Victor and Cazire* balances Percy's love laments to Harriet with Gothic tales of vengeance and atonement. In his personal poems such as "Song" ("Come [Harriet]! sweet is the hour") and "Song: To [Harriet]" ("Stern, stern is the voice"), he depicts himself as passive victim of romantic grief, a "heart-stricken deer" with a "mild heart," whereas the melodramatic narrative poems that he lifts ("St. Edmond's Eve") or derives ("Revenge," "Ghasta") from Lewis allow him to imagine a more violent approach to his role as an outcast (*PS*, I, 103, 86). This early volume, despite the lack of originality claimed by its title, did enable Shelley to explore his identification both with "the pallid stranger" of "Song: Despair," who readily succumbs to "woe," and with the mighty Stranger of "Ghasta," the "majestic" Wandering Jew who seems to relish his alien status (*PS*, I, 94, 33).

In his longest poem to date, *The Wandering Jew* (composed between fall of 1809 and spring of 1810), Shelley creates an Ahasuerus who embodies both the anguish of the personal lyrics to which I have referred and the heroic energies of "Ghasta"'s Gothic Wandering Jew.[88] Like *Zastrozzi* and *St. Irvyne*, this work subverts orthodox Christianity and thus it contributed to Shelley's indoctrination of his cousin/fiancée, to whom he sent the poem before it was even completed.[89] But because *The Wandering Jew* remains more interested in its protagonist's psychology and suffering than in disseminating "Atheistical principles" (*L*, I, 18), it reveals infinitely more about Shelley's own increasingly troubled relationship with Christ than a more polemical work might (and certainly more than the sketchy "Ghasta" does). It also anticipates the parallels between Christ and Ahasuerus that Shelley will draw in his 1821 poem *Hellas*. Lewis's *The Monk*—along with Radcliffe's *The Italian*—still manages to leave its mark on the young author's work, but Shelley departs from those sources to delve into his protagonist's crime against "the meek Lamb" and the punishment he suffered for this offense (*PS*, I, 58: *WJ*, III. 580).

As Shelley portrays him in this poem, the Wandering Jew has become a rather dashing romantic hero named Paulo, who, like Radcliffe's Vivaldi, rescues a young girl, "a fainting novice," from the clutches of the Church (*PS*, I, 46: *WJ*, I. 147). In typical Shelleyan fashion, Paulo exchanges vows of eternal love—but not legitimate wedding vows—with this girl, Rosa, and spirits her to a secluded castle. Eventually, Paulo's villainous friend Victorio, who joins them in Canto II, falls in love with Rosa and accidently murders her when he gives her a "love potion" concocted by a witch. Upon discovering Rosa's lifeless body, Paulo at last resigns himself to the Satanic powers that had been courting him for sixteen hundred years. Although these Gothic trappings provide the framework of Shelley's tale, at the center of the poem is Paulo's canto-long narration of his "sad, [his] cruel destiny," beginning with his fateful confrontation with Christ on the *Via Crucis* (*PS*, I, 57: *WJ*, II. 558).

Remarkably, Shelley presents Jesus in a relatively sympathetic light in this early poem, in part because it predates the explosion of rage against Christ with which Shelley reacted to the "official" dissolution of his engagement to his cousin. Moreover, *The Wandering Jew* is a less polemical work than some of his earlier anti-Christian pieces such as *Henry and Louisa* (1809) and even *Zastrozzi*, both of which, like his 1812–1813 thesis-poem *Queen Mab*, "breathe hatred to government & religion" (*L*, I, 348). By presenting Canto III as an almost uninterrupted soliloquy by Paulo, Shelley can explore his own kinship with both Christ and Paulo-Ahasuerus much more freely than he does, for example, in *Queen Mab*, where both figures must function as grotesque offshoots of "Falshood" (i.e., the Christian religion [*QM*, V. 197]).

While Shelley links Paulo with Milton's Satan by supplying Cantos I and III with epigraphs from *Paradise Lost*, the epigraph that he assigns to the poem itself provides the first hint that the relationship between its protagonist and "the Redeemer" will not be purely adversarial (*PS*, I, 61: *WJ*, III, 656): "If I will that he tarry till I come, what is that to thee? Follow thou me" (John 21: 22). By quoting this particular scripture, Shelley is alluding to an alternative version of the Ahasuerus legend that identifies him as St. John, the "beloved disciple."[90] After the resurrection, Christ prophesies Peter's martyrdom and says to him, "Follow me."

Then Peter, turning about, seeth the disciple whom Jesus loved following; which also leaned on his breast at supper . . .
Peter seeing him saith to Jesus, Lord, and what shall this man do?
Jesus saith unto him, If I will that he tarry till I come, what is that to
thee? follow thou me.
Then went this saying abroad among the brethren, that that disciple
should not die. (John 21: 19–23)

For the young man who in a few months would be apostrophizing the "dearest sweetest power" of love in one breath and thirsting for "the hearts blood
of Xt's hated name" in the next, a legend that allowed him to identify (with)
Jesus' best-loved disciple and his accursed tormenter provided the perfect
foundation for his most ambitious poem to date (*L*, I, 28, 29: 26 December
1810). Shelley may also be invoking St. Paul—"Paulo"—who became
Christ's greatest apostle after gaining notoriety as his greatest persecutor.[91]
Paulo certainly feels "keen remorse" for his crime and expresses real compassion for "the blessed Saviour," but his imitation of Christ's sufferings has
little to do with the self-sacrificing love that Christ, St. John, and St. Paul
advocated (*PS*, I, 60: *WJ*, III. 626, 641). In these early works, where Shelley
first struggles against conventional religion and, perforce, against Christ, he is
more concerned with exploring the sensations of the rebel/martyr than with
supplying his surrogates with a mission that could link their suffering to a zeal
for humanitarian reform. Laon, Cythna, and Prometheus would have to wait.
Shelley would not be ready to reinstate Christ as his moral ideal for quite
some time.

In *The Wandering Jew*, Shelley has at least moved beyond his fascination with pure victimization, which *Zastrozzi*'s Verezzi embodies. Paulo does
courageously challenge the authority of his unappeasable tormenter and thus
earns the kind of limited heroic stature of Milton's Satan as he endures his punishment. Moreover, with its vivid images of martyrdom, this work allows us to
witness an early poetic version of the Passion of Shelley, wherein the poet both
absorbs and challenges the suffering Christ. While a personal lyric such as
"The Retrospect" (1812), in which the speaker laments "The gloomiest retrospects that bind / With crowns of thorn the bleeding mind" (ll. 163–64),[92] presents this Passion directly, in the earlier narrative poem, Shelley filters the
rivalry/identification with Christ through the figure of Ahasuerus. In terms of
his more adversarial stance toward Jesus, Shelley gives the Wandering Jew a
kind of priority over Christ in his suffering by showing us his hero's "drops of
agony" before allowing us to see "the big drops of agony" on the brow of
Jesus, who now seems "belated," as Bloom would put it (*PS*, I, 55, 61: *WJ*, II.
460; III. 644). But the poet draws other, less fraught parallels between Paulo
and Jesus, and these enable him to portray both men, more sympathetically

than in *Queen Mab*, as victims of "Christ's terrific Sire" (*PS*, I, 82: *WJ*, IV. 1441). While Jesus' head is "thorn-encircled," Paulo's is swathed by a "grey encircling band" that hides the burning cross on his forehead (*PS*, I, 61, 66: *WJ*, III. 643, 817). The color of this cross is like "recent blood," which mirrors "the Redeemer's gore" (*PS*, I, 66, 61: *WJ*, III. 819, 655). Furthermore, Paulo explicitly rivals Christ's Passion when he interrupts his narrative to exclaim, "Even now I bleed!—I bleed!" (*PS*, I, 70: *WJ*, III. 967), a cry that anticipates the martyred speaker of "Ode to the West Wind": "I fall upon the thorns of life! I bleed!" (l. 54). Finally, Shelley echoes Isaiah's prophetic description of Christ as "a man of sorrows" (Isa. 53: 3) when he calls Paulo-Ahasuerus "a man of woe" (*PS*, I, 53: *WJ*, II. 386).

These correspondences between Christ and the Wandering Jew allow Shelley indirectly to embrace the former as his proper precursor in suffering and selflessness while at the same time warning his reader of the absurdities of Christian dogma. One of these absurdities, the poem suggests, involves the discrepancy between the vengeful nature of the supposed "God of Mercy" and Christ's (almost) absolute "Forgiveness to his enemies" (*PS*, I, 82, 59: *WJ*, IV. 1435; III. 598). The Wandering Jew seems to be the exception here, for Shelley nearly always has Christ—not Jehovah—pronounce the "curse of immortality" upon his mocker (*Hellas*, l. 151).[93] While the episode in *Queen Mab*, where Christ wears a "smile of godlike malice" as he pronounces sentence on Ahasuerus (VII. 181), is the most well-known, Christ himself also condemns the Jew in *The Wandering Jew* (III. 585–90) and in *Hellas* (ll. 150–51). Schubart's (translated) poem, which Shelley thrice quotes and/or paraphrases, actually takes the onus off of Jesus and ascribes the curse to an "angel of death," at least in the version Shelley includes in the Notes to *Queen Mab* (*PS*, I, 393: Note to *QM*, VII. 67). Moreover, the text that Shelley sent to Hogg even foresees an end to Ahasuerus' punishment. A (presumably different) angel tells the exhausted Ahasuerus that "the wrath of thy Judge is appeased, when thou shalt awake he will be arrived he whose blod thou sawest flow upon Golgotha whose mercy is extended even to thee" (*SC*, II, 650).

In his poems dealing with the Wandering Jew, however, Shelley chose to suppress or relegate to a footnote those passages from his source that thrust a mediator (the angel of death) between Christ and Ahasuerus or that promised an ultimate reconciliation between the two and thus an endpoint for the latter's suffering. Because verse—as opposed to the prose accounts of the legend he composed—may have enabled Shelley better to fuse imaginatively with both of these paired personæ, he wanted to depict direct confrontations between them and thus suggest by their clashes the kind of psychomachia that he will so brilliantly present in *Prometheus Unbound*. Until their hard-won concord in the late work *Hellas*, Christ and the Wandering Jew can no more be reconciled than can Christ and Narcissus, for, as Shelley would implicitly acknowledge in his (first) lyrical drama, this would be reconciling a champion with an oppressor of mankind, the revolutionary principle of Love with the tyrannical principle of Self.

For, despite his affinities with and esteem for Christ, Ahasuerus as he appears in *The Wandering Jew* remains as utterly self-absorbed in his sufferings as the clamorous Ahasuerus of *Queen Mab*. Paulo is not the ancestor of Shelley's martyred Titan, who finally achieves self-transcendence, but of his Beatrice Cenci, who eventually grows like what persecutes her and finally succumbs to "loathsome sympathy" with her vicious father, an earthly version of Paulo's heavenly torturer (*PU*, I. 451).[94] Paulo also resembles Wolfstein and Ginotti, the central characters of *St. Irvyne*, on which Shelley worked the same winter that he wrote *The Wandering Jew*.[95] In fact, Shelley makes the parallels explicit by affixing epigraphs from his poem to the novel's eighth and tenth chapters, which zero in on the inner life of Wolfstein and Ginotti, respectively. Shelley not only connects these three figures through the theme of the undying mortal—Ginotti has the elixir of immortal life and plans to pass it on to Wolfstein—but, what is more important, through their common capitulation to "the dark idolatry of self" (*CW*, I, 362: *LC*, XIII. 192).

Ginotti's chapter-long narrative of his life, which has much in common with Paulo's Canto III soliloquy, suggests that Ginotti's experiences comprise a kind of "secularized" version of the Wandering Jew's rejection of Christ and his subsequent punishment.[96] Moreover, since Ginotti has chosen Wolfstein to be his successor as an immortal Rosicrucian, the novel implies that Ginotti's story is also Wolfstein's.[97] Shelley depicts both men as "*selfish and self-interested*" wanderers who have spurned love as mere "weakness" (*CW*, V, 180: *SI*). Although they desperately cling to material existence while Paulo-Ahasuerus even more desperately tries to escape it, all three men remain imprisoned by the principle of Self, of which their "protract[ed] existence[s]" are merely emblematic (*CW*, V, 181: *SI*).

The novel's analogue to Paulo's confrontations with Christ—one on the *Via Crucis* and one in a vision of Christ's Resurrection/Ascension—appears in the dream that Ginotti recounts to Wolfstein.[98] In it, Ginotti is standing "on the brink of a most terrific precipice," listening to the gorgeous strains of "seraphic" music, when a "form of most exact and superior symmetry" appears before him:

> Rays of brilliancy, surpassing expression, fell from his burning eye, and the emanations from his countenance tinted the transparent clouds below with silver light. The phantasm advanced towards me; it seemed then, to my imagination, that his figure was borne on the sweet strain of music which filled the circumambient air. In a voice which was fascination itself, the being addressed me, saying 'Wilt thou come with me?

wilt thou be mine?' I felt a decided wish never to be his. 'No, no,' I unhesitatingly cried . . . No sooner had I uttered these words, than methought a sensation of deadly horror chilled my sickening frame; an earthquake rocked the precipice beneath my feet; the beautiful being vanished; clouds, as of chaos, rolled around, and from their dark masses flashed incessant meteors . . . it appeared like the dissolution of nature; the blood-red moon, whirled from her sphere, sank beneath the horizon. (*CW*, V, 182, 183)

In the midst of this apocalyptic landscape, which also appears in *The Wandering Jew* and invokes biblical accounts of the Crucifixion, a "deformed" Satanic figure now claims the dreamer, but "in its hideous and detestable countenance" Ginotti discerns something of the radiant being he had rejected (*CW*, V, 184).[99] Read in tandem with *The Wandering Jew*, which Shelley explicitly invites us to do, this episode perfectly evokes the young author's own troubled relationship with Jesus, whom Shelley, like Ginotti and even the penitent Paulo, found himself perversely resisting when his anti-Christian "speculations" began to threaten rather than strengthen his relationship with his Master and with his pupil and fiancée, Harriet Grove. Try as he might, he could not then, or ever, entirely exempt Christ from his attack on the Christian religion, nor could he hold Christ blameless for those blows that Shelley believed Christianity had dealt him. Ginotti's vision of a Christlike visage superimposed on the repulsive face of the demon thus emerges as an emblem of Shelley's increasing ambivalence toward his idealized selfobject, his predecessor on the path of loving self-sacrifice.

Ahasuerus will appear a number of times in Shelley's writings before he makes his dignified entrance into Mahmud's seraglio in *Hellas*. In late 1810, around the time that the poet was feverishly writing letters to Hogg during their Christmas holiday, Shelley composed "The Wandering Jew's Soliloquy," a much fiercer indictment of the Judeo-Christian religious tradition than *The Wandering Jew* had offered.[100] Although this poem does not actually name Christ as Ahasuerus' adversary, Shelley does invoke his presence in the lyric's opening lines: "Is it the Eternal Triune, is it He / Who dares arrest the wheels of destiny / And plunge me in this lowest Hell of Hells?" (*Esdaile* 161). Canto VII of *Queen Mab* finds Ahasuerus—and Shelley himself—challenging Christ much more directly, as might be expected in a poem that takes as its motto "Ecrasez l'Infame." As Holmes has pointed out, "The 'infame' of Voltaire was the Church in general; but the same phrase had also been adopted by the Illuminists as its motto referring specifically to Christ" (*Pursuit* 200). Anxious as he was in *Queen Mab* to condemn everything associated with organized religion and fueled by his chaotic feelings toward Christ, Shelley allows neither the malevolent "Incarnate" nor the strident Ahasuerus to emerge as a heroic figure (*QM*, VII. 163). After staging a brutal confrontation between these two cherished and despised alter egos, Shelley attempts to dismiss them both from the poem as "phantasmal portraiture[s] / Of wandering human thought" in order to usher in the new "paradise of peace" which Mab previews to Ianthe (*QM*, VII. 274–75; VIII. 238).

The Wandering Jew makes a dramatic comeback in the fragmentary tale *The Assassins*, which Shelley began composing during his summer 1814 "honeymoon" on the Continent with Mary Godwin. Stuart Curran has called the Ahasuerus of *Queen Mab* "a barbarous excrescence, an angry young man in death-defying senility" (*Annus Mirabilis* 20–21), and we could apply similar terms to the vociferous stranger whom the young Assassin Albedir discovers in a suspiciously Christlike position: impaled on the broken branches of a cedar tree. This "breathing corpse" (*Prose* 134), whom Mary Shelley identifies as the Wandering Jew (*CW*, V, ix), shouts Illuminist slogans in the midst of the heretofore "uninterrupted quiet" of this primitive Christian community (*Prose* 133). His Zastrozzi-like "bitter smile of mingled scorn abhorrence and scorn" and violent denunciations of religious and political tyranny contend with his "mild" appeal to "the gentle and merciful spirits of sweet human love" (*Prose* 134, 135). Mirroring the Assassins' own bizarre blend of Jacobin revolutionary zeal and the pacifism of their "illustrious master" (*Prose* 131), Christ, this figure incarnates the uneasy marriage of the self-abnegating Christ and the vengeful Ahasuerus in Shelley's consciousness.

Moreover, when he wrote *The Assassins*, Shelley had at last (re)gained in Mary Godwin and Claire Clairmont the "little circle" of female companions/disciples that he enjoyed at Field Place and, briefly, during his marriage to Harriet Westbrook (*L*, I, 292).[101] Perhaps fearing that he might lose Mary and Claire the way he lost his cousin Harriet and sister Elizabeth in 1810 and 1811, Percy imaginatively reenacts in this story the invasion of Christ into his first utopia at Field Place. By yoking together, in this "stranger," Christ and Ahasuerus and then quickly integrating him into the community as "the brother of [Albedir's] soul" (*Prose* 135), Shelley contains his fears as well as Christ himself, who is now inextricably bound to one of his fiercest enemies.

Yet the Wandering Jew's final appearance in Shelley's works finds Ahasuerus and Christ dwelling together in relative harmony.[102] Written in October 1821, *Hellas* comprises one of Shelley's most assured, genuinely self-effacing poems. In this lyrical drama, Ahasuerus *may* be "he whom the great prophet Jesus . . . for his mockery / Mocked with the curse of immortality" (*Hellas*, ll. 149–51). But Shelley also suggests that the Wandering Jew is Enoch, who "walk[ed] with God" and, according to some traditions, was "exempt from Death" (*Paradise Lost*, XI. 707, 709).[103] In *Paradise Lost*, Milton presents Enoch as a type of Christ, an embodiment of the "one just Man"

who prefigures the "one greater Man" that is Jesus Christ (*PL*, XI. 890; I. 4).
Shelley further establishes a positive bond between Christ and the Wandering
Jew in *Hellas* by having Mahmud play Pilate to Ahasuerus' Jesus:

> *Mahmud*. Thou art a man, thou sayest, even as we.
> *Ahasuerus*. No more!
> *Mahmud*.   But raised above thy fellow men
> By thought, as I by power.
> *Ahasuerus*.   Thou sayest so.
>
> (ll. 738–40)

Moreover, Ahasuerus responds to Mahmud's desire to "behold the future" by
echoing Christ's promise in the Sermon on the Mount, "Knock and it shall be
opened" (ll. 804–5).[104] As Shelley presents them, these biblical passages strip
Christ and Ahasuerus of any supernatural aura and thus, in Shelleyan logic,
they help the poet elevate both figures to the lofty status of virtuous, wise, and
utterly *human* beings.[105] We have only to think back on the cruel antagonism
that festered between the phantasmal Christ and Ahasuerus in *Queen Mab* to
realize just how remarkable this humanization of and reconciliation between
these former adversaries really is.

Regenerating Christ

By the time that he composed *Hellas*, Shelley had indulged his deepest narcissistic fantasies not only in a number of love poems and romantic
liaisons but also by constantly imagining and presenting himself as the
"youth / With patient looks nailed to a crucifix" (*PU*, I. 584–85). Following
his break with Christ in 1810–1811, Shelley soon allowed him to re-assert
himself, though generally in the poet's own messianic stances and (sometimes veiled) self-portraits. When we contemplate the relatively unproblematic presence of Christ in *Hellas*, we would be wrong to surmise that time,
maturity, wisdom, and so on, had conquered Narcissus and Ahasuerus and
(re)enthroned Christ as Shelley's guiding spirit—in part, because Shelley
had never fully deserted Christ nor did he ever abandon Narcissus in his
guise as the martyr (as some of his more maudlin lyrics to Jane Williams
remind us). But a "gradual renovation" did occur in Shelley's relations with
Jesus (*QM*, VIII. 143), so that we last glimpse him in Shelley's poetry as one
of "the sacred few" whom the author exempts from the tragic Triumph of
Life (*TL*, l. 128).
It is impossible, however, to trace a clean trajectory from the "horrid
Galilean" of the 1810 and 1811 letters to the "sacred" Jesus Christ of *The Triumph of Life* (*L*, I, 66). The "extraordinary ambivalence" toward Christ that

Stuart Sperry notes in *Queen Mab* remains even in *Hellas*, where one choral lyric calls him "a Promethean Conqueror" who tramples not only "the thorns of death and shame" but also such cherished pagan deities on "Apollo, Pan, and Love" (ll. 212, 214, 232).[106] Moreover, we find positive references to Christ as early as 1812, when Shelley set off with his (first) young wife and sister-in-law to Ireland to evangelize. His Irish pamphlets passionately invoke Jesus as the archetype of "the mildness of benevolence," as well as echo many of his sayings (*Prose* 33: *An Address, to the Irish People*). That Jesus plays a much greater role in *An Address, to the Irish People*, directed to a poor, uneducated and piously Catholic audience, than in the more sophisticated, Godwinian *Proposals for an Association of Philanthropists* suggests that the Savior's presence is partly a strategic one.[107] But Christ's influence on the poet's own self-fashioning is apparent in the amazing verve with which the nineteen-year-old Shelley transformed himself during this campaign into a charismatic orator and social reformer who dispensed moral imperatives such as, "Be in charity with all men" and "When one cheek is struck, turn the other" (*Prose* 16, 30: *An Address, to the Irish People*).

Shelley's early pamphlets manage both to appropriate and to undermine Jesus' authority. In them, and in the essay *On Christianity* (1817), Shelley presents himself as a truer disciple than the Christian audience he is addressing. At the same time, he implies that Jesus essentially failed in his own philanthropic mission, which Shelley himself will now bring to fruition. Jesus, Shelley writes, "fruitlessly endeavoured to teach mankind" the principle of equality (*Prose* 46: *Proposals for an Association of Philanthropists*); later, in *Queen Mab*, Jesus' "attempt to reform the world" is deemed "vain" (*PS*, I, 396: Note to *QM*, VII. 135).

There was to be for Shelley no easy reunion with Christ. In Kohut's terms, Shelley had already suffered severe "narcissistic mortification" when his earlier attempts to "merge into [the] omnipotent figure" of Christ had resulted in his beloved cousin's and sisters' rejection of their young preceptor for the Master himself ("Forms and Transformations" 252; "Narcissism and Narcissistic Rage" 365). Narcissus, whom Shelley had been strenuously resisting during the Harriet Grove crisis of 1810 and 1811, had already found his way into Shelley's psyche through a very unlikely path: the *Via Crucis* of his polar opposite.[108] Possessed once again in 1812 of a female coterie, including his faithful correspondent Elizabeth Hitchener, Shelley was anxious to retain his hold both on his companions/pupils and on Jesus himself, whom he could execrate but never give up. One method of maintaining this fragile new Eden involved taking "editorial control" of his predecessor by composing the *Biblical Extracts*, which Shelley conceived while proselytizing in Ireland.[109] *An Address, to the Irish People*, with its echoes/appropriations of Christ's themes and words, may have received a similar impetus.

More typically, though, he preserved his "proper Paradise" ("On Love" 474) of adoring disciples and safely guarded/absorbed "selfobject" by cultivating those psychological strategies that comprise the fundamental manifestations of his narcissism: the lover who needs a mirroring other and the martyr who noisily renounces Self. These two seemingly antithetical creatures—one a conspicuous progeny of Narcissus, and the other a bastard child of Christ—come together, for example, in *Alastor* and *Epipsychidion*, where the Self-possessed lover receives his punishment in the form of a rather splendid martyrdom, a pattern that subsequent chapters will explore.

Clearly, Shelley recognized Narcissus when he presented himself in his more characteristic attire, but he seems less conscious that his own imitations of Christ-as-martyr often indulge that very "love of *self*" that they are intended to overthrow (*L*, I, 192). Beginning with the 1812 *Letter to Lord Ellenborough*, Shelley explicitly and publicly adopts Christ as his paradigm of the selfless martyr, and, later on, overtly likens himself and such protagonists/personæ as Cythna, Prometheus, and Adonais to this "man of pure life" and glorious death (*PS*, I, 396: Note to *QM*, VII. 135).[110] From the gratuitous sufferings of Verezzi in his first Gothic novel to those Shelleyan heroes "who do endure / Deep wrongs for man," Shelley has certainly refined his conception of martyrdom (*PU*, I. 594–95); but, paradoxically, his lifelong sense that "only the martyr can be sure of his unselfishness" forces him into some inadvertently self-promoting postures (Freeman 117).

The two poems in which Narcissus and Christ collide most disastrously and ensure that the conspicuous suffering that I have alluded to reigns supreme would have to be *Epipsychidion* and *Adonais*. However, the excesses of those poems may actually have helped Shelley gain the much-needed distance from Christ which allowed the poet to treat his rival/ideal with such equanimity in *Hellas* and *The Triumph of Life*. Written within the same year (1821), *Epipsychidion* (January-February), *Adonais* (May-June), and *Hellas* (October) take the poet from the bizarre coalesce of—and with—Christ and Narcissus in the first two poems to the restraint and self-transcendence that grace the lyrical drama. In both *Epipsychidion* and *Adonais*, Shelley portrays his persona as Love itself. In the former poem, the speaker calls himself "This world of love, this *me*" (l. 346), and in the latter the Shelley figure is "A Love in desolation masked" (l. 281). Arguably, this hubristic gesture betrays not so much the poet's narcissism but his desperate attempt to *combat* it, as Love remained for Shelley the converse and potential redeemer of the Self. Yet "the dull vapours of the little world of self" manage to envelop both poems, and it seems to me that Shelley, always acutely aware of his own "egotizing variability," deliberately allows this (*Defence* 497; *L*, I, 44). Shelley's narcissistic merger with the martyred Christ culminates in *Adonais*, both in its versified self-portrait and especially in its (unexpurgated) Preface. This notoriously self-oriented elegy,[11] along with the astonishing excesses of *Epipsychidion*, thus may have enabled Shelley to indulge and at least partially to purge himself of those mighty opposites that alternately and often simultaneously held sway over him.

Thanks in part to these two poems, Shelley could keep both Christ and Narcissus in check within *Hellas* and *The Triumph of Life*, though it is impossible to project how long their relative quiescence would have lasted. It is crucial, though, that we understand their unrivaled place in his imagination, and to do so we must look not to some fictitious future but to his actual past, his boyhood and adolescent past at Field Place. There we can best gauge the depth of those narcissistic wounds he received, first, when as a boy he felt that his mother withdrew her affections from him, and, later, when his cousin/fiancée and his favorite sister rejected him and (re)turned to Christ. The adolescent Shelley's almost simultaneously shattered relationships with Christ, with Harriet Grove, and with his best-loved sister Elizabeth permanently affected his self-conception (in both senses of that phrase). This experience also helped convince him that Love's presence can be "transforming" both in its ever-shifting influence on its votaries and in its own instability and elusiveness.

The failure of his first romantic relationship had an especially powerful and generally underestimated impact on Shelley's development as a man and as a poet, to resort to a Bloomian dichotomy. His romance with his "first Harriet" grew up alongside his anti-Christianity, and the forced termination of their engagement further radicalized his religious views. Moreover, it brought to the surface his latent ambivalence to the "idealized selfobject" who galvanized and thwarted the young Shelley's efforts at self-fashioning. Most likely before and most definitely after his crisis-ridden relationship with Harriet Grove, Shelley did try to effect that with which most later readers credit him: a separation of the wheat that is Christ himself from the tares that his supposed followers later planted. Certainly, as the critical events and emotions associated with the years from 1809 through 1811 receded further into the distance, the much more sympathetic images of Christ that appear in the essay *On Christianity* and *Prometheus Unbound* tended to replace the harshly critical portraits found in the early letters and in *Queen Mab*. *On Christianity* offers an especially glowing tribute to "the mysterious sage of Judæa" (*Prose* 266). In fact, this text manages, linguistically and thematically, to meld the two moralists and poets, moving seamlessly between Christ's words and their quintessentially Shelleyan interpretations and elaborations. Thus the Beatitude "Blessed are the pure in heart, for they shall see God" receives an exegesis that, like so many passages from this essay, anticipates the language of the *Defence*: "[Jesus] affirms that a being of pure and gentle habits will not fail in every object of every thought, to be aware of benignant visitings from the invisible energies by which he is surrounded" (*Prose* 250, 251).

The *Defence* itself offers a similarly harmonious exchange between Christ and Shelley. "Poetry and the principle of Self . . . are the God and the Mammon of the world" (503),[112] Shelley writes, echoing and revising Jesus' words in Matthew 6: 24: "No man can serve two masters . . . Ye cannot serve God and mammon." This passage from the *Defence* simply confirms what even the poet's earliest texts reveal: that Christ profoundly influenced Shelley's thinking about, and his struggles against, Selfhood, that most tyrannical of masters. The constant clashes between the self-sacrificing Christ and the Self-idolizing Narcissus that we witness throughout his writings may have prevented Shelley from formulating—or living by—the consistent "doctrine" of love that he longed to develop, but their fierce and strangely fruitful encounters always remained at the heart of his writings and of his life.

2

SHELLEYAN DOPPELGÄNGER: LOATHSOME SYMPATHY/INDOMITABLE SELFHOOD

If Christ and Narcissus comprise the most significant (and most bizarre) pair that inhabits Shelley's psyche, it is Christ and Ahasuerus who represent quintessential Shelleyan doubles, explicitly linked figures who converge as aspects of one cloven being.[1] I hesitate to use the word *self* here, for when the pair consists of linked opposites, as in *Prometheus Unbound* and *The Cenci*, one member tends to combat the principle of Self by exemplifying Love and self-denial, while his or her double generally (re)asserts sinister Selfhood in guises such as hatred, fear, solipsism, and sexual possessiveness and/or violence. However, as the volatile conjunction of Christ and the Wandering Jew reminds us, Shelley offers no neat bifurcations, allowing the doubles to share certain qualities and to interact dynamically rather than simply to stand as rigid emblems of virtue and vice.

An alternative version of Shelleyan doubling involves his idealized heterosexual couples—those real and imagined "brothers and sisters of the soul"—as well as his penchant for romantic, often homoerotic friendships. Both types of dyad, the loving soul-mates and the yoked antagonists, emerge from a complex matrix comprising Shelley's lifelong sense of psychic division; his conflicting impulses toward self-projection, self-abnegation, and "self-anatomy,"[2] and his ambivalent desire for relation, even merger, with others (*Cenci*, II. ii. 110). What is most important, both configurations signal the return of the repressed in Shelley's life and writings: the strenuously repressed Self as ideal "other" *or* as "foul fiend" (*PS*, I, 450: "O! there are spirits of the air"). We have witnessed such a return in the way that the Self constantly obtrudes into Shelley's efforts to subdue Narcissus, a pattern that generates that ubiquitous figure within the Shelley canon, the ostentatiously selfless martyr, who often functions within one or both of the poet's protypical dyads.[3]

Following Otto Rank, William A. Ulmer points out that "Doubles are always the progeny of repression, projections outside the self of inadmissible impulses and secret guilt" (*Shelleyan Eros* 9). Ulmer focuses on Shelley's repression of the other in his erotic economy. Yet it is actually the poet's almost desperate need to eradicate selfhood altogether—even in such seemingly innocuous forms as personal identity as well as in *propria persona* (self-interest, self-absorption)—that largely generates the plethora of paired characters that people his imagination. This chapter will focus on those antipathetic doubles such as Laon and Othman and Prometheus and Jupiter, while chapter 3 will explore more fully Shelley's myth of erotic twinship. However, I do want to examine here their common origin and the central distinction that Shelley attempts to make between the dark double, referred to hereafter as the "*Doppelgänger*," and what he calls the "second self" (*L*, I, 183).[4] (In the terms I am employing, Prometheus, for example, would have Asia as his second self and Jupiter would be his *Doppelgänger*. We might, then, call Prometheus the "first self.")

Because the malevolent *Doppelgänger* and idealized second self seem to have had a twin birth out of Shelley's ruptured relationships with Harriet Grove, with Christ, and with his family during his late adolescence, the borders between them never remained as clearly drawn as Shelley might have liked. Reeling from those narcissistic blows that his "mirroring" (mother, sister, and cousin) and "omnipotent" (Christ) selfobjects dealt him, Shelley apparently endeavored to soothe himself as well as to dodge subsequent strikes by rooting out the vulnerable—and vengeful—Self altogether. Thus began his lifelong efforts at Self-conquest, and with them the compulsion to shield the "Spirit of love"—as well as his own psyche—from the "the dull vapours of the little world of self" (*S-P*, I. 6; *Defence* 497). And this primary dichotomy—between selfless Love and noxious Selfhood—generally governs Shelley's doubles, be they locked in "mutual hate" or joined by links of love (*CW*, I, 275: *LC*, II. 34).

It is not surprising that Self-idolatry would constitute the kind of "inadmissible impulse" that Rank, Ulmer, and others connect with the *Doppelgänger* phenomenon, and that such a flagrant embodiment of the principle of Self would be displaced from the Shelleyan hero's (and Shelley's own) psyche onto a Count Cenci or a Jupiter. It is also not surprising that another facet of Selfhood, hatred—such as the poet's own toward his ideal of sympathetic love, Christ—would find a fitting vehicle in Ahasuerus. What is remarkable, however, is Shelley's need to project onto an other, be it an actual lover or friend or a fictional character, a desirable attribute such as Self-esteem, cherished in the "Hymn to Intellectual Beauty" as a fleeting but divine gift. This brings us to the notion of the second self, the ostensible obverse of the diabolical double and a precursor of the Shelleyan epipsyche. If the malevolent version of the Shelleyan double offered a complex and disturbing kind of spectrality, involving both the pursuing spectre and the distorting mirror, the second self was for Shelley a "mirror whose surface reflects only the forms of purity and brightness" ("On Love" 474). Or, more radically, the second self became "a Sea reflecting Love" when the "first self" metamorphosed into Love, as the poet often himself yearned to do (*PU*, IV. 384).

The term *second self*, which Shelley first uses in an 1811 letter to Elizabeth Hitchener (*L*, I, 183), is something of a misnomer, for the second self derives its existence from the absence, or at least repression, of a "first self," Shelley's own. In praising and cultivating those virtues in his various "second selves" that he himself longed to embody, Shelley not only played his favorite role of Christlike preceptor, but he also indirectly constructed the identity, the selfhood that he had tried to banish. Thus, for example, Shelley's "esteem" for Miss Hitchener and his concomitant encouragement of her own "Self-esteem" could enable him to partake of this precious quality without slipping into the slough of egotism—and wounded egotism—that seemed to Shelley perilously close to the realm of even the most wholesome manifestations of self-regard.

That Shelley was aware of the narcissistic character of this interpersonal dynamic is evident in an early letter to Hogg, where Shelley laments his own "egotising folly" in praising his sister Elizabeth and thus (deliberately) encouraging his friend to fall in love with her (*L*, I, 29: 23 December 1810). As Elizabeth's physical and spiritual "twin" and the self-appointed guide and guardian of her intellect, Percy realizes here that he had engaged in self-praise when extolling Elizabeth's merits.[5] Yet Percy's need to "create" and interact with mirroring others—usually *female* others—seemed to overcome his scruples about such relationships as the crucial events of 1810 and 1811 unfolded and he found himself bereft of his original "second self," Elizabeth, as well as of his more recent protégée, Harriet Grove.[6] The more furiously he fought against "that egotizing variability" that provoked him to covet the increasingly inaccessible Harriet (and Elizabeth) and thus to supplant "universal imperishable" Love with naked self-interest, the more urgent the demands of the willfully stifled Self seemed to become (*L*, I, 44, 45: 12 January 1811). Although he never abandoned his model of the second self as a conduit for his own self-fashioning and need for Love and Self-esteem, he rarely lost sight of the dangers it posed.

The flash of self-knowledge that we glimpse in the December 1810 letter to Hogg regarding the connection between his own vanity and his celebration of his sister/ second self eventually developed into a complex strategy that allowed Shelley to criticize and yet to preserve this version of doubling as an erotic paradigm. At times this criticism seems to take the form of (self-)parody, as when Laon, with the aid of a compliant Cythna, stridently insists on his status as the source of his sister/second self's very being.[7] Moreover, as we shall see in the following chapters, Shelley often inflicts on one or both of his twinned lovers an annihilation that allows him, by invoking the problematic figure of the radically Self-renouncing martyr, to discipline his own desire for this kind of narcissistic bond.

Most pertinent here, however, is not the common identity—and death—that Shelleyan lovers share, but the way that another kind of pairing haunts

Shelley's consciousness. Either independent of or allied with the ideal, often eroticized first self/second self dyad, the pernicious, usually masculine *Doppelgänger* incarnates the principle of Self much more conspicuously than does the (narcissistic) lover yearning for his mirroring other. Like the figure of the second self, the dark *Doppelgänger* offers the "simultaneous satisfaction and punishment of a repressed desire that is at the core of doubling" (Irwin 44). The former construct, exemplified by Verezzi's Julia and Laon's Cythna, enables the poet to indulge and to chasten his powerful desire for a mirroring other who will confirm/create Shelley's own or his surrogate's perfected selfhood, or, more paradoxically, perfected Selfhood. However, the menacing double, embodied by Verezzi's Zastrozzi and Laon's Othman, provides a vehicle for the more obvious manifestations of "the sordid lust of self" (*QM*, V. 90): vengefulness, hatred, and sexual tyranny (of a less subtle kind than that embedded within the self/second self dynamic).

Yet Rank's emphasis on the double's "catastrophic effect in the relationship of love" reminds us of the essential kinship between the two contrasting types of Shelleyan doubles (*The Double* 11).[8] Although Rank is referring here to the sinister shadow figure who pursues, rivals, and "everywhere balks the self" (11), Shelley's idealized second selves—whether his fictive or his actual alter egos—thwart his efforts to represent sympathetic love just as efficiently as his more recognizably dangerous doubles do. For the second self ensures that Love's "proper Paradise" remained a tightly enclosed haven for the narcissist ("On Love" 474). In fact these competing paradigms of the double, functioning in a way as doubles for each other, often merge (or collide) within both Shelley's personal experience and his fictive worlds. This is not exactly surprising, given that they both seem to have sprung from the emotional chaos that dominated Shelley's late adolescence. Their common roots are most nakedly exposed in his 1810 and 1811 letters to Hogg, where we witness not only Shelley's struggles to destroy and to become Christ but also that troubling entanglement of Love and devastating hatred which his pain and his fury helped effect.

These vivid "transcripts of [his] thoughts"—confessions, rhapsodies, laments, tantrums, (Self-)admonishments—which Shelley dispatches to his beloved friend Hogg offer dizzying displays of Shelley's impetuous leaps between the shrine of hatred and the temple of "love *infinite in extent*" (*L*, I, 176, 35). This last phrase comes from a particularly rich letter, which dramatizes, perhaps deliberately, the young Shelley's torturous dual allegiance to the principle of Self (here eloquently represented by Hatred, Vengeance, and Self-Pity) and to the very power that should defeat this demon: self-abnegating Love. This is the letter of 3 January 1811, discussed in the previous chapter, in which Shelley allies himself with both the Wandering Jew (by echoing Schubart's "Der ewige Jude") and Satan ("Oh how I wish I were the

Antichrist"), discovers that "there is selfishness in the passion of Love," and threatens to adopt the most extreme method to exterminate Selfhood: suicide (*L*, I, 35–36). By identifying with Ahasuerus and with Satan, Shelley is casting himself in the role of Christ's malignant *Doppelgänger*. Yet he encircles and thereby buffers this (literally) central passage on "lasting long revenge" with a Christlike halo: a vision of a unified world-in-relation,[9] an homage to universal, eternal love, and a pledge to spurn selfishness and embrace unconditional sympathy (*L*, I, 35).

Within the bitter core of this letter we find a striking moment of coincidence between these two radically opposed impulses—toward and away from "that *hateful* principle" of Self—when Shelley vows that "every moment shall be devoted to my object" (*L*, I, 34, 35). Although he is referring here to his desire to destroy Christ and Christianity, his language resembles that of a quite different sort of desire. In the language of romantic love, Shelley's "object" ordinarily would be his beloved—at this point Harriet Grove—or those efforts he was making to win her back.[10] Again, a few sentences later, when Percy tells his friend, "I expect to gratify some of this insatiable feeling in Poetry," one would expect such a feeling to be his love for Harriet and/or for humankind itself, if his love were indeed "*infinite in extent*" (*L*, I, 35). While he had for some time been gratifying in various poems and letters (to Thomas and probably to Harriet herself) his "insatiable feeling[s]" of love,[11] it is his "insatiable" appetite for vengeance that erupts into the letter at this point and usurps the language of love which Percy in this letter and elsewhere had been cultivating and with which he had been allying himself (*L*, I, 35). It is as if, in a reversal of Coleridge's enigmatic "conclusion" to Part II of *Christabel*, Shelley must needs express his hate's excess with words of unmeant love; his "rage and pain . . . talks as it's most used to do" and thus inadvertently "force[s] together / Thoughts so all unlike each other" (ll. 676–77, 666–67).

This linguistic conflation of love and hatred suggests the difficulties that Shelley will confront when he attempts to segregate his representatives of sympathetic Love—the virtuous first self and the idealized second self—from the polluting atmosphere of the dangerous *Doppelgänger*. Shelley's most complex and emotionally honest works tacitly acknowlege the impossibility of such strict distinctions between seemingly antithetical impulses (and those who embody them) and in fact allow these two versions of the double to intermingle.[12] And it was his intense emotional involvement with the schoolmistress of Hurstpierpoint, Elizabeth Hitchener, which literally brought home the complex web he had woven between self and double(s).[13]

That Elizabeth Hitchener metamorphoses from the poet's beloved second self to "the Brown Demon" certainly bespeaks Shelley's troubling tendency to elevate and then cruelly demote various friends and lovers according to the shifting tides of his own needs and desires (*L*, I, 336: to Hogg, 3 December 1812). But his disillusionment with her—nearly as soon as she became an inmate of his cottage during the summer of 1812[14]—also reveals the close kinship that connects and even identifies the ideal with the hateful Shelleyan double. The reversal in status that Elizabeth Hitchener suffered within Shelley's imagination and then within his "little circle" (*L*, I, 292) suggests not only that she failed—predictably—to live up to his exalted notions of her, but also that she presented to her preceptor, the "brother of her soul," an almost too precise mirror image of himself.

In her illuminating reading of *Alastor* through the lense of *Frankenstein*, Margaret Homans asks, "What if the hero of *Alastor* actually got what he thinks he wants? What if his desire were embodied?" (107–8). If we apply Homans's query to the Hitchener-Shelley "liaison" as it moved from the realm of epistolary exchange to everyday contact in close quarters, it seems that Shelley got what he thought he wanted: an enthusiastic second self who shared his intellectual and political interests and whose actual conversation and physical presence he could now enjoy.[15] But while it may have delighted Shelley to pore over the letters that echoed his own ideas and even language,[16] it must have been a shock to meet face-to-face his own self-image, a "double" whom he had created—or at least cultivated and onanistically caressed at a distance—and who now stood before him as an embodiment of his irrepressible Selfhood.

Shelley and Elizabeth Hitchener had met only twice—both times prior to his marriage to Harriet Westbrook—before she joined his household in Lynmouth. Thus when he encountered her in the summer of 1812, she had truly become Shelley's "double" and disciple, which only briefly gratified this would-be Christ. Holmes (*Pursuit* 176) rightly discerns sexual revulsion in Shelley's startling description of her as "an artful, superficial, ugly, hermaphrodical beast of a woman" (*L*, I, 336). In spurning her as an hermaphrodite, Shelley is not only referring to Elizabeth's Hitchener's rather masculine features, body type, and facial hair—which Hogg wickedly catalogues in his *Life* (II, 55–57)—but he also seems to be imaging her as an unnatural and repellent composite of himself and Miss Hitchener. A creature of ambiguous gender himself, Shelley would have been troubled by this further evidence that he had somehow "superimposed" himself on this worshipful woman. Lacking the remarkable familial resemblence to Shelley that his other "twins," Elizabeth Shelley and Harriet Grove, shared, Elizabeth Hitchener nonetheless became Shelley's most uncannily accurate—and thus most disturbing—mirror image, zealously imitating his words and activities during her four-month stay with him.

Homans contends in her analysis of Mary Shelley's critique of (masculine) romanticism that embodiment per se—an embodied other or, in terms of visionary poetics, a created product as opposed to creative process—is what

Victor Frankenstein, the *Alastor* Poet, the speaker of *Epipsychidion*, and Percy Shelley himself reject.[17] While I generally concur with Homans' assessment, I credit Percy as well as Mary Shelley with insight into romantic egotism—and into his own odd strain of narcissism, which sprung in part from the poet's "boasted hatred of self" (*L*, I, 77–78). For the tangible second self, the embodied "vision" of an Elizabeth Hitchener, or in *Alastor*, of a conspicuously absent veiled maid, represented for Shelley a grotesque incarnation of his own Self-involvement. As the nexus between the desired second self and the shunned *Doppelgänger*, Elizabeth Hitchener personified the duplicious "spirit of solitude" that will both seduce and torment the Poet of *Alastor*. Stuart Curran's assertion that "The impalpable vision that entices [the Poet] to his eventual death is the perfect ideal of his own mind" emphasizes how the vengeful spirit of solitude and the "cursed man" whom it pursues converge within the two-edged term *alastor* (*Shelley's Annus Mirabilis* 21).[18] I would add that the poem also identifies the Poet's beautiful "Being" with his demonic double (Preface to *Alastor* 69): the veiled maid, or idealized second self, *is* "the fierce fiend" who both lures and pursues the youth to his "untimely tomb" (*Alastor*, ll. 226, 50). In a sense, *Alastor* tells the story of a poet who was not "fortunate" enough to meet the incarnation of his narcissistic desire and thus to recognize it for what it was. Unfortunately, as fodder for Shelley's private mythology, Elizabeth Hitchener herself became for her adored preceptor a demonic *Doppelgänger*, a monstrous incarnation of (his own) Selfhood, who must be expelled from the "proper Paradise" of love ("On Love" 474).[19] It is a testament to her generous spirit—or to her folly—that Elizabeth Hitchener eventually forgave Shelley and cherished her memories of him.[20]

Although Shelley could dismiss this "Brown Demon" with a farewell dinner and the promise of an annual stipend,[21] he had already begun to explore in his writings the tenacity with which such doubles, as Self-projections, clung to their "hosts." Through his experience with Elizabeth Hitchener, he confronted the troubling kinship, even identity between the second self and the *Doppelgänger*, though he never lost his compulsion to seek and/or create idealized and usually feminine "twins." Within Shelley's writings the vicious double, the hideous outgrowth of repressed Selfhood, only rarely reveals, as in *Alastor*, its status as the dark obverse of the second self. As later chapters will emphasize, Shelley found other methods of enacting and punishing his desire for a loving second self besides suppressing and then exposing its intersection with the malevolent *Doppelgänger*.

Besides the second self and the *Doppelgänger*, both of which have at least the fiction of otherness ascribed to them, another type of double emerged from Shelley's imagination as he struggled to supplant the principle of Self with the reign of Love. Sometimes an unthreatening but more often a "ghastly" presence, the double as it appears to the addressee of "O! there are spirits of the air" (*PS*, I, 450),[22] to Laon in his delirium (*LC*, III. 199–207), and to Shelley himself at the Casa Magni (*LMWS*, I, 244–45) functions explicitly as a haunting *self*-image. Although as a boy Shelley had frightened his younger sisters with stories of ghostly pursuers and had populated his earliest writings with various macabre beings,[23] he first identifies such phantoms with the Self during his lonely sojourn in London following his expulsion from Oxford in the spring of 1811. Like so many who feel themselves isolated prisoners within the populous city, Shelley found himself in a particularly painful quandary: both solitude and contact with the urban crowd seemed unbearable. For several months, since the decisive Christmas vacation when he learned that his fiancée had jilted him for the "horrid Galilean"—and for a conventional marriage to "a clod of earth"—Shelley had been continually urging himself to crush all selfish feeling entirely and instead to embrace purely sympathetic love (*L*, I, 66, 41). From Hume and Godwin, for example, Shelley had learned that what Hume calls "disinterested benevolence"[24] could be a feasible individual and communal goal, though the young poet, imitating (and resisting) Christ, strove for a much more radical self-abnegation than his rationalist forbears envisioned or encouraged. Now he discovered just how difficult his personal mission really was. The Self was not so easy to slough off,[25] nor were "co-existent beings" as lovable as one might hope (*L*, I, 77).

A characteristically dense letter to Hogg written during this period displays Shelley struggling with these two interconnected issues, issues that would remain central to the *Doppelgänger* theme as it appears in both his poetry and correspondence. After conveying his first impressions of Leigh and Marianne Hunt, whom he had recently met, Shelley launches into a disquisition on solitude and sympathy. This letter is worth quoting at some length, as it exemplifies Shelleyan self-scrutiny at its most candid and insightful:

> Solitude is most horrible; in despite of the αφιλαυτια [lack of self-love] which perhaps vanity has a great share in, but certainly not with my own good will I cannot endure the horror the evil which comes to *self* in solitude. I spend most of my time at Miss [Eliza] Westbrooks, I was a great deal too hasty in criticizing her character;—how often have we to alter the impressions which first sight or first any thing produces; I *really* now consider her as amiable . . . I most probably now am prejudiced for you cannot breathe you cannot exist if *no* parts of loveliness appear in co-existent beings. I think were I compelled to associate with Shakespeare's Caliban with any wretch, with the exception of Lord Courtney, my father, B[isho]p Warburton or the vile female who destroyed Mary[26] that I should find something to admire; what strange being I am, how

inconsistent, in spite of all my bo[a]sted hatred of self—this moment thinking I could so far overcome Natures law as to exist in complete seclusion, the next shrinking from a moment of solitude, starting from my own company as it were that of a fiend, seeking any thing rather than a continued communion with *self.* (*L,* I, 77–78: 8 May 1811)

Shelley's "hatred of self," the letter implies, could entail "vanity," not only because it may cloak a more fundamental self-conceit,[27] but also because his efforts to repress the self—through willed *aphilautia*[28]—appear futile. For "self" has reappeared as a "fiend," a terrifying twin who initiates a new cycle of repression and flight (Shelley "*start[s]* from [his] own company . . . *seeking* any thing rather than a continued communion" with [him]self).[29] In fleeing from self, though, Shelley must turn to an equally problematic companion, humankind, whom, according to his 1816 spiritual autobiography, he had vowed as a boy to love unselfishly ("Hymn," ll. 83–84).[30]

Although the exiled son regards Timothy Shelley and a select handful of other "tyrants" as irredeemable (and avoidable), his need to discern in his fellow beings at least some "parts of loveliness" emerges not simply from his current loneliness but from his increasing sense that the boundary between self and other is flimsy at best. From disparate sources such as Dr. Adam Walker's lectures on electricity as the sympathetic fluid of the universe, Lucretius' emphasis on the porosity and flux of matter, Christ's supreme, metaphysically based sympathy with his flock, and his own apparent sense of psychic porosity, Shelley had begun conceptualizing the world as a physically and spiritually interpenetrating realm, a "mazy volume of commingling things," as he had put it in a recent poem.[31] One *must* find "something to admire," something to love in others, else those others will inspire what Shelley later terms "loathsome" rather than loving sympathy (*PU,* I. 451). Besides emphasizing through linguistic repetition ("you cannot exist . . . co-existent beings") the connection, or continuity, between self and other, Shelley declares in the letter at hand that "you cannot breathe" if you associate with utterly corrupt beings. For a feature of the Shelleyan sympathetically bonded universe is that, in a very real way, individual members of this vast network supply one another's atmospheres. While the influence one person sheds may be vivifying, another person may emit what Shelley calls in *Epipsychidion* "a killing air" (l. 262).[32]

Though at this point Shelley attempts to segregate and ignore such "enemies" as his father,[33] he had already begun to invoke in his poetry and fiction the figure of the malevolent double as an emblem of his own troubled commitment to what modern feminists have termed a "self-in-relation" model of human interaction.[34] For the *Doppelgänger* enables Shelley to confront and investigate the dark side of his conception of a dynamically interpenetrating world, a world that may involve the subject's vulnerability to and complicity in contaminating (as opposed to salutary) influences. As agents of "the contagion of the world's slow stain," not only do figures such as Othman, Jupiter, and Count Cenci represent their heroic counterparts' self-division and/or displaced aggression, but they also embody Shelley's own ambivalence toward the collapse of self into other that is the hallmark of his erotic verse and the activating force behind the cosmic masque that concludes *Prometheus Unbound* (*Adonais*, l. 366). While the eighteen-year-old Shelley, full of self-pity and self-righteousness, denies his connection with his "enemy," Timothy Shelley, the author of *Prometheus Unbound* and *The Cenci* imaginatively merges with his most vile characters as he explores their disturbing affiliation with his protagonists/surrogates as well as investigates their baneful role within an intimately interconnected world.

As an invasive, diseased creature, the malevolent double in Shelley's mature works spreads poison, and often, more specifically, a poison connected with masculine sexuality.[35] Thus Jupiter's semen is likened to snake's bane and Count Cenci's to a "contaminating mist," while Othman's rapacity—sexual and otherwise—spawns a devastating plague (*PU*, III. i. 39–42; *Cenci*, III. i. 17). In view of the poet's hatred of his father during the crucial years of Percy's late teens and early twenties, it is tempting to see the antagonistic pairings within these works as (re)enactments of oedipal clashes. However, despite Othman's, Jupiter's, and Cenci's obvious function as evil father figures, it is unlikely that Shelley modeled these vicious characters on his own father. Although Shelley did consider his father a hypocrite and tyrant, he never seemed to regard him as an embodiment of sexual power—or blight.[36]

An anecdote about the poet's father recounted by Medwin does suggest, though, that the elder Shelley personified the libertine attitude toward sexual matters that Shelley despised as a feature both of the aristocracy and of masculine arrogance. Timothy Shelley, Medwin reports, "was a disciple of Chesterfield and La Rochefoucauld,[37] reducing all politeness to forms, and moral virtue to expediency; as an instance of which, he once told his son . . . that he would provide for as many natural children as he chose to get, but that he would never forgive his making a *mésalliance*" (*Life* 13).[38] This image of himself scattering his seed with a kind of gentlemanly largesse must have disturbed Shelley greatly, for he was already developing a deep distrust of (his own) masculine sexuality.[39]

From his earliest writings, Shelley links male desire to what he calls in *Queen Mab* "the sordid lust of self" (V. 90), the deadliest of Shelleyan sins and the most salient trait of his most depraved incarnations of the *Doppelgänger*: Othman, Jupiter, and Count Cenci. Even during his most intense anguish over Harriet Grove's rejection of him, he never accused her, or any of the women he portrayed in the literary productions of that period, of sexual betrayal.[40] This seems rather surprising when we consider Shelley's often irrational fury during this crisis and his obvious awareness of female sexual desire,[41] an awareness (and fascination) evinced both in *Zastrozzi* and in *St. Irvine*. Yet while he investigated and even identified with feminine sexuality,[42] he generally reserves for the masculine gender the propensity for sexual infidelity, self-serving sensuality,[43] and sexual violence.

While it is difficult to pinpoint the source of Shelley's pessimism about his own gender, we can probably ascribe it to a combination of factors within the personal, familial, and social realms. To begin with the second category, I have already mentioned Timothy Shelley's presumptions about the masculine "prerogative," an attitude that he no doubt inherited from his own father, Sir Bysshe Shelley, something of a satyr who bequeathed a small part of his fortune to "an unstated number of bastard offspring" (Cameron, *Young Shelley*, 1).[44] Shelley's keen awareness of social conditions also contributed to his antimasculinist cast of mind. One of the most striking images of his early writings is the abandoned woman seeking either "her babe's food at her ruiner's gate" (*Esdaile* 129: "Cold are the blasts") or, as in "Ghasta!!!," vengeance on her false lover.[45] During his brief stay in Keswick in early 1812, Shelley wrote to Elizabeth Hitchener, "Children are frequently found in the River which the unfortunate women employed at the manufactory destroy" (*L*, I, 223).[46] While he might not have known of such extreme cases in his native Horsham, the young Shelley probably heard tell of seduced, impregnated, and abandoned girls from the area, girls who might ultimately have become London prostitutes, a class of women Shelley certainly observed during his boyhood visits to that city.[47] And although he will eventually—and frequently—rail against what he calls in *Queen Mab* "prostitution's venomed bane" (IX. 87), he traces the source of this poison not to feminine concupiscence but to the patriarchal institution of marriage, which, according to Shelley's fragmentary "Essay on Marriage" (?1817), originated from men's efforts to retain women as sexual chattel.[48]

G. J. Barker-Benfield's work on the culture of sensibility helps us see Shelley's rejection of masculinity as reflecting widespread efforts to "soften" and reform a male culture that many saw as "raucous, riotous, appetitive, and brutal" (76).[49] Barker-Benfield observes that the advent of commercial capitalism forced men to try "to make sense of a manhood expressing itself more immediately in commerce than in war" (xxvii). This puts into (a gendered) perspective Shelley's attacks on commerce[50] and on "the selfish and calculating principle," the very "principle of Self, of which money is the visible incarnation" (*Defence* 503). Barker-Benfield's study particularly illuminates how legislation, literature, and religion—especially Methodism—all targeted the unreconstructed male, embodied most notoriously in the dashing, dangerous figure of the rake. While the rake's sexual excesses came under the most scrutiny, Barker-Benfield reminds us that he also personified masculine violence, acquisitiveness, materialism, and egotism. These are all key concerns for Shelley as he conceptualizes his principle of Self—and the dark *Doppelgänger* who incarnate it. Like the rake, or "libertine" as Shelley calls him, such figures as Othman, Count Cenci, and Jupiter are rapaciously sexual creatures, and this aspect of their Selfhood will be of primary importance in the pages that follow. But I want to emphasize that "the *lust* of self," the *Doppelgänger*'s salient trait, works closely with the political tyranny, military aggression, and materialistic greed that characterize Shelley's multifaceted symbols of Selfhood.[51]

When, in the summer of 1812, Shelley writes to James Henry Lawrence (whose antimatrimonial novel *The Empire of the Nairs* Shelley had recently devoured), he reveals an intensely personal stake in his ongoing critique of masculine desire. Justifying his current capitulation to social convention (he and Harriet Westbrook had been married a year), Shelley writes, "seduction, which term could have no meaning, in a rational society, has now a most tremendous one . . . If there is any enormous and desolating crime, of which I should shudder to be accused, it is seduction" (*L*, I, 323). Two years later, writing to Mary Godwin from his dingy London lodgings, Shelley employs similar language to that of both the letter to Lawrence and the 8 May 1811 letter to Hogg lamenting "the horror the evil which comes to *self* in solitude" (*L*, I, 77). "It seems as if you alone could shield me fr{om} impurity & vice," he writes to his new(est) love, "If I were absent from you long I should shudder with horror at myself" (*L*, I, 414: 28 October 1814). Although neither the letter to Lawrence nor to Mary Godwin explicitly invokes the fiendish double that haunted him at Poland Street in the spring of 1811, both letters imply the kind of self-repulsion exposed in the 1811 missive,[52] while the letter to Mary clearly reveals the self-division (or duplication) innate to the *Doppelgänger* phenomenon. Looked at together, these three letters help suggest why the self-divided, self-anatomizing Shelley turned to the double to investigate his own darkest impulses. More specifically, the letters to Lawrence and to Mary Godwin reveal how the baneful *Doppelgänger* in his imaginative works emerged from his deep suspicions about his own sex, a sex all too capable of seduction and of coupling with prostitutes—as these letters emphasize[53]—as well as of the most horrific sexual violence, as powerfully displayed by the tragic history of the Cenci family.

Much more than a vehicle for his protagonists' or his own displaced hatred, self-involvement, or (sexual) aggression, the malevolent double allows Shelley to confront why and how Ruin so often becomes "Love's shadow . . . / Following him destroyingly," both within the poet's own experience and that of humanity at large (*PU*, I. 780–81). As the dark obverse of the longed-for second self, this version of the *Doppelgänger* attests to Shelley's recognition—if not his repudiation—of the narcissism that fuels the quest for a perfectly responsive, compliant, and sympathetic other. As an agent of contamination and destruction, the *Doppelgänger* represents Shelley's troubled but enduring commitment to a self-in-relation model of identity wherein self and other may be joined by "loathsome" or "horrid" rather than loving sympathy (*PU*, I. 451; *CW*, I, 381: *LC*, X. 195). And as an incarnation of the principle of Self more potent than Narcissus, the vicious *Doppelgänger* perfectly embodies the Ruin that stalks Love within the sexual, communal, and spiritual realms. Haunting the pages of Shelley's works from *Zastrozzi* through *The Triumph of Life*, the figure of the sinister double, like that of the self-promoting Shelleyan martyr, emerges as a somewhat paradoxical creature. A vessel of indomitable Selfhood, the Shelleyan *Doppelgänger* is nonetheless emblematic of the poet's willingness to imaginatively identify or "sympathize" with the most hideous "wretch," and, even more difficult, to look inward and recognize that wretch as himself (*L*, I, 77).

Zastrozzi's Distempered Visions

Even during his "votary of Romance" period, Shelley exploits the *Doppelgänger* theme with considerable skill. His first Gothic novel, *Zastrozzi*, composed in the spring and summer of 1809, involves a network of characters that, as Jerrold Hogle has pointed out, includes not only antagonistic male *Doppelgänger*, but also Matilda and Julia, female doubles "who embody in their own ways the angelic and Satanic tendencies in their men" ("Shelley's Fiction" 85).[54] While in the previous chapter I examined this novel within the context of Shelley's struggle to defeat and absorb Christ, I now want to look more closely at *Zastrozzi*'s complex role as Verezzi's dark double.

To call Zastrozzi Verezzi's "dark" *Doppelgänger* may suggest that Verezzi himself is the virtuous half of the pair. But although this early work does anticipate the diametrically opposed doubles that clash within the poems of Shelley's maturity, the young author is not yet able (or willing?) to create a character who embodies that highest of Shelleyan virtues, disinterested love. Perhaps because Shelley had always looked to Christ as the paradigm of self-sacrifice and philanthropy, his chaotic feelings about "the Incarnate" during his adolescence and early adulthood prevented him for many years from fashioning a truly loving, self-abnegating protagonist (*QM*, VII. 163).[55] The only vaguely unselfish inhabitants of *Zastrozzi*'s Gothic landscape, Julia and Claudine, remain shadowy presences. For in the gloomy world of Shelley's first novel, "love" means obsession, possessiveness, and lust—aspects in fact of Selfhood. And it is the principle of Self that remains the book's focus as it unfolds the tragic kinship that binds its two central characters.

This bond is especially tragic because it involves an actual and not simply a symbolic kinship. Oddly enough, commentatators on this work rarely mention that Verezzi and Zastrozzi share the same father and thus are half-brothers. In light of James Bieri's highly reasonable contention that "Shelley had an older half-brother, the illegitimate son of his father Timothy," we could see *Zastrozzi* as an elaborate enactment of a legitimate son's fears about a vindictive bastard brother (29). Regardless of whether Shelley knew of his brother at this time, the young author was well aware of and passionately condemned his father's and grandfather's view of illegitimate children as natural offshoots of masculine and aristocratic privilege. As the progeny and the scourge of social and sexual injustice, the "demoniac" Zastrozzi would allow Shelley to punish the patriarchs of "tumid pride" (linked if not identified with his own progenitors and represented in the novel by the elder Baron Verezzi[56]) as well as to chastize the "legitimate" heirs of their corrupt demesne, such as the young Verezzi and, Shelley may have feared, himself (*CW*, V, 10: *Zastrozzi*; *Esdaile* 44: "Falshood and Vice," l. 18).[57] In a sense, then, Shelley's Gothic villain emerges as an early version of Jupiter's "fatal Child," Demogorgon, though Zastrozzi destroys both his own father and, by orchestrating the younger Baron's suicide, his brother (*PU*, III. i. 19).

It is Shelley's alternating, sometimes simultaneous identification with each of this novel's paired antagonists, who share bloodlines as well as character traits, that enables him imaginatively both to inflict (through Zastrozzi) and to receive (via Verezzi) the kind of punishment that I have been discussing. This dynamic anticipates the interplay between, and Shelley's own psychic interaction with, the paired figures of *The Wandering Jew*, written the following year. This poem, which stages the crucial Shelleyan confrontation/interpenetration between Christ and Ahasuerus, in turn prefigures the dramatic struggles of the warring doubles in the plays of Shelley's maturity, *Prometheus Unbound* and *The Cenci*.[58] In the later works, however, Shelley aligns himself much more decisively with one half of the central pair than he does in the works of his youth such as *Zastrozzi*, *St. Irvyne*, and *The Wandering Jew*, where Shelley's own anger at Christ, his family, and himself eclipses any effort to create and cathect with an embodiment of the love and sympathy that his letters to Hogg will passionately espouse. These early works only adumbrate—through Verezzi's flashes of compassion, Ginotti's and Wolfstein's former "high-souled" nobility (*CW*, I, 113: *SI*), and Christ's "Forgiveness to his enemies" (*PS*, I, 59: *WJ*, III. 598)—the (relatively) idealized member of each of the 1819 dramas' discordant dyads, Prometheus and Beatrice Cenci.

Despite frequent efforts to represent and/or extol unselfishness and love in the productions of his late teens and early twenties, Shelley's most compelling works—then and perhaps always—sprang from his fascination with and bitter hatred of "the sordid lust of self" (*QM*, V. 90).[59] When, in a letter to William Godwin, Shelley calls *Zastrozzi* and *St. Irvyne* "distempered . . . visions," he suggests that their composition involved a kind of purgation of his "intellectual sickliness" (*L*, I, 266: 8 March 1812). The fact that both novels focus on a pair of *Doppelgänger* whose mutual devotion to the principle of Self provides their salient link reveals that Shelley's "distemper" involved his own struggles to escape the bonds of that most "relentless gaoler," the tyrannical Self (*CW*, V, 7: *Zastrozzi*).[60]

When we first meet the two key players of *Zastrozzi*, their only link seems to be that of victim and victimizer, an affiliation whose supreme significance becomes apparent when we encounter those genuine Shelleyan martyrs who, unlike Zastrozzi and Verezzi, strive to subdue and even destroy rather than indulge Self. Because Shelley does not disclose these characters' familial relationship until the novel's final pages, it would be easy to sustain our initial impression of Verezzi simply as Zastrozzi's "hapless victim of unmerited persecution" (*CW*, V, 6). Verezzi's extreme passivity could not provide a more striking contrast with his enemy's indefatigable energy, while Zastrozzi's "towering and majestic" manliness constantly counters Verezzi's remarkably feminine sensibility and behavior (*CW*, V, 34). Yet Shelley subtly establishes their spiritual affinity throughout the novel as he exposes the various guises the principle of Self can wear as well as explores the loathsome sympathy that unites Verezzi with both his tormentor and his tormentor's female mirror image, Matilda.

One of Shelley's more direct methods of yoking Verezzi and Zastrozzi as *Doppelgänger* is to provide a linguistic link between them. Thus, for example, both Verezzi and Zastrozzi have "soul-illumined countenance[s]" and both die "exulting," Verezzi with "a bitter smile of exultation" and Zastrozzi with a "convulsive laugh of exulting revenge" (*CW*, V, 86, 88, 103). Moreover, Shelley invokes the notion of the double as conscience that Freud emphasizes in "The Uncanny" when, for instance, Zastrozzi tells his "prey," that "following us in submissive silence can alone procure the slightest mitigation of your punishment," a punishment that involves not only Zastrozzi's revenge on his mother's ruiner and "his progeny for ever" but also—proleptically—the sexual trangression that Zastrozzi ensures the young Verezzi will commit with Matilda (*CW*, V, 5, 6, 102). And when Zastrozzi tears his victim "from the society of all he held dear on earth" (*CW*, V, 5), particularly his beloved Julia, he provides the "catastrophic effect" on love that Rank associates with the *Doppelgänger* (*The Double* 11). Finally, after Verezzi temporarily escapes his persecutor's clutches, Zastrozzi becomes the kind of pursuing double that Godwin had portrayed in *Caleb Williams*[61] and that his daughter would depict in *Frankenstein*: Verezzi "thought that he heard Zastrozzi's voice in every gale. Turning he thought Zastrozzi's eye glanced over his shoulder" (*CW*, V, 15). When Verezzi then "start[s]" at his own reflected image," his (self-) identification with Zastrozzi seems complete (*CW*, V, 15).[62]

And in fact Verezzi comes to resemble Zastrozzi more and more as the novel unfolds. The "painful captivity" Verezzi suffers in the first chapter suggests that he undergoes a kind of metamorphosis while in his enemy's custody (*CW*, V, 7). Chained to a rock within a "desolate and dark cavern" (*CW*, V, 11), the miserable Verezzi prefigures Prometheus on his crag and Cythna in her sea cave, while his "resurrection" from this "grave" (*CW*, V, 6) recalls Christ's liberation from his sepulchre and foreshadows Cythna's miraculous release from her "strange dungeon" (*CW*, I, 348: *LC*, VII. 124).[63] Yet Verezzi emerges no redeemed martyr from his womb-tomb. Instead, he is (re)born in the image of "his most rancorous, his bitterest enemy," whose unmasked face he beholds only after his interment in the cave (*CW*, V, 35).

Jerrold Hogle has rightly identified the crucial impulse that unites these doubles as "the cancerous self-hatred that urges the mind to stay locked within the labyrinth of its personal desire for what is lost" ("Shelley's Fiction" 85). As Cythna will tell the mariners who rescue her from her shattered cavern, hatred and self-contempt spring from the same poisonous root, "the dark idolatry of self" (*CW*, I, 362: *LC*, VIII. 192). Both Zastrozzi's thirst for revenge and Verezzi's obsessive grief reflect such self-idolatry, which impels them, like all Shelleyan narcissists, towards (self-inflicted) death. For Verezzi, as Hogle points out, it is the loss of Julia that inspires his self-involvement/self-loathing, which takes the form first of regressive, almost autistic withdrawal and finally of suicide (*CW*, V, 84). In Zastrozzi's case, it is the loss of his adored mother, coupled with the terrible promise she exacts from him, that plunges him permanently into the abyss of the Self, where vengeance and (self-)hatred reign supreme.[64]

Perhaps the most ingenious way that Shelley links these antagonistic (though not antithetical) doubles is by providing them with a mediator in the form of a beautiful and absurdly libidinous woman, Matilda. Her presence in the novel brings to light the subterranean homoeroticism that flows through both *Zastrozzi* and Shelley's second Gothic novel, *St. Irvyne*. When he composed these works, Shelley had not yet met Hogg, to whom he would someday confess, "Ah! how I have loved you. I was even ashamed to tell you how!" (*L*, I, 172: 10 November 1811).[65] Yet his fragmentary "Essay on Friendship" (?1822) and his 1819 remarks on a sculpture of Bacchus and Ampelus reveal that Shelley's penchant for romantic friendship began at Eton, or even as early as his Syon House days.[66] On one level, *Zastrozzi* plays out the troubling eroticism that lurked beneath the idealized schoolboy friendships he vividly remembers more than ten years later, same-sex "attachments" that Shelley insists—in the "Essay on Friendship" as well as in his *Discourse on Love* (1818)—are "wholly divested of the smallest alloy of sensual intermixture" (Clark 338: "Essay on Friendship"). In Shelley's first Gothic novel, the sexually voracious—and sexually ambiguous—Matilda serves as the conduit for such an "alloy," a crucial ingredient in the muddied stream of loathsome sympathy that unites Verezzi with his irresistible masculine double.[67]

As Zastrozzi's partner in crime, his eager student in atheistical doctrine, and his flagrantly self-oriented spiritual twin, Matilda by all accounts should be his sexual partner as well. Yet Zastrozzi has replaced "love"—that is, sexual desire—with revenge as his *raison d'être*: "Love is worthy of any risque," he tells Matilda, "I felt it once, but revenge has now swallowed up every other feeling of my soul—I am alive to nothing but revenge" (*CW*, V, 47). Matilda thus becomes Zastrozzi's surrogate in his sexual and spiritual seduction of Verezzi—"your cause is mine" Zastrozzi tells her (*CW*, V, 25)—and she embodies a sexual ambiguity that befits her role as the namesake of Monk Lewis's tranvestite witch.[68] She is female but not feminine. She has a "commanding countenance" and "bold expressive gaze"; she must affect the "meekness and sensibility" she does not possess; she sexually hounds and perhaps rapes Verezzi;[69] and she murders her rival Julia "with repeated stabs" of a phallic knife (*CW*, V, 29, 30, 102).[70] Her overpoweringly masculine (and libidinous) character makes her, rather than the effeminate Verezzi or her own spiritual mate, the revenge-obsessed Zastrozzi, the true heir of Verezzi Sr.'s cruel libertinism.[71]

As the bizarre vehicle for Shelley's earliest indictment of masculine power and sexuality, issues that Shelley almost invariably raises in his depictions of *Doppelgänger*, this "phallic woman" suggests that for even the adolescent Shelley masculinity and femininity did not necessarily correspond to biological categories. While this is largely true, as Verezzi's "womanliness" underscores, one gets the sense that Shelley would have liked to portray Verezzi's seductress as a man, or dispense with her altogether and allow the two male antagonists to come together on a sexual as well as a psychological battleground. The "disgusting ideas, the unacountable detestations which often, in spite of himself, filled [Verezzi's] soul towards" Matilda (*CW*, V, 35–36) remind one of the "images of pain and horror" that Shelley later associates with sodomy, which in the *Discourse on Love* he calls an "operose and diabolical . . . machination" (Notopoulos 411). It is as if Matilda, who just barely qualifies as a woman, represents in part the forbidden possibility of homosexual desire that Shelley would examine, and transcendentalize, most thoroughly in his *Discourse*.

The violent disgust coupled with "irresistible fascination" that the novel's protagonist feels toward Matilda mirrors his morbid psycho-sexual attraction to Zastrozzi, and Verezzi's eventual capitulation to Matilda's onslaught of "seductive blandishments" represents the ultimate consummation of his unholy marriage to his "majestic" but demonic brother (*CW*, V, 32,

34, 58, 100). Matilda's voluptuous but strangely repugnant body, then, is the site of the sensual and spiritual union of the novel's male *Doppelgänger*. Although Shelley certainly does not limit the loathsome sympathy that flows among his three central characters to an interpenetrating sexual current, the strange displacements and eruptions of sexuality within this complex triangle serve as potent metaphors for the irresistible influence that these figures exert over one another.

Shelley made many subsequent efforts to recuperate this dark vision of sexual dominance, invasion, and infection[72] by portraying sexual attraction and intercourse in terms of a "magnetic sweetness" that flows from "frame" to "frame," most memorably in *Prometheus Unbound* IV and *Epipsychidion* (*Esdaile* 85: "To Harriet" ["It is not blasphemy"], l. 15). Yet he never lost his conviction that sexual passion "conceal[s] / A deadly poison . . . / Uniting good and ill," and he discovered in his earliest published work that the figure of the malignant double provided the perfect vehicle through which to explore his suspicion that sexual desire, particularly masculine desire, operates as one of Selfhood's most duplicitous offspring (*Esdaile* 41: "Passion" [1811]). As an incarnation and—through his "second self," Matilda—disseminator of the selfish (sexual) appetite that spawned him,[73] Zastrozzi emerges as a direct ancestor of Jupiter and Count Cenci, Self-worshipping rapists whose poisonous semen emblematizes both Shelley's deep distrust of the male eros and his ambivalence toward the world-in-relation paradigm that even his earliest works envision—and question.

Written when Shelley was only sixteen and understandably lacking in aesthetic polish, *Zastrozzi* nonetheless provides us with a remarkably thorough map for investigating the gloomy domains of subsequent Shelleyan *Doppelgänger*. Like *Zastrozzi*, later works such as *Laon and Cythna*, *Prometheus Unbound*, and *The Cenci* invoke the sinister, invasive presence of the *Doppelgänger* to explore such issues as Self-idolatry, loathsome sympathy, and the dangers of sexual desire. Yet Shelley's first protagonist, "the wretched Verezzi," is a far cry from the idealized heroes and heroines of Shelley's mature works, figures who are stalked by their own version of Zastrozzi (*CW*, V, 5). Verezzi never comes close to expressing the selfless love that might disarm his enemy, and it would be quite awhile before Shelley could fully conceive his warring doubles as opponents fighting his own archetypal battle between Love and Selfhood.

The Night of the Mind: *The Voyage*

The figure of the malevolent *Doppelgänger* will appear several more times before he turns up as Othman in the first of Shelley's depictions of doubling that focus not on the dark twin, the embodiment of tyrannous Selfhood, but on a "first self" who strives to dethrone his or her enemy by exemplifying what Laon calls "love's benignant laws" (*CW*, I, 310: *LC*, V. 81). Yet Shelley begins to adumbrate the crucial distinction between his idealized protagonists and their vicious doubles in his second Gothic novel, *St. Irvyne*, and in one of his earliest long poems, *The Wandering Jew*, both completed in the spring of 1810.

In the former work, as in *Zastrozzi*, it is their devotion to the principle of Self that bonds the two central male characters,[74] but the beckoning phantasm that Ginotti encounters in his dream encapsulates in its contrasting visages the fundamental schism that will distinguish a self-abnegating Prometheus from a self-worshipping Jupiter. Seen in my previous chapter as an icon of Shelley's ambivalence toward Christ, this alternately and then simultaneously "beautiful" and "hideous" being reflects Ginotti's—and, implicitly, Wolfstein's—potential for unselfishness and love, on the one hand, and self-idolatry and hate on the other (*CW*, V, 183, 184). A powerful symbol of these characters' deeply divided natures, this figure would have to be cut in two, like Aristophanes' egg, before Shelley could explore the relational dynamic that pitted the impulses and embodiments of sympathetic Love against those of the Self.

In *The Wandering Jew* Shelley does distribute these antithetical impulses between two characters. The relationship between Christ and Ahasuerus in this poem prefigures to a certain degree that between Prometheus and Jupiter, for example. This early poem, though, like the Gothic novels, places at center stage not the incarnation of selfless love but the "monument" of self-involved despair and guilt (*PS*, I, 65: *WJ*, III. 797).[75] The prototype of each of Shelley's idealized martyr-heroes/heroines, Christ hovers in the background of this poem, pitied but ultimately absorbed by his dark double. The Wandering Jew's own "exquisitely torturing pain" as a rebel and outcast best suited the adolescent Shelley's feelings of alienation both from family and from Christ (*PS*, I, 60: *WJ*, III. 624).

The virtuous "first self" and the evil *Doppelgänger* share almost equal time in a bizarre production entitled *The Voyage*. Written in August 1812 and inspired by an unusually difficult sea journey from Dublin to Wales, this poetic fragment involves a young visionary, clearly Shelley himself, who is accompanied by his beloved (Harriet Shelley) and a "sister" (Eliza Westbrook) and menaced by a "pitiless landsman" (*Esdaile* 103: l. 173). Shelley presents the "rapacious, mean, cruel and cowardly" landsman as an older, corrupted version of the idealistic youth, whose salient characteristic is his capacity to love "deeply" and passionately (*Esdaile* 103: l. 158).

At the center of the fragment is the Shelley figure's dream that he and his vicious double engage in a violent struggle on a "barren island rock" (*Esdaile* 103: l. 167). The landsman, wielding weapons such as "strong

Power" and "malice"—offshoots of Shelleyan Selfhood—overcomes the young dreamer, who embodies a love that though "quenchless" is nonetheless "despairing" (*Esdaile* 103, 104: ll. 176, 185, 175). With his devotion to love and his strangely passive "defiance" and "fortitude," this "Victim" certainly resembles a Shelleyan martyr, whose plight inspires "human Nature [to] pause awhile / In pity to his woe" (*Esdaile* 104: ll. 183, 185, 195–96).[76] Yet when we turn to another figure in the poem whose blood is shed, we realize why "truth, love, and courage" (and their ostensible representative) are literally crushed beneath the stony selfishness of "the dastard of relentless soul" (*Esdaile* 103, 104: ll. 176, 212).[77]

Excepting perhaps Percy's visionary double who strangled Mary in her bed at the Casa Magni, the landsman of *The Voyage* offers the most naked example of a Shelleyan *Doppelgänger* who embodies the poet's own repressed aggression. In 1813 the catalyst and recipient of this aggression was Eliza Westbrook, the omnipresent sister-in-law who exerted, as Holmes writes, a "maternal hold" over Harriet Shelley and who helped ensure that Shelley's beloved Hogg remained a safe distance from "her" household after his attempt to seduce Harriet in late 1811 (*Pursuit* 89).[78] We recall that Eliza was the representative other whom Percy invested with redeeming qualities as he contemplated his interconnection with "co-existant beings," around whom "you cannot breathe you cannot exist if *no* parts of loveliness appear" in them (*L*, I, 77: 8 May 1811). The instinctive dislike which he initially felt for Eliza had not, after living with her for nearly a year, evolved into the love and sympathy to which his 1811 letter aspired. Instead it had become the hatred that bubbles to the surface of *The Voyage*, ultimately to explode into "disgust and horror" as his marriage to Harriet disintegrated (*L*, I, 384).

Shelley unleashes this hatred by allowing his protagonist/surrogate's *Doppelgänger* to stab "in security of malice" and with "dastardly revenge" the "Sister" who "accompanied [the young idealist's] voyagings" (*Esdaile* 104: ll. 186, 190, 210, 187). By placing the landsman's attack within the relatively innocuous context of the young man's "wild, woeful dream" and, moreover, incapacitating and rendering unconscious the dreamer within that dream,[79] Shelley appears to absolve his surrogate from responsibility for the landsman's (imagined) violence (*Esdaile* 103: l. 157). Yet Shelley had recently begun a poem in which dreams reveal a reality more true than the world to which consciousness has access. Seen in the light of *Queen Mab*'s visionary atmosphere, which exposes not only humanity's potential for redemption, but also, and more memorably, its most vicious impulses, the poet's dismissal of the bloody tableau at the heart of *The Voyage* as "but a dream" seems disingenuous, or at best, ironic (*Esdaile* 105: l. 214).

More likely, Shelley is ascribing this attempt at defusing the violent vision to the dreamer himself, who is eager to distance himself from his mur-

derous aggression toward his "Sister," as well as from the self-hate that kindled his fantasy of his own (futile) martyrdom. By moving from the young
man's point of view—culminated by the somewhat desperate series of excla-
mations that interrupts his dream—to that of the ship's company as a whole,
Shelley suggests that his protagonist's dream actually infected the experience
of his fellow passengers:

> And this is but a dream!
> For yonder—see! the port in sight!
> The vessel makes towards it!
> The sight of their safety then,
> And the hum of the populous town
> Awakened them from a night of horror
> To a day of secure delights.
>
> (*Esdaile* 105: ll. 214–20)

That the "night of horror" could refer either to the stormy sea crossing or to
the spiritual darkness which enveloped and was exuded by the dreamer underscores the possibility that the protagonist's mental condition—his "night of
the mind"—exerted as powerful an influence over the "little vessel's company" as the meteorological phenenomena that threatened the ship (*Esdaile*
98, 99: ll. 18, 37). Shelley seems to set up a chain of causality that begins with
the landsman, whose "insecure malignity" contaminates the young visionary,
who in turn infects the whole ship with the venom he absorbs from his *Doppelgänger* (*Esdaile* 102: l. 119). Yet early in the poem Shelley refers to the
"mingled mass of feeling" that flows among the various "human spirits" on
this allegorical voyage (*Esdaile* 99: l. 30). He thereby invokes the paradigm
of a network of mutually interpenetrating consciousnesses, all of which share
in the drama of influence, self-projection, and "susceptibility," to invoke a
favorite Shelleyan term, that the central pair of *The Voyage* symbolically
enacts.

In one respect, however, Shelley's protagonist does bear a larger burden
than his fellow "human spirits" within the web of influence they all inhabit.
As a privileged recipient of "pristine visions" (*Esdaile* 103: l. 156) and thus a
prototype of the romantic poet-prophet, the young idealist could inspire the
kind of "communal dreaming"[80] that would supplant the principle of Self with
the power of Love—and of Love's great offspring and instrument, poetry—in
the minds and, ultimately, the actions of his "co-existent beings." If, instead,
he cultivates the hatred and self-contempt that spawn the type of vision into
which he "fell" during this particular voyage, he could generate a collective
nightmare of a "woe-fertilized world" dominated by venomous creatures such
as the landsman, the youth's own dark double to whom he too easily suc-

cumbs within his own nightmare (*Esdaile* 103: ll. 162, 128).

An uneven blend of allegory and barely-veiled autobiography, *The Voyage*, like its protagonist, is overwhelmed by the "infectious gloom" that Shelley will vow to dispel when he turns to his revolutionary epic *Laon and Cythna* in the spring of 1817 (*CW*, I, 242: Preface to *LC*). In the Preface to that work, Shelley identifies an "essential attribute of Poetry"—and of the poet—as "the power of awakening in others sensations like those which animate [his] own bosom" (*CW*, I, 244). When the poet's "sensations" predominately involve his own personal vendettas, against an other such as his annoying sister-in-law,[81] or, more crucially, against Christ, his precursor on the path to selfless love, his compositions may kindle in his readers "those violent and malignant passions of our nature" which the landsman and other Shelleyan doubles freely indulge (*CW*, I, 247: *LC*, Preface). In *Laon and Cythna*, Shelley develops the paradigm he establishes in *The Voyage* of an idealistic protagonist, "nerved . . . with love," who must grapple with an enemy who is both a "co-existent being" with his own history and a lurking presence within the soul of the hero himself (*Esdaile* 103: *The Voyage*, l. 174). However, the spotlight will now turn from the Self-idolatrous *Doppelgänger* to the "first self" who strives to exemplify the Christlike love that Shelley never relinquished as his highest ideal of moral excellence.

Dreadful Sympathy in *Laon and Cythna*

It was the ambitious epic of *Laon and Cythna*, composed during a time of domestic tranquility with his second wife at Marlow in 1817, that provided the transition away from the hate-fueled depictions of *Doppelgänger* by enabling the poet to conceive, if not fully develop, his adversarial doubles in terms of his own primary dialectic between Love and the Self. The brief appearances of Othman in the epic and Shelley's refusal to probe too deeply into his psyche suggest that he needed to distance himself from this icon of Selfhood, who might otherwise overwhelm a work that celebrates Love "as the sole law which should govern the moral world" (*CW*, I, 247: *LC*, Preface). Shelley evidently sensed the danger that Othman, a source of "deep pollution" (*CW*, I, 317: *LC*, V. 282), might prove too overpowering, too "infectious" a presence for himself, for his protagonists, and for his readers. As he writes in his Preface,

[G]loom and misanthropy have become the characteristics of the age in which we live, the solace of a disappointment that unconsciously finds relief only in the wilful exaggeration of its own despair. This influence has tainted the literature of the age with the hopelessness of the minds from which it flows . . . Our works of fiction and poetry have been over-

shadowed by the same infectious gloom . . . I have avoided all flattery
to those violent and malignant passions of our nature, which are ever on
the watch to mingle with and to alloy the most beneficial innovations.
(*CW*, I, 242, 247)

The language of this passage is that which Shelley associates with those
malevolent *Doppelgänger*, from Zastrozzi through Count Cenci, who "taint"
and "infect" not only the spiritual mates to whom they are yoked but everyone who enters their sphere of influence. In this, his "first serious appeal to
the Public,"[82] Shelley acknowledges the writer's power to influence his age
and strives to cleanse the stream that "flows" from his own mind (*CW*, I, 245:
LC, Preface). He thus dissociates himself for the time being from those agents
of "the world's slow stain" who dominate his earliest novels and poems,
including *Queen Mab*, a work pervaded with powerful images and personifi-
cations of poison, contagion, and pollution (*Adonais*, l. 356).

As the less perfect of the sibling revolutionaries who star in Shelley's
sprawling epic, Laon is more demon-haunted than his heroic sister.[83] During
the course of the poem he must face malevolent *Doppelgänger* both in the
person of the tyrant Othman and in the form of "foul, ceaseless shadows" that
torment him with his own self-image (*CW*, I, 295: *LC*, III. 204). A zealous
champion of "love's benignant laws," Laon nonetheless capitulates to the
principle of Self by casting those closest to him as "second selves" who hover
in the background of his own personal drama (*CW*, I, 310, 281: *LC*, V. 81; II.
209).[84] As an idealized yet subtly ironized self-portrait, Laon enables the poet
imaginatively to enact such fantasies as charismatic leadership, sibling incest,
and glorious martyrdom while exposing and chastening the egotism inherent
in these facets of Shelleyan love. However, a work that Shelley describes as
"a succession of pictures illustrating the growth and progress of individual
mind aspiring after excellence, and devoted to the love of mankind" cannot
get too bogged down in private exorcisms of the poet's own demons (*CW*, I,
239: *LC*, Preface). Throughout the epic, we never lose sight of the fact that
Laon remains firmly on the side of "the great Spirit of Good," while Othman
and his cohorts spring from and sustain "the conquering Fiend" that for the
time being reigns over the earth (*CW*, I, 265: *LC*, I. 247, 252).[85] Moreover,
Shelley never penetrates too deeply the tyrant's "pollute[d]" breast, lest the
poisonous vapours of the little world of self overwhelm the purifying incense
of the martyr-heroes' funeral pyre (*CW*, I, 345: *LC*, VII. 36).

Shelley sets up in his first Canto the conflict that governs his "Vision of
the Nineteenth Century," a conflict that pits his hero and heroine against "the
sceptered wretch" Othman and, more specifically, that fosters the antagonism
between Laon, as idealized first self, and Othman as his sinister *Doppelgänger* (*CW*, I, 325: *LC*, V. 217). The Woman who pilots the narrator to the

Temple of the Spirit recounts to him the ongoing struggle of the two primordial powers that "o'er mortal things dominion hold," Manichean or Zoroastrian "Twin Genii" whose clashes determine whether Good or Evil will gain ascendency over the world (*CW*, I, 264: *LC*, I, 221, 225). Shelley avoids turning this dualistic myth into an ossified dichotomy by invoking two images of these powers' battle that allow for some blurring of the boundaries between them.[86] In their original form, the Spirits of Evil and of Good burst into the purview of the world's "earliest dweller" as a "blood red Comet and the Morning Star / Mingling their beams in combat" (*CW*, I, 264: *LC*, I. 226, 230–31). As the poem opens in Shelley's own post-Revolutionary theater, these gods have become "an Eagle and a Serpent wreathed in fight," with "feather and scale inextricably blended" (*CW*, I, 259: *LC*, I. 67, 75).

That seemingly antithetical principles in fact intersect or "mingle," as Shelley puts it, certainly did not come to him as a revelation in 1817. As early as 1811 he was musing on (sexual) passion as the source both of ecstacy and of "misery . . . / Uniting good and ill" (*Esdaile* 42: "Passion," ll. 49–50). More recently, in the "Hymn to Intellectual Beauty" (1816), he questions "why man has such a scope / For love and hate, despondency and hope" (ll. 23–24). In fact, Shelley's most effective depictions of antagonistic doubles emerge from his recognition that dichotomies constantly collapse, even the one to which he most stubbornly clings, the opposition of the Self to Love.

The relationship between the hero and the rapacious tyrant of *Laon and Cytha*, however, comes perilously close to rigid allegory when Shelley foists upon his rather ineffectual protagonist the strict standards of his preface. Trumpeting love as "the sole law which should govern the moral world," calling for "the bloodless dethronement of . . . oppressors" and refusing any "quarter [for] Revenge"—which in the Shelleyan lexicon is nearly synonymous with Selfhood—this polemical piece requires of the poem's hero a moral perfection that he never achieves (*CW*, I, 240, 247). When "the earliest dweller of the world" witnesses the archetypal battle of the malevolent Comet and the beneficent Morning Star, his own thoughts wage "mutual war, / In dreadful sympathy," a sympathy all the more dreadful because he "shed[s] his brother's blood" upon the victory of the Comet (*CW*, I, 264: *LC*, I. 226, 232–33, 234). While the logic of the poem (and of Laon's character) does not require that Laon mimic this Adam-Cain figure and consummate his own "mutual war" with Othman by murdering him, we need more convincing evidence that the hero's own "dreadful sympathy" with his and Cythna's oppressor has indeed become loving compassion when Laon enters the tyrant's Imperial House in Canto V.

There is something spurious in Laon's Christlike forgiveness of Othman in this episode; in fact, by sparing his *Doppelgänger*'s life, Laon sabotoges the revolution while at the same time ensuring that his own noble destiny as a sacrificial lamb will be fulfilled.[87] For the "dreadful sympathy" that flows between these doubles does not correspond merely to their competing roles as earthly representives of the warring "twin Genii" but also involves the much more intimate bond of victim and victimizer that Shelley explored in his first Gothic novel, *Zastrozzi*. As the most elaborate and undisguised enactment of Shelley's own *imitatio Christi* to date, *Laon and Cythna* requires of both its hero and his feminine counterpart the perfect extinction of self that Shelley attributed only to the martyr.[88] Whereas the ferocious Zastrozzi, prototype of all Shelleyan *Doppelgänger*, torturously prolongs his victim's life in order to become the quintessential incarnation of Selfhood,[89] Laon must preserve his persecutor in order to achieve radical self-abnegation on his "bier / Of fire" (*CW*, I, 397: *LC*, XII. 42–43). When, near the end of the epic, Laon returns to the Golden City disguised as the Stranger, he has in effect coalesced with Othman, who for all practical purposes disappears from the poem. In his eagerness to embrace his martyrdom, Laon becomes his own *Doppelgänger* and the Judas to his own Christ. "I am Laon's friend," he tells the bloodthirsty multitude, "And him to your revenge I will betray" (*CW*, I, 395: *LC*, XI. 186–87).[90]

Laon's symbolic merger with his double does not, however, signify a reconciliation of this Shelleyan Champion with the Oppressor of mankind. Laon merely usurps Othman's adversarial role in his impatience to reach "the pyre of expiation," the bridal bed where he and his feminine second self can achieve their ecstatic "one annihilation" (*CW*, I, 386: *LC*, X. 335; *Epi.*, l. 587). Their final erotic union in Canto XII liberates Laon and Cythna from the material bodies that obstruct their perfect commingling as well as purges them of any remnants of Selfhood which would bar them from the pantheon of "love-devoted" Shelleyan martyrs (*JM*, ll. 373).[91] More specifically, this fiery *Liebestod* allows the lovers finally to escape the shadow of masculine (sexual) aggression that Othman has cast throughout the poem.[92]

Cythna has borne "the tyrant's heaviest yoke" by suffering both Othman's sexual violation of her and his cruel enforcement of his paternal "rights," which deprive his victim of her baby daughter (*CW*, I, 303: *LC*, IV. 159). Yet Laon too feels the sting of "the cold tyrant's cruel lust," particularly when it festers in his own veins (*CW*, I, 345: *LC*, VII. 29). As he traces his hero's progress toward his proper Shelleyan goal of complete self-annihilation, the poet simultaneously dissociates Laon from and implicates him in his *Doppelgänger*'s phallic aggression. Ulmer points out that the poem "includes a shadowy Oedipal theme by associating Laon and Othman as competitors for Cythna, rivals for the prerogatives of fatherhood" (*Shelleyan Eros* 64). Like Zastrozzi before him and Jupiter after him, Othman separates the male protagonist from his beloved, and even more devastating, he actually drafts her into his own seraglio and savagely rapes her. While the constellation of characters that dominate *Zastrozzi*—Matilda, Zastrozzi, and Verezzi—suggested a displaced homoeroticism with Matilda as middle man-woman, the sexual triangle of *Laon and Cythna* involves instead the hero's fears of his own (hetrosexual) desire for his sister.

This desire not only must override the incest taboo—which the rather defensive final paragraph of Shelley's Preface addresses in oddly abstract terms—but it also requires of Laon that he confront his sexual differentiation from his "second self" (*CW*, I, 281: *LC*, II. 209).[93] Along with shattering the illusion of utter continuity with his beloved that Laon cherishes, this difference assigns to him the more violent role in consummating this desire. As a kind of invited intruder, Othman—represented by his soldiers armed with bare and "glittering swords"—will arrive just in time to intercept Laon's erotic fears and desires, as well as to seize their catalyst, Cythna, who is spirited away to the king's "polluted halls" (*CW*, I, 290, 345: *LC*, III. 53; VII. 30).

As Laon's passion for Cythna threatens to assert itself, he has "monstrous dreams" of sexually suggestive "foul and ghastly shapes" (*CW*, I, 290: *LC*, III. 45, 42). Laon awakens from "the impotence / Of sleep" to find himself and his sister surrounded by armed soldiers, magically summoned by Laon's unconscious (*CW*, I, 290: *LC*, III. 46–47). In a redirection of his sexual energy, Laon stabs and kills three of the men. Along with his "shadow" Cythna and the "foul, ceaseless shadows" of his own self-images,[94] these figures will turn up in his hallucinations during his imprisonment as manifestations of the self-idolatry that interferes with his philanthopic mission as well as with his love for Cythna (*CW*, I, 281, 295: *LC*, II. 208; III. 204).[95]

After emerging from this purgatory, Laon repudiates the violence he indulged during this early crisis and, donning the mantle of self-abnegating love, he refuses to execute Othman after (briefly) unseating him from his throne. While I have stressed how the hero's preservation of his *Doppelgänger* enables Laon ultimately to receive the crown of the self-sacrificing Shelleyan martyr, Ulmer finds that Othman's lurking presence in fact allows Laon and Cythna finally to unite sexually:

> [Shelley's] protagonists consummate their love amid the desolation and debris of the revolution's failure, and there is a disconcerting logic to that apparent coincidence. Laon's arrival at the Golden City accompanies the resurgence of Othman because eros can fulfill itself only under the auspices of a triumphant male power in *The Revolt of Islam*. (63–64)

Ulmer's argument rightly recognizes the deep pessimism that pervades Shelley's conception of sexuality, particularly of the male eros. After completing his epic, Shelley will tend to spiritualize and/or displace onto a cosmic canvas the sexual encounters between his ideal characters, and he will also increasingly feminize his heroes/surrogates to distance them further from the aggressive carnality that the rapist-tyrants of *Laon and Cythna, Prometheus Unbound,* and *The Cenci* epitomize. Beatrice Cenci thus becomes the most extreme example of the feminized Shelleyan hero. Unfortunately, she also becomes Shelley's worst victim of loathsome sympathy with her rapacious *Doppelgänger.*

The Heart's Dark Caverns:
Prometheus Unbound and *The Cenci*

It is no coincidence that the period which produced the apotheosis of the Shelleyan world-in-relation, *Prometheus Unbound,* also generated the poet's most probing investigation of loathsome sympathy. Written between Acts III and IV of *Prometheus Unbound, The Cenci* qualifies and darkens Shelley's celebration of sublime intermingling, which then re-asserts itself in the exuberant finale of the lyrical drama.[96] Together these works display the culmination of the *Doppelgänger* theme in Shelley's works, a theme that did not disappear but that Shelley never again presented as an objectification of his dialectic between Love and the Self.

After delving into Beatrice Cenci's appalling transformation into her "unnatural" father's true daughter (*Cenci,* I. iii. 54), Shelley abandons the idealized first self/evil *Doppelgänger* paradigm. This is in part because he had come full circle from his first publication in 1810, *Zastrozzi,* a novel that insists on identifying rather than dissevering its seemingly antithetical characters. Shelley's circuitous journey back to the Gothic horrors of *Zastrozzi,*[97] however, took him through the failed revolution of *Laon and Cythna* and the redeemed cosmos of *Prometheus Unbound.* With varying degrees of success, Shelley struggled in these two works to envision, embrace, and encourage in his readers the kind of self-transcendent love that *Zastrozzi* does not begin to intimate. Although Count Cenci is certainly a more vile figure than any of Shelley's previous *Doppelgänger,* Shelley's portrait of him is nonetheless the most probing, most "sympathetic" depiction of the evil double in that it emerges from his willingness to imaginatively enter "the most dark and secret caverns of the human heart"—and not simply as an exercise in Self-indulgence or Self-purgation (Preface to *The Cenci,* 239).

While the earliest incarnations of the Shelleyan double—Zastrozzi, the Wandering Jew, Ginotti, and the landsman—remained for the most part creatures of the young writer's private exorcisms, Count Cenci, and, to a lesser extent, Othman and Jupiter, emerge from Shelley's recognition that the "streams of sympathy" so vital to his ideal of a lovingly interconnected world may in fact be polluted (*Prose* 233: *On the Death of the Princess Charlotte* [1817]). Shelley refuses to neutralize Francesco Cenci's vivid presence in the play by restricting him to the wings, like Othman, or dropping him through a trap door, like Jupiter. While we can only describe Shelley's own sympathy for the Count as "loathsome," it nonetheless allowed him to integrate into his model of mutually interpenetrating beings the "strange, savage, ghastly, dark, and execrable" (*PU*, III. iv. 182). Yeats calls Cenci "an artificial character, the scapegoat of [Shelley's] unconscious hatred," but I think that he emerges from the play as an emblem of Shelley's emotional courage and philosophical honesty (*Essays and Introductions* 421: "*Prometheus Unbound*"). In delving into Count Cenci's "dark spirit," Shelley had to preserve an essential compassion, "the sense of love" he had been exalting in *Prometheus Unbound* (II. iv. 102), in order to confront without capitulating to "the moral deformity" that disfigures Beatrice's *Doppelgänger* and eventually Beatrice herself (*Cenci*, I. ii. 61; Preface, 240). That is, Shelley—and, in turn, his audience—had to become the ideal, loving "first self" that his heroine fails to remain.[98]

Prometheus' harrowing encounters with his own *Doppelgänger* and with the Furies—Jupiter's "tempest-walking hounds"—provide a paradigm for the kind of interaction with and purgation of evil that Shelley demanded of himself and of his audience in *The Cenci* (*PU*, I. 331). Such interplay is conspicuously absent in the earlier *Laon and Cythna*, where the doubles remain rather inertly linked instead of vigorously clashing. Despite his (somewhat) purifying madness during his captivity, Laon lacks credibility as a redeemed redeemer in part because he never really *sees* and thus never actually grapples with his *Doppelgänger*. Othman is an incorrigible despot whom Laon automatically (and foolishly) pities, describing this rapist-tyrant in absurdly inappropriate terms as a "poor lonely man" (*CW*, I, 317: *LC*, V. 293).[99] However, Prometheus never loses sight of the fact that Jupiter is a "cruel King," even after hate and disdain have turned to pity (*PU*, I. 50).[100] Contrary to what Laon might believe, pity is not the magical "spell," to use Demogorgon's term, that will dethrone—or better yet, reform—a "Foul Tyrant," but merely a hesitant first step toward genuine compassion and thus toward the "transforming presence" of love (*PU*, IV. 568; I. 264, 832). Even after Prometheus' moment of insight at I. 53, the "elaborate machinery of power rumbles on," as John Rieder declares, "not simply in the visits of Mercury and the Furies, but more importantly, in the roundabout enactment of the curse under the aspect of necessity" (783).[101] For my purposes, though, it is the Furies' physical and psychological onslaught on Shelley's hero that best reveals Prometheus' complicity in and ultimate victory over this "machinery of power."

Before addressing this issue, which will involve the interactive paradigm that Shelley devises for Prometheus and for the readers of both his lyrical drama and his tragedy, I want to say a word about Jupiter's role as Prometheus' double. Shelley's readers agree almost unanimously that the play presents Jupiter as a projection of Prometheus' own divided mind, a manifestation of the Titan's "self-love, with its concomitant lust for dominion and tyranny," as M. H. Abrams puts it (302). Along with the landsman of *The Voyage*, Jupiter certainly emerges as the closest thing to an "epiphenomenon" of the Shelleyan hero himself (Rieder 778).[102] Yet in the interest of exploring the relational dynamic these antithetical doubles have established, Shelley still insists on what C. F. Keppler would call Jupiter's "simultaneous outwardness and inwardness, . . . difference from and identity with the first self" (10), Prometheus, a pattern that characterizes each previous pair of Shelleyan *Doppelgänger* we have examined.

As the drama opens, Prometheus and Jupiter seem more alike than "antithetical." Not until the conclusion of the first act, after Prometheus has faced his antagonist both in the form of the "tremendous Image" summoned from the spectral world and of the "execrable shapes" of the Furies does he achieve the status of the selfless, ideal member of the dyad (I. 246, 449). By the end of this act, the exhausted, humbled Prometheus finally turns from Selfhood—emblemmed by Jupiter, by the loudly self-justifying Prometheus, and by their composite image, the great Phantasm—toward Asia, whom the poem identifies with love.[103] Shelley's invocation of the Zoroastrian figure of the Fravashi, a spiritual double which protects the earthly self, prepares us— and Prometheus—for the apparition that confronts the Titan with his own terrible self-image superimposed on the form of Jupiter.[104] This Phantasm, despite its horrible visage and pronouncements, does fulfil the role of "active guardian spirit" by enabling Prometheus to recognize and repudiate "his curse and the mental kinship with his oppressor" (Curran, *Shelley's Annus Mirabilis*, 73, 74).[105] However, Prometheus cannot immediately turn away from Jupiter, or his own Jupiterean self, for Shelley will require that his hero discover and control the power of loathsome sympathy in order to look more closely at the destructive forces that he has inadvertently unleashed by embracing Jupiter rather than Asia as his soul-mate.

As Jupiter's hench-monsters and surrogates, the Furies present the Titan with another opportunity to behold and interact with his *Doppelgänger*. Prometheus in fact welcomes these hideous creatures—"call up the fiends"— as weird tour guides through a devastated (and devastating) psychological and historical landscape (I. 432). While the Phantasm of Jupiter/Prometheus showed the Titan how he had empowered and merged with his foe and thus blighted himself, the Earth, and all her people,[106] the scenes of ruin that the Furies unveil suggest to Prometheus that his divorce from Jupiter will only heighten his own and mankind's torments. Shelley emphasizes his hero's active interplay with these "Hounds / Of Hell" by invoking two participatory formats, the catechism and the (anti)masque (I. 341–42).[107] The poet allows Prometheus himself, however, the most direct expression of his willingness to enter and be entered by the Furies' "loathed selves" (I. 461).

When the Furies charge the Titan with a rush of "countless wings," Prometheus remains remarkably cool headed, though certainly not frozen by the "calm hate" that he had cultivated for their master (I. 441, 259):

> Horrible forms,
> What and who are ye? Never yet there came
> Phantasms so foul through monster-teeming Hell
> From the all-miscreative brain of Jove;
> Whilst I behold such execrable shapes,
> Methinks I grow like what I contemplate
> And laugh and stare in loathsome sympathy.

(I. 445–51)

While the ever-timid Ione warns his sister to "close thy plumes over thine eyes, / Lest thou behold and die," the Titan refuses to avert his gaze from these grotesque beings (I. 439–40). Prometheus embraces a paradigm of perception that closes the gap between "behold" and "become," a model that, as this passage underscores, can be extremely dangerous. Yet his "loathsome sympathy" with the Furies—and thus with Jove, whom he invokes here—remains conscious and skillfully modulated throughout his encounter with them.[108] He enters their polluted atmosphere, probing the nature of their deformity, but preserves his essential distinction from them, as in these antithetically balanced assertions: "Pain is my element as hate is thine; / Ye rend me now: I care not" (I. 477–78). As Ione observes, "A low yet dreadful groan/ . . . tear[s] up the heart / Of the good Titan" when he beholds the horrible spectacle of human misery and violence the Furies present, yet instead of succumbing to their temptation to despair, Prometheus moves closer to his destiny as the self-abnegating and explicitly Christlike "saviour and . . . strength of suffering man" (I. 578–80, 817). In the aftermath of the Furies' siege, Prometheus appropriately addresses his fierce double, with whom he has been struggling via Jupiter's "miscreations," the Furies themselves and the horrors they have shown him: "The sights with which thou torturest gird my soul / With new endurance" (I. 643–44).

By emphasizing Prometheus' ability to conceptualize his reaction to the Furies—"*Methinks* I grow like what I contemplate"—as well as to articulate his shifting sensations during this agonizing episode, Shelley proposes a strategy for empathically participating in without being overwhelmed by the "dark passions" that will provide the focus of his next work, *The Cenci* (Preface to *The Cenci* 240). In that work, Beatrice's inability, or refusal, to articulate her suffering or to name the rape itself pushes her closer to violence and thus makes permanent the loathsome sympathy that binds her to her father. "I . . . can feign no image in my mind / Of that which has transformed me," she tells the horrified Lucretia, while to Orsino, she declares:

> I have endured a wrong so great and strange,
> That neither life or death can give me rest.
> Ask me not what it is, for there are deeds
> Which have no form, sufferings which have no tongue.
>
> (*Cenci*, III. i. 108–9, 139–43)

Enormously sympathetic with his heroine, Shelley nonetheless suggests that had Beatrice been able psychologically to confront and shape into words and images the "formless horror" of the rape, she ultimately might have shattered the mesmeric and "distorted mirror" that displayed "Her image mixed with what she most abhors," the "hideous likeness" of her father (*Cenci*, III. i. 111; IV. i. 147, 148, 146).

Yet in a sense it was Beatrice's failure to preserve her angelic nature that attracted Shelley to her history.[109] Previous protagonists/surrogates such as Laon and Prometheus allowed Shelley to bask vicariously in the admiration and sympathy that they, as heroic martyrs, inspired in others toward them. But the crimes that Beatrice does, not suffers, compelled Shelley to modify his instinctive identification with her and to "awaken and sustain" his own and his audience's more reflective compassion *for* her rather than to solicit sympathy for himself *through* her (*Cenci*, Preface, 239).

In pursuing her "dark and deliberate revenge"—for Shelley a horrible outgrowth of Selfhood—Beatrice relinquishes her status as the antithesis of her father and thus leaves a gap in Shelley's archetypal structure of ideal first self and malevolent double (*CW*, I, 120: *SI*). While *Prometheus Unbound* begins with the hero utterly paralyzed by loathsome sympathy with his *Doppelgänger*, from whom the Titan seems almost indistinguishable, *The Cenci* opens with Beatrice and her father/double as moral opposites.[110] The plays thus trace contrasting trajectories, with Prometheus moving steadily away from Jupiter and toward self-transcendence and Beatrice slipping closer toward the "Strange ruin" that unites her physically and then spiritually with Count Cenci (*Cenci*, IV. i. 26). By dismantling the framework of antithetical doubles that *Prometheus Unbound* keeps intact, *The Cenci* allows the author himself and his reader/spectator to embrace the role of loving first self. Moving from pity for the heroine through loathsome sympathy with her vicious father and the fallen Beatrice, Shelley and, he hoped, his audience ultimately achieves genuine compassion for Beatrice and for those who have suffered similar assaults.[111]

Her gender and the particular violation she suffered may have contributed to Shelley's ability to modify and modulate his identification with Beatrice as a persona/surrogate. As a woman, not simply a feminized male, like Prometheus, for example, La Cenci retains a crucial difference from her male dramatist, a difference most strikingly underscored by her rape. Shelley can empathize with but never actually experience the anguish that so transforms Beatrice. Her incoherence following the rape corresponds in part to Shelley's own struggle to imagine and express a torment that remains largely inaccessible to him: her "wild words" and conspicuous lacunæ are his (*Cenci*, III. i. 66).

Yet if Beatrice's "strange horror" hovers just beyond the grasp of the poet's experience and language, her rape graphically buttresses his ongoing indictment of masculine sexuality (*Cenci*, IV. iv. 97). From his first investigation of the *Doppelgänger* theme, 1809's *Zastrozzi*, Shelley identified masculine (sexual) aggression and violence as the quintessential characteristics of the malevolent double. If the Shelleyan *Doppelgänger* emerges in its broadest outlines as the return of the repressed Self, Shelley's own or his self-abnegating surrogate's, on a more specific level, the dark double (re)asserts the kind of phallic power that Shelley always deeply distrusted, in himself and in others.

Jupiter's resurgence in the person of Count Cenci involves just such a return. Our last glimpse of Jupiter is his descent into the abyss—with the help of his "fatal Child," Demogorgon—and the principle of Self and the aggressive masculine libido supposedly went with him (*PU*, III. i. 19). Yet in Shelley's original ending to the play, Jupiter and his bloody legacy dominate the ostensibly joyous report of the Spirit of the Hour (III. iv. 98–204), who vividly conjures this "ghastly . . . tyrant of the world" even as he recounts his defeat (III. iv. 181–83). When Francesco Cenci appears in all his diabolical splendor in the first scene of *The Cenci*, it is as if Jupiter has taken on a new, even more gruesome shape. That Shelley assigns the Count a soliloquy in his first scene indicates the poet's willingness to expose and explore much more thoroughly than he did in the lyrical drama the "moral deformity" of his villain (Preface to *The Cenci* 240). Shelley heightens our sense of Cenci as a (re)incarnation of Jupiter by explicitly linking the sexual crimes they perpetrate. As the "God of rape," Jupiter fittingly closes his reign by boasting of his assault on Thetis (Ulmer 82). The poisonous semen that burns and "dissolve[s]" Jupiter's consort becomes in *The Cenci* the "clinging, black, contaminating mist" that "dissolves / [Beatrice's] flesh to a pollution" (*PU*, III. i. 41; *Cenci*, III. i. 17, 21–22).[112] Shelley also provides a structural parallel between these rapes by describing—or, in *The Cenci*, failing to describe—them at the center of each play (Act III, scene i).

Thetis' rape at the hands of Jupiter is not the only violation in *Prometheus Unbound* to which Shelley compares Beatrice's attack. Prometheus himself undergoes a form of sexual assault when the "crawling glaciers pierce [him] with the spears / Of their moon-freezing chrystals" as he hangs from his precipice (*PU*, I. 31–32). What is more important, Jupiter ravages and pollutes Prometheus via his surrogate "rapists," "Heaven's winged hound," the voracious eagle, and those "tempest-walking hounds," the Furies (I. 34, 331). In a brilliant move, Shelley symbolically reverses the genders of Prometheus and the hags who furiously assail him. Prometheus thus becomes the "feminine" rape victim whom the invasive Furies penetrate and poison, like "blood with [his] labyrinthine veins / Crawling like agony" (I. 490–91).[113] The spawn of the blood that flowed from the castrated Uranus, the "masculine" Furies are apt emblems of the sexual (and oedipal) violence from which Shelley longed to dissociate himself and his feminized heroes.

In his dramas of 1818 and 1819, Shelley took his final and most elaborate journey into the corroded heart and mind of the pernicious *Doppelgänger* while at the same time allying himself with the victims of the double's sexual, psychological, and spiritual attacks, the martyred first self. We tend to link the poet with the virtuous protagonists of those works that pit a "love-devoted" hero or heroine against a self-obsessed double, and Shelley certainly encourages us to do so (*JM*, l. 373). Yet in a moving letter to the Gisbornes that Shelley wrote not long after the death of his adopted or illegitimate daughter, Elena Adelaide, the poet tells his friends, "My Neapolitan charge is dead. It seems as if the destruction that is consuming me were as an atmosphere which wrapt & infected everything connected with me" (*L*, II, 211: ?7 July 1820). This letter simply makes explicit what the works we have looked at suggest: that he felt a disturbing kinship—a loathsome sympathy—with those poisonous souls that had fascinated him since boyhood. Never reformed, never integrated into a harmonious community, the dark Shelleyan *Doppelgänger* stands as a powerful incarnation of the poet's recognition that the principle of Self would always lurk beneath Love's "awful throne of patient power," whether that throne stood in his own heart or at the heart of a liberated world (*PU*, IV. 557).

3

A Band of Sister-Spirits

With the downfall of Jupiter in Act III of *Prometheus Unbound*, the serpent of Selfhood is shut out from Paradise, at least for the time being. A favorite, and appropriately fluid, Shelleyan symbol, the snake appears in this work as the sublime, morally neutral "snake-like Doom coiled" beneath Demogorgon's throne (II. iii. 97), as the ambiguous amphisbænic snake (III. iv. 120), and as the poisonous Numidian seps which Thetis likens to the Self-worshipping Jupiter's "penetrating presence" (III. i. 39).[1] In its final incarnation within the play, the potentially destructive power poised to invade the Promethean empire, the serpent evokes each of its previous guises, though none more disturbingly than that of the rapist-god Jupiter. While he never *identifies* Jupiter as this coiled "Doom," Shelley does ascribe a strikingly Jupiterean temperament to this lustful, and oedipal, snake who threatens to "clasp . . . with his length" the feminine Eternity, "Mother of many acts and hours" (IV. 569, 567, 566).[2]

This final image of a phallic force endangering both the maternal power and the feminine paradise over which she presides is an archetypal one for Shelley. (With a Holy Family—including the feminized Prometheus—that is a kind of divine sorority, the Promethean Age promises to be a gynarchic one.) This reptilian image becomes even more complex, and self-revelatory, when we recognize that snake as one of Shelley's familiars. Since spellbinding his young sisters with tales of the Great Old Snake which "had inhabited the gardens at Field Place for several generations," Shelley felt a special affinity with this most maligned of creatures (Hogg, I, 22).[3] Barbara Charlesworth Gelpi offers a suggestive reading of what she rightly calls Hogg's "peculiar little aside" describing Shelley's "Old Snake" legend, which she links with myths of the Great Mother (*Shelley's Goddess* 100). While Gelpi plausibly argues that "Hogg's own comments on the 'old Snake' suggest his awareness of its association with the Mother Goddess" (*Shelley's Goddess* 100), I would contend that Shelley identified the snake with himself, a masculine intruder into the feminine Eden at Field Place which Gelpi evokes and analyzes so well. Moreover, Hogg's (embellished) account of the snake's violent demise implies that Shelley had to destroy that part of himself which prevented complete integration into the maternal and sisterly circle—his gender: "[The Snake] was killed, accidentally, through the carelessness of the gardener, in mowing the grass; killed . . . by that two-handed engine, the scythe" (Hogg, I, 22).[4] Shelley will resurrect this serpent throughout his writings, not only as the venomous and irredeemable Jupiter, but also as the benignant snake who swims through "The Assassins" (1814) and Canto I of *Laon and Cythna*.

As Richard Holmes points out, "the pre-Lapsarian land of Field Place was constructed from a society of sisters" (*Pursuit* 12), Elizabeth (b. 1794), Mary (b. 1797), Hellen (b. 1799), and Margaret (b. 1801). Holmes's vivid portrait of Shelley's early years makes excellent use of a series of letters written in 1856 by Hellen Shelley to Lady Jane Shelley and included in the opening chapters of Hogg's *Life of Shelley*. Hellen's letters offer us glimpses of the poet in the midst of an adoring "band of sister-spirits,"[5] entertaining, instructing, and, as Kenneth Neill Cameron writes, "gently shepherding" them in their "private Arcadia" (*Young Shelley* 6). The Percy whom we see in his sister's epistolary narrative is an integral, if somewhat domineering, member of the Field Place sorority. For the first ten years of his life, until he was sent off to boarding school, the boy remained within the predominantly female household of Field Place. As Barbara Gelpi has shown, by the standards of the period, Shelley "spent an extraordinarily long time within [the] closed, feminine circle presided over by a strong mother" (*Shelley's Goddess* 80). But the poet found himself rudely expelled from his sororal retreat, first in 1802, when he was transported to the exclusively male world of Syon House Academy,[6] and finally, decisively when Harriet Grove and Elizabeth Shelley withdrew their precious sympathy. It appears that Shelley's deep-seated ambivalence toward his own gender—the masculinity that may have always barred him from the "intimate inner circle" of the Field Place women (Cameron, *Young Shelley*, 5)—developed into intense antipathy when in his nineteenth year he lost his membership in the sisterly coalition. Although it was largely his religious skepticism and budding political radicalism that aliened "his" young women, Percy responded not by embracing orthodoxy but by launching a vigorous attack on (his own) masculinity and, concomitantly, on "that hateful principle" of Self, which he would always yoke with masculine aggression, acquisitiveness, and sexual appetite (*L*, I, 34). Thus Shelley the serpent, always lurking within the childhood Eden, rises to his full mythic stature as the poet enters his post-Lapsarian life.

That the Shelleyan snake winds up cradled in a fair and female bosom in "The Assassins" and in *Laon and Cythna* suggests something about the poet's own primal desires and about his strategies for satisfying them. Even more suggestive, however, is the fact that this serpent must be infantilized (in

"The Assassins") or "wounded" (in the epic) before the the woman "unveil[s] her bosom" and invites it to enter (*CW*, I, 262: *LC*, I. 154, 176).[7] For Shelley's (ambivalent) identification with his serpent totem not only generated a whole fraternity of malefactors—*Doppelgänger* such as Jupiter, who emanate from and stalk his literary surrogates—but it also compelled the poet to develop more radical strategies to purge himself of the masculine taint that he believed barred him from the "magic circle" of love ("To Jane. The Recollection," l. 44).

The poem alluded to in my opening sentence, "The Serpent Is Shut Out from Paradise," exemplifies how Shelley—"the serpent"—raises the spectre of (his own) masculinity, only to suppress it by the lyric's second line:

> The serpent is shut out from Paradise—
> The wounded deer must seek the herb no more
> In which its heart's cure lies—
> The widowed dove must cease to haunt a bower
> Like that from which its mate with feigned sighs
> Fled in the April hour.—
> I, too, must seldom seek again
> Near happy friends a mitigated pain.
>
> (ll. 1–8)

Actually, Shelley does not simply neutralize—or, rather, *neuter*—but he also feminizes the serpent's phallic presence in this opening stanza. Instead of just wounding/castrating the serpent, as in *Laon and Cythna*, Shelley transforms it into a "wounded deer," another of the poet's favorite self-images and a conspicuous emblem of his "feminine"—and Christlike—nature.[8] This deer in turn becomes more explicitly feminine as the poem progresses, metamorphosing first into a "widowed dove" and later into a "crane [who] o'er seas and forests seeks her home," her "quiet nest" (ll. 41–42). The entire poem, in fact, is enveloped within a womblike "bower" of feminine sensibility: the poet's own.[9]

Written in 1822 and addressed to his "beloved Jane" (Williams), "The Serpent Is Shut Out from Paradise" distills a brief lifetime's worth of meditations on and experiences with what Shelley calls elsewhere the "course of love" ("With a Guitar. To Jane," ll. 90, 33). Yet this late lyric is remarkably close in spirit and language to one of his earliest poems, a "Song" addressed to Harriet Grove and written in August 1810. Looked at together, these lyrics, the one addressed to his first and the other to his last great love, display the poet's "will-to-femininity" as a crucial, constant presence in Shelley's works.

Song: To—

Stern, stern is the voice of fate's fearful command,
    When accents of horror it breathes in our ear,
Or compels us for aye bid adieu to the land
    Where exists that loved friend to our bosom so dear;
'Tis sterner than death o'er the shuddering wretch bending,
And in skeleton grasp his fell sceptre extending,
Like the heart-stricken deer to that loved covert wending
    Which never again to his eyes may appear.

And ah! he may envy the heart-stricken quarry,
    Who bids to the friend of affection farewell,
He may envy the bosom so bleeding and gory,
    He may envy the sound of the drear passing knell;
Not so deep is his grief on his death couch reposing,
When on the last vision his dim eyes are closing!
As the outcast whose love-raptured senses are losing
    The last tones of thy voice on the wild breeze that swell!

Those tones were so soft, and so sad, that ah! never
    Can the sound cease to vibrate on Memory's ear;
In the stern wreck of nature for ever and ever,
    The remembrance must live of a friend so sincere.

                                    (*PS*, I, 103–4)

We recall that in the summer of 1810 Shelley was dreading—and perversely
encouraging—his cousin/fiancée's ultimate break with him, a loss that devastated the poet the following winter. Intent on perceiving and presenting himself
as a romantic victim,[10] if not of Harriet, then of "fate," Percy embraces here for
the first time the (self-)image of the "heart-stricken deer," the same deer whose
"feeble steps" he traces in the 1822 lyric to Jane (*Adonais*, l. 277).[11] Associated
with traditionally feminine qualities such as gentleness, innocence, and grace,
as well as with Shelley's prototype of selfless love, Christ, the wounded deer
in the "Song" to Harriet resembles another familiar Shelleyan figure, the feminized Christ. The quintessential emblem of Shelley's lifelong struggle against
(masculine) Selfhood, the feminized Christ will play a central role in later
works such as *Laon and Cythna*, *Prometheus Unbound*, and *Adonais*.

    In the 1810 lyric, Percy's desire to be both Christlike and feminine vio-
lently intersect in the "bleeding bosom" of the wounded deer.[12] A sensationalized version of Cowper's portrait of himself and of the compassionate Christ
as "stricken deer" (*The Task*, III. 108), Shelley's "heart-stricken quarry"
allows him simultaneously to merge with the martyred Christ and to out-suf-

fer him with wounds and grief even more "deep." A similar pattern of coalescence and competition defines the poet's dynamic with his lover and audience, Harriet. First of all, Percy allies himself with Harriet, and her femininity, in the phrase "our bosom." The plural pronoun logically refers to the speaker and anyone else facing a similar exile, but it actually belongs to Percy and Harriet, linked emotionally and anatomically by a shared female bosom. That Shelley's deer-surrogate also possesses a "bosom" further links the poet to the feminine realm of maternity, sensibility, and sympathy that this term invokes.

Yet the word "envy," (literally) central to line 9 and repeated in line 11, introduces a dissonant note into this mellifluous, if melodramatic, "Song." While the poet claims to envy the dying deer because its anguish is less than his own, Shelley in fact "may envy the bosom so bleeding and gory" because it represents not only his aspirations toward femininity and Christlike selflessness but also the inevitable failure of those aims. We might even use the term *breast envy* here, a phrase that has special resonance in light of Percy's desperate attempt to suckle his and Harriet's baby Ianthe when Harriet refused to do so herself.[13] This episode, in which the feminine-tending Shelley finds himself thwarted by the tyranny of biology, sheds a good deal of light on the poet's sense of gender and its relationship to sex. Considering his own remarkably fluid sense of gender and his apparant lack of what psychoanalyst Robert Stoller would call a "core gender identity,"[14] it is tempting to impose on Shelley a radically constructivist viewpoint à la Judith Butler.[15] Yet Shelley inherited from the culture of sensibility that so influenced him a medical-aesthetic theory that emphasized features such as nerves and fibres, hybrid entities, like "spirits," that fall somewhere between the physiological and the metaphysical.[16] And, as G. J. Barker-Benfield and others have demonstrated, the more impressionable, the more sensitive and "susceptible" of these attributes were thought to belong to women.[17] The "psychoperceptual scheme" of sensibility (Barker-Benfield xvii), with its focus on the nervous system, would allow Shelley, as a "man of feeling," to see himself as sharing though never *equaling* the psychic and somatic receptivity and "delicacy" that was ascribed to women.[18] Thus the femaleness, and not just the femininity, of his sister-spirit, is crucial to the poet's sex-crossing imaginings. In her, he found the mirror that made feminine that which was masculine.

Much as he might try, though, Shelley could never become entirely feminine, nor could he become Christ. But he did develop some ingenious ways to explore and even gratify these affiliated desires. As I argued in my opening chapter, the adolescent Shelley attempted to absorb rather than merely emulate his "idealized selfobject," to employ Kohut's term, when he felt Christ slipping away from him. He responded in a comparable, though not identical, way when confronted with the impending loss of his "mirroring selfobjects,"[19] his cousin Harriet and, soon thereafter, his sisters, losses that themselves reflected his earlier (perceived) privation of his mother's emotional nurturance. Whereas Percy, until quite late in his career, felt no qualms about tyrannically assimilating and punishing the rival/ideal who stole the poet's original flock of female disciples,[20] he was more careful to preserve a female "other" or, preferably, "others" with whom he could re-create—in art and in life—the "magic circle" of feminine love from which he was expelled in 1811.[21] And in order to re-create, rejoin this circle, Shelley had to remake himself in the image and likeness of its legitimate members: the women from whom he craved love.

To return to the 1810 "Song," a proleptic account of Shelley's eventual expulsion from Paradise, we witness in this lyric patterns of merger and rivalry with the feminine beloved that will become more pronounced as Shelley becomes less confident in his ability to keep his "little circle[s]" intact (*L, I*, 292). The image of the "envied" bosom epitomizes how Shelley's sympathetic union with his feminine cousin in the first stanza becomes, in effect, muted resentment of his *female* cousin in the second. In order to match Harriet's inherent, and physiologically certified, femininity, Percy had to downplay it and instead to highlight his own feminine temperament.[22] Thus, *his* are the "love-raptured senses," his the sentimental attachment to the "friend so sincere." Overwhelmed by his own acute sensibility, the poet cunningly usurps the feminine subject position from Harriet,[23] despite—or because of—the fact that he assigns himself the traditionally masculine role of romantic exile, casting off from land and love for the "wild breeze." As the poem closes, competition gives way to the coalescence that governed the first stanza. Feminine audience and feminized speaker come together harmoniously in the "soft," "sad" tones that belong both to Harriet's voice and to the poem itself.

A telling episode involving this lyric finds Shelley taking the woman's part in a more radical way. Hogg reproduces in his biography two poems which he tells us Shelley wrote down from memory when they were at Oxford. The second of these is a kind of composite poem comprised of three lyrics (or parts thereof) from the *Victor and Cazire* volume, including the "Song," "Stern, stern is the voice." The penultimate stanza of this odd creation reads:

> And, ah! she may envy the heart-shocked quarry,
>   Who bids to the scenery of childhood farewell,
> She may envy the bosom all bleeding and gory,
>   She may envy the sound of the drear passing-knell.
> Not so deep are his woes on his death-couch reposing
>   When on the last vision his dim eyes are closing,
> As the outcast—
>
>   (Hogg, I, 126)

This passage, derived from the second stanza of "Stern, stern is the voice," reveals how easily Shelley, and the "Song" itself, adopts the feminine pronoun as a natural outgrowth of the original version's remarkably feminine perspective.[24] But Shelley had his own reasons for making this perspective more explicitly feminine: he was (re)writing his poem in the persona of his sister, Elizabeth Shelley. At this time and throughout the first several months of his friendship with Thomas Hogg, Shelley was encouraging, to put it mildly, his friend to fall in love with his sister, and he wanted Hogg to believe that *she* had written these and the other verses from the siblings' *Victor and Cazire* volume that Shelley copied and revised for Hogg.[25] But on a less conscious level, this subterfuge allowed Percy to transform the sympathetic bonding with Harriet that permeates the earlier version of "Stern, stern is the voice" into an unrestrained fusion with his best-loved sister.

The time frame involved here helps explain the shift from a largely relational dynamic to one in which coalescence prevails. In August 1810, the original date of the poem's composition, Percy's relationship with Harriet was still relatively intact and his sister's love as warm as ever, but by the time he recast the poem for Thomas Hogg in the winter of 1811,[26] "the dearest of [his] ties" had either been severed (his engagement to Harriet) or badly frayed (his sister's loyalty to her "deistifying" brother) (*L*, I, 27, 42).[27] When he rewrites "Stern, stern is the voice" for Thomas, Percy is now holding onto Harriet-Elizabeth the only way he can: by becoming her.[28]

Accounts of the poet's rocky transition from Field Place's feminine ambience to the often brutal boy-world of boarding school suggest that he was "woman identified" since boyhood.[29] But his radical fusion with his feminine "twin(s)" in late adolescence must have contributed immensely to Shelley's remarkable ability to create and inhabit vibrant, complex heroines and personæ such as Cythna, Asia, Beatrice, and the Witch of Atlas.[30] His identification with Harriet, Elizabeth, and, to a lesser extent, his younger sisters also helped inspire the feminist sympathies that inform *Queen Mab*, *Laon and Cythna*, *A Discourse on Love*, and his fragmentary "Essay on Marriage" (?1817). Yet Shelley's unshakable sense of woman's elusiveness and inconstancy, instilled first by his mother's and then by his cousin's and sisters' "abandonment" of him, helped prevent him from championing the revolutionary feminism with which Nathaniel Brown, for example, credits him.[31] Although Shelley has both Queen Mab and Laon envision a feminist millennium where "free and equal man and woman greet / Domestic peace," the poet himself feared that women—"his" women—were in fact too free: free to leave him, free to hurt him, free to disappoint him (*CW*, I, 285: *LC*, II. 329–30; cf. *QM*, IX. 89–92). The spectacle of an immobile Prometheus languishing on his crag while Asia embarks on her amazing journey dramatically captures Shelley's sense of impotence and psychic paralysis in the face of feminine energy and autonomy. Formerly his to "mould," first Harriet Grove and then Elizabeth Shelley declared their independence from their preceptor, leaving him to his own devices, his own designs for recapturing his fugitive sisters of the soul (*L*, I, 163).

One of Shelley's strategies, as I have been arguing, involves cultivating his own feminine qualities in an effort to mirror those of his female beloved(s).[32] As an initiated and confirmed "sister," he could then slip back into the Field Place sorority, or at least re-creations of it in his art and in his life.[33] Yet Shelley also needed his "sister-spirits" to mirror *him*, that is, to obediently (and flatteringly) reflect his ideas, his personality, and his desires, as well as to confirm his sense of self-worth in the normative way that the "approving" or "mirroring" Kohutian selfobject does. Although I do not want to reduce Harriet and Elizabeth to mother-surrogates, it does seem that the elder Elizabeth Shelley's apparent "failure" as the first and most important "mirroring selfobject" for her emotionally demanding son compelled him to transfer his now intensified needs for approval and love to his sister(s) and cousin.[34]

While Percy felt a deep and genuine affection for them both, his favorite sister, Elizabeth, and his beautiful cousin, Harriet, were perhaps most crucial to the young poet as nurses who helped heal the narcissistic wounds left by Lady Shelley's apparent retreat from him when he began attending Syon House Academy, if not earlier.[35] Daughterly as well as maternal,[36] Elizabeth and Harriet also became for Percy responsive "twins," the prototypes of the Shelleyan "second selves" who continuously drift through his psychic landscape. Yet it is significant that Percy did not conceptualize or consciously embrace the notion of a feminine second self until *after* his sister and cousin pulled away from him. Their withdrawal, a devastating re-enactment of his mother's (perceived) rejection of him, may have convinced Shelley that "the most tenderly loved of [his] soul," who had always been women, would inevitably flee from him, leaving him the perennial victim of "repulse and disappointment" (*Esdaile* 124: "Dares the Lama"; "On Love" 473). When his cousin's and sister's immediate successors—named, appropriately, Harriet (Westbrook) and Elizabeth (Hitchener)—arrive on the scene, Shelley is extremely anxious that they remain with him "*forever*" (*L*, I, 131).[37] While Miss Hitchener calls him "the Brother of [her] soul" and he zealously adopts her terminology, Shelley himself invents an even more intimate kinship, one that can radically and, he hopes, permanently unite him with his "new sister[s]" (*L*, I, 145n2: E. H. to Shelley, 11 October 1811; *L*, I, 152).[38]

When first Elizabeth Hitchener and then Harriet Westbrook Shelley "graduate" to the rank of "second self," they participate in a Shelleyan dynamic that will govern most of his subsequent experiences with and artistic depictions of romantic love.[39] Usually an idealized, feminine double for the poet or for his (feminized) heroes, the second self plays a number of interrelated roles that tend to elude any kind of fixed hierarchy involving the first and second selves that we, or even Shelley himself, try to impose. As a "second" self, she appears to be a mere "shadow" or extension of the first self, but when, for instance, Laon's "shadow," Cythna, begins to overshadow him, we begin to question the stability of the terms Shelley and his hero have adopted (*CW*, I, 281, 274: *LC*, I. 534; II. 208). As a woman, the second self may seem doomed to a supporting role in a sexist scenario, but when we recognize femininity as the "far goal" both of Shelley and of his male protagonists, the Shelleyan hero appears less powerful, less realized, and less complete than his feminine double (*PU*, III. iv. 174). Or, to blend a Bloomian with a Shelleyan paradigm, the feminine second self rather than the masculine first self emerges as the great original of "everything excellent or lovely" in human nature, an "ideal prototype" whom her masculine counterpart can only hope to reflect as her (belated) "antitype" ("On Love" 473, 474).

Shelley's idealization of the feminine is inscribed in his eloquent essay "On Love," from which I have just quoted. Though composed in the summer of 1818, its ideas suffuse even Shelley's earliest works. Images of birth and of nursing mothers help the poet illustrate his notion of perfect sympathy or "correspondence," while his description of the inner ideal or prototype suggests a child *in utero*, a "miniature" being within our being, or "soul within our soul" ("On Love" 474, 473, 474).[40] Shelley's favorite (self-)image of an Eolian harp also enhances the feminine aura of this piece. He longs for a lover "with a frame whose nerves, like the chords of two exquisite lyres strung to the accompaniment of one delightful voice, vibrate with the vibrations of [his] own" (474). Though according to Shelley's often slippery syntax, the two lyres represent the nerves of the longed-for antitype, this highly-wrought passage compels us to see the twin harps as the speaker and his mate, perfectly, *erotically* attuned and alive with feminine sensibility, receptivity, and tenderness.

As we shall see when we turn to works such as *Rosalind and Helen* and *Laon and Cythna*, the woman-identified poet and his heroes must interact dynamically with their feminine second selves, communing, coalescing and even competing with these sister-spirits if they are to achieve the sisterly twinship that the essay "On Love" hints at. That the feminine second self's own roles are varied, her own identity unstable is quite appropriate, considering her strange birth. Her inception certainly occurred earlier than the crucial winter of 1810–1811, as we can surmise from Percy's intense involvements with his "twins" Elizabeth Shelley and Harriet Grove and from his creation of Verezzi's pliant Julia and Fitzeustace's perfectly sympathetic Eloise.[41] But the second self first became an acknowledged, vital presence in the poet's relational model in the aftermath of the Harriet Grove crisis. Emanating from

Shelley's need for mirroring females to replace his mother, cousin, and sister, the idealized, feminine double is also a progeny of the war against Selfhood that began to obsess Shelley during this period. As Percy lost first Harriet and then Elizabeth, he tried to overcome his hurt and rage by purging himself of self-interest, jealousy, possessiveness, and even desire itself, and his violent exertions to root out that "*hateful* principle" of Self helped produce a figure who shares qualities with both the Shelleyan martyr, the focus of my first chapter, and the baneful masculine *Doppelgänger*, examined in chapter 2 (*L*, I, 34).

     Like the Shelleyan martyr, the second self originates in part from the "willed selflessness" that the poet and his protagonists often strive to achieve (Curran, *Shelley's Annus Mirabilis* 139). And just as the self-advertising martyr might be Narcissus in the guise of Christ, the Shelleyan second self may be the mirror into which Narcissus gazes in rapt self-worship.[42] Like the male *Doppelgänger*, the female second self allows Shelley to project and explore aspects of himself that interfere with or strengthen his ability to envision and participate in a sympathetically interacting world. Both dark double and ideal second self represent the poet's deep reservations about the ceaseless interminglings that comprise such a world, but oddly enough, the former figure, who inspires "loathsome sympathy," embodies Shelley's commitment to a world-in-relation model much more powerfully than does the loving twin (*PU*, I. 451). In creating and empathically merging with malefactors such as Ahasuerus, Jupiter, and Count Cenci, Shelley resolutely enters the noxious atmosphere that others may emit as well as acknowledges his own contribution to this psychic pollution. The ideal second self, however, often allows the poet to evade "the polluting multitude," and his membership therein, by offering self-communion disguised as radical interpenetration with an other ("Euganean Hills," l. 356). Thus it is not Shelley's recurring nightmare of his own and others' infectious evil that most relentlessly undermines his visions of sympathetic exchange, but rather his persistent dream of a sister-spouse[43] who would shelter him with her innocuous, familiar consanguinity from "the contagion of the world's slow stain" (*Adonais*, l. 356).

Peculiar Susceptibility

     That the ideal twin usually remains an elusive dream or inspires dark fantasies of mutual annihilation attests to the poet's own profound doubts about this crucial ingredient of Shelleyan love. As early as December 1810, Percy saw that "egotising folly" lead him to present his sister Elizabeth to his friend Thomas Hogg as a kind of ideal self-projection (*L*, I, 29).[44] But because his urgent desire to recapture the feminine Paradise of his boyhood never abated, the poet could not abandon his ideal of a feminine second self, a figure who represents both his own feminine qualities and the loving mother-sister who invites the (feminized) poet back into the Field Place sorority. Shelley did, however, constantly address and try to break through the hermeticism, narcissism, and hierarchism inherent to his cherished first-self/second-self model.

When Shelley inflicts a "mutual annihilation" on the incestuous lovers in *Laon and Cythna* and on the spiritual siblings of *Epipsychidion*, he is passing his harshest judgement on his own forbidden desires—the desire to (sexually) possess the sister-mother and the desire for the "Narcissus' looking-glass" included in her dowry (Thorslev, "Incest as Romantic Symbol," 56).[45] While (self-)punishment comprises Shelley's most extreme method of purging his erotic paradigm of "the sordid lust of self," he also devised strategies that allowed him to battle the principle of Self from within his favorite configuration (*QM*, V. 90). In *Prometheus Unbound*, for example, Shelley expands the consanguineous lovers' potentially "anti-social union" until it embraces and animates the entire cosmos (Richardson, "The Dangers of Sympathy," 751).[46] And in *Laon and Cythna* and *Epipsychidion*, he continually inverts the hierarchy implied in the terms *first* and *second self*, thereby destabilizing the couples' power dynamics and preventing either partner from congealing into the embodiment of grasping, tyrannical Selfhood.

But Shelley's most ingenious method of enlisting these erotic doubles in his war against Selfhood involves much more than the pairs' ever-shifting power relations. Shelley could justify his idealized depictions of twinned, potentially self-sequestered lovers only if these figures helped him erode the very foundation of Selfhood: personal identity. For Shelley, one of the more effective means of combating the principle of Self entailed pre-empting its most terrible, and most familiar, manifestations by sabotaging it in its least recognized, ostensibly innocuous guises. While greed, self-idolatry, hatred, and violence provide obvious targets for the social reformer who wants to replace the Mammon of Selfhood with the "Spirit of love," individual identity seems an utterly acceptable, and even desirable acquisition (*S-P*, I. 6). But when Shelley urges Elizabeth Hitchener to "divest [herself] of individuality," he *means* it, and has been struggling to do so himself, not just since his recent break with his cousin and family but since his conversion to "the religion of Philanthropy" as a boy at Syon House (*L*, I, 151; *Prose* 42: *Proposals for an Association of Philanthropists*).[47] And here is where Shelley's valorization of femininity really comes into play.

Like many theorists of his own and of our day, Shelley credited women with "permeable" ego boundaries and a fluidity of identity that would enable them to dispense more readily than men with the notion of a discrete, rigidly defined self.[48] In compelling heroes such as Laon, Prometheus, and the voluble speaker of *Epipsychidion* to mirror the femininity of their supposedly "second" selves, the poet distances his surrogates from (masculine) conceptions of personal autonomy, fixed gender, and static identity, from the principle of Self that Shelley's dangerously virile, monomaniacal, and "self-closd" *Doppelgänger* embody.[49] Together, as chameleons, as martyrs, or as both, the feminized Shelleyan hero and his female twin assail the male-born myth of impervious, monolithic selfhood.

Attacks on (masculine) Selfhood via feminine self-sacrifice, empathy, and multiplicity do not, of course, cancel out the self-indulgent aspects of the Shelleyan fantasy of ideal twinship, as the poet himself was well aware. Moreover, the notions of feminine receptivity and flexibility held an obvious appeal for someone with Shelley's lifelong penchant for "moulding" female disciples.[50] But by his own and others' accounts, Shelley himself exemplified the kind of "susceptibility," or acute sensitivity, to outside impressions that traditionally belongs to the feminine gender (*L*, I, 228).[51] His depictions of women—both within the first-self/second-self dyad (Cythna, Emilia) and beyond it (Beatrice Cenci)—thus involve a more complex form of authorial self-projection than is generally recognized. If Shelley's malevolent male *Doppelgänger* embody the invasive, poisonous Self that lurked within the poet's own psyche and in the world at large, his heroines, second selves, and female personæ often represent his "feminine" openness to the "surrounding universe," a universe whose inhabitants may supply an "atmosphere of light" and love or emit "vapours . . . which have strength to kill" ("On Life" 477; *PU*, IV. 323; *S-P*, III. 75).

Two references to Shelley's "impressible soul" in T. J. Hogg's biography of his friend suggest how Shelley could have regarded his own psychic porosity as both a gift and a curse.[52] I will begin with a passage that displays Shelley's "exquisite sensibility" in a completely favorable light, despite the pall of irony that Hogg's relentless mock-reverence toward the "Divine Poet" always threatens to cast (I, 83; II, 34). Like other contemporary accounts of the "feminine" Shelley, including the poet's own, Hogg's employs the physically-tinged language of sensibility. First, Hogg describes "how profoundly the resistless beauties" of the natural world "entered into [Shelley's] inmost soul" and became "integral portions of himself and of his existence" (II, 48). The remarkable spiritual and aesthetic receptivity that Hogg emphasizes here and elsewhere reminds us of how the poet in his "passive youth" opens himself to the "Spirit of BEAUTY" that nourishes, purifies, and consecrates each "human thought or form" it visits ("Hymn," ll. 79, 13, 15). And Shelley's own consecration of such words as *soft, penetrable, susceptible, melt, dissolve* reveals how much he cherished an ideal of (his own) supple—and strikingly feminine—responsiveness.

The biographer then turns to a less passive, though equally feminine form of Shelley's sensibility: his power of imaginative self-transformation.

"[T]he poetic faculty of turning himself mentally into the subject of his poem," Hogg writes, "of metamorphosing himself internally into an attendant spirit, into Titania, Queen Mab herself, was conspicuous and astonishing" (II, 48). Not only does Shelley imaginatively become a female character in the example that Hogg cites, but evidence from Shelley's own texts suggests that the poet viewed the power of self-alteration as itself a distinctly feminine gift that he was privileged to share. Shelley's shape-shifting "daughter of Earth and Water" in "The Cloud" (l. 73); the (self-)transforming presence of the radiant Asia; the capricious Witch of Atlas; and the protean, metaphor-spawning Emily all epitomize the feminine multiplicity that enables them to elude ossified, uniform Selfhood and, in Asia's case, to personify and disseminate the "Spirit of love" (*S-P*, I. 6).[53]

In Hogg's next example of what Shelley himself calls his "peculiar susceptibility," the poet's feminine fluidity returns to the essentially passive plasticity or permeability that allowed nature's "resistless" beauty to "enter into" the poet's soul (*L*, I, 228):

> In trifling matters, moreover, which were unconnected with, or unworthy of, poetic themes, [Shelley] could become, I should say rather he became, involuntarily and unconsciously, the very personage of whom any remarkable incident was related, however trivial it might be, that forcibly struck his impressible soul. (II, 48)

Hogg's remarks here on Shelley's "disposition and habit to adopt the situation, the feelings, the colour of other persons" (II, 48) parallel and even echo one of Shelley's own comments on "the poetical Character," to borrow a phrase from Keats (*Keats's Letters*, I, 386: 27 October 1818): "Poets, the best of them—are a very camæleonic race: they take the colour not only of what they feed on, but of the very leaves under which they pass" (*L*, II, 308: 13 July 1821). Whereas Hogg's reference to the poet's sympathetic identification with his own characters implies conscious effort on Shelley's part—he "metamorphos[es] himself," he "turn[s] himself" into "the subject of his poem"—both his final emphasis on Shelley's "impressible soul" and the poet's own remarks on the "camæleonic race" of poets underscore Shelley's "involuntary" or "unconscious" receipt of influence from an outside source.

At this point, it would be worthwhile to turn our attention to Keats, whose spirit has been hovering over the discussion for quite some time. It is Keats rather than Shelley with whom we associate the notion of "the camelion Poet," for Keats seemed much more capable than Shelley of empathically entering the world of concrete particulars and thereby obliterating the self (*Keats's Letters*, I, 387: 27 October 1818). But Keats's famous letter on the poetical Character, heavily influenced by Hazlitt, traces the same movement from active self-transformation to passive self-surrender as that charted by Hogg's subtly contrasting descriptions of Shelley's identification *with* his own characters and his susceptibility *to* "other persons" (Hogg, II, 48). "A Poet is the most unpoetical of any thing in existence," Keats writes, "because he has no Identity—he is continually in for[ming?]—and filling some other Body" (*Keats's Letters*, I, 387: 27 October 1818). Although the Keatsian poet "has no self," this passage implies that at least some active self-projection is involved in entering and then "filling" the object or individual he is exploring. This is especially evident when we look at a very different aspect of the camelion Poet that Keats brings up later in the letter:

> When I am in a room with People if I ever am free from speculation on creations of my own brain then not myself goes home to myself: but the identity of every one in the room begins to press upon me that, I am in a very little time annihilated—not only among Men; it would be the same in a Nursery of children. (*Keats's Letters*, I, 387)

Here is where the "weak ego boundaries" that psychologist Nancy Chodorow ascribes to women and that Barbara Gelpi and Adrienne Rich link with Keatsian Negative Capability become a somewhat troubling attribute.[54] While Keats revels with "gusto" in his own ontological elasticity, he hints at something claustrophobic in his vulnerability to other identities which "press upon" him, perhaps even "fill" him the way that he imaginatively "fill[s] some other Body."

The distinction that psychologist Gail S. Reed makes between intrusive and receptive empathy is pertinent here. According to Reed, "intrusive" empathy involves a kind of phallic trespass into the psyche of another—in Reed's example, the analysand—in order to "gather" information or "grasp" meaning ("Antithetical Meaning of the Term 'Empathy'" 17, 14). She associates "passive" or "receptive" empathy, on the other hand, with "the mythological figure of the perfectly attuned, resonating, responsive mother" who provides "an atmosphere, medium, or surround" for the other to enter and explore (16, 17)—in conjunction with the empathic "host(ess)"—his or her own psychic landscape. Reed does not place value judgements on these "masculine" and "feminine" modes of empathy, and she points out that in practical experience they constantly intersect and, ideally, complement each other.[55] Similarly, I would like to apply her categories descriptively rather than prescriptively in my comments on the complex nature of both Keatsian and Shelleyan empathy.

I hesitate to label as "phallic" or "penetrative" the kind of impulse that, for instance, enabled Keats to imaginatively enter a sparrow and "pick about the Gravel" with it, or, rather, *as* it, but this example does involve a less passive, less "feminine" kind of empathy than that which characterizes Keats's experience in the crowded room (*Keats's Letters*, I, 186). Significantly, it is when Keats stops "speculating on creations of [his] own brain" that other identities "press upon" and "annihilate" him. Turning away from the parthenogenetic activities of his own "working brain," the poet is suddenly, frighteningly subject to invasion by other selves, other consciousnesses (*Keats's Poems* 277: "Ode to Psyche," l. 60). The pores or, as Shelley might say, "interstices," of Keats's being are now completely open: even nursery-age children have more firmly demarcated, aggressively intrusive egos than the camelion Poet in his most feminine guise. Keats's mind *was* "susceptible," his heart *was* made of "penetrable stuff," though not in the way that Shelley implies throughout *Adonais*, his self-projective myth of Keats's tragic victim-ization at the hands of vicious reviewers (Preface to *Adonais* 391).[56]

The image of the radically, defenselessly receptive Keats in a room full of more self-contained, self-assertive identities brings us to the second of Hogg's references to his friend Shelley's "impressible soul":

> In a crowded stage-coach Shelley once happened to sit opposite an old woman with very thick legs, who, as he imagined, was afflicted with elephantiasis, an exceedingly rare and most terrible disease, in which the legs swell and become as thick as those of an elephant, together with many other distressing symptoms, . . . and indeed a whole Iliad of woes, of which he had recently read a formidable description in some medical work, that had taken entire possession of his fanciful and impressible soul . . . He also took it into his head that the disease is very infectious, and that he had caught it of his corpulent . . . fellow-traveller; he presently began to discover unequivocal symptoms of the fearful conta-gion in his own person. I never saw him so thoroughly unhappy as he was, whilst he continued under the influence of this strange and unac-countable impression.[57] (Hogg, II, 38–39)

Although Hogg is emphasizing Shelley's imaginative susceptibility to the medical book describing elephantiasis when he mentions the poet's "impress-ible soul," the phrase implicitly describes Shelley's own sense of utter vul-nerability to "the contagion of the world's . . . stain," here embodied by a grotesque, diseased old woman (*Adonais*, l. 356). Peacock, who confirms Hogg's account in substance if not in all its details, dates the episode "about the end of 1813" (*Memoirs* 326).[58] Seven years later, at the close of 1820, Shelley is still exhibiting symptoms of his "peculiar susceptibility," this time at the Carnival in Pisa. As Thomas Medwin, who was staying with the Shel-leys at the time, tells us: "So sensitive was he of external impressions, so mag-netic, that I have seen him, after threading the carnival crowd in the Lung'

Arno Corsos, throw himself half fainting into a chair, overpowered by the atmosphere of evil passions, as he used to say, in that sensual and unintellectual crowd" (268).[59]

These two examples, along with Shelley's own complaint of his "terrible susceptibility to objects of disgust and hatred," reveal the dark underside of the remarkable receptivity and "delicate sensibility" celebrated, for example, in the "Hymn to Intellectual Beauty," "Ode to the West Wind," and the *Defence* (*L*, I, 383: 16 March 1814; *Defence* 505). In each of these works, the poet receives "evanescent visitations" from a "diviner nature" (*Defence* 504) that cleanse and "quicken" ("WW," l. 64) him, as well as unveil to him the self's true nature: "an atom to a Universe" (*Defence* 505). These moments of inspiration enable him, at least briefly, to transcend "the dull vapours of . . . self" (*Defence* 497) and to glimpse and even be "interpenetrated" by a beautiful ("Hymn") or sublime ("Ode to the West Wind") spiritual presence, but only if he offers himself up as a "still instrument" that awaits the breath "of some unseen Power" ("Hymn," ll. 34, 1). By identifying in the "Hymn" and elsewhere with the Aeolian harp—the "exquisite lyre" of the essay "On Love" (474)—the poet is yet again embracing a conspicuously feminine self-image, modeled on the Coleridgian harp as "coy maid yielding to her lover" ("The Eolian Harp," ll. 43, 15).[60] Like the (self-)image of the wounded deer, discussed earlier, the Shelleyan lute resonates both with the poet's innate affinity with the feminine gender and with his desperate desire to purge himself completely of the masculine taint that prevented him from joining his archetypal "band of sister-spirits" as a full-fledged member. In order to compensate for that last infirmity of the feminized male—the irreducible, inexpurgable kernel of masculinity—Shelley often exaggerates his own feminine sensibility, and this is exactly what he does when he adopts the role of an utterly passive lute.

Coleridge's reference to the Aeolian harp as "this subject Lute" and his later depiction of an agonized, screaming harp tortured by a "Mad Lutanist" underscore the dangers inherent to the kind of extravagant passivity that both he and Shelley tended to exemplify ("Eolian Harp," l. 43; "Dejection: An Ode," l. 104).[61] In a letter that he wrote to Mary Godwin in late 1814, Shelley acknowledges that as a "fragile lute," he is vulnerable both to refreshing winds and to destructive blasts: "I am an harp responsive to every wind. The scented gale of summer can wake it to sweet melody, but rough cold blasts draw forth discordances & jarring sounds" (*Alastor*, l. 667; *L*, I, 418).[62] While this letter is playful in tone, Shelley's mood during this period often verged on deep despair. From October 23 through November 8, Percy and Mary were forced to take separate lodgings so that Percy could elude the bailiffs hired by his angry creditors.[63] As the impassioned letters that the exiled Percy wrote his most recent "treasured love" reveal (*L*, I, 414), the dejection that threatened to overwhelm him involved much more than mere loneliness or "separation anx-iety." For the spiritual, emotional, and sexual dynamic that allowed Percy to abandon himself to the role of responsive, "delicately organized," and femi-nine harp was suddenly missing its most crucial component: the sister-spirit who not only mirrors/confirms the poet's own femininity but who also "shields[s] [him] fr{om} impurity & vice," both his own and others' (*Defence* 507; *L*, I, 414: 28 October 1814).[64] Bereft of Mary, he now felt terribly exposed to the pestilential vapours of the "miserable city" rather than delight-fully susceptible to the vivifying and purifying breath of his beloved second self (*Esdaile* 53: "On leaving London for Wales," l. 1).[65]

And Percy clearly thought of his newest love, then at the height of her reign, as his ideal twin. The letter referring to "impurity & vice" exemplifies how the poet pitted his own darkest urges, always for Shelley products of cor-rupt and corrupting Selfhood, against his feminine self-image and his alliance with a female double:

> Mary love—we must be united . . . Your thoughts alone can waken mine to energy. My mind without yours is dead & cold as the dark midnight river when the moon is down. It seems as if you alone could shield me fr{om} impurity & vice. If I were absent from you long I should shud-der with horror at myself. My understanding becomes undisciplined without you. I believe I must become in Marys hands what Harriet was in mine—yet how differently disposed how devoted & affectionate: how beyond measure reverencing & adoring the intelligence that governs me—I repent me of this simile it is unjust—it is false. Nor do I mean that I consider you much my superior—evidently as you surpass me in orig-inality & simplicity of mind.—How divinely sweet a task it is to imitate each others excellencies—& each moment to become wiser in this sur-passing love—so that constituting but one being, all real knowledge may be comprised in the maxim γνωθι σεαυτον (know thyself) with infi-nitely more justice than in its narrow & common application. (*L*, I, 414)

A kind of anatomy of Shelleyan love in miniature, this urgent letter unveils the intricate undergirding of the poet's most treasured erotic paradigm. We see how Mary, as ideal second self, protects him from external contaminants as well as fends off the spectre of Percy's own Selfhood ("If I were absent from you long I should shudder with horror at myself").[66] We also observe how Percy's initial self-abasement and self-repression become Self-Esteem when he merges at the end of the passage with Mary, whom the poet almost sys-tematically elevates, both in this letter and in others that he wrote during this emotionally and erotically-charged autumn.[67] This pattern, moreover, involves the "subordination to female power" that had often characterized his relationship with Elizabeth Hitchener and that suggests a desire for a maternal and not simply a sisterly mate (Paglia 372).[68] But if Mary is mother, Percy is not son but rather daughter, for in a remarkable sleight of hand, the poet slides into Harriet's feminine subject position, becoming "in Marys hands what Harriet was in [his]." As the passage ends, the mother-daughter dyad at last metamorphoses into the kind of relationship that Percy yearned for all along: the perfect, sympathetic correspondence of sisters who "imitate each others excellencies" and so "constitute but one being."

"The excellence of sisterly affection" is at the heart of an intriguing episode that Hogg recounts in great detail early in his biography of Shelley (I, 81). While the eloquent, not always reliable biographer may have invented some of this detail,[69] the elaborate speech about sisterly love that he has the young poet deliver has an authentic Shelleyan feel to it, in spirit and even in style. While exploring the countryside around Oxford in the autumn or winter of 1810,[70] Hogg tells us, he and Shelley stumbled onto an enclosed garden, still lovely in its desolation. Shelley was captivated, and he soon conjured suitable gardeners to tend this enchanting retreat:

> "[T]he seclusion is too sweet, too holy, to be the theatre of ordinary love; the love of the sexes, however pure, still retains some taint of earthly grossness; we must not admit it within the sanctuary . . . The love of a mother for her child is more refined; it is more disinterested, more spiritual; but," he added, after some reflection, "the very existence of the child still connects it with the passion, which we have discarded"; and he relapsed into his former musings.
>
> "The love a sister bears towards a sister," he exclaimed abruptly, and with an air of triumph, "is unexceptionable."
>
> The idea pleased him, and as he strode along he assigned the trim garden to two sisters, affirming, with the confidence of an inventor, that it . . . was their constant haunt; the care of it their favourite pastime, and its prosperity, next after the welfare of each other, the chief wish of both. (I, 80–81)

The hierarchy of love that Shelley embraces here is one that subtly or overtly informs central works such as *Laon and Cythna*, *Prometheus Unbound*, and *Epipsychidion*. Heterosexual desire, "however pure," occupies a low rung on the Shelleyan ladder of love because it invariably "retains the taint of earthly grossness," the "passion of animal love" that for Shelley remained inextricably linked with physical decay and with (masculine) aggression and "self love" (*L*, I, 208). A mother's love for her child is more commendable, but because the child is an offspring of sexual passion, maternal love, according to Shelley, cannot be entirely "disinterested" and "spiritual." It is the mutual devotion of sisters that receives Shelley's highest praise in this impromptu discourse. This "unexceptionable" love alternates and at times coincides with the self-sacrifice of the Christlike martyr as the highest expression of the Shelleyan "Spirit of love" (*S-P*, I. 6).

Shelley's lofty, and not very convincing, dismissal of the sexual instinct as "that passion, which we have discarded" clues us in on the poet's own desire to participate in and not simply to observe or imagine the sisterly ideal, which he then goes on to characterize:

> [Shelley] described [the sisters'] appearance, their habits, their feelings, and drew a lovely picture of their amiable and innocent attachment; of the meek and dutiful regard of the younger, which partook, in some degree of filial reverence, but was more facile and familiar; and of the protecting, instructing, hoping fondness of the elder, that resembled maternal tenderness, but had less of reserve and more of sympathy. In no other relation could the intimacy be equally perfect; not even between brothers, for their life is less domestic; there is a separation in their pursuits, and an independence in the masculine character. The occupations of all females of the same age and rank are the same, and by night sisters cherish each other in the same quiet nest. Their union wears not only the grace of delicacy, but of fragility also; for it is always liable to be suddenly destroyed by the marriage of either party, or at least to be interrupted and suspended for an indefinite period.
>
> He depicted so eloquently the excellence of sisterly affection, and he drew so distinctly, and so minutely, the image of the two sisters . . . that the trifling incident has been impressed upon my memory. (I, 81)

As undeniably sentimentalized as it is, there is real pathos in Shelley's portrait of the garden's "tutelary nymphs" (I, 80). His reference to maternal "reserve" reminds us why he so craved sisterly "sympathy," while his vivid evocation of that sympathy reminds us that even before his actual exile from the "magic circle" of Field Place (I, 78),[71] his gender excluded him from the perfect intimacy that his own sisters shared. Soon enough, though, he would become the serpent shut out from paradise in a much more decisive way. When he loses his cousin, Harriet Grove, his sisters, and thus his place as an honorary member of their sorority, Shelley embarks on a lifelong mission to re-create his feminine Eden, both in his writings and in his life. But it is in his poetry that he will refashion this paradise with a crucial difference. Through a relentless siege on his own masculinity, the poet will imaginatively enter that "quiet nest" of delicately sensual sister-love, not as a voyeur, but as a sexually transformed member of that dyad, a sister-spirit who mirrors and at times exceeds "her" second self's radiant femininity.

Dear Woman's Love: *Henry and Louisa*

Shelley's first long poem, *Henry and Louisa*, composed in the fall or winter of 1809, bears an epigraph that tersely announces the young poet's decisive alliance with the feminine gender: "She died for love—and he for glory" (*Esdaile* 131). The "glory" that Shelley disparages throughout this work is the "titles and wealth and fame" that military "Heroes" earn when they "mingle in [their] country's battle tide" rather than remain in "love's most blissful bower" (*Esdaile* 131, 133, 135: I. 2, 45, 109). The echo of *The Faerie Queene* that we hear in the last phrase—amplified by the fledgling poet's rather impressive use of Spenserian stanzas—could suggest a satirical take on "[d]ear Woman's love," but the "ruling grace" who presides over this poem's bower of bliss is a faithful Una rather than a Circean Acrasia (*Esdaile* 133: I, 60; *S-P*, II. 2). In fact, Louisa, quite unlike Spenser's "faire Enchauntresse," encourages her knight to take up his "warlike armes" and to forsake the feminine sphere of love for the masculine world of violent action (*FQ*, II. xii. 81. 8; xii. 80. 1). The poet himself, it turns out, is the only one who properly values the feminine paradise in which his hero and heroine once wove their "soul-spun ties of tenderness" (*Esdaile* 132: I. 16).

Written during or shortly after the initial crisis in Shelley's relationship with Harriet Grove—a crisis to which this fiercely antireligious work both contributes and responds—*Henry and Louisa* attempts to be the kind of politically and philosophically subversive epic that *Laon and Cythna* will more successfully exemplify.[72] But the outbursts that Shelley as "narrator" constantly interjects—ranting sermons against religion and selfishness and in favor of "dear Love!"—link this poem most closely to the emotionally explosive, nakedly self-revelatory letters that he would write to Hogg the following winter (*Esdaile* 137: I. 149). Whereas in those remarkable missives, the jilted poet usually directs his (narcissistic) rage at Christ, who severed "the dearest the tenderest of [his] ties," in *Henry and Louisa*, Shelley buttresses his indictment of religion, not yet a full-blown onslaught against Christ himself, with a powerful attack on masculinity, here epitomized by military enterprise ("legal murder") and imperial conquest (*L*, I, 35; *Esdaile* 131: I. 4). When he identifies masculinity with action, travel, and (suspect) accomplishment and femininity with domesticity and love, Shelley is certainly not invoking a gender paradigm that is in any sense revolutionary. However, the savage indignation with which the poet assails masculine "selfishness" and the fervour with which he embraces the feminine bower that the hero deserts reveal an almost desperate desire to (sexually) cross over and play the woman's part within this inherited model (*Esdaile* 131: I. 8). If the macho warrior spurns the feminine world of "purest love," Shelley himself will (re)enter it by donning the "womanly dress" that his misguided heroine exchanges for manly attire as she too leaves her Paradise (*Esdaile* 132, 139: I. 20; II. 189). Louisa, to her credit, heads for the battlefield not for any selfish purpose, but to repair the "soul-spun ties of tenderness" that her lover had brutally severed when he exchanged "dear Love" for the "dear loved work of battle" (*Esdaile* 132, 137, 140: I. 16, 149; II. 208).

Even before his own "tender tie" with his cousin Harriet is irreparably torn, Percy tends to regard their engagement from the perspective of a bereft, exiled lover (*Esdaile* 132: I. 25).[73] The closer Shelley moved toward a final crisis in his relationship with his cousin, the more justified seem the laments for lost love that we find in nearly every poem that implicitly or explicitly addresses their engagement. More puzzling is the sense of devastating separation from the beloved that pervades the earlier poem, *Henry and Louisa*, which is written as though the breakup was already a fait accompli. Percy's unshakable dread that Harriet would someday abandon him seems to emerge, at least in part, from her affiliation in the poet's mind with the elusive mother, the first woman whom Percy strove to (re)capture through emulation/assimilation. In her perceptive reading of *Epipsychidion*, Angela Leighton has commented on the "sense of mourning" that colors this strange poem (229). We can apply her phrase to nearly all of Shelley's meditations on (romantic) love, from his earliest productions through his last grim vision of human desire, *The Triumph of Life*. If, however, most of Shelley's love poems are really elegies—for the lost mother, for the fugitive sister-spirit(s), for the feminine Eden that excluded the postpubescent poet—he goes about his work of mourning in a remarkably innovative and energetic manner.

In *Henry and Louisa*, for example, Shelley allows the warrior to indulge in a protracted and sentimental farewell, first to his tender lover and then to the fragrant garden where he had often basked in her "sacred presence" (*Esdaile* 135: I. 116). In these moments, Henry becomes a surrogate for the poet, whose own "bitter tear[s]" his (temporarily) softened hero cathartically sheds (*Esdaile* 136: I. 123). But if in the poem's first part, Shelley "bid[s] a long adieu" to "love's most blissful bower," in "Part Second," he re-enters/re-creates it on the arid soil of an Egyptian battlefield (*Esdaile* 136, 135: I. 122, 109). The poet's stern, often censorious attitude toward his protagonists melts into pure sympathy when Louisa discovers her lover dying in the desert. All their previous concern with military glory, imperial power, and "Religion's tie" vanishes completely, and in their last moments, they rebuild in "a ruin's shade" the bower of love they had both foolishly abandoned (*Esdaile* 143, 140: II. 296, 221). In a move that prefigures Kathema's suicide on the gibbet which bears the carcass of his dead lover and that anticipates Laon and Cythna's mutual martyrdom, the "love-nerved" Louisa joins her lover in death and thus ensures that the "spot from which their spirits fled" will be a place "[s]acred to Love" (*Esdaile* 133, 143: I. 44; II. 305).

As the poem closes, Henry, Louisa, the "silent ruins" where they died, and the poet himself are all enveloped by the feminine atmosphere that reigned at Louisa's country home and at its probable model, the poet's own Field Place (*Esdaile* 142: II. 267). The "soul-illuming ray" of "Dear Woman's love" that Shelley celebrates in the poem's first part re-asserts itself in this final tableau as "Affection's purer ray," the feminine and feminizing power that, Shelley hoped, would allow him, like his protagonists, to "Despise self" and to "know / All the delight love can bestow" (*Esdaile* 143: II. 298–99). That this self-feminization and permanent (re)union with the beloved woman often require that both partners die is only one of the troubling aspects of Shelley's strategies of mourning and recompensing the loss of mother, cousin, and sisters, as we shall see when we turn to some of the poet's later works.

Strange Harps: Rosalind and Helen and Alastor

Before leaving *Henry and Louisa* behind, however, we should note one more way that Shelley manages to identify himself with the feminine, or, more precisely in this case, with a specific female martyr. He concludes the poem's first half with a diatribe against "Religion! hated cause of all the woe / That makes the world this wilderness," an intensely personal passage that veers sharply away from narrative and toward confessional lyric (*Esdaile* 136: II. 144–45). The final stanza does not even attempt to fulfill its Spenserian requirements, as if the poet could not contain his fury against "selfish Prejudice" within his poem's formal constraints:

> For by the wrongs that flaming deep
>   Within this bosom's agony,
> That dry the source whence others weep,—
>   I swear that thou shalt die!
>
> (Esdaile 137: II. 151, 153–56)

The poet, it seems, suddenly has become St. Teresa of Avila, the ecstatically tormented nun whose flaming heart captivated the baroque imaginations of Bernini and Richard Crashaw. Unlike "the warrior's war-steeled breast," Shelley's own soft bosom is utterly penetrable, susceptible to the "fiery dart" that made "delicious wounds" in St. Teresa's breast.[74] The "wrongs" that torture Shelley include the universal misery that he believed Christianity propagated and, more specifically, as the penultimate stanza reveals, his impending loss of the fundamentally orthodox Harriet Grove. His startling self-identification with St. Teresa enables Percy simultaneously to incorporate both the femininity of the retreating Harriet and the glorious martyrdom

of his own, and St. Teresa's, Great Original: Christ. This passage thus comprises Shelley's first (self-)portrait of the feminized Christ, a figure whom he
would meet face to face when he visited the Bagni di Lucca almost nine
years later.

Lucca's most famous relic is a twelfth-century crucifix on which hangs
a bronze likeness of Jesus that is remarkably feminine, in figure if not in
face.[75] Dressed in a long tunic and equipped with gently swelling breasts, the
Volto Santo ("Saint Face") must have confirmed the poet's deep-seated sense
of Christ as an essentially feminine figure. This crucifix also helped inspire, I
believe, the most bizarre passage of Shelley's "Modern Eclogue," *Rosalind
and Helen*, completed while he sojourned at Lucca with Mary and Claire during the summer of 1818. On the grounds of Lionel's childhood home, where
the ineffectual Shelleyan revolutionary retreats with his beloved Helen, stands
a temple dedicated to Fidelity:

> And in the shrine an image sate,
> All veiled: but there was seen the light
> Of smiles, which faintly could express
> A mingled pain and tenderness
> Through that ethereal drapery.
> The left hand held the head, the right—
> Beyond the veil, beneath the skin,
> You might see the nerves quivering within—
> Was forcing the point of a barbed dart
> Into its side-convulsing heart.
> An unskilled hand, yet one informed
> With genius, had the marble warmed
> With that pathetic life . . .
> . . . .
> . . . it was Lionel's own hand
> Had wrought the image.
>
> (*CW*, II, 37: *RH*, ll. 1056–68, 1074–75)

Although Helen, who is describing this figure for her friend Rosalind, uses a
neuter pronoun here, the statue's "ethereal drapery" and veil signal in a typically Shelleyan manner its feminine gender.[76] This "dying statue fair and wan"
thus pays tribute both to Lucca's womanly Volto Santo and to St. Teresa, with
her "barbed dart," as well as to Spenser's veiled *Venus Hermaphroditus* (*CW*,
II, 38: *RH*, l. 1987).[77] At the same time, this image of feminine "pain and tenderness" is a portrait of the artist(s), the perennially suffering Lionel and,
behind him, the "fair and wan" Shelley. Ostensibly inspired by a dog's heroic
rescue of Lionel's mother from the sea, this temple and its statue are in fact

dedicated to Lionel himself, whose "own hand" the poet, through repetition of this noun, subtly identifies with the dart-wielding hand that the statue uses to torture/pleasure itself. Finally, in one of his more outrageous moves, Shelley has Lionel's mother in effect worshipping the image of her martyred son when she performs the "rites of a religion sweet" in "this lone fane," both before and presumably after the young man actually dies (*CW*, II, 38: *RH*, ll. 1077, 1076). Crucifixion and Pietà rolled into one, this strange set-piece from *Rosalind and Helen* makes the Shelleyan fantasy of maternal pity that opens *Prometheus Unbound* seem positively restrained.

But Lionel does not just allow the poet imaginatively to become a feminized version of Christ who regains and reflects the mother, but he also helps transport the poet through a series of metempsychoses back to the idealized feminine paradise of his boyhood.[78] The first stage of this process involves Lionel's spiritual, and erotic, migration into the body of his faithful Helen. In a scene that recasts in a less ludicrous fashion the climax of the 1810 "Epithalamium of Francis Ravaillac and Charlotte Cordé," Helen imbibes the soul of her lover, Lionel, whose "thin and languid form" can finally succumb to death (*CW*, II, 33: *RH*, l. 909). In both the "Epithalamium" and *Rosalind and Helen*, the beloved woman acts as a kind of benevolent succubus: her "[e]ndless kisses steal [the] breath" of her mate, who is then reborn within/as his feminine counterpart (*PS*, I, 121: "Epithalamium," l. 89). For Shelley, with his inexorable will-to-femininity, this is a resurrection devoutly to be wished. In fact, Lionel himself arranges an elaborate ceremony in his self-dedicated temple for this transmigration of his soul, a ceremony in which Helen plays the role of *Alastor*'s "veiled maid," luring the effeminate youth toward final (re)union with the longed-for female (l. 151).[79] After Helen concludes her "wild song," Lionel deliberately seeks dissolution in her embrace, feeding on the lips that are drinking in his soul (*CW*, II, 40 : *RH*, l. 1175). As Helen explains to her friend Rosalind: "words I dare not say / We mixed, and on his lips mine fed / Till they methought felt still and cold" (*CW*, II, 40: *RH*, ll. 1176–78).

For several months after Lionel's death, Helen's soul kept "the impress of [his] being" (*CW*, II, 41: *RH*, l. 1219). Despite the madness and grief that enveloped her, "Thy image ever dwelt on me," she assures her departed yet ever-present lover (*CW*, II, 42: *RH*, l. 1222). Shelley offers a naturalistic as well as a mystical explanation for his hero/surrogate's occupation of Helen's body and soul, which brings us to the next step in the poet's vicarious journey to his woman-centered Eden. Despite his extraordinary physical frailty, Lionel has managed to impregnate his beloved with a miniature version of himself, a "sweet child" who becomes "all the solace of [Helen's] woe" (*CW*, II, 42: *RH*, ll. 1224, 1227). Helen herself speaks of this young boy as if he were a reincarnation of her adored Lionel:

> "Observe, that brow was Lionel's,
> Those lips were his, and so he ever kept
> One arm in sleep, pillowing his head with it.
> You cannot see his eyes, they are two wells
> Of liquid love."
>
> (*CW*, II, 43: *RH*, ll. 1265–69)

After inhabiting the body of his feminine beloved, Shelley's hero now returns to his original (ambiguous) gender: the effeminate male.[80]

Alan Sinfield's recent work on the shifting historical definitions of "effeminacy" helps illuminate this most Shelleyan of figures, simultaneously heterosexual and self-feminizing. Sinfield writes,

> Up to the time of the Wilde trials—far later than it is widely supposed—it is unsafe to interpret effeminacy as defining of, or as a signal of, same-sex passion. Mostly, it meant being emotional and spending too much time with women. Often it involved excessive cross-sexual attachment. (27)

Lionel's—and Shelley's own—"cross-sexual attachment(s)" would not, then, necessarily clash with his cross-sexual *identification*. Heterosexual lovemaking, and even procreation, was an option for Shelley's feminized protagonists; though the rather hazy love scene at hand suggests how the poet, a father many times over, might psychically have elided his own (paternal) role in the latter. *Effeminacy*, though not as taboo as it would become in the wake of Wilde's downfall, was still a derogatory term, as the Sinfield passage makes clear, even during an age which celebrated the "man of feeling." G. J. Barker-Benfield's look into "The Question of Effeminacy" reveals how the fear of emasculation lurks beneath many eighteenth-century (male) authors' celebrations of sensibility.[81] Barker-Benfield's commentary on writers such as Shaftesbury, Hume, and Mackenzie, along with Marlon Ross's analysis of how Shelley's fellow male romantics coped with the "threat" of the feminine,[82] allows us to see Shelley's own *lack* of ambivalence toward the feminine realms of sensibility and sentiment as remarkable, even revolutionary.

If *Rosalind and Helen*'s "effeminate" Lionel is a (self-)portrait of the artist as a young man, his beatific son represents Shelley's ideal of himself as a boy. Shelley underscores his identification with this child by calling him "Henry," a name that had long held a mysterious fascination for the poet and which he had embraced since his earliest writings as a kind of alias, most recently in *Queen Mab*.[83] Shelley also likens this "fair child" to himself by assigning Henry his own penchant for launching delicate miniature boats: "Oft in a dry leaf for a boat, / With a small feather for a sail, / His fancy on

that spring would float, / If some invisible breeze might stir / It's marble calm"
(*CW*, II, 12: *RH*, ll. 173, 182–86).

Henry's genealogy and role in *Rosalind and Helen* are particularly
intriguing. We must recall the genesis of this poem, begun in 1817 at Marlow,
in order fully to appreciate the boy's tangled lineage. Originally inspired by
Mary's painful rupture with her girlhood friend Isabella Baxter (now Isabella
Booth),[84] the eclogue implicitly casts Mary in the role of Helen, ardently
devoted to her ostracized poet-lover.[85] As the child of Helen-Mary and of
Lionel-Percy, then, Henry allows the poet to reincarnate himself as his own
wife's child and to dwell peacefully with her as the sole (infantilized) male in
her feminine "circle" (*CW*, II, 43: *RH*, l. 1282). Not only does Lionel-Percy,
now Henry-Percy, enjoy the unconditional love of a mother-wife, but he also
receives the attentions of a loving "aunt" (Rosalind) and a sister-cousin, Rosalind's daughter, who eventually ripens into the cousin-sister-spouse that Harriet Grove never became.

Rosalind and Helen, which Mary treasured as her "pretty eclogue," thus
emerges from some of Percy's most primal fantasies of oedipal communion,
Christlike suffering, and sexual metamorphosis (*LMWS*, I, 43). Read alongside *Alastor*, written two years before Shelley began composing *Rosalind and
Helen*, this strange "Modern Eclogue" becomes even more rich in Shelleyan
self-revelation. The striking parallels between these works particularly help
illuminate the ways that the poet simultaneously indulges and criticizes his
most cherished fantasy: the dream of an ideal, feminine second self. In the
first half of *Rosalind and Helen*, this dream seems reduced to ashes, destroyed
as decisively and violently as the doomed love of Rosalind and her brother
and of the nameless brother and sister who fall prey to the rage of the "unen-
lightened" multitude.[86] But the relationship between Lionel and Helen, to
which Shelley devotes most of the poem's 1,300 lines, resurrects this erotic
ideal, with Helen playing symbolic sister-spirit rather than actual sister.

While Kenneth Neill Cameron has argued that the idealistic, passionate,
and physically fragile Lionel embodies a politically active version of the *Alastor* Poet,[87] William Ulmer recently has offered a suggestive, but only partially
accurate assessment of Helen's contribution to the kinship between these two
works: "*Rosalind and Helen* can be taken as an *Alastor* variation in which the
questing Poet (Lionel) ends his travels and accepts an actual woman (Helen,
acting as a surrogate Arab maiden)" (*Shelleyan Eros* 44). Though it is true that
Helen is an "actual woman" and that her nurturing, loving ministrations
resemble the selfless devotion that the Arab maiden offers the (literally and
figuratively) unconscious Poet, Lionel remains just as incapable as his fellow
visionary of abandoning his narcissistic quest for a idealized, feminine mirror
image. In fact, as his final act, Lionel tyrannically transforms his warmly
human lover into a divine, but death-dealing veiled maid, the original of

whom he apparently met while on his *Alastor*-like wanderings through "the world's vast wilderness" (*CW*, II, 28: *RH*, l. 738). Lionel has not, after all, broken the *Alastor* Poet's "self-centred" and self-destructive erotic cycle, though Shelley initially encourages us, and perhaps even himself, to believe that he has (*Alastor*, Preface, 69).

During his travels, the protagonist of the earlier poem meets (but never really sees) a potential mate who "minister[s] with human charity / His human wants" (*Alastor*, ll. 255–56). He is shortly thereafter visited by the visionary second self who will prevent him from ever accepting an ordinary woman such as the Arab maiden.[88] In *Rosalind and Helen*, Shelley reverses the order of these encounters and thus sets the stage for the kind of domestic idyll that he knew Mary longed for and that he believed he craved as well. The young Lionel, like the Poet, leaves his "native land" and while on his journey receives "silver dreams" of erotic fulfillment in his (literally) "liquid sleep" (*CW*, II, 28, 29: *RH*, ll. 739, 768, 769). And like the Poet, Lionel "wake[s] to weep," for he was "deceived / By some strange show" akin to the command performance of the elusive veiled maid in *Alastor* (*CW*, II, 29: *RH*, ll. 775, 758–59). That Lionel's vision involved a narcissistic self-projection similar to the one that the Poet had conjured is evident in the "mournful verses" that he composes: "I love, but I believe in love no more, / I feel desire, but hope not. O, from sleep / Most vainly must my weary brain implore / Its lost flattery now" (*CW*, II, 29: *RH*, ll. 762, 772–75). But Lionel, unlike the hopelessly (self-)obsessive Poet, has the potential to break free from his "self-centered seclusion" (*Alastor*, Preface, 69), and from his desperate quest for his "flatter[ing]" mirror image, by accepting and reciprocating the "sweet human love" of a real woman (*Alastor*, l. 203).

Whereas the *Alastor* Poet encounters his "enamoured" Arab maiden before he erotically communes with his "own treacherous likeness," Lionel meets Helen, a sexually and intellectually liberated incarnation of the Arab maiden, after his bitter experience with (self-)love (*Alastor*, ll. 133, 474). Extremely receptive to her attentions, Lionel seems at last to leave "desolation" behind (*CW*, II, 30: *RH*, l. 786). However, after submitting to his requisite Shelleyan martyrdom—in his case, imprisonment in a "dreary tower"— Lionel resumes his fatal quest for his perfect twin (*CW*, II, 32: *RH*, l. 859). His steadily declining health and the feverish infatuation with death that accompanies his erotic mission remind us of the *Alastor* Poet.[89] But instead of abandoning, like the Poet, his mortal maiden, Lionel takes her with him and eventually transforms her into the object of this quest. Moreover, Lionel's desire for the ultimate merger with his second self takes him back to his ancestral home rather than farther away from it, as in the earlier work. Lionel, in fact, experiences the *nostos* that Shelley himself, permanently exiled from Field Place, could never enjoy. But if Lionel's return functions in some respects as a wish fulfillment for the poet, it also obliges Shelley to confront the most troubling aspects of his compulsive need to recreate his boyhood Eden, with its Percy-centered circle of sister-spirits.

This chronic nostalgia is at the root of the strongest charge that Shelley makes against himself in *Rosalind and Helen*: his failure to find satisfaction with even an extraordinary woman such as his second wife, the eclogue's most important audience. Lionel's re-enactment of the *Alastor* Poet's self-involved and self-destructive communion with his spectral twin serves as Percy's confession to himself and to Mary that he would never break free from his (regressive) desire for fusion with his original mirroring female,[90] his mother, or her immediate heirs, the sister-spirits who flocked around him at Field Place. When Lionel-Percy leads Helen-Mary into the Temple of Fidelity, he turns her into an impassioned veiled maid who is explicitly a maternal figure.[91] The "strange harp" that Lionel compels Helen to play is "his mother's harp," and his spirit's (re)entry into his beloved represents the ultimate homecoming (*Alastor*, l. 166; *CW*, II, 39: *RH*, l. 1114).

The "symphony" that Helen-as-veiled-maid performs for her beloved, moreover, indulges her lover's rampant narcissism as well as his oedipal yearnings (*CW*, II, 39: *RH*, l. 1143).[92] As she performs her "wild song," Helen's voice is like the voice of Lionel's own soul, her singing and playing inspired by his "keen eyes," his radiant countenance, and his ardent gestures (*CW*, II, 40, 39: *RH*, ll. 1175, 1134). But in Shelley's strict moral economy, the price of admission for this concert is death. As a worshipper at the shrine of Self, Lionel is decisively shut out from the domestic "circle" that Shelley celebrates in the poem's conclusion (*CW*, II, 43: *RH*, l. 1282). Before he can become a selfless member of the harmonious sorority that Rosalind and Helen establish, Lionel must be reborn as the "gentle boy" Henry, whose remarkably empathic temperament the poet underscores early in the poem (*CW*, II, 12: *RH*, l. 180).[93] While once it was Lionel and Helen whose souls were "interwoven" and whose "fingers intertwined," as the poem closes, it is the reunited sister-spirits Rosalind and Helen who walk "[w]ith equal steps and fingers intertwined" toward Helen's lovely cottage, where they will rebuild the Paradise that Lionel—and Shelley—has lost (*CW*, II, 35, 34, 42: *RH*, ll. 979, 940, 1244).

Shelley could criticize but never forsake his quest for his ideal twin, a "second self" whose femininity he in turn mirrored as antitype to her prototype. Both *Alastor* and *Rosalind and Helen* explore the dangers and strange rewards of this quest, and both poems allow their protagonists to complete their circuitous journeys (back) to their "sweet mate[s]" (*Alastor*, l. 282). In their last moments, both the Poet and Lionel shed the last vestiges of their already diluted masculinity. Radically feminized into "fragile lute[s] on whose harmonious strings / The breath" of the powerful mother-lover-sister wanders, these two figures finally achieve the coveted status of sister-spirit for which Shelley himself so yearned (*Alastor*, ll. 667–68). That they do so only at the instant of their deaths reminds us that the "far goal" of the woman-identified male may be yet another essentially "unattainable point to which [Shelleyan] Love tends" (*PU*, III. iii. 174; "On Love" 474).

Imaginative Transsexualism in *Laon and Cythna*

Rosalind and Helen's intricate interweaving of crucial Shelleyan themes such as narcissism, martyrdom, erotic doubling, and (feminine) Paradise lost owes a good deal to the poem that Shelley completed just before beginning work on his eclogue. Once the most neglected of Shelley's major works, *Laon and Cythna* has been at the center of the current critical debate about Shelley's attitudes toward women, sexuality, and gender roles.[94] Two of the key players in this controversy, Nathaniel Brown and Stuart Sperry, have recently gone head to head over Shelley's purported advocacy of an androgynous ideal of gender identity. With *Laon and Cythna* as the critical battleground, Sperry argues that Shelley's hero and heroine embody "distinct but complementary male and female attributes," while Brown contends that in his epic and elsewhere the poet promotes "a sexual monism transcending gender differences—'these detestable distinctions,' as Shelley labelled them."[95]

Brown comes closer to the truth when he discerns in Shelley a yearning for unisexuality, but the word *androgyny*, which Brown constantly invokes, is a misnomer when applied to the Shelleyan ideal. For Shelley's politics of androgyny, to borrow a phrase from Barbara Gelpi,[96] leaves little or no room for the masculine, let alone for the "true ideal of masculinity" that Sperry believes Laon finally exemplifies (*Shelley's Major Verse* 62). By renouncing his own gender and identifying his heroes, and himself, with the feminine, Shelley tries to erase those distinctions between self and other, male and female that he considered "detestable" but that in fact allow us to "respect the differences" as well as "the similitudes" (*Defence* 480) between ourselves and our "co-existent beings" (*L*, I, 77). However, far from making him the feminist saviour that Brown canonizes, Shelley's aspirations toward and idealization of femininity often prevented him from clearly seeing the painful struggles that real women faced in a patriarchal culture, a culture that Shelley despised but from which he benefitted nonetheless.[97] In my view, if *Laon and Cythna* fails as a feminist manifesto, it succeeds brilliantly as an exercise in imaginative transsexualism,[98] with poet and hero crossing gender lines to meet and finally merge with their feminine mirror images.

Shelley's Dedication to the poem intimates why the poet would want to defect from his own gender and cleave to his mate—here, his "dear

Friend," Mary Shelley—on her own sexual turf (*CW*, I, 251: *LC*, Dedication, l. 19). As an "ardent and tender-hearted" champion of humanity, Percy wants to ally himself with the realm of feminine sensibility and love, which Mary, the "Child of love and light," governs in this opening poem (*CW*, I, 242, 251: *LC*, Preface; Dedication, l. 9). Moreover, as one for whom love has been a "blight and snare," Percy wants to smooth away the (sexual) difference between himself and his current "Queen" in order to recreate within "her inchanted dome" the sisterly atmosphere that the poet found most congenial (*CW*, I, 252, 251: *LC*, Dedication, ll. 46, 3, 4). That Shelley was thinking of previous sister-spirits when he composed this Dedication is evident in the canceled stanza that alludes to Harriet Grove and Harriet Shelley, whose "hard hearts" contrast with their former and Percy's and Mary's current feminine softness:

> Nor ever found I one not false to me:
> Hard hearts and cold, like weights of icy stone,
> That crushed and withered mine.
> She whom I found was dear but false to me,
> The other's heart was like a heart of stone
> Which crushed and withered mine.
>
> (*CW*, I, 255)

While ostensibly based on the heterosexual passion of a brother and sister, the sibling incest that the Dedication hints at and that the poem itself, in its original version, explicitly depicts has more in common with the sisterly love that Shelley envisioned in that Oxford garden he visited with Hogg in the winter of 1810. The opening two stanzas of the Dedication illustrate how Shelley carves out his own feminine space to mirror Mary's domestic haven and thereby returns to her from his "summer-task" as a sister-spirit rather than as a virile quester for poetic fame:

> I
> So now my summer-task is ended, Mary,
> And I return to thee, mine own heart's home;
> As to his Queen some victor Knight of Faëry,
> Earning bright spoils for her inchanted dome;
> Nor thou disdain, that ere my fame become
> A star among the stars of mortal night,
> If it indeed may cleave its natal gloom,
> Its doubtful promise thus I would unite
> With thy beloved name, thou Child of love and light.

II
The toil which stole from thee so many an hour
Is ended,—and the fruit is at thy feet!
No longer where the woods to frame a bower
With interlaced braced mix and meet,
Or where with sound like many voices sweet,
Water-falls leap among wild islands green,
Which framed for my lone boat a lone retreat
Of moss-grown trees and weeds, shall I be seen:
But beside thee, where still my heart has ever been.

(*CW*, I, 251: *LC*, Dedication, ll. 1–18)

That Shelley employs chivalric imagery, with its rigid gender divisions, suggests how deliberately he sets about to collapse these "detestable distinctions," here and throughout his writings (*L*, I, 195). Marlon Ross has argued that Shelley affiliates himself in this Dedication with the world of "masculine combat" by employing "the chivalric trope," but in fact the poet invokes in order to exorcise the spectre of masculinity from his own soul and from his domestic Eden (*The Contours of Masculine Desire* 137). While initially Percy seems to play a traditionally masculine role—the "victor Knight" with "bright spoils"—in the second stanza these spoils become the "fruit" of his labors within a womblike bower that replicates Mary's "inchanted dome."[99]

A letter that he wrote William Godwin not long after poem's completion suggests that the author of *Laon and Cythna* thought of its composition in terms of parturition, and, more dramatically, of Jesus' anguish at Gethsemane. Irked by his father-in-law's harsh criticism of his epic, Shelley indignantly informs him that this work "grew as it were from 'the agony & bloody sweat' of intellectual travail" (*L*, I, 578: 11 December 1817). This letter contains another illuminating connection with the poem's Dedication. Shelley was particularly annoyed that Godwin had lavishly praised "a little scrap" that he had written about Godwin's most recent novel, *Mandeville*, while "censur[ing]" the poet's ambitious epic (*L*, I, 576, 577). An oedipal clash with his often infuriating father-in-law threatened to erupt, but Shelley defuses it with the kind of diplomatic flattery that he used in 1812 when Godwin heatedly denounced the young poet's Irish campaign.[100] One vehicle of that flattery was the glowing review of *Mandeville*, an expansion of the remarks Shelley had earlier sent Godwin, which the poet submitted to Hunt's *Examiner* and signed "E. K." for "Elfin Knight."[101] When we recall that "Elfin Knight" was one of Mary's pet names for her husband, we realize that Percy is stepping back from the arena of masculine rivalry that Ross describes so well and is assuming a noncombative, childlike stance toward his pugnacious father-in-law. Returning to *Laon and Cythna*'s dedication, we see that the poet as an adorable, and diminutive, "Knight of *Faëry*" is domesticating the realm of manly action the instant he brings it into his poem. Like the serpent in Canto I who has access to the feminine bosom only after it is wounded, the Shelleyan knight must be domesticated and emasculated in order to enter his Queen's "inchanted dome." As he portrays himself in the Dedication, this questing hero deliberately sticks pretty close to hearth and home, "where still [his] heart has ever been."

The swerve away from oedipal strife that we witness in Shelley's encounter(s) with Godwin occurs in the poem itself when Laon confronts his good and bad fathers, the Hermit and Othman, respectively. Laon's tender communion with the Hermit and his refusal to dispatch the tyrant Othman distance him from the world of father-son conflict and help return him to what Sperry rightly calls the "idyllic, harmonious, maternal world" that he shares with his sister in the poem's second canto (*Shelley's Major Verse* 47). This "beloved spot," with its "star-light smile of children, the sweet looks / Of women, the fair breast from which [Laon] fed" glances back longingly to Field Place, as Sperry recognizes (*CW*, I, 274, 285: *LC*, II. 1–2, 350).[102] Moreover, the "tangled bower of vines" that the hero describes as an integral feature of this Edenic scene resembles the bower wherein the poet composed his epic, a "lone retreat" now rendered even more feminine through its association with the maternal world that "nurse[d]" Laon's "folded powers" (*CW*, I, 274: *LC*, II. 1–2, 5; Dedication, l. 16; II. 9). While the incarnation of phallic aggression, Othman, helps eject hero and poet from this feminine haven, the gentle, benign, and nurturant Hermit guides them back by providing a model of feminized (i.e., "redeemed") manhood.[103]

When Othman, represented by his malevolent soldiers, invades Laon and Cythna's cottage in Canto III, he externalizes and aggravates the hero's own fears about his lust for and sexual differentiation from his young sister.[104] Othman's henchmen/surrogates also embody the principle of Self which Laon has been indulging by arrogantly considering himself Cythna's "only source of tears and smiles" (*CW*, I, 291, 280: *LC*, III. 74; II. 189). Although Laon and the poem's original narrator employ the terms *second self* and/or *shadow* when they describe Cythna,[105] Shelley acknowledges the perils of this dynamic when he inflicts on his imprisoned hero the "foul, ceaseless shadows: . . . / All shapes like [his] own self, hideously multiplied" that "bemock themselves" as well as Laon's compulsion for self-projection (*CW*, I, 295: *LC*, III. 204, 207). Laon will not have to relinquish the ideal of erotic twinship so dear to Shelley himself, but as the poem unfolds, he must learn to destabilize, even invert its implied hierarchy.[106] He must, in short, recognize that as Cythna is his second self, so he is hers, the "mirror of her thoughts," the reflection of "the [feminine] grace / Which her mind's shadow cast" (*CW*, I, 307: *LC*, IV. 269–70). Only then can the "quire of devils," the grotesque self-images that

torment him in his madness, become the "female quires" that surround the triumphant Cythna and welcome him as a "votary" at his sister's "high shrine"
(*CW*, I, 295, 320, 321: *LC*, III. 200; V. 380, 418, 411).[107]

That Laon's gender dissevers him at the opening of Canto III from his
sister-spirit and from the feminine world over which she presides is evident in
the lurid dreams that precede—or, as Ulmer suggests, produce[108]—his skirmish with the soldiers who abduct Cythna. Laon's first dream finds him sit-
ting "upon the threshold of a cave" with his sister, whose "pure and radiant
self was shown / In this strange vision, so divine . . . / That if [he] loved
before, now love was agony" (*CW*, I, 289: *LC*, III. 15, 25–27). The "nameless
sense of fear" that grips Laon involves his realization that his masculinity,
erupting here as the "hyena lust" that Cythna had vowed that same evening to
combat,[109] represents both a barrier and a key to the "secret depths" of the
female womb-world whose threshold beckons the young man (*CW*, I, 284,
289: *LC*, II. 323; III. 31). His epiphany of Cythna's purity and radiancy suggests Laon's realization that the very things he treasures in her and in the
"pristine world" she governs will have to be defiled if he is to penetrate this
border (Sperry, *Shelley's Major Verse*, 48).

His next dream and its violent aftermath in the waking world reveal the
divergent paths Laon can take (back) to his feminine Eden:

> The scene was changed, and away, away, away!
> Thro' the air and over the sea we sped,
> And Cythna in my sheltering bosom lay,
> And the winds bore me;—thro' the darkness spread
> Around, the gaping earth then vomited
> Legions of foul and ghastly shapes, which hung
> Upon my flight; and ever as we fled,
> They plucked at Cythna—soon to me then clung
> A sense of actual things those monstrous dreams among.
>
> And I lay struggling in the impotence
> Of sleep, while outward life had burst its bound,
> . . . .
> . . . breathless, pale, and unaware
> I rose, and all the cottage crowded found
> With armed men, whose glittering swords were bare,
> And whose degraded limbs the tyrant's garb did wear.
>
> (*CW*, I, 289–90: *LC*, III. 37–47, 51–54)

Hearing Cythna's cry, Laon "grasp[s] a small knife" and, ignoring her pleas
for pacifism, plays impetuous Peter to his sister's serene Christ: "I drew / My

knife, and with one impulse, suddenly / All unaware three of their number slew" (*CW*, I, 290, 291: *LC*, II. 59, 86–88).[110] The dream's rather repulsive sexual imagery[111] has materialized as the phallic weapons that both Laon and the soldiers wield. Here, then, is one potential route into the feminine space that is both Cythna's now utterly vulnerable body and the cottage-haven these "bloody men"—among whom Laon is temporarily numbered—have invaded (*CW*, I, 291: *LC*, III. 74). But Laon's dream has also shown him another path, the path of feminine encirclement, or enwombment. When Laon envisions Cythna lying within his "sheltering bosom," he is adopting a maternal role toward his beloved, a role that allows him to mirror/coalesce with Cythna rather than penetrate her as her (sexual) opposite.

Before Laon meets the gentle Hermit who will help bring his submerged femininity to light, Shelley subjects him to an inferno/purgatory that burns away the last remnants of his masculine identity.[112] Othman's men strip him naked and chain him to the top of "a mighty column," an appropriate site for the phallus-haunted Laon to face his demons (*CW*, I, 100: *LC*, III. 100).[113] Exposed to the elements, the protagonist of Shelley's epic, like Prometheus after him, suffers "piercing agonies," though it is the merciless sun rather than the Titan's cruel glacier that stabs Laon with "shafts of agony" (*CW*, I, 293, 294: *LC*, III. 162, 174). The "foul and ghastly shapes" of his earlier nightmare revisit Laon as "the foul, ceaseless shadows" that represent both his self-obsession and his (unmodified) masculinity—"entangling evils" that for Shelley remained inextricably entangled with each other (*CW*, I, 290, 295: *LC*, II. 42; III. 204, 205). Finally, in his madness, Laon imagines that his captors present him with "four stiff corpses," the "swarthy" soldiers he had killed and the "fair" Cythna whose loving, Christlike nature he had betrayed by resorting to violence (*CW*, I, 29: *LC*, III. 218, 221).[114] As Ulmer observes, these "'stiff,' libidinally potent bodies [are] dead themselves but symbols of psychic forces alive within Laon" (*Shelleyan Eros* 61). These forces—outgrowths of the principle of Self—allowed Laon to commit three actual murders as well as to kill, or at least paralyze, his own potential for feminine softness, embodied by his ideal "twin," his sister Cythna.

Confronted with, pierced by, and (literally) chained to patriarchy's most sacred relic, the phallus, Laon finally can topple this idol, at least in his own consciousness, when he experiences his most morbid vision: his consumption of the body of his beloved. By ingesting Cythna's flesh, Laon takes communion at a new altar, where woman and Christ—or woman as Christ—reign supreme.[115] When Cythna's "cold and blue" flesh becomes warm in Laon's mouth, he is, in effect, reviving his absent/dead sister, or, rather, he is resurrecting her spirit within him.[116] Now Laon is ready to begin his journey back to his beloved, with the aid of the compassionate Hermit who rescues the young man from "the lone column on the rock" (*CW*, I, 301: *LC*, IV. 91).

This "stately and beautiful" old man, whose name links him with Shelley himself in his role as the benevolent Hermit of Marlow,[117] demonstrates that even the most muscular and "giant" representative of the male sex can exemplify feminine qualities (*CW*, I, 296: *LC*, III. 243, 257). When he later recounts his adventures, Laon will fondly recall how "that aged man, so grand and so mild, / Tended [him], even as some sick mother seems / To hang in hope over a dying child" (*CW*, I, 298: *LC*, III. 294–95). The "sylvan solitude" to which Laon's new mother-father brings him offers the young man yet another allegorical landscape that affects and reflects his own evolving psychosexual terrain (*CW*, I, 299: *LC*, IV. 44). At first the Hermit's home, a "tower of stone," seems to duplicate Laon's former prison, but this potential monument to what Marlon Ross would call "masculine self-possession"[118] is actually a "crumbling heap" that has collapsed (back) into the arms of Mother Nature: its portal is overgrown with "blooming ivy"[119] and its floor strewn with "spangling sands" and "rarest sea-shells" that "the mother of the months" has deposited via her "slave," the tide (*CW*, I, 298: *LC*, IV. 2–7). "A changeling of man's art, nursed amid Nature's brood," this drab grey tower has become a beautiful, ever-changing shrine to feminine creativity, variety, and nurturance (*CW*, I, 298: *LC*, IV. 9). It even contains a subterranean bower whose womblike ambience transports Laon back to the embowered paradise of his childhood and early youth. This "small chamber" tapestried with "mosses rare," moreover, mimics the cave-prison in which Cythna gives birth, succumbs to insanity, and, with no help from a kindly nurse such as Laon's, regains her reason (*CW*, I, 299: *LC*, IV. 16).[120] In its final manifestation, the canopied ruin that serves as the siblings' bridal chamber, the Shelleyan bower has become common ground for the feminized hero and his feminine "second" self: it is a woman- and love-identified space wherein Laon can at last "mingle" with his beloved sister-spirit (*CW*, I, 337: *LC*, VI. 301).

While he is drinking in the influence of the maternal Hermit and convalescing in his pastoral retreat, Laon is also re-acquainting himself with Cythna by answering his guardian's queries about her: "like mine own heart, / Of Cythna would he question me, until / That thrilling name had ceased to make me start, / From his familiar lips" (*CW*, I, 300: *LC*, IV. 47–50). That name will become even more thrilling when Laon learns of the alias his sister has adopted since their separation. As his sojourn with his gentle nurse-therapist comes to an end, Laon, convinced at this point that Cythna must be dead, listens with great interest to the Hermit's account of a courageous young woman who has instigated a feminist uprising in the Golden City (*CW*, I, 303: *LC*, IV. 157). After softening Laon with excessive praise of his "strong genius," the Hermit smoothly segues into a glowing account of this "maiden fair," whose (feminine) pacifism and self-abnegation stand as an implicit reproach to the (masculine) egotism and violence Laon had earlier embraced (*CW*, I, 302, 303: *LC*, IV. 133, 157).

The Hermit's adroit transition from "Laon's name" to the "nameless" young woman symbolically enacts the self-transformation that the young man must undergo if he is to reunite with Cythna as *her* sister-spirit under the auspices of the magical name *Laone*:

> ". . . Laon's name to the tumultuous throng
> Were like the star whose beams the waves compel
> And tempests, and his soul-subduing tongue
> Were as a lance to quell the mailed crest of wrong.

XVIII

> "Perchance blood need not flow, if thou at length
> Wouldst rise; perchance the very slaves would spare
> Their brethren and themselves; great is the strength
> Of words—for lately did a maiden fair,
> Who from her childhood has been taught to bear
> The tyrant's heaviest yoke, arise, and make
> Her sex the law of truth and freedom hear;
> And with these quiet words—'for thine own sake
> I prithee spare me,'—did with ruth so take

XIX

> "All hearts, that even the torturer, who had bound
> Her meek calm frame, ere it was yet impaled,
> Loosened her weeping then."

(CW, I, 313, 303: LC, V. 164; IV. 150–65)

The Hermit's ostensibly flattering description of Laon's revolutionary rhetoric as "a lance to quell the mailed crest of wrong" becomes a criticism of his phallic "soul-subduing tongue" when the old man suggests in line 154 that this tongue might provoke actual bloodshed.[121] As he readies his ward for re-entry into the world, the Hermit holds up as an ideal alternative to Laon's incendiary speech and behavior the "awful sweetness" of the meek maiden's voice, which compels even her foes to "cast the vote of love in hope's abandoned urn" (*CW*, I, 304: *LC*, IV. 196, 198). "Veiled / In virtue's adamantine eloquence," this young woman, as the Hermit describes her, exemplifies the gentleness and loving self-sacrifice that the old man, himself a "gentle grandsire," hopes Laon will emulate (*CW*, I, 303, 297: *LC*, IV. 167–68; III. 278). Moreover, like Asia after her, this maiden exudes a kind of "ether" that heals, refreshes, and unifies those who "dwell beside" her (*PU*, I. 831; *CW*, I, 304: *LC*, IV. 186). In her "transforming presence," to borrow Panthea's rich phrase,

"Lovers renew the vows which they did plight / In early faith, and hearts long parted now unite" (*PU*, I. 832; *CW*, I, 304: *LC*, IV. 188–89).[122]

Having established this young woman as the prototype Laon should follow, both as a disciple and as an antitype,[123] the Hermit sends him on his way with the command, "uplift thy charmed voice, / Pour on those evil men the love that lies / Hovering within those spirit-soothing eyes—/ Arise, my friend, farewell!" (*CW*, I, 306: *LC*, IV. 246–49). That Laon has been attentive to his mentor's lessons is evident in the typically Shelleyan moment the young man experiences just before setting off to join the rebel forces. Gazing at his reflection in a "reposing lake," Laon sees how his years of suffering have aged him, but what is more important, he discerns in his own withered countenance the lineaments of his sister, the "second" self whom he must now mirror in order to regain (*CW*, I, 306, 269: *LC*, IV. 252, 269).

Shortly after his arrival at the rebel camp, Laon finds a characteristically self-dramatizing method of proving his twinship with the revolutionary maiden whom he rightly suspects to be "[his] own Cythna" (*CW*, I, 307: *LC*, IV. 293). The Hermit has told Laon, "Perchance blood need not flow," but it already has—in the tyrant's "polluted halls" where Cythna and countless other woman were savagely robbed of their virginity (*CW*, I, 303, 345: *LC*, IV. 154; VII. 30). Although unaware at this point of Cythna's horrible ordeal, Laon instinctively mimics her violent defloration by rushing toward a spear meant for another. He also reenacts the scene that took place years before in their cottage when Cythna joyously embraced her fate as a martyr for truth and love. Now it is Laon who, like his Christlike sister before him, cries "Forebear, forbear!" to the purveyors of violence and ratifies with his own blood "love's benignant laws" (*CW*, I, 310: *LC*, V. 72, 81). As observed in the previous chapter, Laon's strident claims to self-abnegation undermine his credibility as an embodiment of sympathetic love, but if his strenuous efforts cannot match his sister's more spontaneous acts of selflessness, they do at least finally reunite him with her, first in name and then in deed.

One of the most remarked-upon aspects of *Laon and Cythna* is the fact that Shelley compels his heroine to rename herself "Laone."[124] Many readers have argued that this new appellation confirms Cythna's status as her brother's self-projection,[125] but I would suggest a different terminology that acknowledges Laon's, and Shelley's, desire for a mirroring female as well as the poet's and hero's need to mirror the female.[126] As a kind of compound being, "Laone" allows Cythna to enwomb her brother and transmute him into a sister-spirit, while at the same time he-she enables Laon, via his narrative, to enwomb his sister and thereby participate in her "strange tale of strange endurance," with its sufferings and triumphs that are uniquely female (*CW*, I, 344: *LC*, VII. 19). That enwombment becomes containment when Laon fails to turn over the duties of primary narrator to Cythna bespeaks both his own and Shelley's desperate desire to preserve control over the elusive and powerful female.[127]

When Laon finally beholds Laone at the Festival of Equality, she is seated, goddess-like, "upon an ivory throne," with a "veil shroud[ing] her countenance bright" (*CW*, I, 320: *LC*, V. 387, 398). As he approaches her altar, Laon is "blind / And silent, as a breathing corpse," ready to be reborn in his sister's image and likeness (*CW*, I, 321: *LC*, V. 402–3). Laone pronounces him dead on the scene and then ceremoniously resurrects him as her sister-spirit:

> "thou art our first votary here," she said:
> "I had a brother once, but he is dead!—
> And of all those on the wide earth who breathe,
> Thou dost resemble him alone—I spread
> This veil between us two, that thou beneath
> Should'st image one who may have been long lost in death."

> (*CW*, I, 321: *LC*, V. 418–23)

Although *she* is wearing the veil, Laone's locution here turns her brother into a veiled maiden, not unlike the veiled statue that serves as Lionel's feminized self-portrait in *Rosalind and Helen*. Laone's heroic rescue of Laon from the tyrant's forces the following day confirms the sexual alchemy performed in this ritual. As his sword-wielding sister sweeps him onto her giant courser, Laon becomes for a moment even more feminine than his beloved. Anxious to preserve the sisterly dynamic that has begun to flow between these sibling-lovers, however, Shelley quickly revokes Laone's masculine status by focusing on her long, dark hair, "dispread / Like the pine's locks upon the lingering blast" (*CW*, I, 334: *LC*, VI. 185–86). A Shelleyan emblem, like her veil, of Laone's femininity, her flowing hair spreads its "shadowy strings" over Laon's eyes as well, iconically fusing him with his beloved beneath a private canopy that proleptically images the canopy of their "bridal couch" (*CW*, I, 334, 343: *LC*, VI. 187, 486).

Obeying their "feminine" homing instincts, Laon and Laone discover a "marble ruin" that contains within its walls "a green and lone recess," a wedding bower in which *both* spouses can "celebrate a bridal night" as brides (*CW*, I, 334, 338, 339: *LC*, VI. 196, 327–28, 347). After confirming Laone's identity as his "own sweet sister," Laon at last unites with her in the "mute and liquid ecstasies" of sexual passion (*CW*, I, 334, 337: *LC*, VI. 215, 295). Yet Shelley makes sure that no hint of penetrative imagery slips into his portrait of erotic bliss. Instead, he emphasizes the lovers' "linked frames," the intermingling of their "common blood," and the "likeness of [their] features" as he allows them (sexually) to explore their "close sympathies" (*CW*, I, 338, 336, 339: *LC*, VI. 329, 276, 277, 348).

This brings us to the question of procreation, or, more precisely, paternity, which Shelley displaces onto the poem's representative of masculine lust, Othman. Not only does Laon's vicious (and virile) double, the "sceptered wretch" who rapes Cythna, enable the young man to avoid the potentially onerous task of piercing Cythna's hymen, but he also allows Laon to father a child without actually inseminating his sister-spouse (*CW*, I, 315: *LC*, V. 217). As E. B. Murray argues, the young girl whom Laon greets in Othman's palace "with a father's kiss" and who joins the sibling lovers on their post-mortal voyage, is "at once the fruit of [Cythna's] spiritual communion . . . with Laon and her physical rape by the Tyrant" (*CW*, I, 315: *LC*, V. 215; "'Elective Affinity' in *The Revolt of Islam*" 578).[128] Like Fitzeustace, the effeminate Shelley figure of the early Gothic production *St. Irvyne*, Laon "cherish[es]" his adoptive child "with the affection of a father" but evades the physiological role in its generation that would conspicuously confirm the masculine identity he is struggling to slough off (*CW*, V, 195: *St. Irvyne*).[129]

If Shelley deliberately removes his hero from the troubling realm of (biological) fatherhood,[130] he transports him directly into the maternal sphere that belongs to Cythna. As Canto VII opens, the now sated lovers exchange their stories of suffering and self-discovery.[131] As if his sister's account of her rape were too harrowing and the "fearful imagery" of "the cold tyrant's cruel lust" too similar to his own self-revelatory nightmares, Laon tells us Cythna's story in the third person up to her plunge into the "green silence" and "dark lairs" of her new underwater abode (*CW*, I, 345, 346: *LC*, VII. 48, 29, 84, 86). Now, until the close of Canto IX, Cythna will take over the narrative, though, as Ulmer reminds us, "she speaks only through Laon's Romantic ventriloquism" (*Shelleyan Eros* 71).[132] Enveloped by the "protective" sac of Laon's own discourse, Cythna's autobiography becomes his, a child *in utero* that emerges from Laon's womb as he delivers his-her story to us. It is in these three cantos, then, that "Laone" really comes into his-her own.

Not only does Shelley's hero get to reenact his sister's pregnancy, childbirth, and breast-feeding within her underwater cave-bower, but he also (vicariously) experiences one of the supreme moments of feminine communion in the Shelley canon. "Her touch would meet / Mine," Laone says of her tender interplay with her infant daughter, "and our pulses calmly flow and beat / In response while we slept" (*CW*, I, 349–50: *LC*, VII. 184–86). She then invokes one of Shelley's most cherished images, a scene that takes us back to the Oxford garden tended by Shelley's imaginary sisters and ahead to *Prometheus Unbound*'s intertwined Oceanides, Panthea and Ione: "Weary with joy, and tired with our delight, / We, on the earth, like sister twins lay down / On one fair mother's bosom" (*CW*, I, 350: *LC*, VII, 191–93).[133] This tableau poignantly reveals Shelley's deep desire to participate in the mother-daughter—or sister-sister—dyad, while at the same time it highlights his status as an outsider, a wistful onlooker barred from what Claire Clairmont had once called "the subterraneous community of women" (here a subaqueous sorority).[134] Canto XII's emotional reunion between mother and daughter in the realm of the Spirit further underscores the father-brother's exclusion from their private moments of feminine communion: "The glossy darkness of [Cythna's] streaming hair / Fell o'er that snowy child, and wrapt from sight / The fond and long embrace which did their hearts unite" (*CW*, I, 403: *LC*, XII. 205–7). The same flowing locks that had graphically feminized Laon and fused him with his sister as they galloped toward their embowered bridal chamber now curtain his sister-spirits from his view.

Shelley himself had ample opportunity to witness the kind of intense bonding between mother and child that he portrays in Canto VII and again in Canto XII. While he seemed to underestimate his first wife's attachment to their baby daughter Ianthe—interpreting Harriet's refusal to breastfeed as a failure of love—he had no reason to doubt Mary's commitment to and passionate involvement with the two children she had borne and to the baby she carried while her husband gave birth to his epic.[135] On the contrary, Mary's deep connection with her children, and her profound grief over her first daughter's death, must have reassured the Percy who idealized femininity and maternity while it unsettled the Percy who felt himself excluded from the domestic circle, from the feminine space where mother and child—and perhaps especially mother and daughter—forge a bond that he could never know.[136] Paradoxically, by attempting to recreate in his own household and in such a work such as *Laon and Cythna* the feminine Paradise of his boyhood, he also (re)experiences a painful sense of exclusion from the magic circle of feminine love, a malady that no amount of self-feminization could completely remedy. Although a number of factors contributed to Shelley's failure to establish "a fixed, settled, eternal home,"[137] we cannot rule out as a crucial source of his wanderlust his fear that not only was his childhood Paradise lost but that it never *had* been his domain (*L*, I, 491: 17 July 1816).

Ever the resourceful mythologizer of his own life, however, Shelley manages at the close of *Laon and Cythna* to provide his surrogate-hero with a supramundane Paradise that abolishes the "detestable distinctions" from his beloved women—now truly sister-*spirits*—that Laon's material, ineluctably male body had imposed. Spirits all, Laon, Cythna, and their "bright child," transformed into a "plumed Seraph," journey toward the poem's first and final Shelleyan bower (*CW*, I, 403: *LC*, XII. 208). The ultimate destination of these cosmic travelers and the site of their birth, the Temple of the Spirit, with its "vast dome," radically transcendentalizes the many womb-worlds through which Shelley's epic guides us (*CW*, I, 271: *LC*, I. 442).[138] While the Hermit's mossy hospital-bower, Cythna's subaqueous cave, and the verdurous dome of the sibling-lovers' bridal chamber obviously held a strong attraction for Shelley, poet and hero can only achieve their apotheosis as sister-spirits in the "hollow hemisphere" of the Temple, a brilliantly illuminated "dome in air" where biology is no longer destiny (*CW*, I, 272: *LC*, I. 468).[139]

As we turn back—or, rather, forward—to Canto I, where we get our first glimpse of the poem's central protagonists, we notice that of the "two mighty spirits" who have just returned "from the world's raging sea," it is Laon's and not Cythna's femininity that seems most pronounced (*CW*, I, 273: *LC*, I. 519, 520). With his "curved lips" and his "outspread hair," the "beautiful" Laon now sets the standard for feminine loveliness for the sister who in the mortal realm he struggled to emulate (*CW*, I, 274: *LC*, I. 530, 532, 533).[140] Although the narrator who describes the siblings for us pronounces Cythna "far lovelier" than her brother, he also describes her as Laon's "shadow," whose "floating locks" mimic his long, flowing hair (*CW*, I, 274: *LC*, I. 535, 534, 537). A work in which Shelley's hero constantly vacillates between competition and coalescence with his female beloved, *Laon and Cythna* ultimately appears to endorse the former strategy for the self-feminizing male. Moreover, Laon's failure to turn over to Cythna the duties of primary narrator in the poem proper certainly reveals how coalescence can itself become containment, of the elusive sister-spirit and of her feminine sphere. Yet in the final few lines of Canto I, among the last that Shelley composed for the poem, it is the Shelleyan ideal of sisterly communion that reigns supreme, with Cynthna's eyes waking in Laon precious, painful, and most of all, *shared* memories.[141] Enveloped by Cythna's "[g]lances of soul-dissolving glory," Laon can at last savor the unremitting interchange with his sister-twin that is both the source and the reward of his hard-won femininity (*CW*, I, 274: *LC*, I. 538).

A sprawling, politically resonant epic that expresses Shelley's "wider sympathy" with the world, *Laon and Cythna* nonetheless remains most deeply committed to the intimate sympathies of home, the "haven" that the divine family finds in the poem's last line (*CW*, I, 284, 408: *LC*, II. 318; XII. 369). No exemplary feminist, Shelley nonetheless envisions in *Laon and Cythna* a vital sisterhood of love, community, and self-sacrifice that evades and even subverts the "brotherhood of ill" which the patriarchal tyrant Othman creates (*CW*, I, 376: *LC*, X. 47). That Shelley finally transports his radiant band of sister-spirits into a transcendental, highly aestheticized Temple of the Spirit suggests how fragile he believed this ideal sorority, and especially his own place in it, really was.

Shelley's most elaborate exercise in imaginative transsexualism, *Laon and Cythna* illuminates how the poet's sororal ideal helps shape later texts. Turning away now from Shelley's sibling lovers and their transcendental Paradise, I will briefly examine how two of the poet's mature works, *Prometheus Unbound* and *Epipsychidion*, build on and revise his epic's method of enrolling poet and protagonist in a band of sister-spirits, a "hallowed circle" that can expand ever outward or shrink to the tiny compass of the little world of self (*JMS*, I, 35 [Percy's phrase]).

Far Eden: Sororal Utopias in
Prometheus Unbound and *Epipsychidion*

Like *Laon and Cythna*, Shelley's lyrical drama and his effusive, autobiographical love poem each trace the hero's journey (back) to his feminine "second self," who then accompanies him to the secluded Paradise where they will cultivate undisturbed "the excellence of sisterly affection" (Hogg, I, 81). However, these later works can dispense with one of the epic's central elements: the hero's metamorphosis from phallic aggressor to "male heroine."[142] Having exhaustively explored this process in *Laon and Cythna*, Shelley can examine in *Prometheus Unbound* and *Epipsychidion* the rewards and pitfalls inherent to the fulfillment of the self-feminizing hero's quest. Moreover, because his tormented Titan and his (sexually) passive persona in *Epipsychidion* establish their feminine identities almost from the outset, the poet is able in these later works to devote more attention to the precise qualities that these protagonists' female counterparts exemplify. Thus *Prometheus Unbound* and *Epipsychidion* move beyond the notion of gender crossing as an end in itself, as it sometimes seems to be in *Laon and Cythna*.

For a poet whose struggles to shake off the "burr" of Self were lifelong and frequently unsuccessful, self-transcendence was the most crucial feminine quality to cultivate, a quality that Cythna, Asia, and, in a very different manner, Emily all embody (*L*, II, 109). It was Laon's desire to achieve feminine selflessness, Shelley's epic suggests, that helped inspire his efforts to mirror his Christlike sister. But when compared to Cythna's spontaneous activities as the poem's true "prophetess of love," Laon's attempts at self-abnegation appear feeble and unconvincing (*CW*, I, 370: *LC*, IX. 174). Furthermore, because Cythna herself remains trapped within her brother's narrative, the "light / Of liquid tenderness" she emanates seems confined to Laon's personal solar system, a preview of *Epipsychidion*'s worst excesses (*CW*, I, 390: *LC*, XI. 41–42). Prometheus, on the other hand, does eventually overcome (his own) Selfhood as he moves in the play's first act from Jupiterlike hatred through feminine pity to, finally, Asia-like love.[143] And when he finally reunites with his beloved, he helps her diffuse rather than hoards—like Laon—the love she has come to represent. Together, Prometheus and Asia, as sister-spirits, can now inspire others to shed "self-love [and] self-contempt," the twin poles of Shelleyan self-idolatry (*PU*, III. iv. 134).

But it is Shelley himself, in the guise of *Epipsychidion*'s anonymous Writer, who achieves the most bizarre and radical *Selbsttödtung* as he strains to reach the height of self-feminization. His attempts to eradicate his own Selfhood come, however, only after, and because, he has (ab)used his affinity with the feminine gender to enact in this poem an elaborate narcissistic fantasy. As a "passive Earth" ruled and ravished by a number of powerful female planets—Emily the Sun, Mary the Moon, Claire the fierce Comet[144]—the poet strikes a posture that almost parodies the feminine stances that he has adopted and celebrated since his earliest writings (l. 345). In fact, throughout the poem Shelley exploits for self-indulgent purposes the very traits—feminine receptivity and tenderness—that usually arm him in his battle against Selfhood. And instead of associating Love itself, as he usually does, with a sister-spirit such as Cythna, Panthea, or Asia, in *Epipsychidion* he elevates himself to "a world of love," but a world that only receives rather than gives off a "living light" (ll. 346, 342). Thus, with his "fruits and flowers" awakened by the "bright regents," Emily and Mary, who "govern [his] sphere of being," the poet himself becomes in lines 345 through 387 the "far Eden" of feminine fecundity and love for which he has been yearning since his exile from Field Place (ll. 346, 360, 361).[145] Since he is now his own "delicious isle," complete with "faint bowers" and "trees of Paradise," his imaginary voyage with Emily to the Ionian island may seem somewhat superfluous (ll. 478, 353, 361). Yet the island sojourn remains a vital part of the Shelleyan formula, for he still needs his "heart's sister" (l. 415)—in the draft, his "band of sister-spirits"—to mirror/confirm his hard-won feminine identity (*CW*, II, 382: "Fragments Connected with *Epipsychidion*," l. 173).[146]

In this "idealized history of [Shelley's] life and feelings," Self-chastisement follows hard on the heels of Self-indulgence, and the poem concludes humbly, almost contritely, with the speaker's recognition in his *envoi* that he is Love's guest and not Love itself (*L*, II, 434). Within the poem proper, Shelley suffers "annihilation" when he engages in the autoerotic experience of making love to a sister-spouse whom he imagines to be his own twin (l. 388). And by killing himself off via his fictive persona in the poem's "Advertisement," he continues his symbolic atonement for his orgy of self-obsession and perverse appropriation of feminine subject positions.

Shelley's appearance in the Advertisement as an "unfortunate" (and deceased) "friend" reveals that the poet's desire to distance himself from this autobiographical work began as soon as it was completed, and this desire grew stronger with the passing of time (*NCE* 373). In June 1822, a year and a half after he wrote the poem, Shelley tells John Gisborne, "The 'Epipsychidion' I cannot look at; the person it celebrates was a cloud instead of a Juno; and poor Ixion starts from the centaur that was the offspring of his own embrace" (*L*, I, 434). While the poet's repudiation of his former idol carries on the usual Shelleyan pattern of jettisoning the once-adored twin as the damning evidence of his own narcissism, it is his revulsion from the poem itself that comes across most clearly here. *Epipsychidion* was monstrous, Shelley realized, not because Teresa Viviani fell short of his ideal, but because its six hundred lines of gorgeous verse created a radiant Paradise that encompassed little more than the poet's own narrow world of Self. And he reacts to his hideous "offspring" just as, eleven years before, he had responded to the shadowy *Doppelgänger*, the incarnation of Shelleyan Selfhood, that haunted him in his London rooming house: he "start[s] from" it as though it were a "fiend" (*L*, I, 78: 8 May 1811).

But even within this most Percy-centered text, the poet chips away at the foundations of Selfhood by celebrating and participating in the (feminine) power of self-alteration that his sister-spirit embodies.[147] A chameleon who transports her lover through a series of dizzying metamorphoses, Emily as Seraph, bird, lute, and sun helps him "avoid becoming fixed, immobilized" into Cenci- or Jupiter-like Self-possession (Irigaray 103). Shelley must follow this "soul out of [his] soul" through each of her lightning-swift self-alterations if he is to (re)unite even briefly with her "as two meteors of expanding flame" that explode almost as soon as they come into contact (ll. 238, 576). When Shelley, in pursuit of Emily's (self-)transforming presence, imaginatively transforms himself within five lines from "dizzy moth" to "dead leaf" to "lamp of earthly flame," he is imitating his sister-spirit's constant shifts from one identity to another (ll. 220, 221, 224). But in fixating on the role of "passive Earth," the still center of his lovers' orbit, the poet abandons the dynamic strategy that would enable him to preserve his feminine posture(s) while radically undermining the principle of Self, a principle to which the poem too often capitulates (l. 345).

Perhaps *Epipsychidion*'s frankly autobiographical nature prevented Shelley from achieving the kind of self-transcendence that he celebrates and exemplifies in *Prometheus Unbound*, whose more impersonal genre enabled him to disperse his imaginative energies into various figures that are involved in a vast cosmic revolution.[148] In his lyrical drama, Shelley manages to integrate his own myth of feminine Paradise lost into a larger pattern of universal longing—for peace, for liberation, for love's transforming presence. And the fulfillment of the poet's and his hero's desire to (re)join/coalesce with his sister-spirits not only coincides with but actually causes the universal regeneration that occurs in Acts II and III. The consummate vision of the Shelleyan bower, the Promethean cave (lovingly described in III. iii), is a far cry from the "self-centred seclusion" to which the poet retires in the final section of *Epipsychidion* (*Alastor*, Preface, 69). In this enchanted dwelling where the "trailing odorous plants" of nature blend beautifully with the "progeny immortal" of human culture, the unbound Prometheus creates with his "[f]air sister nymphs" Asia, Panthea, and Ione a feminine Eden that not only envelopes and unites them but that exudes a healing ether which permeates the entire cosmos (III. iii. 11, 54).[149] Just as in the Gospel of St. Mark the "virtue" of Christ "[went] out of him" and instantly healed a woman who touched his garment (Mark 5: 30), the "virtue" of the Promethean and Asian cave emanates ever outward to purify the dull vapours of (Jupiterean) Self-hood that had polluted the atmosphere for so long (*PU*, III. iii. 63). But this cave also allows Prometheus to isolate himself from the multitude that often thronged his Galilean counterpart. Hermetic and yet sympathetic, Prometheus can, with his sister-spirits, radiate an "atmosphere of light" and love while remaining within their secluded womb-world, joined in a magic circle that both connects them with and protects them from the trembling throng (IV. 323).

As the late lyric that most poignantly invokes the Shelleyan magic cir-cle reminds us, the artistic visions and personal experiences of its "Elysian glow" offered the poet only "momentary peace" ("To Jane. The Recollec-tion," ll. 47, 74). Thus even Shelley's final works—his beautiful lyrics to Jane Williams and his troubled vision of a feminine "shape all light" in *The Tri-umph of Life*—give no hint that his twin quests for a feminine and feminizing "second self" and for her embowered Eden were coming to an end (*TL*, l. 352). But "To Jane. The Recollection," written to the last "Radiant Sister" who inspired his passion, overtly recognizes both in its title and particularly in its prologue the nostalgic nature of his lifelong quest for "one fair form that [would fill] with love / The lifeless atmosphere" ("To Jane. The Invitation," l. 47; "To Jane. The Recollection," ll. 51–52). Shelley's description of this lyric as an "epitaph of glory fled" could describe each of the artistic works and romantic liaisons through which he tried to recapture the feminine Eden of his childhood (l. 6). At the end of his life, Shelley the serpent still remained shut out from Paradise, slowly sloughing off the scaly hide of his (masculine) Self-hood as he wove the threads of memory and desire into shadowy bowers— bowers from whose "deep recesses" yet another sister-spirit beckoned (*Witch*, ll. 153).

4

SEX, SYMPATHY, AND SCIENCE

If the idealized world of feminine intimacy held an irresistible allure for Shelley, he in turn elicited considerable interest from the various women and girls who could offer him entrée into their "hallowed circle[s]" (*JMS*, I, 35). Even sight unseen, the author of a series of vivid, impassioned, and often charming letters to his recently adopted mentor could intrigue the women of the Godwin household. "Our family have been taught by yourself and Mrs. Shelley to be anxious about the place where you shall fix your abode," writes Godwin in the summer of 1812, "The moment when I may now call the well-known hand was seen, all the females were on the tiptoe to know" (*L*, I, 313n1). This brief scene at 41 Skinner Street nicely captures the rich range of responses that Percy Shelley invited, often deliberately, from current or potential female companions, in this case (Mrs.) Mary Jane Godwin, Fanny Imlay, and Jane Clairmont.[1] The women's anxiety about the Shelleys' rootlessness, no doubt heightened by Percy's frequent complaints of ill health, seems to emerge from a kind of maternal and/or sisterly concern; while Godwin's reference to "all the females . . . on the tiptoe" suggests that the young correspondent has become for them something of a romantic, even erotic figure.

As we shift our gaze back in time to Field Place in, say, 1804, or forward to 1814 and the Bracknell home of Mrs. Harriet Boinville and her daughter Cornelia Turner, we will recognize a similar pattern: Percy co-creating with various sisterly and maternal figures a haven in which the familial and the erotic subtly interfuse.[2] Yet the urgency and ingenuity with which Shelley sought to recreate, artistically and experientially, his original Eden reminds us how precarious the poet's, and his fictive surrogates', place was in every feminine circle he entered. The role of the self-feminizing poet or hero would always remain ambiguous; the type of erotic current he generated (and received) would differ not simply in degree but in kind from the sisterly sensuality that Shelley's visionary nymphs enjoy in their Oxford garden (Hogg, I, 77–81). In fact, the poet's sex-crossing impulses often seem at cross-purposes both with the desires of the sister-spirits whose sororities he hoped to join and with his own susceptibility to "passion's trance,"[3] an issue I will address a bit later. While the woman-identified Shelley longed to mirror and merge with an ideal "second self" who would bestow on him some of her own feminine grace, it was his sexual difference that sparked the erotic *frisson* in the real women who glimpsed "the well-known hand" of Godwin's latest disciple. They found themselves drawn not to a "sisterly" figure, but to a young, charismatic *man*.

Here a suggestive passage from Hogg's preface to his *Life of Shelley* is worth quoting at length:

> [Shelley] was most conspicuously great in that particular excellence, which, in all ages and in all nations, has been invariably the characteristic distinction of the greatest of mankind—he was pre-eminently a lady's man. The following pages will show . . . that he was uniformly the chosen favourite of the charming sex. The moment he entered a house, he inspired the most lively interest into every woman in the family; not only the mistress of the house, her daughters, and other lady relatives, but even the housekeeper and the humblest females in the establishment were animated alike by an active desire to promote and secure his well-being, in every way and to the utmost in their power . . . The young poet's fortunes would certainly have been less rude—they would have been mitigated, and softened, and brightened, if a due preponderance had been conceded to the gentle and humanizing patronage and fond devotion of his countless lady friends. (Hogg, I, 13–14)

Even through the layers of sticky sentiment and prickly irony that blanket this "tribute" to the Divine Poet we can discern a kernel of truth, though perhaps not the "truth" that Hogg would have us glean. The biographer's phrase *lady's man* conjures absurd images of Shelley as a suave drawing-room rake who adroitly engages the attention of "the charming sex," or, in Hogg's next epithet, "the fair" (14). (The term *lady's man* may also hint at Shelley's own feminine qualities, which the biographer periodically emphasizes.) While Hogg's bloated, pseudo-chivalric descriptions both of the poet and of "his countless lady friends" presents an overly genteel picture of a young gallant and his female devotees, his description nonetheless conveys Shelley's own notions about women's "soften[ing]" and "humanizing" power, and it invokes Shelley's desire to benefit from these qualities as "the chosen favourite" of various feminine "patrons." This passage also gains credibility from the fact that Shelley *did* earn the "fond devotion" of many of the women whose homes he entered. And, finally, Hogg's gender-specific language ("lady's man," "the fair sex") recognizes that the "lively interest" the poet inspired in his various "lady friends" had quite a bit to do with a (mutual) attraction fueled by sexual difference.

As Shelley himself certainly was aware, his masculinity, the very thing he strove to repress or at least transform, could sometimes serve as a passport into the maternal-erotic-sisterly circles that so enchanted him. This holds true both for his original sorority at Field Place and for each of its successors. It is to the former that we will now turn. A passage from one of Hellen Shelley's invaluable letters transports us back to Field Place in about 1804 and allows us to observe what Barbara Charlesworth Gelpi calls the house's "electric family atmosphere" in its most literal form (*Shelley's Goddess* 93).

The greater portion of Hellen's letter reveals a devoted sister fondly recalling the pranks and stories with which an adored older brother delighted both himself and his young sisters. No doubt Percy's gender as well as his status as the eldest Shelley child helped earn him the kind of sisterly loyalty and even adulation that he enjoyed in his boyhood home—and that emanate from most of Hellen's letters to Lady Jane Shelley. Yet Hellen's account of one of Percy's "eccentric amusements" suggests how the boy might exploit his masculine glamour not simply to entrance but to dominate his little sisters (Hogg, I, 22):

> When my brother commenced his studies in chemistry, and practised electricity upon us, I confess my pleasure in it was entirely negatived by terror at its effects. Whenever he came to me with his piece of folded brown packaging paper under his arm and a bit of wire and a bottle . . . , my heart would sink with fear at his approach; but shame kept me silent, and, with as many others as he could collect, we were placed hand-in-hand round the nursery table to be electrified; but when a suggestion was made that chilblains were to be cured by this means, my terror overwhelmed all other feelings, and the expression of it released me from all future annoyance. (Hogg, I, 23)[4]

While at first glance, these frightening experiments might resemble elaborate exercises in child abuse, they in fact illuminate how Percy could rely on his masculinity, and his seniority, in order to (re)create and (re)join the feminine circle from which the now pubescent boy felt himself increasingly excluded. As these episodes probably occurred in late 1803 or early 1804, Percy's sense of separation/isolation would have emerged not just from the dramatic physical changes he was undergoing, but also from his very real exile from Field Place that began in 1802 when his parents sent him off to Syon House Academy. In the passage at hand, the boy's "studies in chemistry," commenced at boarding school, provide the sign of both his displacement from the home and his sexual difference from his young sisters. Yet Percy's initiation into the "masculine" realm of knowledge,[5] and especially of science,[6] offered him a powerful means of reasserting his place in his sisters' world when he returned home for the holidays.

As countless chroniclers of Shelley's boarding-school misery have observed, one thrilling voice did interrupt the "harsh and grating strife of tyrants and foes" that emanated from the school rooms at Syon House (*CW*, I, 251: *LC*, Dedication, 27). Amateur scientist, inventor, astronomer, and "itinerant, eccentric lecturer," Mr. Adam Walker "opened to Shelley a new universe of speculations,"[7] in Tom Medwin's words, when he delivered his stimulating series of lectures at Syon House during Shelley's second year there (Holmes, *Pursuit*, 16; Medwin 28).[8] From Walker, Shelley not only learned the techniques for carrying out the kind of homemade experiments that his sister describes, but what is more important, he also gained both intellectual and practical access to what Walker rapturously dubbed "the paragon of elements": electricity (*System of Familiar Philosophy*, II, 74). Celebrated in Walker's lectures as "a vivifying spirit," a "vital fluid," and, most strikingly, "the soul of the material universe," this "wonderful agent" permeated and quickened Shelley's imagination the way Walker and other contemporary scientists claimed it imbued and animated the physical world (*System*, II, 72, 49, 74, 72).[9]

While Walker identified the sun as the ultimate source of "this subtil and powerful matter," he argues in his lecture on "animal electricity" that all animated beings[10] contain reservoirs of "the electric fluid," transmitted throughout the body by what Walker calls "the animal nerve" (*System*, II, 49, 42).[11] Although he never overtly invokes the term *sympathy*, Walker's discussions of both atmospheric and somatic electricity emphasize allied principles such as affinity, "local affections," and "cohesive attraction" (*System*, I, 153, 157).[12] When he muses on "the relationship between electricity and magnetism" and speculates on the existence "of an electrio-magnetic fluid," he comes closest to making the comparison between sympathy and electricity that was, as Roy R. Male points out, "a commonplace" among contemporary scientists (*System*, I, 52, 55; Male 200).[13] When Shelley read further in the sciences and, perhaps most important, attended the London lectures of Dr. John Abernethy in 1811, he would encounter much more explicit, more elaborate parallels between the power of electricity and the power of sympathy. But even in 1804, the novice scientist who "practised electricity" on Hellen and his other young sisters seemed to intuit that, physiologically and metaphorically, sympathy and electricity were close kin, even identical twins.

When the "poet and experimentalist," as Hellen ruefully calls him, rounded up his little subjects for a hands-on introduction to the wonders of electricity, he was, first of all, bringing to life *and* bringing into the home the scientific theories that the fascinating Mr. Walker elucidated in his Syon House lectures. Thus, as I suggested earlier, the unhappy boarding-school denizen nonetheless discovered in that exclusively masculine world a compensatory and empowering body of knowledge which he then imported into the feminine realm of Field Place. He also seemed to have found in Adam Walker an appealing male role model whose pedagogy *and* whose "Experiments, Miscellaneous and Entertaining" the budding chemist could recreate on his own home turf (*System*, II, 51).[14] Although electrifying one's students is not the most common way of conducting a class, the nursery-room sessions Hellen describes spotlight Percy playing the (masculine) role of teacher-scientist[15] that Walker performed so brilliantly at Syon House.[16]

The fact that Shelley's female pupils also served as the subjects—or victims—of his experiments with electricity exaggerates almost to the point of parody his masculine posture. The scene Hellen unveils has a kind of archetypal feel to it: the willful male scientist, oblivious to everything but his own thirst for knowledge and power, seizes his female victim (a stand-in for Mother Nature herself) and subjects her to cruel but brilliantly conceived experiments. When, in her next letter to Lady Jane Shelley, Hellen remarks, "The tranquillity of our house must have frequently been rudely invaded by experiments," she may be referring obliquely to her own sense of bodily invasion as she endured the electric shocks that her brother administered (Hogg, I, 23).

Walker's statement in one of his lectures that electricity "is capable of making many opaque bodies transparent by impregnating them with temporary light" indicates that this "vital fluid" could in fact be seen as a (literally) seminal agent, an invasive *and* life-giving power (*System*, II, 58, 50).[17] As the "child of the sun," in Walker's cosmic genealogy, electricity absorbs and disperses some of its father's masculine energy (*System*, II, 1). The following passage, from Walker's lecture on magnetism, highlights the sun's masculine nature and presents electricity—and its siblings, light and fire—as a kind of solar ejaculate:

If electricity, light, and fire, be modifications of one and the same principle . . . , and they have their origin, or fountain, in the sun, it is natural to suppose, in issuing from that luminary, they proceed from him first in their purest state, or in the character of electricity; that joining the particles of our atmosphere, electricity becomes *light*, and uniting with the grosser earth, *fire*. (*System*, I, 66)

Although all the players in the drama that Hellen recounts were very young, it is probable that for the novice scientist himself, the electricity he harnessed and distributed carried a powerful sexual charge. Electricity certainly emerges from Adam Walker's lecture series as its most captivating star, able to excite life and motion in the material world,[18] unbounded enthusiasm in the seasoned natural philosopher, and, in Shelley himself, a lifelong fascination with its irresistible, and erotic, force field. Looked at from one angle, then, Hellen's anecdote reveals Percy penetrating his sisters' world *and* bodies with a sexually tinged substance that emblematized as well as enhanced his own virility (*System*, II, 36).

Yet Walker's comparison of electricity to Proteus, in the stirring conclusion of Lecture VIII, should caution us against assigning this most elusive of substances a rigid (gender) identity (*System*, II, 74). If "this wonderful agent" could emit a masculine aura, as "the paragon of elements" it was also the handmaiden of Nature, obedient to and infused with her maternal power (*System*, II, 72). Walker's discussion of electricity's journey from the pulsating solar "fountain" to the "grosser earth" suggests how this "subtil matter" might adapt to and adopt the more "feminine" character of its new home (*System*, II, 1):

> That electricity after penetrating through the atmosphere, and approaching the earth, has its affinities like other matter, and becomes a latent principle in bodies till called into activity by frictions or heat, is more than probable, from the readiness with which some bodies part with it, and the tenacity with which others retain it. Hence the earth has been considered as the grand reservoir of electricity. (*System*, II, 14)

Originally a power that, as Walker puts it a bit later, "force[s] its way" through the earth's atmosphere, electricity metamorphoses here into a kind of amniotic fluid, pooled within and around the earth as well as within the various bodies that populate her realm (*System*, II, 36). Throughout Walker's lectures, electricity and its close ally, magnetism, remain (sexually) ambiguous entities, full of "perplexing subtleties" that, while sometimes frustrating, allowed even a recent initiate into the mysteries of electromagnetism to explore and exploit its physical power and, what is most important, its metaphorical richness (*System*, II, 74).[19]

In the nursery-room laboratory where he "practised electricity" on his little sisters, Shelley is acting out, with his very reluctant supporting players, a remarkable psychosexual drama whose script he found in the unlikeliest of places: an introductory course on natural philosophy. Thus far, I have been stressing Shelley's roles as director, scientist, and schoolmaster, roles that place him rather conspicuously in a masculine subject position. That the fledgling chemist arms himself with a "subtil and powerful" agent that can "impinge on," or penetrate, the (female) bodies of the earth and of his own sisters seems only to ratify his hyper-masculine status (*System*, II, 36). Yet a closer look at the exact nature of the experiment Hellen describes suggests how the electricity Percy helps generate ultimately carries a feminine charge—and inducts him (back) into the sisterly circle/circuit he left behind when he was shipped off to Syon House.

When Shelley tested Walker's theories of electromagnetism during his holidays at Field Place, he was in essence conjuring a marvelous, shape-shifting genie from a bottle (in this case, a primitive version of the Leyden jar).

But the real magic began, at least for Percy himself, when he placed his little sisters "hand-in-hand round the nursery table to be electrified." As the current flowed from Percy's homemade condenser into the human conductors he had recruited, "the marvellous powers of electricity" created an equally marvelous circle of sympathy, in which each member receives *and* bestows what the poet will later call the "contagious fire" (Hogg, I, 56; "Ode to Liberty," 1. 4).[20] As a literally cohesive power that forges separate individuals into one magic circle, electricity takes on its most feminine guise, and thus, for the young scientist himself, its ideal form. Shelley, like so many of his contemporaries, saw sympathy as a distinctly feminine (and feminizing) force, in part because he was steeped in cultural myths of female virtue. And here "virtue" would denote not simply "goodness" but also, and most crucially, "power"—power to influence, power to unify, power to heal.[21] (When Walker, in his lecture on magnetism, describes the earth's subtle "effluvium" or "aether" as its "magnetic virtue," he is tapping into these rich layers of meaning [*System*, I, 60, 59].) Although "men of feeling" certainly could participate in and even exude this wonderful unifying force, Shelley himself would always prefer to drink his own draughts of the sympathetic fluid in its purest form, that is, as the undiluted liquid fire which emanated from a sister-spirit. And the nursery-room experiments with electricity and (terrified) female siblings allowed him to do just that. Because it issued not just from an electrically charged bottle but also from the reservoirs of "animal electricity" stored within his sisters' bodies, the electro-sympathetic energy that darted around the sisterly circle(s) Shelley designed would have been almost exclusively feminine. Even if the young scientist did not literally join the circle, its pulsing sympathetic energy would have embraced/infused Shelley himself, thus inducting him in both a scientific and a metaphorical sense.

Although, as Shelley learned from his earliest scientific studies, electrical or magnetic induction simply required proximity and not contact with "an electrified or magnetized body,"[22] his penchant for self-electrification—recorded most memorably by Hogg—suggests that he may have wired himself more directly into this magic circle/circuit. One of the first feats that the Divine Poet performs for his new friend at Oxford is to demonstrate "the marvellous powers of electricity" by becoming a real-life version of Blake's "Glad Day":

> [Shelley] proceeded, with much eagerness and enthusiasm, to show me the various instruments [in his Oxford rooms], especially the electrical apparatus; turning round the handle very rapidly, so that the fierce, crackling sparks flew forth; and presently standing upon the stool with glass feet, he begged me to work the machine until he was filled with the fluid, so that his long, wild locks bristled and stood on end. (Hogg, I, 56)

Like the "circuit of several people" receiving and conveying an electric shock, the "human battery" appears in Walker's lectures and was thus familiar to Shelley during the Syon House period discussed here (*System*, II, 46; Crook and Guiton 50). Though the self-electrification Walker describes ostensibly falls under the rubric of "medical electricity," there is something profoundly (auto)erotic in this radical method of "increas[ing] the circulation of the blood, and the pulsation of the heart" (*System*, II, 64).[23] Erasmus Darwin, whom Shelley read in 1809,[24] or perhaps, as Grabo suggests (*Newton* 3), even earlier, makes electricity an explicitly erotic force in the first canto of his *Economy of Vegetation*. Here a "fearless beauty" fills herself with "etherial floods" in order to exchange an electric kiss with a "fond youth," while a "circling band" of "youths and timorous damsels, hand in hand" are "thrill'd" by a subtle fire that is both their own sexual energy and the electric charge from a Leyden jar (*The Botanic Garden*, *Economy of Vegetation*, I. vii. 349, 335, 355, 361, 362, 365).

Even without the elaborate "philosophical apparatus" necessary for the particular experiment Hogg witnessed—and Shelley probably did not acquire his own machine until his matriculation to Eton—the enterprising young chemist certainly dabbled in such self-stimulation before summoning his sisters to his makeshift laboratory (Hogg, I, 57). But it was their presence that would allow Shelley to create and experience something that no solitary self-transfusions of "the vital fluid" could ever offer: "the unreserve of mingled being" (*System*, II, 50; *PS*, I, 511).

This phrase, from his 1816 poem "The Sunset," concisely captures the Shelleyan ideal of absolute coalescence: sensual, spiritual, emotional, and intellectual. As I emphasized in my analysis of the poet's masculine and feminine doubles, this paradigm can be extremely frightening, especially to someone like Shelley with remarkably permeable or "weak" ego boundaries.[25] Yet it can also be immensely liberating, at least when the "mingling" is between two (or more) sympathetically attuned "beings." (As we shall see, this rather abstract and all-compassing term—prominent in texts such as *Alastor* [Preface] and *Epipsychidion*—best describes the diverse group of humans and non-humans who actually achieve "mingled being" in Shelley's writings). For Shelley himself, his younger sisters and their spiritual heirs would always epitomize the loving, familiar, and—what is crucial—*pure* companions with whom he could freely and joyously "interfuse" (another favorite expression).

"Hand-in-hand" with his beloved siblings in the Field Place nursery or hovering at the edges of their vibrant force field, the "poet and experimentalist" had stage-managed masterfully what was to become an archetypal Shelleyan scene (Hogg, I, 23). A band of kindred spirits—or, better yet, sister-spirits—sharing one another's "electric life," burns through the borders that divide self and other to create a highly-charged circle of sympathy (*Defence*

508). As it spins ceaselessly through Shelley's literary imaginings, this circle at times will contract to enclose a pair of secluded lovers, as in *Alastor* or Canto VI of *Laon and Cythna*, or dilate to encompass and purify the "polluting multitude" (in "Lines written among the Euganean Hills") and even, most remarkably, all of creation (in *Prometheus Unbound*). Ideally, *rarely*, the "fertilizing streams of sympathy" that pulse through these circles remain uncontaminated by psychic, spiritual, and sexual poisons (*Prose* 233: *On the Death of Princess Charlotte*). Chances are, if the "vital fluid"—a potent brew of electrical, sympathetic, and sexual energy—does become tainted, it is because the very ingredient Shelley hoped to expunge has slipped into the mix: the toxic vapor that emanates from "the little world of self" (Walker, II, 50; *Defence* 497).

Unselfing Desire:
"On Love," *The Banquet*, and *A Discourse on Love*

According to the Dedication to *Laon and Cythna*, where the poet recalls "the hour which burst / [His] spirit's sleep" as he walked "upon the glittering grass" at Syon House,[26] the principle of Self had by 1804 penetrated Shelley's imagination and his newly born social consciousness, announcing itself as a powerful enemy that flourished in the external "world of woes" as well as within his own soul (*CW*, I, 251: *LC*, Dedication, ll. 21–22, 23, 26). Shelley's struggle to overcome through Christlike love and sympathy the "harsh and grating strife" of (his own) unchecked selfishness was thus already underway when he conducted his experiments with electricity and a band of sister-spirits during his holidays at Field Place (*LC*, Dedication, l. 27).

The nursery-room episodes that I have been scrutinizing so minutely reveal how Shelleyan sympathy and the Shelleyan Self might clash, or more accurately, "commingle" in a rather bizarre fashion. Temporarily reprieved from his exile at Syon House, Percy was attempting to re-enter his beloved sorority by staging a series of experiments that, it turned out, simultaneously enhanced and dissolved his own Selfhood. Parading through Field Place in the guise of the domineering, aggressively masculine scientist, (Shelley's) Selfhood "rudely invaded" the sisterly circle in order, paradoxically, to undergo a radical meltdown within its high-voltage, feminine force field (Hogg, I, 23). Theoretically, the very hierarchies—male/female, scientist/subject, schoolmaster/pupil—that Shelley enforced in order to carry out his nursery-room experiments would collapse once the magic circle of sympathy is (electrically) generated. Yet the Self, progenitor of these hierarchies, is still in the mix, still in the loop, relentlessly imposing its own will, even if it *is* a will-to-sympathy. Similarly, the inexorable will-to-selflessness of the Shelleyan martyr often helps ensure that he remains trapped within the prison of the Self. As

I emphasized in my discussion of Shelley's strange *imitatio Christi*, the poet's most strenuous efforts to disentangle himself from the coils of Selfhood could cause these coils to tighten, tormenting him (and his fictive surrogates) even more terribly. The Shelleyan "quest for sympathy," to borrow Alan Richardson's helpful phrase, like his correlative quest for selflessness, could, if pursued too desperately, bind the poet and his heroes more steadfastly to the Self they had hoped to flee ("Sibling Incest" 753).

Whether Shelley's search for sympathy involved his longing to receive, to bestow, or, as in his Field Place exploits, to interchange this precious elixir, he often found it difficult to describe this quest save in the language of the Self. His 1818 essay "On Love" exemplifies and may even (Self-)consciously allude to this dilemma:

> I know not the internal constitution of other men, or even of thine whom I now address. I see that in some external attributes they resemble me, but when misled by that appearance I have thought to appeal to something in common and unburthen my inmost soul to them, I have found my language misunderstood like one in a distant and savage land. The more opportunities they have afforded me for experience, the wider has appeared the interval between us, and to a greater distance have the points of sympathy been withdrawn. With a spirit ill fitted to sustain such proof, trembling and feeble through its tenderness, I have every where sought, and have found only repulse and disappointment. (473)

In this paragraph, a kind of autobiographical prologue to the essay proper, the principle of Self (here issuing forth as self-absorption and self-pity) and the desire to conduct the electric spark of sympathy seem inextricably intertwined. (The electricity-sympathy parallel is present in the phrase *points of sympathy*, which suggests Franklin's pointed conductors, precursors to his lightning rod.)[27] Looked at one way, in fact, this entire passage is overwhelmed by the language of Self. Yet Shelley's lament that he has "found [his] language misunderstood like one in a distant and savage land" could be challenging *us*, his current audience, to read more carefully, more sympathetically. Written during a prolonged dry spell in which Shelley composed almost no poetry, though he completed his superb translation of the *Symposium*, "On Love" certainly reflects the poet's gnawing (and growing) doubts about his own audience, an audience that, as Shelley was too well aware, could never rival that of his friend Lord Byron. Did he indeed *have* one and, if so, could he safely "unburthen [his] inmost soul" to readers who might "sympathise not" with his ideas and feelings (474)?

It is over the prologue's final, soul-baring pronouncement that these questions most anxiously hover: "With a spirit ill fitted to sustain such proof, trembling and feeble through its tenderness, I have every where sought, and have found only repulse and disappointment." On the surface, one of Shelley's most starkly confessional and flagrantly self-indulgent sentences, this miniature prose poem in fact resembles a highly wrought, beautifully controlled *complainte*.[28] The kind of sympathetic reader it demands is not one who will promiscuously shower the speaker with pity, though pity is a first step toward the kind of sympathetic identification between reader and speaker Shelley is trying to negotiate.[29] The responsive, supple reader that Shelley hoped for will move beyond a purely emotional reaction to the passage—and pity is one of the more *generous* responses this sentence usually elicits—toward an aesthetic appreciation of the writer's artistry, and finally to a recognition of herself, her own yearnings, pain, and "tenderness," in the "airy children" of the author's brain, now "born anew" within her own (473).

Whether or not we so willingly enter into the text and help close "the interval between us"—that is, between ourselves and the author—Shelley is left with another question about his audience: Could he accurately "read" *us*, understand our "internal constitution"? Despite Shelley's confession in the prologue that he has often misread his fellow humans and that they remain essentially mysterious to him, the essay itself answers this question with a resounding "yes." First of all, as he moves into the essay proper Shelley abandons the "I" of the prologue for "we," thus drawing his reader into the portrait of Love that comprises the rest of the piece:

> *Thou* demandest what is Love. It is that powerful attraction towards all that we conceive or fear or hope beyond ourselves when we find within our own thoughts the chasm of an insufficient void and seek to awaken in all things that are, a community with what we experience within ourselves. (473)

Moreover, the "internal constitution" of "other men," in general, and that of his reader, in particular, is precisely what Shelley claims to discern when he sympathetically, *empathically* probes the deepest recesses of the human heart and mind. With astonishing authority, not only does the poet elucidate the inner necessity that impels us toward beings and ideals "beyond ourselves," but he also provides us with a detailed map of our own psychic terrain, where in one spot "the chasm of an insufficient void" gapes and, in another, "a soul within our soul . . . describes a circle around its proper Paradise" (474). Although a good deal of the self-revelation that characterizes the essay's prologue carries over to its main body—after all each of the "we"s and "our"s that Shelley utters implicate him as well as us in the text—it is the reader who may feel most exposed by the author's penetrating gaze.

The power of sympathy that Shelley must wield in order to peer into our "internal constitution," our "intellectual nature," our most intimate feelings and desires resembles the seminal stream of electricity that, as Walker asserted, "is capable of making many opaque bodies transparent by impregnating them with temporary light" (*System*, II, 58). This form of sympathy also corresponds to the "masculine" empathy that Gail S. Reed (mentioned in the previous chapter), links with phallic "intrusion" and "'trespass,' that is, entry into forbidden territory . . . at the service of discovering a hidden reality" (17). The element of domination that we observed in Shelley's attempts to conduct, in both senses of the word, his sisters' electro-sympathetic energy thus informs even the gentle sentiments of the essay "On Love," where "tears of mysterious tenderness" barely blur the writer's remarkable X-ray vision (474). But again, as with his nursery-room experiments, the ultimate goals the poet pursues in "On Love" are self-feminization and the unreserve of mingled being (though this time sexual mingling is an "acknowledged and visible" component of the Shelleyan formula [Notopoulous 409: *Discourse*]). The "feminine" tenderness and susceptibility Shelley displays in the prologue remain his self-ideal throughout the text, while the image of lovers' eyebeams "mix[ing]" and "melt[ing]" together synechdocally expresses the poet's desire for more elaborate forms of spiritual and physical fusion with his beloved.

Why, then, if the (intersecting) aims of self-feminization and self-other coalescence govern this text (and the author himself), does Shelley need to "impregnate" us—not just his readers but other "co-existent beings" as well—with the light of his own penetrative sympathy (*L*, I, 77)? First of all, we must recall the dramatic fissure that divides the prologue, where his fellow beings remain disturbingly opaque to the poet, from the essay itself, in which he confidently illuminates the depth of our deepest mysteries, to paraphrase the Narrator of *Alastor*. The boldness, even bravado with which the essay informs us how *we* feel, how *we* love almost overrides the despair that suffuses the prologue. But Shelley's profound doubts about our "internal constitution" and his own ability to see it clearly linger, particularly where the poet concedes how difficult, even impossible it is to discover (and dis-cover) one's ideal lover, for Shelley his ideal "likeness" (473).

This brings us to the central purpose of the restlessly probing, sympathetic "searchlight" that Shelley turns on his reader/other as the essay itself unfolds. Although the poet had long felt himself part of an intimately interconnected world, that "mazy volume of commingling things" he sometimes celebrates and sometimes fears, the kind of communion he envisions in "On Love" differs in some important ways from the "ordinary" interchange this highly susceptible poet usually presupposes (*PS*, I, 119). Genuine "mingled being" is, for one thing, a deliberately, vigorously, even obsessively *pursued* communion, not the accidental exchange of miscellaneous emissions that, in

Shelley's interpenetrating cosmos, meant business as usual. Moreover, the Shelleyan lovers who inhabit the essay "On Love" and several of his other works enthusiastically and *thoroughly* "mix" and merge on several levels: the intellectual, the imaginative, and the physical (or, more precisely, the sexual).[30] In *Civilization and Its Discontents*, Freud writes that "At the height of being in love the boundary between ego and object threatens to melt away" (13). Shelley's emphasis, in the text at hand and elsewhere, on the "unreserve," rather than the *threat*, of mingled being might seem incompatible with Freud's skeptical, sometimes hostile, view of such a state, yet Shelley harbors his own suspicions toward the very experience he so idealizes throughout his writings. The two facets of mingled being that I have just identified—its status as the object of an impassioned quest and its radical, multidimensional quality—often prove most worrisome to the poet.

To begin with the second aspect, the thoroughgoing interpenetration that he imagines is potentially horrifying to someone with Shelley's deep-seated obsession with contagion, be it moral, spiritual, or, perhaps worst of all, sexual. Familiarity, consanguinity, and extreme youth ensured that the sister-spirits with whom the novice scientist had intermingled in an electrified circle would pose no such threat. *Their* "animal electricity" could thus be nothing more—or less—than "vestal fire" (*CW*, I, 254: *LC*, Dedication, l. 99). The unknown, perhaps unknowable "thou" whom Shelley addresses in "On Love" is a different story, however. The poet must attempt to unveil and illuminate the "internal constitution" of this other, who haunts the essay as a being who may offer the writer "repulse and disappointment" or, worse yet, the kind of dangerous interchange that Shelley linked with the notion of "loathsome sympathy." Ideally, this reader/other will turn out to be the poet's longed-for "antitype," immaculate heir to the poet's original sister-spirits.[31] We can in fact read Shelley's essay as enacting his own quest for this spiritual twin. This brings me to the other crucial component of Shelleyan mingled being mentioned earlier: the fact that it is an experience, a state that one may eagerly—perhaps too eagerly—pursue. And here is where the poet's own self-suspicion (or Self-suspicion) comes into play.

If Shelley felt compelled to screen potential partners in mingled being, he was just as anxious to scrutinize his own "inmost soul" to make sure that the "something within [him] which . . . thirsts after its likeness" was not simply the spectre of Narcissus clamoring for his mirror image (473). What the poet hopes to see, if only "dimly," when he turns his gaze inward is "a miniature . . . of [his] entire self, yet deprived of all that [he] condemn[s] or despise[s]," which for Shelley would include anything smacking of self-involvement. This "ideal prototype" would in fact be a self that is purged of Selfhood—that is, of selfish desire as well as of rigid personal identity, which Shelley's use of the first person plural attempts to erase (and which my brack-

eted interpolations re-inscribe). In both the key passage introducing the prototype and the subsequent description of the antitype, Shelley's language is
oddly impersonal, or rather, supra-personal, as though he were trying to
"overleap" the mire of Selfhood, of narcissistic desire that threatens to engulf
the model of loving interchange he is constructing.[32] But when the poet abandoned the "I" of the prologue, he did not escape his own craving for perfect
sympathy, perfect "correspondence," an urgent "want" that bursts forth as the
relentless "demands" attributed to the supposedly serene and pure prototype
(474). The "type within," in turns out, is a pretty severe taskmaster, and it is
difficult to distinguish its quenchless "thirst" for its antitype from the "self
devoted self-interested" love that Shelley so passionately condemned and that
he explicitly linked with sexual desire (*L*, I, 173).

When Shelley composed "On Love," he had just finished translating
Plato's *Symposium*, a text whose ideas suffuse Shelley's brief essay.[33]
Aristophanes' account of how Jupiter surgically split primitive human
beings—circular creatures with eight limbs, two faces, and two sets of genitals—and thus doomed them (and us) to a perpetual quest for wholeness
provides the most obvious link with Shelley's piece, where prototype and
antitype seem joined by some ancient bond. But Pausanias' and Eryximachus' comparisons of Uranian and Pandemian Love are just as vital to
Shelley's own attempts, in the essay at hand and throughout his writings, to
answer the timeless question "What is Love?" ("On Love" 473). The distinction that Plato's banquet-goers make between these two types of love
was especially crucial to Shelley as he explored how "passion's trance"
might promote *or* prevent the triumph of ideal sympathy, unalloyed and
noninvasive, over tyrannous Selfhood.[34]

As Pausanias tells his companions, the two Loves he will discuss correspond to and accompany the two Venuses, "one, the eldest, the daughter of
Uranus, born without a mother, whom we call the Uranian; the other younger,
the daughter of Jupiter and Dione, whom we call the Pandemian" (Notopoulos 421–22). Uranian Love Pausanias celebrates as the more exalted of the
two, for it inspires us to move beyond (merely) personal, sensual desires
toward the selfless adoration of another's beautiful soul. Votaries of the Uranian divinity joyfully submit to "the servitude of love," for by devoting themselves to "a person of virtue,"[35] they too become "more virtuous and wise"
(425, 424, 425). The "unity and communion of stedfast friendship" that the
Uranian lovers enjoy ultimately infuses the whole social and political sphere
in which they dwell; the "mutual love" they privately cultivate spawns harmony and cohesion in the world at large, or, in Platonic terms, "the state"
(426). As Eryximachus, expanding on Pausanias' discourse, declares, "the
more benignant Love . . . prepares for his worshippers the highest happiness
through the mutual intercourse of social kindness which it promotes among

them, and through the benevolence which he attracts to them from the Gods our superiors" (428).

Though their ladder of love does not rise so high, these celebrants of Uranian Love anticipate the ascending steps "toward the wide ocean of intellectual beauty" that Socrates will trace in his climactic "encomium of Love" (449, 450). Shelley's own version of Uranian Love, which he had begun to conceive long before he immersed himself in Plato during the summer of 1818,[36] certainly incorporates Socrates' transcendentalism as well as Pausanius' and Eryximachus' concern with the "right government of Love" here on earth (428). As early as 1811, when despair over his loss of Harriet Grove threatened to overwhelm him, Shelley was fervently invoking a love that was "*infinite in extent*, eternal in duration," a power that could offset his fear that "there is selfishness in the passion of Love" (*L*, I, 36). This brings me to the other half of that "double Love" we meet at the Platonic banquet (427). The Love "which attends upon Venus Pandemos" emerges from both Plato's dialogue and Shelley's own often scathing remarks as the very essence of "self-centred, self-possessing" and self-serving appetite (Notopoulos 422; *L*, I, 171).[37] As Pausanias explains, Pandemian Love "is, in truth, common to the vulgar, and presides over transient and fortuitous connexions"; its votaries "seek the body rather than the soul, and the ignorant rather than the wise, disdaining all that is honourable and lovely, and considering how they should best satisfy their sensual necessities" (422). Eryximachus' judgement is much harsher; he labels Pandemian Love "evil and injurious" and "excessive and disorderly" (428). As it spreads its baneful influence, says Eryximachus, it disrupts and pollutes not just the human realm but "all things which are" (426). (Uranian love, too, Eryximachus tells us, exerts a universal influence; and, as we shall see, these two contending powers alternate sway over the various "beings" that populate some of Shelley's best-known poems.) In Shelleyan terms, it is the Pandemian divinity that spawns a particularly crude version of "self love": the "passion of animal love" (*L*, I, 208).

However, for Shelley, as for his Platonic forebears, Pandemian Love and "the sexual impulse" per se were by no means synonymous, not in theory, at any rate (Notopoulos 408: *Discourse*). In fact, the desire for "sexual connection," as Shelley puts it in *A Discourse on Love*, had its rightful place even in the sublime realm of Uranian Love (Notopoulos 408). Followers of this "more honourable Love" do not spurn physical beauty or erotic gratification;[38] they just make sure that "the flower of the form" is not "the sole object of . . . desire" and that "sensual necessities" do not overwhelm the all-important "zeal of virtue" (Notopoulos 428, 424, 422, 426: *The Banquet*). Thus, Uranian Love, though it "enkindle[s]" intense passion, nonetheless "exempts us from all wantonness and libertinism"—at least this is what Shelley longed to believe, and never quite could (423, 422).

It is worth noting that the last quoted term, *libertinism*, is one of Shelley's additions to the dialogue, an interpolation which another intriguing departure from the original text helps illuminate (Notopoulos 574). Where the Loeb and Bollingen translations declare, respectively, that Uranian Love is "untinged with wantonness" and "innocent of any hint of lewdness,"[39] Shelley writes that this Love "exempts *us* from all wantonness and libertinism" (emphasis mine). Here we can see how Shelley's own anxiety to distance himself from the horrid taint of the libertine insinuates itself into the Platonic text—and, what is more important, into the sacred precincts of Uranian Love.[40] As suggested in chapter 2, Shelley regarded the libertine as a particularly loathsome incarnation of Selfhood, a creature who stalked the poet as one of his own darkest doubles.[41] This is how he appears in *A Discourse on Love*, companion piece to Shelley's translation of *The Banquet*: "Few characters are more degraded than that of an habitual libertine; that is, a person who is in the custom of seeking a relief from the impulse of the sexual instinct, divested of those associated sentiments which in a civilized state precede, accompany, or follow such an act" (Notopoulos 410). While the "civilized" or "sentimental" lover, the Uranian lover, "thirsts for communion not merely of the senses but of our whole nature, intellectual, imaginative, and sensitive," the depraved devotee of Pandemian Love seeks only "gratification of the senses" (Notopoulos 408: *Discourse*). The only kind of "mingled being" that interests the libertine, then, would be merely sexual, whereas the ideal Shelleyan (and Platonic) lover desires, or, rather, requires "that all sympathies . . . be harmoniously blended" (410). Presumably, the enlightened lover, having conscientiously followed the dictates of his or her own "higher faculties" as well as the "imperious" demands of love itself (410, 408), can with joy and "unreserve" commingle with the beautiful "person selected as the subject of [sexual] gratification" (410), a loaded locution that underscores the subject/object biases of language (and erotic love) at the same time that it tries to erase them.

However, despite Shelley's strenuous efforts throughout the *Discourse* to link the sexual impulse to "the highest emotions of our nature," physical desire emerges in this piece, and in a good many of Shelley's writings, as an "unworthy alloy,"[42] one that pollutes even the most elevated, beautifully orchestrated interminglings (410, 413). The material body, with its too easily inflamed senses, its (literal) decadence, and its susceptibility to infectuous disease—particularly sexually transmitted ones[43]—inhabits Shelley's sexual imagination as the palpable symbol of this alloy. But a more subtle contaminant lurks behind both the body itself and the desires it generates. (That the human body is the most conspicuous site of the "detestable distinctions" of gender certainly heightened the feminine-tending poet's ambivalence toward it [*L*, I, 195].) Even in his earliest writings—the "distempered" Gothic novels, the ardent letters to Hogg and Elizabeth Hitchener, the melodramatic lyrics—

it is Selfhood that usually provides the driving force behind sexual appetite, or, to use a more Shelleyan term, sexual "thirst." In fact, Shelley's first reference to the principle of Self is in connection with the principle of sex.

It was New Year's Day 1811, and Shelley, despondent over his recent breakup with Harriet Grove, had just received a letter from Hogg offering a peculiar sort of consolation. Why not, Hogg suggested, seek "perfection in love" and "perfectiblity" of oneself by embarking on a series of erotic liaisons (L, I, 34)?[44] In his impassioned reply Shelley admits that though he found Hogg's ideas provocative and even tempting he must condemn them as sacrilege to the true spirit of love: "Oh your theory cost me much reflexion, I have not ceased to think of it since your letter came . . . Is it not however founded on that *hateful* principle—Is it *self* which you propose to raise to a state of superiority by your system of eternal perfectibility in love[?]" (L, I, 34). Shelley wraps up what turns out to be round one of an ongoing debate with his friend by yoking Selfhood with the "thrilling sensualities of Epicurism" that Hogg evidently had recommended (L, I, 34).[45] To these twin evils, the young poet opposes "Love! dear love," which demands sacrifice and not indulgence of Self. In what was fast becoming a typically Shelleyan move, the young poet embraces "torments" and "agony" rather than risk that selfishness which, in his next letter, he discerns even in "the passion of Love" (L, I, 34, 36). This does not mean, however, that Shelley found his own sexual urges easy to resist; on the contrary, he often seemed to find them overpowering.[46] In fact, his admonitions to Hogg, who eventually followed his own Pandemian muse and tried to seduce Shelley's new bride, often seem like self-chastisements and not simply Self-chastisements.

As we shall see when we turn to some representative texts, Shelley was already attempting, at least imaginatively, to reconcile his strong desire for sexual "mingling" with his need to conquer (his own) Selfhood. At his most optimistic, the poet recognized that "the transports of love"—a phrase from one of his earliest poems—could lift one out of the little world of Self and into a privileged realm of "exstatic" *and* generous interchange (PS, I, 11: "Song. Translated from the German" [October 1809]). But the kind of self-transcendence Shelleyan lovers achieve often has more to do with the "agony" and "torments" of the martyr than with the blissful abandon of the love-adept. Sexual martyrdom—the postcoital deaths we witness in "The Sunset," *Laon and Cythna*, and *Epipsychidion*, the terrible dissolution the fierce dancers suffer in *The Triumph of Life*—ultimately emerges as one of Shelley's most ingenious concepts, one that allowed him decisively, *violently*, to expel the Self from the hallowed realm of mingled being.

When we look back to Shelley's boyhood attempts to fuse his own "electric life" with that of his sisters, we may be most struck by the pathos, the desperation, or the sheer ingenuity of his efforts (*Defence* 508). Sympathetic and not sexual interchange is the young scientist's goal, but his struggle to "weave a bondage of . . . sympathy" in the Field Place nursery illuminates how willfullness and domination might infect the more explicitly erotic forms of mingled being he will explore (*CW*, I, 278: *LC*, II. 137). That Shelley was well aware of this danger is evident in his searing depictions of rape (or, in *The Cenci*, of its terrible aftermath). However, as my allusion to the ideal "transports of love" suggested, Shelley did envision a way to escape these Self-spawned cycles of will, dominance, invasion, and victimization.

If the sexual charge that flows between Shelleyan lovers is to transmit "magnetic sweetness" and not "electric poison," both lovers must surrender their individual wills and desires to a kind of presiding deity who sanctions and even sanctifies the mingled being they enjoy (*Esdaile* 85: "To Harriet" ["It is not blasphemy"]; *Epi.*, l. 359). Whether it appears as Intellectual Beauty—"messenger of sympathies, / That wax and wane in lovers' eyes" ("Hymn," ll. 41–42)—as the Uranian Venus, or even as a mortal "Lady" who tends a paradisal garden (*S-P*, II. 5), this benignant Power requires of its beneficiaries the sort of feminine receptivity and wise passiveness that Shelley himself exemplifies in the "Hymn to Intellectual Beauty."[47] Regretfully, except in the radically transformed worlds that Shelley imagines in *Queen Mab* and *Prometheus Unbound*, the "SPIRIT fair" visits "this various world with as inconstant wing / As summer winds that creep from flower to flower" ("Hymn," ll. 83, 3–4). But when it does, it graciously "consecrate[s]" and purifies each lover's heart, enabling him or her, at least briefly, to luxuriate in the unreserve of mingled being, unscathed by Selfhood's "sordid lust" ("Hymn," l. 13; *QM*, V. 90). Or it may allow the lovers to become, in the words of Shelley's essay "On Love," "two exquisite lyres strung to the accompaniment of one delightful voice"—to become, that is, two sister-spirits soothed by the song of their common mother (474).

Pandemian Love in *Zastrozzi*

Just about the time that Shelley was exploring the wonders of electricity with his little sisters at Field Place, he met the beautiful girl who would really ignite the circle of feminine sympathy that intermittently enveloped the young "poet and experimentalist." When his cousin Harriet Grove joined the poet's sisterly coterie,[48] it was more often in spirit, via her lively letters, than in body, but that did not diminish the profound effect she had on Shelley's conception of mingled being. In fact, her (physical) absence during their courtship was just as crucial to Shelley's sexual imagination as her abrupt disappearance from his life would be. Judging from family members' reminiscences as well as from Shelley's own literary commemorations, the cousins' rare meetings were highly-charged, especially for the volatile young poet. On at least one occasion, Shelley became a "wild boy" in his beloved's company, pulling pranks and upsetting a bottle of wine at a staid family gathering (Hellen Shelley, quoted in Hogg, I, 27). Almost from the beginning of their romance, Harriet Grove existed for Shelley as a dreamlike figure who lived in their letters to each other and in the torrid Gothic novels and sentimental lyrics that she helped inspire.[49] She also dwelt in her cousin's (erotic) dreams and thus became the first of Shelley's visionary maidens, gorgeous, elusive creatures who managed to be both voluptuous and ethereal. It was almost as if actual contact with Harriet were too intense for the ardent suitor who had already met and perhaps mingled with her in his "visioned slumber" (*PS*, I, 128: "Melody to a Scene of Former Times").[50]

In Shelley's earliest writings as well as in many of his mature works, "passion's trance" is just that, an extraordinary state in which "normal" sensations and perceptions remain suspended and conscious thought gives way to the mind's subterranean rumblings.[51] The adolescent Shelley, involved in a heated but largely epistolary romance, had plenty of opportunity to explore the various intersections between sexual desire and dream-states. The works that he composed during this crucial period reveal the poet (and novelist) grappling with an issue that will continue to haunt him even in his final writings: the distinction between the "distempered dream[s]" planted by Pandemian Love and the blissful, benign visions that Uranian Love grants its votaries. The poem just quoted, *Alastor* (l. 224), acknowledges that these dream categories may intermingle as freely as the dreamer and his veiled maid, and it is this quandary that Shelley confronts in his first Gothic novel, *Zastrozzi*.

Shelley eventually would label both *Zastrozzi* and *St. Irvyne* "distempered altho unoriginal visions," but the earlier work best fits the description of a lurid, often hallucinatory fever-dream (*L*, I, 266). While the "hero" Verezzi often remains unconscious, the victim of sleeping potions, fainting fits, and dire illness, the lustful Matilda is constantly swept away by voluptuous dreams and reveries that feature "the hapless Verezzi" as her sexual prey (*CW*, V, 37). Initially devoted to the lovely, virtuous Julia, Verezzi ultimately succumbs to Matilda's "seductive blandishments" and enters a nightmare world of erotic obsession and violent death (*CW*, V, 58). Nora Crook and Derek Guiton, who rightly identify "the passion of lust" as the novel's central theme, read *Zastrozzi* as a "glamorised" confessional account of Shelley's own sexual lapse, his own seduction at the capable hands of a Matilda-like figure (35). We need not, though, wholeheartedly accept Crook and Guiton's speculations, which they candidly present as such, in order to recognize Shelley's astonishingly empathic depictions not just of Verezzi's terrible inner turmoil but of Matilda's as well. In fact, the novel's own blurring of the psychic (or psychotic) realm with external "reality" suggests that hunting for a particular biographical incident is unnecessary: it is his characters' "palpable dreams" and "disturbed visions" of sexual commingling that captivate the author, while the act itself fades into relative unimportance, to paraphrase a key line from the *Discourse on Love* (*CW*, V, 71; Notopoulos 410).

From the onset, Matilda's erotic fantasies are Pandemian in nature: tempestuous, depraved, and utterly self-oriented. But Verezzi falls into libertine love (and into Matilda's fierce embrace) from a much loftier height. Though apparently bereft of the "wider sympathy" and remarkable spiritual aspiration that characterize genuine Uranian Love (*CW*, I, 284: *LC*, II. 318), Verezzi's devotion to Julia does resemble the kind of sentimental or "civilized" love that Shelley so idealized. "Sympathy and congeniality of sentiment" rather than selfish sexual appetite govern their relationship; in fact, the tender affection that Verezzi feels toward his "idolised Julia" seems to preclude the fervent physical passion that he (briefly) shares with Matilda (*CW*, V, 59, 52). "The fire of voluptuous, of maddening love supplants the "chaste and mild emotion [that] characterized his love for Julia" when Verezzi exchanges his soothing visions of his first love for the distempered dreams that he and Matilda create together (75).

It would be easy to read Verezzi's defection from Julia to Matilda in terms of the protagonist's (or author's) need to split the beloved woman into a spiritualized soul mate on the one hand and a fiery temptress on the other, and this literary and psychological cliché certainly leaves its mark on the novel. But Shelley's precocious insights into his own sexual psychology and his experimental attitude toward his characters' gender roles push *Zastrozzi* far beyond this dead-end theme. I touched on the gender issue in my second-chapter commentary on the novel's *Doppelgänger*, Verezzi and Zastrozzi. This earlier discussion stressed the aggressively masculine Matilda's role as a carrier/conduit of the homosexual charge that flowed between Verezzi and his demonic pursuer, Zastrozzi. However, whether linked through loathsome and strangely erotic sympathy with Zastrozzi or harassed by Matilda's tireless sexual advances, the extravagently passive Verezzi, zealously playing the maiden in distress, remains at the opposite end of the sexual spectrum from his "towering" adversaries, that is, until his captor(s) actually deflower him (14). Only then—or to be more precise, only when he "return[s] [Matilda's] embrace with ardour"—does Verezzi acquire the tincture of masculinity that qualifies him for a same-sex marriage with Zastrozzi-Matilda (75).[52] Thus, rather than preserving or enhancing his feminine aura the way we might expect, Verezzi's surrender to an insatiable man-woman of "strong passions" infuses him with the selfish appetite that Shelley consistently yoked with masculine desire (29).

The highly susceptible Verezzi needs to preserve his sympathetic connection with his gentle sister-spirit Julia if he is to retain his feminine identity without succumbing to the various psycho-sexual violations that the young novelist rather gleefully details. In Shelleyan terms, as well as in the discourse of sensibility, if Verezzi's soft heart, "generous passions," and highly developed emotional and aesthetic sensibility reveal admirable aspects of his feminine nature, his hopeless vulnerability to his ultra-virile enemies suggests how this same femininity may prove extremely dangerous to those who, like Shelley himself, deliberately cultivate it (31). Camille Paglia's remarks on unmodified, "malleable femininity" in *The Faerie Queene* help illuminate the sexual dynamic at work in Shelley's Gothic romance:

> [W]eakness inspires attack. Vulnerability generates its own entrapments, creating a maelstrom of voracity around itself. Nature abhors a vacuum. Into the spiritual emptiness of pure femininity in Spenser rush a storm of masculine forces. Florimell, for example, is a professional victim . . . And Amoret is grotesquely defenseless against the sorcerer Busyrane. (186)

Substitute "spiritual porosity" for "spiritual emptiness" and you have a pretty accurate picture of the dilemma Shelley confronts not just in *Zastrozzi* but also in mature works such as *The Cenci* and *Prometheus Unbound*, where heroines and male heroines alike suffer invasive "storm[s] of masculine forces." But where Spenser's worthiest protogonists "internally subsume the chastened extremes of masculine and feminine" and thereby transcend the "savage circular world of rape" (Paglia 186), Shelley's ideal characters, or "beings," preserve their radical femininity *and* their essential purity even when subjected to the most horrific violations. The very virtues that Shelley saw as feminine—selflessness, love, compassion—allow Cythna, for example, to remain undefiled by a crime *against* her femininity. Her metamorphosis from rape-victim, trapped in Othman's "polluted halls," to the almost virginal bride who enjoys with Laon "mute and liquid ecstacies" within their wedding bower is an astonishing one (*CW*, I, 345: *LC*, VII. 30; VI. 295). Despite her ordeals, her inmost soul, her "ideal prototype" still "reflects only the forms of purity and brightness," including the ideal (feminized) form of her beloved Laon, with whom she can finally mingle in complete unreserve ("On Love" 473, 474).

Verezzi, too, though it may seem absurd to compare him with such an illustrious Shelleyan heroine, has the potenial to keep his own prototypical "soul within [his] soul" pristine as well as to chart a Cythna-like course toward the glories of mingled being ("On Love" 474). Despite the constant physical and mental invasions he suffers at the hands of his rapacious enemies, the feminine-tending Verezzi (temporarily) escapes lethal contamination by allying himself with "his adored Julia," the "mild" and "heavenly" sister-spirit who screens him from Matilda's "fatal, resistless passion" (*CW*, V, 36, 29, 28). Because the lovers remain forcibly separated throughout most of the novel, Julia must protect and commune with Verezzi *in absentia*, and he in turn must keep her spirit alive within him through memory and, most important, through the dreams and reveries that are so crucial to the Shelleyan eros.[53] Only then can he preserve his own "unspotted spirit" (or ideal proto-type) and enjoy "the sweet, the serene delights" of commingling with his exquisite Julia (52, 51).

To his credit, Verezzi does stay true to Julia, and thus to his own ideal self, for quite some time. Subjected to Matilda's sexual bullying, Verezzi nonetheless mentally cherishes Julia's "fragile form," "mild, heavenly coun-tenance," "interesting softness," and "unaffected sweetness" (*CW*, V, 29, 33, 58). Zastrozzi's admonition to his partner in crime nicely sums up the way Verezzi has internalized his feminine second self: "'Tis but the image of that accursed Julia . . . revelling in his breast, which prevents him from becoming instantly yours. Could you but efface that!" (61).[54] This is exactly what Matilda has already set out to do, and her ingenious strategy brings me to the issue mentioned earlier: Shelley's remarkable understanding of his own erotic sensibility. In the Dedication to *Laon and Cythna*, Shelley identifies himself as one of "those who seek all sympathies in one," and as early as 1809, when he composed *Zastrozzi*, Shelley recognized that love could be "a blight and snare" for such uncompromising votaries of sentimental love (*CW*, I, 252: *LC*, Dedication, ll. 47, 46). Long before he wrote his Platonically inspired exposi-tion of sentimental or "civilized" love, the eloquent *Discourse on Love*, he inserted into his Minerva Press–spawned thriller a cautionary tale of senti-mental love gone sour.

As a Shelleyan sentimental lover, Verezzi "thirst[s] for a communion not merely of the senses but of [his] whole nature, intellectual, imaginative, and sensitive" (Notopoulos 408: *Discourse*). If anything, the "chaste and mild emotion which . . . characterize[s] his love for Julia" contains too lit-tle rather than too much "sensual intermixture," to borrow a phrase from "An Essay on Friendship" (*CW*, V, 75; Clark 338). Significantly, it is Verezzi's appetite for sympathy and not for sex that the ever-scheming Matilda targets as she lures him into her web and into her bed. Not only does she mimic the feminine delicacy and tenderness that Verezzi so treasures in Julia, but Matilda also weaves "syren illusions" of "sympathy and conge-niality of sentiment":

> To touch his feelings had been her constant aim; could she find anything which interested him . . . or could she succeed in effacing another from his mind, she had no doubt but that he would quickly and voluntarily clasp her to his bosom.

By affecting to coincide with him in everything—by feigning to possess that congeniality of sentiment and union of idea which he thought so necessary to the existence of love, she doubted not soon to accomplish her purpose. (*CW*, V, 31, 59)

Skillfully penetrating her victim's inmost being, reading his every mood and idea, Matilda wields the power of (invasive) sympathy in order to fabricate the kind of soulful communion that Verezzi requires. "[T]he wily Matilda" successfully ensnares as well as blights her prey, in part because he cannot or will not, to borrow the Walkerian term, "impregnate" her with the irradiating spark of his *own* sympathetic/empathic energy (58). Initially suspicious of and even repelled by Matilda, Verezzi nonetheless refuses to look into her corroded heart and instead remains obsessed with the imperious demands of his own "softened soul" (31). Posing as his ethereal soul-mate, Matilda draws the duped Verezzi into the world of libertine lust through the portals of sentimental love. As his shrewd seductress is well aware, "the hapless Verezzi" is susceptible in more ways than one (5).

In one of the novel's more vivid set-pieces, Matilda's "syren illusions" involve an actual siren song:

"Suffer me to retire for a few minutes," said Matilda.

Without waiting for Verezzi's answer, she hastily entered a small tuft of trees. Verezzi gazed surprised; and soon sounds of such ravishing melody stole upon the evening breeze, that Verezzi thought some spirit of the solitude had made audible to mortal ears etherial music.

He still listened—it seemed to die away—and again a louder, a more rapturous swell, succeeded.

The music was in unison with the scene—it was in unison with Verezzi's soul; and the success of Matilda's artifice, in this respect, exceeded her most sanguine expectation. (*CW*, V, 59)

That Matilda plays Verezzi as easily as she plays her harp suggests a rather sophisticated skepticism on the young Shelley's part toward his own ideal of sympathetic correspondence. With her angelic instrument and "voice of celestial sweetness," Matilda is able to create "soul-touching melod[ies]" that prefigure the enchanting music that flows from *Alastor*'s veiled maid, from *Rosalind and Helen*'s central heroine, and from Claire Clairemont in "To Constantia" (57). Seen as descendents not of the virtuous sister-spirit Julia, but rather of the fierce imposter Matilda, these idealized Shelleyan singers look a bit more sinister, a bit more dangerous, a danger which the nexus between music and mingled being enhances.

In each of these works, *Zastrozzi* included, the male listener is ravished by the music he hears. He "dissolves in . . . consuming extacies" that anticipate, symbolize, or coincide with the sexual union he enjoys with the beautiful singer ("To Constantia," l. 12). This music, however, also ushers him into death, and not just the little death of sexual climax. In "To Constantia," Shelley eventually interrupts Claire's song and thus his own "voluptuous flight" toward dissolution (l. 22), but Lionel, the Poet, and Verezzi all ride the waves of sound past life's "dim boundaries" (*CW*, II, 39: *RH*, l. 1127). Yet Shelley's fear that the sister-spirit may prove to be a femme fatale is not the main issue here; or, rather, this suspicion emerges from a more overwhelming anxiety about his own propensity for self-involvement, his own tendency toward narcissistic desire. All three protagonists/personae just mentioned—Verezzi, the *Alastor* Poet, and Lionel—exemplify sentimental lovers whose utterly Shelleyan quests for sympathy actually keep them trapped within Selfhood: they discover, or conjure, gorgeous songstresses whose familiar voices chime with their own inner music. They are, in essence, narcissists who finally overcome the limits of the Self only after being serenaded by an impassioned Echo; their punishment—literally "consuming extacies"—turns out to be their reward.[55] They suffer/enjoy the erotic martyrdom that Shelley assigns to the most "self-possessed" seekers of mingled being (*Alastor*, Preface, 69).

The "affinity of eros and death" in Shelley, an issue at the heart of William Ulmer's recent study, thus involves more than regression fantasies, romantic despair, or even the problem of "desire-as-violence" that Ulmer so fruitfully explores (61, 60). Although Shelley saw sexual mingling as a potential escape route from the world of Self, he was all too aware that the noxious Selfhood of either partner could fatally contaminate this communion. It is important to note here that Shelley always regarded the Self as inextricably bound to the mortal realm and to the prison of the physical body.[56] Thoroughly annihilating or "dissolving" this "clay-formed dungeon" was for Shelley the most radical and effective method of exterminating the Self and Self-spawned appetite(s) (*L*, I, 35). The postcoital deaths he inflicts on so many of his characters serve—literally, in the case of Laon and Cythna—to burn away the final remnants of selfish desire as well as "the last clouds of cold mortality" that both envelop and emanate from the material Self (*Adonais*, l. 486). In some works, such as *Epipsychidion*, this fiery consummation involves the kind of Self-chastisement that Verezzi, the Poet, and Lionel must endure, while in *Laon and Cythna*, for example, Shelley launches a kind of pre-emptive strike on the lovers, whom he allows one blissful, Self-transcendent night of lovemaking but cannot quite trust with another.

Yet if postcoital fatalities abound in Shelley's poetic universe, postmortal coitus is also featured, most prominently and explicitly in the torrid "Epithalamium of Francis Ravaillac and Charlotte Cordé." Even in *Zastrozzi* it is the dead who unreservedly enjoy mingled being; in fact, postmortal mingling is the only kind of lovemaking that the novel freely endorses. Like so many of the "fierce transports" which pulsate through the novel (*CW*, V, 75), the literally "celestial transports" that Shelley depicts here occur within the enflamed imaginations and anticipations of his central characters (49). The young author introduces the theme of heavenly intercourse just at the point when Matilda, stepping up her attack on Verezzi's chastity, informs her victim that his beloved Julia is dead. Matilda's hoax—for the exquisite Julia still lives—allows her, it seems, to ravish Verezzi as he collapses once again into a state of "torpid insensibility" (11). Yet her scheme backfires in that Verezzi emerges from his swoon even more devoted to Julia than before. And, what is more, he has for the first time in the novel worked up some real passion for his angelic soul mate:

> "Julia! Julia!" exclaimed he, starting from the bed, as his flaming eye-balls were unconsciously fixed upon the agitated Matilda, "where art thou? Ah! thy fair form now moulders in the dark sepulchre! would I were laid beside thee! thou art now an ethereal spirit!" And then, in a seemingly triumphant accent, he added, "But, ere long, I will seek thy unspotted soul—ere long I will again clasp my lost Julia!" Overcome by resistless delirium, he was for an instant silent—his starting eyes seemed to follow some form, which imagination had portrayed in vacuity. (38)

Verezzi's outburst contains more than a hint of necrophilia: none too eager to seek out his adored Julia while she walks in beauty among the living, he now longs to lay down beside her mouldering body in that fine and private place, the grave. (Verezzi's desire to "clasp" the dead Julia really betrays his newly discovered sexual ardor. A Shelleyan buzzword that suggests a rather fierce erotic embrace, *clasp* is a key term in the "Epithalamium" and "Hymn to Intellectual Beauty," and in Demogorgon's admonitory speech at the close of *Prometheus Unbound*.) Yet for these Gothic lovers, the tomb is but a way station; their ultimate consummation will take place not in the world *of* but in the world "*beyond* the grave," where mortal Selfhood's "chain of clay" no longer binds (*PS*, I, 6: "Written in Very Early Youth" [emphasis mine]; *PS*, I, 120: "Epithalamium," l. 49). The alacrity with which Verezzi moves from Julia's "form," be it "fair" or foul, to her "ethereal spirit" reveals that incorporeal mingling is the only kind that really interests this quintessentially Shelleyan lover.[57]

That it was Julia, the novel's only "unspotted" character, who had introduced Verezzi to the notion of postmortal love confirms that this idea, "hallowed by the remembrance of . . . Julia," also enjoys the author's own imprimatur (*CW*, V, 73). With "her mild, heavenly countenance" and radiant aura of (feminine) selflessness, Julia offers Verezzi the kind of mild, heavenly, and

eternal love that Shelley himself, with his precocious awareness of love's violence and mutability, was already idealizing (29). (In *St. Irvyne*, for example,
the sage young author observes that Wolfstein's love for Megalena, "though
fervent and excessive, at first, was not of that nature which was likely to
remain throughout existence; it was like the blaze of a meteor at midnight,
which glares amid the darkness for awhile, and then expires" [*CW*, V, 136].)
And just as Julia's image, "revelling in [Verezzi's] breast," shields him from
the electric poison of Matilda's embrace, so too does Julia's theory of postmortal mingling and marriage seem to protect him from the spurious "earthly
paradise" that Matilda promises him (61, 87). Confronted yet again by what
Matilda terms her "faithful and ardent attachment" to him, Verezzi fervently
embraces—and dramatically embroiders—Julia's vision of a honeymoon in
heaven (52):

> "Think you . . . that because my Julia's spirit is no longer enshrined in
> its earthly form, that I am the less devotedly, the less irrecovably
> hers?—No! no! I was hers, I am hers, and to all eternity shall be hers:
> and when my soul, divested of mortality, departs into another world,
> even amid the universal wreck of nature, attracted by congeniality of
> sentiment, it will seek the unspotted spirit of my idolised Julia . . ."
>
> Matilda's whole frame trembled with unconquerable emotion, as
> thus determinedly he rejected her. (52)

In Verezzi's indignant speech, postmortal becomes postapocalyptic mingling,
a theme Shelley picks up in *St. Irvyne* and *The Wandering Jew*, and, ultimately, in *Prometheus Unbound*. Verezzi, like Wolfstein and Paulo/Ahasuerus
after him, rather histrionically gestures toward the end of the world as he
protests his literally undying love for his soul mate. The caddish Wolfstein
exploits apocalyptic imagery—the lovers will enjoy their "eternal, indivisible,
although immaterial union" against the backdrop of "nature's latest ruin" and
the "the face of heaven"—in order to ensure that Megalena obeys passion
rather than "prejudice" (*CW*, V, 135, 136: *SI*); while the tormented, death-
seeking Paulo, who also envisions postapocalyptic "rapture without measure"
with his beloved, has a more legitimate reason to look forward to the end of
the world (*PS*, I, 51: *WJ*, I. 319). Verezzi's motive for invoking apocalypse is,
on the face of things, much more straightforward, and more laudable, than
those of his fellow prognosticators: he simply wants to impress upon Matilda
just how unshakable his dedication to Julia really is.

Yet Verezzi's extravagent rhetoric, his insistence on embellishing Julia's
idea of posthumous love with references to "the universal wrecks of nature"
displaces/postpones so radically his (sexual) union with his beloved that
Matilda's ultimate triumph over her increasingly remote rival seems

inevitable. Though it is the "interesting softness" and "etherial form" of both the living and the (supposedly) dead Julia that press "on [Verezzi's] aching senses" throughout most of the novel, by the time Matilda sets her final trap,[58] Julia and the celestial minglings she promises have become for Verezzi "an unreal vision" (*CW*, V, 33, 48).[59] Potentially a precursor of the *Alastor* Poet, who follows his "Vision and Love" to the ultimate bower of bliss (l. 366), Verezzi falls victim to a more sordid fate. Susceptible at last to the temptations of the flesh, Verezzi succumbs to the "fatal passion" that consumes Matilda and that long ago compelled his father to seduce Olivia Zastrozzi (74). Thus, the revenge of Olivia's bastard son, Pietro Zastrozzi, hinges on the fact that Verezzi, Jr., proves himself to be his father's true son and a votary of libertine love. (Actually, Zastrozzi's vengeance is even more diabolical and more clever in that he has arranged for Verezzi to step into the role of ruined maiden that Olivia had tragically played.)

In the novel's bloody climax, Verezzi and his true love do finally achieve mingled being, though not of the sort either had anticipated. When Julia surprises Verezzi and Matilda in their Venetian hideaway, the horrified young man faints dead away. He returns to consciousness long enough to plunge a dagger into his bosom: "His soul fled without a groan, and his body fell to the floor, bathed in purple blood" (*CW*, V, 88). Just as she had acted as a go-between in Zastrozzi and Verezzi's psychosexual combat, Matilda now negotiates a union between the two lovers she had tried so desperately to dissever: her eyes "scintillat[ing] with a fiend-like expression,"

> She advanced to the lifeless corse of Verezzi—she plucked the dagger from his bosom—it was stained with his life's blood, which trickled fast from the point to the floor. She raised it on high, and impiously called upon the God of nature to doom her to endless torments, should Julia survive her vengeance. (88)

After a perfunctory chase around the chamber, Matilda succeeds in capturing her rival and "stabb[ing] her in a thousand places" (89). The "life's blood" of Verezzi, which covers the dagger, now flows into Julia's own "ensanguined stream," though it is Matilda who revels in "exulting pleasure" during this bizarre orgy of erotic violence (89). The sensational marriage of carnality and carnage that Shelley stages in this, his first substantial composition, finds its ultimate form in the Dionysian dance that the dreaming poet witnesses in his last great work. But in *Zastrozzi*, Shelley allows his martyred couple a kind of triumph that he withholds from the promiscuous "maidens and youths" who mingle in the later work (*The Triumph of Life*, l. 149). Though Verezzi had betrayed his soul-mate and the ideal of spiritual love she exemplified, in his final act he regains some credibility as sentimental lover, eager to flee the prison of libertine love he had foolishly entered. In a tableau that Shelley will recreate and rearrange in many works to come, the dead lovers at last lie together, their nuptial bed presided over by the "mighty Shadow" of death, perhaps the most sublime sponsor of Shelleyan mingled being (*Alastor*, l. 306).

Postmortal Mingling: "Epithalamium"

Though it is another "awful shadow," that of Intellectual Beauty, which hovers over the bridal bower of Laon and Cythna, the voluptuous garden of *The Sensitive-Plant*, and the silent pine forest of "To Jane. The Recollection," death remains the preeminent matchmaker in Shelley's early texts. *Henry and Louisa*, an ambitious poem which Shelley wrote just after completing *Zastrozzi* and just after Harriet Grove's initial retreat, transplants the novel's Gothic *liebestod* onto an Egyptian battlefield. Here again, it is the hero's masculine "selfishness" and lust—this time for military glory—that tears "the soul-spun ties of tenderness" that bind him to his beloved (*Esdaile* 131, 132: I. 8, 16). (However, Henry, racked with "remorseful pain" by poem's end, definitely overtakes Verezzi on the road to redemption [*Esdaile* 140: II. 223].) As pointed out in the previous chapter, *Henry and Louisa* allowed the poet both to lament the loss of his cousin-fiancée and imaginatively to reunite and merge with her as a sexually transformed recipient *and* donor of "Dear Woman's love" (*Esdaile* 133: I. 60). This poem also enabled Shelley to move beyond the hollow sensationalism that defines the final exit of *Zastrozzi*'s doomed lovers. Henry and Louisa's double death not only catapults them into the realm of postmortal, incorporeal love that the novel celebrates—"Despising self, their souls can know / All the delight love can bestow"—but it also achieves a larger significance within the world of religious fanaticism, political tyranny, and military strife that they leave behind (*Esdaile* 143: II. 298–99). More akin to Laon and Cythna than to Verezzi and Julia, these romantic martyrs will help perpetuate "Virtue" and "Affection"—antitheses of "selfish Prejudice"—in the hearts of those who hear their story (*Esdaile* 143, 137: II. 295, 301; I. 151). The site of their sacred consummation also will be a kind of holy place that instills fear and dread in the soldiers and despots who pass by and that comforts the victims of these "human hounds of blood" (*Esdaile* 143: II. 306). Martyrdom, mingled being, and social amelioration: this will prove to be an almost unbeatable combination in the strange world of Shelleyan eros.

We encounter this magical nexus in the "production" that the new resident of Oxford's University College hoped would make his most recent volume, *Posthumous Fragments of Margaret Nicholson*, "sell like wildfire" (*L*, I, 23). "Fragment. Supposed to be an Epithalamium of Francis Ravaillac and Charlotte Cordé," composed in October or November 1810, perhaps can best

be described as a piece of visionary pornography, a dream vision in which the
sleeper becomes a voyeur who witnesses the heavenly intercourse of the
poem's title characters. But Shelley elevates both the dreamer's (un)con-
sciousness and the couple's "maddening passion" by infusing the poem with
political and social significance (*PS*, I, 121: l. 85). The poem's context, as well
as its content, establishes its republican credentials[60] and thus links the lovers'
celestial minglings with radical reform on earth. "Epithalamium" follows an
untitled poem that energetically attacks the "Ambition, power, and avarice"
embodied by the "Monarchs of earth" (*PS*, I, 115, 116: ll. 1, 37). Shelley, or,
rather, the pseudonymous John Fitzvictor, singles out this poem in his
"Advertisment" as being "intimately connected with the dearest interests of
universal happiness" (*PS*, I, 114). "Epithalamium" picks up its predecessor's
themes—"the woes of lost mankind," "the ceaseless rage of Kings"—and
even treats the reader to the sight of Satan welcoming defeated despots into
their new home, a scenario that "Ambition, power, and avarice" anticipates in
its concluding lines (*PS*, I, 118: "Epithalamium," ll. 5, 6). Shelley's boldest
stroke, in terms of politicizing his erotic wedding poem, is to select as the
bride and groom two tyrannicides, Charlotte Corday d'Armont, murderer of
Marat, and Francois Ravaillac, who assassinated Henry IV. Executed themselves, Charlotte and "Francis" become in Shelley's poem martyred revolutionaries who have earned "an endless night . . . of bliss" in their heavenly
"nuptial bed" (*PS*, I, 122, 121: ll. 101–2, 72). We can only speculate whether
Laon and Cythna, pacifist descendents of this rather bloodthirsty Shelleyan
couple, mingle in "eternity's bowers" as ecstatically as the lusty Francis and
Charlotte (*PS*, I, 177: "Song: 'Ah! Faint are her limbs'").[61]

     If the postmortal lovers of "Epithalamium" share a family resemblence
to Laon and Cythna, and, to a lesser degree, Zeinab and Kathema,[62] Francis
and Charlotte also mirror, and idealize, the poet and his own "dearest angel,"
Harriet Grove (*PS*, I, 121: "Epithalamium," l. 82).[63] On the verge of a final
break with Harriet, Percy casts her in the role of "sisterly co-revolutionary," a
role she had once seemed eager to play, and stages a glorious consummation
with her in a rather voluptuous version of heaven (Crook and Guiton 162):

FRANCIS

'Soft, my dearest angel, stay,
Oh! you suck my soul away;
Suck on, suck on, I glow, I glow!
Tides of maddening passion roll,
And streams of rapture drown my soul.
. . . .
Endless kisses steal my breath,
No life can equal such a death.'[64]

CHARLOTTE

'Oh! yes, I will kiss thine eyes so fair,
    And I will clasp thy form;
Serene is the breath of the balmy air,
    But I think, love, thou feelest me warm.
And I will recline on thy marble neck
    Till I mingle into thee.'

(*PS*, I, 121–22: ll. 82–86, 89–96)

This "Symphony" turns Percy-Francis and Harriet-Charlotte into beings who are at once more rarified and more carnal than the "frail mortals" they once were (*PS*, I, 121: l. 79).[65] It is as though Shelley has merged the "carnal pleasure" which Milton's Raphael warns Adam against with the "heav'nly Love" that the genial angel extols and experiences (*Paradise Lost*, VIII. 593, 592). Raphael's discreet portrait of angelic intercourse certainly left its mark not only on the "Epithalamium," where mingled being literally describes the lovers' communion, but also on later, major works such as *Alastor*, *Prometheus Unbound*, and *Epipsychidion*. Raphael tells his eager pupil,

Whatever pure thou in the body enjoy'st
(And pure thou wert created) we enjoy
In eminence, and obstacle find none
Of membrane, joint, or limb, exclusive bars:
Easier than Air with Air, if Spirits embrace,
Total they mix, Union of Pure with Pure
Desiring; nor restrained conveyance need
As Flesh to mix with Flesh, or Soul with Soul.

(*PL*, VIII. 622–29)

The angel's emphasis on purity would have appealed to the "susceptible" poet whose horror of contamination—including, and perhaps especially, sexual contamination—I explored in my previous two chapters. And as the "Union of Pure with Pure" which Raphael celebrates requires that both partners be pristine, the poet could imagine that he, too, and not simply his dream maiden, had cast off the ultimate Shelleyan contaminant, mortal Selfhood, bound by a "chain of clay" and emitting noxious vapors (*PS*, I, 120: "Epithalamium," l. 49).

While Milton's angel helped Shelley, and Adam, imagine the purity and thoroughness ("Total they mix") of heavenly mingled being, one of Shelley's favorite heroines lent his conception of spiritual intercourse a more voluptuous edge. She also lent Shelley some of the more memorable imagery that ignites the "Epithalamium." Pope's Eloisa melds "pleasing sense" and soulful communion during her rapturous dreams of Abelard—"All my loose soul unbounded springs to thee"—as well as envisions a postmortal reunion with her beloved that evades "sin" (*Eloisa to Abelard*, ll. 69, 228), which for Shelley would mean "the sordid lust of self" (*QM*, V. 90): "Death, only death, can break the lasting chain; / And here, even then shall my cold dust remain, / Here all its frailties, all its flames resign, / And wait, till 'tis no sin to mix with thine" (*Eloisa to Abelard*, ll. 173–76).[66]

A paradigm, in Shelley's eyes, of feminine self-sacrifice, as well as a woman of decidedly strong sexual desires, Eloisa guides Shelley through the treacherous "tides of maddening passion" and helps him envision a luxurious form of mingled being that nonetheless involves self-transcendence rather than "selfishness and every hateful passion" (*L*, I, 81).[67] By identifying, in the "Epithalamium" and elsewhere, not only with feminine selflessness but also with feminine desire,[68] Shelley hoped to enter imaginatively into a communion with his real-life *and* his fictive "second selves," a communion that was at once sisterly, sensuous, and spiritual. Eloisa had shown Shelley how to replace the sexual body with the sexualized soul, and neither "weak matter" nor the "detestible distinctions" of gender that the flesh inscribes could interfere with the rapturous mingling of Shelleyan (sister-)spirits (*PS*, I, 120: "Epithalamium," l. 44; *L*, I, 195).[69]

Death, dreaming, and mingled being intersect in "Epithalamium" and other early Shelleyan texts, in part because the poet's first love, Harriet Grove, proved to be such an elusive figure. Seldom seen, more seldom touched, Harriet, from the beginning of the cousins' relationship, seemed a shimmering, vanishing apparition which Percy in the end failed to arrest. "My Harriet is fled like a fast-fading dream," he laments in early 1810, and by the end of the year he must recognize that she is "for ever gone": "I thank thee dearest for the dream . . . I see a dark and lengthened vale, / The black view closes with the tomb," a fitting epitaph for their love and for all the dreamy and grave-obsessed lyrics and Gothic tales that it inspired (*PS*, I, 85: "To St. Irvyne," l. 17; *PS*, I, 127, 128: "Melody to a Scene of Former Times," ll. 1, 29, 35–36). Feverish visions, the shadow of death, *and* the spectre of Selfhood will follow Shelley into his relationship with his second Harriet, but the most famous dream poem of the Harriet Westbrook Shelley era will attempt to exorcise and even transfigure some of the demons that haunted the poet's erotic imagination.

Consentaneous Love: *Queen Mab*

As *Queen Mab* and the numerous lyrics addressed to his "fair girl" make clear, Shelley at times saw Harriet Westbrook as a kind of bright angel who irradiated and purified both his world, and, more important, himself (*PS*, I, 227: "To Harriet" ["Never, O never shall yonder Sun"]). If Percy rescued Harriet from (perceived) paternal tyranny, she in turn rescued him from the despair and self-contempt that enveloped him following the loss of Harriet Grove. And the emotional security and sense of regeneration that the poet's first marriage temporarily offered him allowed him to move beyond the merely personal concerns and complaints that had dominated his writings during his cousin's ascendency. That his marriage to Harriet coincided with Percy's most energetic and wide-ranging efforts as a hands-on political activist suggests that her unwavering love enabled the poet vigorously to cultivate "a wider sympathy" (*CW*, I, 284: *LC*, II, 318).[70]

"Whose eyes have I gazed fondly on, / And loved mankind the more? / Harriet! on thine," Shelley asks and answers in the Dedication to *Queen Mab* (ll. 7–8).[71] This Dedication picks up the theme that runs through all of the lyrics entitled "To Harriet"—the protective and revivifying power of her "love-beaming gaze"[72]—as well as goes a bit farther in that it identifies Harriet as her husband's "purer mind" (*PS*, I, 228: "To Harriet" ["Never, O never"]; *QM*, Dedication, l. 9).[73] In one half-line, Shelley accomplishes that Self-transformation so crucial to his sexual psychology: he discards two of (his own) Selfhood's most visible incarnations—the corrupt body and the masculine gender that this body has imposed on him—by merging with a loving and *pure* sister-spirit. In this gently erotic lyric, Harriet and Percy achieve mingled being through a metaphysical sleight-of-hand, but *Queen Mab* itself suggests that Shelley may be ready to admit "sensation" into the sanctuary of love.

A poem that ultimately offers a redeemed and redemptive sexuality, *Queen Mab* does not make a very auspicious start. The familiar Shelleyan dichotomy of body and soul is in full bloom here, with the heroine's "sinless soul" literally splitting off from her "bodily frame" (I. 11, 133). Though the poet describes Ianthe's form as "lovely," "fair," and even "heavenly," he cannot help but imagine "putrefaction's breath" as infecting it with "loathsomeness and ruin" (I. 16, 19, 18, 21). Despite the potentially erotic situation of the dream-vision's frame—Ianthe's lover Henry hovering over her couch as she slumbers—Shelley initially deflects the poem's sexual energies away from the body and toward its ideal double, the "free, . . . disembodied soul" (I. 165).

The passage wherein Mab liberates Ianthe's spiritual from her physical being ends up featuring the sexualized soul, so prominently displayed in the "Epithalamium." "All beautiful in naked purity," Ianthe's voluptuous Soul "Pants for its sempiternal heritage, / And ever-changing, ever-rising still, / Wantons in endless being" (I. 132, 149–51). (This in contrast to her body, which "Fleets through its sad duration rapidly; / Then, like a useless and worn-out machine, / Rots, perishes, and passes" [I. 154–56].) Yet Ianthe's "glorious change" is a temporary one (I. 192); while earlier Shelleyan figures such as Verezzi and Julia, Henry and Louisa, and Charlotte and Francis chart a one-way course toward postmortal (mingled) being, Ianthe goes on a circuitous journey that culminates in her return to material existence and her reunion with her mortal lover. Implicit in this revised flight pattern is Shelley's new-found hope in the power of love, including (sanctified) sensual love, to radically transform earth and all its "grovelling passions" (L, I, 208).[74]

Throughout *Queen Mab*, Shelley underscores just how crucial such a transformation is. Ianthe's guided tour, in Cantos II through VII, of the premillenial world, allows her, and Shelley himself, to confront humanity's darkest passions without participating in them. Imaginatively coalescing with his heroine's pristine Spirit just as he did with his wife's "purer mind," Shelley scrutinizes mortal crimes and woes while lifting himself above the "taint of earth-born atmospheres" (IV. 153). When the Fairy Mab "rend[s] / The veil of mortal frailty," Shelley and Ianthe, like Prometheus in his encounter with the Furies, behold terrible sights that torture yet "gird [their] soul[s] / With new endurance, till the hour arrives / When they shall be no types of things which are" (*PU*, I. 643–45).

Although sexual corruption is but one of the vices that Mab puts on display, its "venomed exhalations" permeate the entire dystopia she exposes (IV. 84). Even in the final celebratory canto, we are reminded that "prostitution's venomed bane" has "Poisoned the springs of happiness and life" (IX. 87, 88);[75] each of the poem's references to pollution, pestilence, contagion, and poison—and there are many—thus partakes of this primal taint. When it comes to "the connection of the sexes," the Pandemian Venus is clearly in charge (*PS*, I, 370: Note to "Even love is sold" [V. 189]). Her "evil and injurious Love," to borrow from Shelley's translation of the *Symposium*, infects the human and natural worlds with "blights and diseases" that only the purifying flame of Uranian love can heal (Notopoulos 428).

Worst of all, Venus Pandemos is the handmaiden and mirror image of selfishness. Though selfishness and Pandemian love are implicitly joined throughout the poem, Shelley linguistically binds them in phrases such as "the sordid lust of self" and "gross and sensual self" (V. 90; VII. 96). And in Canto V, when Shelley formally introduces his personified version of selfishness, he presents it as feminine—"Twin-sister of religion"—and as "Unblushing, hardened, sensual, and vile," a perfect character sketch of the Pandemian Venus herself (V. 22, 32). Yet by the end of this canto, selfishness, as well as her boon companion sensualism, has undergone a sex change; now the masculine figure of Time, iconically and verbally linked with "hoary-headed selfishness,"[76] becomes the representative both of Self and of Self-serving sexuality: "a penitent libertine" who will "Look back, and shudder at his younger years" (V. 249, 258, 259). Anxious to set the stage for a feminine utopia, Shelley had to free the feminine principle from Venus Pandemos' blighted precincts and displace this "selfish beauty's" sins onto her male counterpart, the diseased and decrepit libertine (V. 191).

Time, the "hoary giant" and paradigm of masculine Selfhood (IX. 24), makes his final exit in Canto IX, where, as Barbara Gelpi points out, this "patriarchal destroyer of destructive patriarchal rule" flees "and the earth comes under the sway of a force given a feminine gender" (*Shelley's Goddess* 78):

> . . . slow and gradual dawned the morn of love;
> . . . .
> Then steadily the happy ferment worked;
> Reason was free; and wild though passion went
> Through tangled glens and wood-embosomed meads,
> Gathering a garland of the strangest flowers,
> Yet like the bee returning to her queen,
> She bound the sweetest on her sister's brow,
> Who meek and sober kissed the sportive child,
> No longer trembling at the broken rod.[77]
>
>   (IX. 38, 49–56)

Gelpi's astute reading of this beautiful passage illuminates how the feminized figure of Reason, linked as a "mother/sister" to the girlish figure of passion, exemplifies "the idealized feminine, the ensphered goddess . . . who offers an alternative to the violence and injustice of the patriarchal given of the world" (*Shelley's Goddess* 78, 79).[78] In fact, Reason is but one of the members of what turns out to be a powerful collective feminine entity: peace, radiant in her "vestal purity," earth, with her newly "fertile bosom," Necessity, the "mother of the world," and, most important, love, with her beautiful and protective "canopy," all band together to transform the "wild and miserable world" into a vibrant "paradise of peace" (III. 68; VIII. 109; VI. 198; IV. 7; VI. 12; VIII. 238).

Anticipating the maternal, or sororal, paradise that Prometheus and his beloved Oceanides create, *Queen Mab*'s new Eden also glances back to the postmortal playgrounds where earlier Shelleyan lovers frolicked and erotically intermingled. Like the heavenly bowers that Shelley envisions in works such as *Zastrozzi* and "Epithalamium," the renovated world he presents in *Queen Mab* is a "haven of perpetual peace" and, more crucially, a "sweet place of bliss / Where friends and lovers meet to part no more" (IX. 20, 15–16). Shelley's tributes in his final canto to the "sacred sympathies of soul and sense" and "sensation's softest tie" indicate that, in the poem's perfectibilian plot, the (purified) material world ultimately will provide a healthful climate for the unreserve of mingled being, a pristine atmosphere that in previous works had been furnished solely by heaven's "viewless ether" (*QM*, IX. 36, 77; *PS*, I, 119: "Epith.," l. 26). As Mab reveals in the passionate apostrophe that opens Canto IX, the "happy Earth" will at last become the "reality of Heaven" (l. 1). And where selfish sensualism was, consentaneous love shall be.

Even before the climactic final cantos, Shelley offers us a few hints as to how this new erotic order might express itself. Early on in the poem, Ianthe's celestial journey affords her a panoramic view of the entire universe, whose planets and stars dance together as "infinite orbs of mingling light," much like the "Ten thousand orbs involving and involved" which whirl into the fourth act of *Prometheus Unbound*:

> Below lay stretched the universe!
> . . . .
> Countless and unending orbs
> In mazy motion intermingled,
> Yet still fulfilled immutably
> Eternal nature's law,
> Above, below, around,
> The circling systems formed
> A wilderness of harmony;
>
> (*QM*, VI. 146; *PU*, IV. 241;
> *QM*, II. 70, 73–79)

Similar to the earth(l)y interchanges that Shelley will celebrate in poems such as *The Sensitive-Plant* and "Love's Philosophy," this harmonious cosmic mingling—which becomes more explicitly eroticized in *Prometheus Unbound* IV—sets the standard for sexual "connexion" in the human realm. As the Fairy Mab points out, humanity so far has failed miserably to live up to this lofty standard: "The universe / In nature's silent eloquence, declares / That all fulfil the works of love and joy,—/ All but the outcast man" (III. 196–99). But, in a passage that glances back to Canto II's vision of a lovingly interpenetrating cosmos, Mab assures the despondant Ianthe that the earth and her inhabitants eventually will join this universal dance, this cosmic marriage:

> How sweet a scene will earth become!
> Of purest spirits, a pure dwelling-place,
> Symphonious with the planetary spheres;
> When man, with changeless Nature coalescing,
> Will undertake regeneration's work.
>
> (VI. 39–43)

While here it is with Nature that humankind coalesces, Mab previews in Canto IX the sexual mergers that men and women will enjoy with each other, when "that sweet bondage which is freedom's self, / . . . rivets with sensation's softest tie / The kindred sympathies of human souls" (IX. 76–78). The Fairy's references—in Canto VI and again in Canto IX (line 8)—to the regenerated earth as the pure abode of "purest spirits" suggests that the sublunary paradise will be merely a repetition in the finite world of the incorporeal Edens and "etherial palace[s]" that Shelley so lovingly constructs in his early works (*QM*, II. 29). But Mab's promise that "sensation" will help secure the sympathetic union of "human souls" hinges on the (sexual) body's honored place in this "paradise of peace" (VIII. 238).[79] "The sacred sympathies of soul *and* sense" are thus destined to overcome both "dull and selfish chastity" and "unenjoying sensualism" (IX. 36 [emphasis mine], 84; V. 195).

In the "Epithalamium," we have seen how Shelley blends the sensual and the spiritual to create his ideal form of mingled being, a phrase that, as the editors of *The Poems of Shelley* point out, expresses the poet's "sense . . . of combined sexual and spiritual mutuality" (*PS*, I, 511: note to "The Sunset," line 8). But in "Epithalamium" and, more explicitly, in *Queen Mab*, it is the spark of feminine energy, or love, that infuses this ideal with "Life, light, and rapture," the gifts Ianthe is to bestow upon her lover Henry when she returns from Mab's Hall of Spells (IX. 211). A lyrical interlude that the poet inserts midway through Mab's long lecture illuminates how the spiritual, the sensual, and the feminine coalesce within the realm of Shelleyan eros:

> All touch, all eye, all ear,
> The Spirit felt the Fairy's burning speech.
> O'er the thin texture of its frame,
> The varying periods painted changing glows,
>   As on a summer even,
> When soul-enfolding music floats around,
>   The stainless mirror of the lake
>   Re-images the eastern gloom,
> Mingling convulsively its purple hues
>   With sunset's burnished gold.

(VI. 1–10)

Here is one of those quintessentially Shelleyan moments of intersubjective communion, or "affect attunement," that Barbara Gelpi has described so well in her remarkable reading of *Prometheus Unbound*.[80] "Affect attunement" is developmental psychologist Daniel Stern's version of Lacanian mirroring between mothers and infants; in Gelpi's pithy summary, it "builds on the

infant's . . . capacity for amodal perception," Stern's term for "the infant's
extraordinary and active power to perceive and organize experience across
different sensory modalities":

> [Affect attunement] involves the mother's showing the infant that she
> shares the feeling of a moment, such as sudden joy or slight bewilder-
> ment or disappointment, not by mimicking the infant's acts of facial
> expressions but by a virtually instantaneous response in another sensory
> modality. (*Shelley's Goddess* 18, 19)

In Mab's and Ianthe's empathic "dialogue," not only do the Fairy and the
Spirit share one another's feelings, emotions *and* sense perceptions, but they
also share the infantile and maternal roles that Stern and Gelpi elucidate.

On the one hand, the Queen of Spells is also Queen of the linguistic
domain, much like "the mother-educator" whom Gelpi profiles in the first two
chapters of *Shelley's Goddess* (66). With her divine omniscience and her
"burning speech," Mab is a kind of supreme mother to the malleable, daughterly Soul of Ianthe; in the passage I have quoted, language is her mode of
expression, while Ianthe, like Stern's amodally responsive infant, "perceive[s]
and organize[s]" and *expresses* herself somatically, if we can call her etherial
"frame" a body. But Gelpi's account of Sternian "affect attunement" also
allows us to see how Ianthe herself takes on the maternal role when she shows
Mab, now in the child's (subject) position, that she literally feels the import of
the Fairy's "burning speech." Ianthe conveys to Mab "that she shares the feeling of [the] moment," not by "mimicking" or echoing Mab's mode of communication—language—"but by a virtually instantaneous response in another
sensory modality": "O'er the thin texture of [the Spirit's] frame, / The varying periods [of Mab's speech] painted changing glows."

It seems strange to be discussing the "sensory modalities" of spiritual
beings, but Shelley's own language forces us to embrace such a paradox. The
complexity and thoroughness of the intersubjective exchange, as seen through
the lens of psychoanalytic theory(s), gains even greater resonance in Shelley's presentation, which adds a spiritual dimension that psychoanalytic
accounts generally ignore. In the passage at hand, "the functions of sense,"
and even the organs themselves ("all eye, all ear"), flourish within the realm
of the spirit (*Alastor*, Preface, 69); and this allows Mab and Ianthe to achieve
a truly extraordinary form of sympathetic attunement, one that resembles the
"rapport" that the mesmerist or "magnetist" must achieve with his patient.
When, at the beginning of the poem, Mab "pour[s] the magic of her gaze /
Upon the maiden's sleep," she seems to be infusing Ianthe with her own magnetic fluid, the mesmerist's chief elixir (I. 77–78). Moreover, their wonderful
moments of heightened intersubjectivity, as in the interlude discussed here,

suggest that Mab and Ianthe are, like the mesmerist and her patient, "in communication" or "in rapport."[81] Finally, Mesmer's notion of "mixed action" illuminates the way the Fairy and the Spirit interact both sensually and spiritually. In J. P. F. Deleuze's summary of one of animal magnetism's key principles, "Man is composed of a body and a soul; and the influence he exerts participates the properties of both. It follows that there are three actions in magnetism: first, physical; second, spiritual; third, mixed action" (21). Mesmerism and Shelleyan mingled being will intersect more dramatically in the second act of *Prometheus Unbound* and in the late lyric "The Magnetic Lady to Her Patient"; in *Queen Mab*, the vital fluid of animal magnetism flows gently and almost imperceptively between the Fairy and the Spirit.

Mab and Ianthe's is an exemplary interchange, one that the poem suggests must be imitated within earth's precincts as well. Sensual and spiritual, it is also, perhaps most crucially, feminine. Coming as it does just after the Fairy's promise that "hoary-headed selfishness" and "libertine" Time, both gendered male, ultimately will suffer defeat, the communion of sister-spirits that opens Canto VI emerges as the new paradigm of self-other relationship, with feminine mutuality supplanting masculine Selfhood and domination.[82]

The poet's glowing portrait of Mab and Ianthe's "reciprocal attunement"—psychoanalyst Jessica Benjamin's term—thus evokes the Shelleyan ideal of sisterly intimacy as well as the primary bond of mother and child, but it also conjures the more overtly erotic interplay of perfectly attuned lovers (27). The intricate simile Shelley develops in the second half of the stanza quoted earlier brings out the subtle eroticism that suffuses the opening lines. Mesmerized, perhaps literally, by her mentor's visionary sermon, Ianthe feels and reflects back to Mab the Fairy's own meanings and emotions,

> As on a summer even,
> When soul-enfolding music floats around,
> The stainless mirror of the lake
> Re-images the eastern gloom,
> Mingling convulsively its purple hues
> With sunset's burnished gold.

> (VI. 5–10)

As mentioned in the discussion of *Zastrozzi*, music, especially when composed or performed by women, is almost always for Shelley a potent erotic force, an aphrodisiac that inspires and accompanies some of his texts' most memorable moments of mingled being. In this passage, Mab's "varying periods" become "soul-enfolding music" that echoes the "soul-touching melod[ies]" of *Zastrozzi*'s Matilda and anticipates the ravishing harmonies that the veiled maid, Helen, and Claire-Constantia each create (*CW*, V, 57).

Yet unlike the "life-dissolving sound[s]" that her sister-symphonists produce, Mab's music does not prove to be a death knell for her audience (*CW*, II, 40: *RH*, l. 1166). Ianthe will chart a very different trajectory than that of her male counterparts—Verezzi, the Poet, Lionel, and Shelley himself—who must actually die to their own masculine Selfhood as they experience the "consuming extacies" of music and mingled being ("To Constantia," l. 11). Already a feminine exemplar of "sweet and sacred love," Ianthe is illuminated and (inter)penetrated but not annihilated by the flame of love (and knowledge) that Mab shares with her (*QM*, IX. 208). Her task is to return to earth in order to transmit Mab's lessons and, most important, the spark of "consentaneous love" that accompanies them (VIII. 108); that her lover Henry is to be the first recipient of this boon suggests that for him, unlike his aforementioned Shelleyan brethren, the vital spark will kindle "soft fires" and "flames innocuous," such as those that Darwin's electrified lovers experience (*The Botanic Garden, Economy of Vegetation* I. vii. 356, 352).

The beautiful imagery at the heart of Shelley's elaborate simile helps us envision this flame that burns but consumes not. Recasting Mab and Ianthe's intimate communion as the interplay between a glowing sunset and a calm lake, the poet fashions one of his earliest reflexive images.[83] The watery mirror of the lake reflects—or "re-images," in Shelley's more active locution—the sunset's "burnished gold," while remaining unharmed by the "orb of fire" itself (*PS*, I, 360: Note to *QM*, I, 242–43). Moreover, the lake not only mirrors/merges with the sunset, but it also allows, by uniting on its own surface eastern "gloom" with western "gold," various elements of the sunset to come together visually, and, as the phrase *mingling convulsively* suggests, sexually.[84] Technically, the verb *mingling* could have as its subject the gloom or the lake, a grammatical ambiguity that nicely captures the way all of the primary elements—stainless water, purple gloom, and burnished sunlight—interact as agents *and* recipients of a sublime sympathetic-erotic power, emblematized here as "soul-enfolding music." Three and a half years later, in the "Hymn to Intellectual Beauty," "the hues and harmonies of evening" that Shelley invokes in this passage appear as avatars of the "Spirit of BEAUTY," whose own unseen shadow "floats" like the music that caresses the lake and the sunset in *Queen Mab* ("Hymn," ll. 8, 13, 2). In the millennial cantos of the earlier work, this sublime but "inconstant" Power, or a force analagous to it, will take up permanent residence on the radically transformed earth and thus ensure that the passionate minglings that occur here express only the "sacred sympathies of soul and sense" and not the appetites of "gross and sensual self" ("Hymn," l. 3; *QM*, IX. 36; VII. 96).

Reading backward to the original referents of the *Queen Mab* simile—the Fairy and the Spirit of Ianthe—we can now see their communion as intensely erotic; having discovered, with Mab's help, what Benjamin calls "the intersubjective foundation of erotic life," Ianthe can and *must* share her knowledge and her joy with those who remain within "the mortal scene" (*The Bonds of Love* 29; *QM*, I. 88). As Mab tells her pupil early in the poem, it is not "virtue's only meed, to dwell / In a celestial palace, all resigned / To pleasurable impulses": "Learn to make others happy," she admonishes, "This is thine high reward" (II. 59–61, 64, 65). Mab's final instruction to Ianthe will be a more specific version of this sweeping command: "Go, happy one, and give that bosom joy / Whose sleepless spirit waits to catch / Light, life and rapture from thy smile" (IX. 209–11).[85] The Queen of Spells even equips the Spirit with this efficacious smile. Shortly after her "burning speech" envelops and irradiates Ianthe's ethereal frame, Mab silently assuages the Spirit's lingering despair over the "wild and miserable world": "The Fairy calmly smiled / In comfort, and a kindling gleam of hope / Suffused the Spirit's lineaments" (VI. 2, 12, 23–25).[86] Again, as in their previous exchange, communication is instant, "amodal," and radically empathic. Most crucial here is the "kindling gleam of hope," which glances back to Harriet's "gleaming" love in the poem's Dedication and forward to the "flame / Of consentaneous love" that Ianthe and Henry must help light (Dedication, l. 1; VIII. 107–8). In the circuit of sex and sympathy that the poem sets up, Mab, with her glowing form,[87] "burning speech" and incandescent smile, communicates the vital spark to Ianthe, who must then, like Shelley's own sister-spirits in the Field Place nursery, transmit this "electric life," and love, to her beloved Henry (*Defence* 508).

Yet, as the poem closes, Henry is still waiting to be inducted into the magic circle; as Sperry points out, "there is something extraordinarily tentative about the posture of the attendant Henry as he bends over Ianthe . . . At the end of *Queen Mab* Ianthe barely awakens, and the smile which Henry so patiently awaits is intimated but never actually arrives" (*Shelley's Major Verse* 18). "The joys which mingled sense and spirit yield"—joys vividly present in Ianthe and Mab's exchange(s)—remain just out of reach for the suppliant Henry, worshipping like the poet himself at the shrine of "Dear Woman's love" (*QM*, IV. 158; *Esdaile* 133: *Henry and Louisa*, I. 60). So too do "spring's awakening breath" and "sunny smile" hover just outside the frame of the poem, promising but not yet delivering the universal regeneration that Mab allows the "surpassing Spirit" of Ianthe to glimpse (IX. 167, 170; III. 15). In *Queen Mab*, Shelley has almost, but not quite, imported the unreserve of mingled being into the earthly sphere, almost revealed how the "flame of consentaneous love" can burn both passionately *and* purely for its votaries.

This fragile faith in an unselfish, exalted form of sexual love, crucial both to the thesis and to the emotional core of Shelley's first utopian poem, will soon be shattered by the poet's own compulsion to "Pick flaws" in the "close-woven happiness" with Harriet that the poem's Dedication celebrates (*PS*, I, 433: "Evening: To Harriet"). As the Shelleys' marriage crumbles and

Percy directs his own sexual energy elsewhere—first toward Mrs. Boinville's lovely daughter Cornelia Turner and then toward the even more magnetic Mary Godwin—the "delirious and distempered dream[s]" of Pandemian love return in full force, always ready to eclipse the poet's increasingly elaborate and rapturous visions of Uranian Venus' voluptuous but "undefiled Paradise" (*L*, I, 384; *S-P*, I. 58).

5

THE UNRESERVE OF MINGLED BEING

All Sympathies in One

Not until 1819 and the completion of the fourth act of *Prometheus Unbound* would Shelley orchestrate a purely celebratory scene of sexual union, one in which death plays neither matchmaker (as in "Epithalamium") nor sinister shadow (as in, for example, *Alastor*, "The Sunset," and *Laon and Cythna*).[1] But even in Shelley's consummate vision of mingled being, it is heavenly rather than human bodies that perform the Dionysian dance that signals universal liberation, universal ecstacy. Having time and again witnessed, experienced, and imaginatively explored passion's "wondrous power / To wither *or* to warm," Shelley, as he concludes his lyrical drama, seems compelled to elevate sexual desire into the cosmic realm, where innocently incestuous planets can perhaps instruct even "Spirits whose homes are flesh" how to winnow out Self-spawned desire from redemptive sexual love (*PS*, I, 191: "Passion: To the [Woody Nightshade]," emphasis mine; *PU*, IV. 544).

Yet, as we shall see when we turn to *Prometheus Unbound* IV, the nuptial masque performed by the Earth and the Moon, with all its stylized moves and transcendental impulses, still manages to convey a sense of felt experience. Shelley does not refine out of existence the human passions that inspired this astonishing erotic vision; the cosmic intercourse that the Earth and Moon enjoy is the climactic episode in an ongoing mythic saga starring, in various guises, the poet and his own sister-spouse, Mary Wollstonecraft Shelley. Written five and a half years after the couple's momentous first meeting, this ebullient setpiece captures better than any other Shelleyan text the "animation of delight"—*sexual* delight—that enveloped Percy and Mary during their first giddy months together (*PU*, IV. 322). In late 1819, after a series of personal tragedies and emotional upheavals that radically undermined their already volatile relationship, Percy and Mary, the original models for *Prometheus Unbound*'s planetary paramours, must now take their cue from their own idealized, textualized images if they hope to regain the "surpassing love" they once knew (*L*, I, 414).

In the play's fourth act, Percy has truly created a "prismatic and manysided mirror," one that "collects the brightest rays" from his and Mary's past, beautifies their distorted present, and projects "majesty and beauty" and *love* into their future (*Defence* 491). Of course, Shelley's concerns in *Prometheus Unbound* involve his "wider sympathy" with humankind and not merely his personal bond with Mary; but, as always for this poet, the sweeping political, social, and spiritual change forecast in his lyrical drama must find its impetus in individual desire, and must have as its daystars, to use another of Shelley's astronomical metaphors, such luminous and linked spirits as Prometheus and Asia, Earth and Moon—and Percy and Mary (*CW*, I, 284: *LC*, II. 318).

It was with the young Mary Godwin that the poet appears to have experienced "the unreserve of mingled being" for the first time. While Harriet Grove certainly inspired an intense ardor in her impetuous cousin, their erotic unions remained perforce within the realm of (his) dreams and literary productions. And one senses, in reading the poems and letters chronicling Shelley's first marriage, a certain lack of sexual fire between the poet and his "second" Harriet.[2] If "friendship & not passion was the bond of [his] attachment" to Harriet Westbrook Shelley, "a violent" and, he believed, "*lasting* passion" united him with the beautiful, brilliant daughter of William Godwin and Mary Wollstonecraft (*L*, I, 390, 394, emphasis mine). In these and other letters that Percy scribbled off to Harriet, Thomas Hogg, and Mary herself during the tempestuous summer and fall of 1814, sexual love emerges as a kind of salvific, transformative force: "How wonderfully I am changed!" Shelley exclaims in an effusive letter to Hogg, "Not a disembodied spirit can have undergone a stranger revolution!" (*L*, I, 403: 4 October 1814). Having met and mingled with his ideal spiritual twin, Shelley is "deeply persuaded that thus ennobled, [he will] become a more true & constant friend, a more useful lover of mankind, a more ardent asserter of truth & virtue" (*L*, I, 403). At this point, in the midst of his "pure and celestial felicity" with Mary (*L*, I, 403), all sympathies, to adapt a phrase from the *Discourse*, appear to be harmoniously blended: the couple's own emotional, intellectual, *and* physical sympathies have converged and thus allowed Percy's—and, one presumes, Mary's—sympathetic love for humanity to blossom as well. Akin to the symbiotic link between personal and humanitarian love Shelley establishes in the Dedication to *Queen Mab*—"Whose eyes have I gazed fondly on, / And loved mankind the more?"—the marriage of intimate and generalized sympathy celebrated in the letter to Hogg now integrates the eroticism that hovers just outside the borders of his epic poem, and, as it turned out, of his first marriage (*QM*, Dedication, ll. 7–8).

Not surprisingly, sex and sympathy merge most memorably in Shelley's 1818 fragment "On Love":

> If we reason, we would be understood; if we imagine, we would that the airy children of our brain were born anew within another's; if we feel,

we would that another's nerves should vibrate to our own, that the beams of their eyes should kindle at once and mix and melt into our own, that lips of motionless ice should not reply to lips burning with the heart's best blood. This is Love. This is the bond and sanction which connects not only man with man, but with every thing which exists. (473)

In this passage, *all* love is Eros—expansive, passionate, cohesive, life-affirming. Here, psychoanalyst Jean Laplanche's distinction between Eros and sexuality is pertinent:

Eros . . . differs from sexuality, the first discovery of psychoanalysis. Eros is what seeks to maintain, preserve, and even augment the cohesion and the synthetic tendency of living beings and of psychical life . . . [What] appears with Eros is the *bound and binding* form of sexuality . . . In the face of this triumph of the vital and the homeostatic, it remained for Freud . . . to reaffirm . . . a kind of antilife as sexuality, frenetic enjoyment [*jouissance*], the negative, the repetition compulsion . . . For the death drive does not possess its own energy. Its energy is libido. (Laplanche, *Life and Death in Psychoanalyis*, 123, quoted in Benjamin 263n25)

In her commentary on this passage, Jessica Benjamin writes, "Thus Laplanche argues, rightly, I think, that sexuality can be alloyed either with Eros or with death and destruction" (263n25), an insight which will be crucial when we look, briefly, at works such as *Alastor*, *Laon and Cythna*, "The Sunset," and, in greater detail, *Prometheus Unbound*.[3] To return to the Shelleyan text just quoted, no dark shadow of selfish (sexual) appetite comes between the intense interpersonal desire—one form of Eros—described in the first sentence and the sympathetic, vital, and, likewise, erotic love for "every thing which exists" invoked in the last. Moreover, in the essay's conclusion, union with the world—specifically, the natural world—abundantly recompenses the lover who fails to discover and mingle with his or her proper mate or "antitype":

[I]n solitude, or in that deserted state when we are surrounded by human beings and yet they sympathise not with us, we love the flowers, the grass and the waters and the sky. In the motion of the very leaves of spring in the blue air there is then found a secret correspondence with our heart. There is eloquence in the tongueless wind and a melody in the flowing of brooks and the rustling of the reeds beside them which by their inconceivable relation to something within the soul, awaken the spirits to a dance of breathless rapture, and bring tears of mysterious tenderness to the eyes. (474)

Again, a sympathetic *and* erotic current passes between and binds lover and (nonhuman) beloved. In a text so pervaded with melancholy and even despair, it is astonishing to find such an affirmation of a "sustaining Love" that inter-penetrates us even in our seeming solitude (*Adonais*, l. 481).[4]

As we survey the erotically themed texts that cluster around the essay "On Love" and the central relationship that inspired both its pessimism and its hope, we will see just how difficult it was for Shelley to maintain his faith in Eros, the "*binding* form of sexuality" which harmonizes with and stimulates our "wider sympathy" with all life. The October 1814 letter to Hogg quoted earlier reveals that this faith largely depended on the poet's "entire union" with an ideal sister-spirit, a feminine second self who protects him from (his own) sexuality's darker side (*L*, I, 402). This letter allows us to observe both versions of Shelleyan sexuality: the vital, cohesive force that emerges from time to time in the essay "On Love" and "the negative form of sexuality" wherein corrupt Selfhood and—as Benjamin observes—"death and destruc-tion" reign supreme (263n25). In fact, in his mythopoeic account of his segue from Harriet to Mary, Percy also portrays himself as moving from death-tend-ing sexuality, now yoked with the once-adored Harriet, to life-affirming Eros, whose avatar is the newest "object & sharer of [his] passion" (*L*, I, 390):

> I saw the full extent of the calamity which my rash & heartless union with Harriet: an union over whose entrance might justly be in[s]cribed
>   Lasciate ogni speranza voi ch'entrate!
> had produced. I felt as if a dead & living body had been linked together in loathsome & horrible communion . . . I wandered the fields alone. The season was most beautiful. The evenings were so serene & mild—I never had before felt so intensely the subduing voluptuousness of the impulses of spring. Manifestations of my approaching change tinged my waking thoughts, & afforded inexhaustible subject for the visions of my sleep. I recollect that one day I undertook to walk from Bracknell to my father's, (40 miles). A train of visionary events arranged themselves in my imagination until ideas almost acquired the intensity of sensations. Already I had met the female [Mary Godwin] who was destined to be mine, already had she replied to my exulting recognition, already were the difficulties surmounted that opposed an entire union. (*L*, I, 402)

Barbara Gelpi points out that "Jones's insertion of the name 'Mary Godwin' confuses Shelley's meaning, though he is more faithful than Shelley to the facts. The import of the passage . . . is that the image of an ideal woman *as yet unmet* obsessed him" (*Shelley's Goddess* 126). As Gelpi reminds us, at the time Shelley made this excursion to Field Place in late May or early June, he had already been introduced to Mary Godwin (during one of his frequent visits to Skinner Street). "We can be virtually certain, then," Gelpi continues, "that the fantasies of female perfection that occupied his long walk had not a little to do with the actual young woman he had recently met" (127). Gelpi rightly notes Shelley's "manipulation of the truth," both in his letter to Hogg and in his attempts to "mask his immediate and obsessive passion for Mary Godwin" while he visited with his mother and sisters at Field Place (126). Her reading of the letter and of the visit itself suggests how this new "spectral presence" might have interacted in Shelley's mind with other "phantasms from a shared period of intense past emotion," phantasms that would include his mother, his sister Elizabeth, and his beloved cousin Harriet Grove (126).

Yet in manipulating the facts, the chronology of events, Shelley remains loyal to a different kind of truth about his relationship with his new love. Mary did enter the poet's life as part of a "train of visionary events" involving a "destined" female, a prototypical "Being whom he loves" and who loves him (*Alastor*, Preface, 69). Glimpsed in dreams both ecstatic and distempered, briefly embodied by Harriet Grove, Harriet Westbrook, and even Cornelia Turner, and imaginatively (re)created as Julia, Louisa, Charlotte Cordé, and Ianthe, this sister-spirit had at last—or so it seemed to Shelley at the time—appeared in her full and radiant glory as the sublime Mary Godwin. While the unfortunate Harriet, the latest but not the last victim of the "Shelleyan declension from idealization to disillusion,"[5] is relegated to the hell of gross materiality and death-tending sexuality, Mary joins her mate in the privileged realm of Eros, where "ideas" and "sensations," the spiritual and the sensual, intermingle and where the individual lover participates in the general "voluptuousness of the impulses of spring."

Read alongside the poet's later accounts of his boyhood epiphany of Intellectual Beauty, this prose passage reveals how tightly Percy wove Mary into his own mythic autobiography and into his vision of an all-encompassing love, one that integrates philanthropy, eroticism, and sympathy (with the natural world as well as with other human beings). As Crook and Guiton argue, the "mystical experience" that Shelley describes, for example, in the "Hymn to Intellectual Beauty" and the Dedication to *Laon and Cythna* involves an "arousal of sexuality" as well as a "moral, intellectual, and imaginative" awakening (134). Ideally, then, sexuality need not interfere with other forms of love, including the Christlike selfless love which Shelley continuously struggled to embody. But an "awful LOVELINESS," a radiant "messenger of sympathies" must descend upon the heart of the questing lover in order to ensure that his or her desire remain pure, free of self-idolatry and "malignant . . . sensuality" ("Hymn," ll. 71, 42; *Prose* 142: "On *Memoirs of Prince Alexy Haimatoff*").

In the "Hymn" itself, the "SPIRIT fair" is a mysterious, impersonal, and genderless Power, but in *Laon and Cythna*'s dedicatory verses, this evanescent entity merges with the lyric's feminine subject and recipient, the "Child of love and light," Mary Shelley (*CW*, I, 251: *LC*, Dedication, l. 9). More precisely, Mary, Intellectual Beauty, and the season of renewal, springtime, interfuse in order to vitalize or "revive" the somnolent poet (*CW*, I, 252: *LC*, Dedication, l. 54). Looking back to his boyhood days at Syon House Academy, Shelley writes, "I do remember well the hour which burst / My spirit's sleep: a fresh May-dawn it was, / When I walked forth upon the glittering grass, / And wept" (*CW*, I, 251: *LC*, Dedication, ll. 21–24). When we recall that Percy first met Mary in May (1814) and that "sweet Maie" was one of his "cosy nicknames" for her (Holmes, *Pursuit*, 275), we see that the poet is transporting his beloved back to his own childhood, or early adolescence, where, in "a pure anticipated cognition," he first glimpsed her luminous spirit (*L*, II, 321, 438). Already linked in Percy's 1814 letter to Hogg with "the subduing voluptuousness of . . . spring," Mary is further identified with "that sweet time" in the Dedication's seventh stanza: "Thou Friend, whose presence on my wintry heart / Fell, like bright Spring upon some herbless plain, / How beautiful and calm and free thou wert / In thy young wisdom" (*L*, I, 402; "Hymn," l. 56; *CW*, I, 252: *LC*, Dedication, ll. 55–58). With the advent of Mary Wollstonecraft Godwin, "spring's awakening breath," foretold but never actually felt in *Queen Mab*, has finally arrived, and sex, sympathy, and selfless love should now harmoniously blend, at least in the poet's own experience (*QM*, IX. 167).

But if Percy linked Mary with springtime and its presiding deity, Intellectual Beauty, he also identified her with a more problematic image, that of the moon. As early as the fall of 1814, during their traumatic period of separation and debt-dodging, Shelley assigned to his beloved what would become her permanent symbol, one that plays a prominent and troubling role in the 1821 production, *Epipsychidion*:

> Mary love—we must be united. I will not part from you again after Saturday night. We must devise some scheme. I must return. Your thoughts alone can waken mine to energy. My mind without yours is dead & cold as the dark midnight river when the moon is down. It seems as if you alone could shield me fr{om} impurity & vice. If I were absent from you long I should shudder with horror at myself. (*L*, I, 414: 28 October 1814)

Images and ideas from this and other equally urgent letters that the poet wrote to his redemptive Mary during that wretched autumn find their way into *Alastor*, which contains Shelley's most vivid sex scene since the one that crowns the "Epithalamium." Though I do not want to suggest an equation between Percy and the Poet and Mary and the veiled maid, I do think that the "solitariness and desolation of heart" that Shelley experienced in late October and early November of 1814 significantly colored the tale of sexual discovery and loss that he composed a year later (*L*, I, 407). Having known with Mary the "pure & celestial felicity" of mingled being, the poet now felt desperately alone and, as his October 28 letter reveals, utterly exposed to "the impurity and vice" that comprises the flip side of the unalloyed erotic delight he enjoyed with his beloved (*L*, I, 403, 414). In order to ward off the negative, selfish, contaminating forms of desire—sexuality as "antilife," in Laplanche's term—that beseiged him at the time, Shelley basked in the soft, cleansing light of his ensphered lover whenever he could. And in her absence, he kissed her "εἰδῶλον κὲνον"—her insubstantial image or Lucretian simulacrum— before going to sleep, presumably to ensure that his dreams would quell rather than heighten the "feverish agitation & sickening disquietude" that he suf- fered during his "comfortless estrangement" from Mary (*L*, I, 420, 419, 414).

The Phases of the Moon

A simulacral lover, postcoital despair, and a hovering moon all figure prominently in *Alastor*, a poem that questions whether erotic love, so ideal- ized in the letters documenting Shelley's and Mary Godwin's courtship, really can rescue us from "unprofitable solitude," lift us out of the world of Self, and thus elevate us above "this dark scheme of things finishing in unfruitful death" (*L*, I, 419: 4 November 1814). The Poet's dream intercourse with his veiled maid contains all the crucial ingredients of an archetypal Shelleyan love scene: it takes place in a "natural bower," haunt of the cov- eted sister-spirit; it involves an entire union—intellectual, spiritual, and sen- sual—between a young man of feeling and his feminine second self; and its imagery is drawn in part from the world of science, where electricity's "per- meating fire" suffuses an erotically charged universe and, according to Dar- win's lyrical homage, kindles in the human frame a thrilling flame akin to sexual rapture (*Alastor*, ll. 147, 163; *The Botanic Garden, Economy of Veg- etation*, I. vii. 335–70). Moreover, the key question that the poem asks after presenting passion's trance is one that will echo throughout works such as "The Sunset," *Julian and Maddalo*, and *Epipsychidion*: "Were limbs and breath, and being intertwined / Thus treacherously?" (ll. 208–9). At his most optimistic, Shelley believed that "the sexual impulse" exemplified and but- tressed "all types of human and extrahuman attraction" (Notopoulos 408: *Discourse*; Abrams 298).[6] But it is sexuality's alliance with isolated Selfhood and not with communal ideals that *Alastor* in particular exposes. Rather than strengthen the Poet's putative bond with nature or his (extremely frail) ties to his fellow humans, his sexual initiation plunges him further into the "self- centred seclusion" that had prevented him from recognizing the "sweet human love" which the Arab maiden and other enamoured virgins offered (*Alastor*, Preface, 69, 203).

Intense, rapturous, and tragically brief, the Poet's passionate mingling with his veiled maid, though confined to the realm of dream, is nonetheless representative or "allegorical" of the real-life cycles of human desire (*Alastor*, Preface, 69). Having experienced "irresistible joy" and marvelous oneness with an ideal (in both senses of the word) lover, the Poet abruptly falls back into division, a condition which he had never before felt so keenly (l. 185). Estrangement, despair, and loneliness—these are some of the progeny of this and other Shelleyan sexual unions.[7] Even the sibling lovers Laon and Cyntha, blessed by the Uranian deity, can bridge the chasm between them only momentarily as they become "two restless frames in one reposing soul":

> Was it one moment that confounded thus
> All thought, all sense, all feeling, into one
> Unutterable power, which shielded us
> Even from *our own cold looks*, when we had gone
> Into a wide and wild oblivion
> Of tumult and tenderness?
>
> (*CW*, I, 337: *LC*, VI. 307–12, emphasis mine)

The aftermath of Laon and Cythna's lovemaking underscores the essential separateness of even those who share "such close sympathies":

> Cythna's sweet lips seemed lurid in the moon,
> Her fairest limbs with the night wind were chill,
> And her dark tresses were all loosely strewn
> O'er her pale bosom:—all within was still,
> And the sweet peace of joy did almost fill
> The depth of her unfathomable look;
>
> (*CW*, I, 338: *LC*, VI, 334–39)

Commenting on the two stanzas cited above, Richard Holmes writes, "The psychological acuity retained in 'even from our own cold looks' . . . and of '*almost* fill' . . . is remarkable in such a molten passage of erotic intensity" (*Pursuit* 396). Shelley is admitting, both in his visionary epic and in *Alastor*, one of "the sad realities of life" and love, one that constantly undermined his efforts to depict and experience absolute sexual and spiritual fusion: no matter how strenuously we try to create "one being" out of two linked souls, the way Percy once hoped to do with Mary, the sly serpent of difference inevitably invades the dream of primal unity (*CW*, I, 198: Mary Shelley's Note on *Alastor*; *L*, I, 414: 28 October 1814).

In *Laon and Cythna*, any residual distance or "coldness" between the lovers—starkly imaged by the "chill," corpselike Cythna of VI. 334–37—is dissolved by the "consuming flames" of their funeral pyre (*CW*, I, 403: *LC*, XII. 217). Leaving behind "life's envenomed dream," with its burden of material, isolated Selfhood, Laon and Cythna can commune endlessly as (sister-)spirits in their vast aërial dome, spectacular site for the postmortal mingling that Shelley had been envisioning since the 1809s Gothic production *Zastrozzi* (*CW*, I, 404: *LC*, XII. 242). Despite his efforts—and, in his early months with Mary Godwin, his *ability*—to divorce Eros and Thanatos,[8] Shelley's deep distrust of human sexuality usually compels him to escort his fictive lovers through "the dark gate of death" before he allows them the consummate (Shelleyan) form of mingled being: transcendental intercourse (*Alastor*, l. 211).

Moreover, Shelley finds several ways to draw his own sister-spouse into the pattern of deathly desire that he weaves in works such as *Alastor*, *Laon and Cythna*, and "The Sunset." While Mary's spirit shines through the central female figures of each work—the veiled maid, Cythna, and Isabel—it is her lunar incarnation that strikes me as particularly suggestive. In "The Sunset," the "broad and burning moon" presides over both sex and death: a young man ends up "dead and cold" after enjoying with his beloved "the unreserve of mingled being" (*PS*, I, 511);[9] while a paler moon casts a rather sinister light on the bridal bowers of *Alastor* and *Laon and Cythna*. In these last two texts, as Shelley presents the aftermath of sexual union, Cythna's lips seem "lurid in the moon," and the hills near the Poet's lonely dell appear "garish" as "the blue moon" hangs over the scene (*CW*, I, 338: *LC*, VI. 334; *Alastor*, ll. 194, 193). A beneficent, animating force in the October 1814 letter quoted earlier, Shelley's "presiding moon" has become in these passages a sign and source of alienation, emptiness, disillusion, and even decadence, both literal and figurative (Sperry, *Shelley's Major Verse*, 25).[10] Yet in both poems Shelley ultimately recuperates his lunar muse by linking her not only with mortality, but also with *post*mortality and the "mysterious paradise" that lies beyond "the foul grave" (*Alastor*, ll. 212, 217). Though such a paradise remains in *Alastor* merely an enticing possibility, for the Poet himself the shimmering form of the veiled maid and the visionary realm to which she belongs take on more reality, more substance than the "phantasmal," "vacant" world which now imprisons him (*Alastor*, ll. 697, 195). And it is "the great moon" whose receding gleam he follows into oblivion or rapture, a cresent moon whose "two lessening points of light" merge with the "beloved eyes" of the veiled maid (*Alastor*, ll. 646, 654, 332). Moon, maid, and, hovering behind them both, Mary thus conduct the Shelleyan Poet through the last threshold and, ideally, (back) into the passionate embrace of his feminine second self.

A redeemed, redemptive moon is also crucial to the conclusion of Shelley's visionary epic. In *Laon and Cythna*, the poet actually presents the postmortal Eden that his earlier protagonist only glimpsed in the "pathless desart of dim sleep" (*Alastor*, l. 210). The moon that led the *Alastor* Poet into the final dark sheds a holy radiance on the "scene of joy and wonder" that the sibling revolutionaries enter after their fiery martyrdom (*CW*, I, 406: *LC*, XII. 298). Having exposed, with its glaring white light, the fissures that threatened to mar the lovers' (sexual) union in the mortal realm, the "sphered lamp[. . .] of . . . night" now blesses and illuminates Laon and Cythna's perfect and *permanent* oneness in the world of the Spirit (*CW*, I, 407: *LC*, XII. 336). In fact, Mary's primary emblem is everywhere in this Shelleyan Paradise: "moonlike lamps, the progeny / Of a diviner heaven" reveal "new glories" to the new denizens; "moonlike blooms" adorn the beautiful trees that canopy an idyllic pool; a "roof of moonstone" crowns the entryway of the Temple of the Spirit itself; and, finally, the boat that takes Laon, Cythna, and their seraphic daughter to this Temple is a "divine canoe" carved in the shape of a cresent moon:

> The boat was one curved shell of hollow pearl,
> Almost translucent with the light divine
> Of her [Cythna's child] within; the prow and stern did curl,
> Horned on high, like the young moon supine,
> When o'er dim twilight mountains dark with pine,
> It floats upon the sunset's sea of beams,
> Whose golden waves in many a purple line
> Fade fast, till, borne on sunlight's ebbing streams,
> Dilating, on earth's verge the sunken meteor gleams.[11]

(*CW*, I, 407, 401, 271, 405, 402: *LC*,
XII. 338–39, 337, 161; I. 457; XII. 181–89)

Stuart Sperry points out that this boat resembles a nautilus, a lovely sea creature which visits Cythna in her underwater cave and one with which Shelley himself identified (cf. *L*, II, 288, where the poet calls himself "the Nautilus").[12] This "boat of pearl" therefore imagistically melds Mary and Percy, moon and mollusk, who then together "glide in peace down death's mysterious stream," a dark, quintessentially Shelleyan fantasy that Sperry's excellent reading does not quite grasp (*CW*, I, 406, 404: *LC*, XII. 307, 240). Mary, like nearly all of Percy's lovers and heroines, must be imported imaginatively into the postmortal realm before he can think of answering in the affirmative the question that haunts nearly all of his erotic writings: "Tomorrow blest creature I shall clasp you again—*forever*. shall it be so? Shall it be so?" (*L*, I, 417: to Mary, 3 November 1814).

Magnetic Sweetness, Electric Life: *Prometheus Unbound*

"Henceforth we will not part," a seemingly mundane statement in the midst of the sublime lyricism that distinguishes *Prometheus Unbound*, is in fact one of the play's most quietly triumphant assertions (III. iii. 10). Reunited at last with his radiant bride, Prometheus promises Asia, her "Fair sister nymphs," and himself that the sympathetic-erotic communion they enjoy in their lush cave-bower will be an everlasting one (III. iii. 8). The Shelleyan quest for sympathy, sisterhood, and mingled being, which has taken the poet from the mortal to the postmortal world, now transports him to the *immortal* sphere; yet the play itself, unlike his 1817 epic and his first utopian text, *Queen Mab*, allows us to see how the divinely inspired "sense of love"— erotic, feminine, Self-dissolving—transforms the Earth itself (and its sister-spirit the Moon) (III. iv. 102). While *Laon and Cythna* radically dichotomizes the Temple of the Spirit and, to borrow from Erasmus Darwin, the Temple of Nature (and of humanity), in *Prometheus Unbound*, the divine and the material worlds interpenetrate one another and thus *share* the sweet ether of love's "transforming presence" (I. 832). And whereas *Queen Mab* merely anticipates how "spring's awakening breath will woo the earth," and allow her creatures joyously to woo each other, the beings who inhabit Shelley's lyrical drama actually experience the "happy changes" brought about by this season of renewal (*QM*, IX. 167; *PU*, III. iv. 84).

According to the poem's Preface, Shelley himself felt the invigorating effects of the spring as he composed *Prometheus Unbound*:

> This Poem was chiefly written upon the mountainous ruins of the Baths of Caracalla, among the flowery glades, and thickets of odoriferous blossoming trees which are extended in ever winding labyrinths upon its immense platforms and dizzy arches suspended in the air. The bright blue sky of Rome, and the effect of the vigorous awakening of spring in that divinest climate, and the new life with which it drenches the spirits even to intoxication, were the inspiration of this drama. (133)

In fact, only Acts II and III were produced in this paradisal setting, but this passage reveals Shelley's ardent desire to baptize the entire poem in the same vernal fount that had "drenched" his own spirits during March and April of 1819—and during the spring of 1814, when he first fell in love with Mary Godwin. And the "subduing voluptuousness of the impulses of spring" (*L*, I, 402), inextricably linked with Mary's fateful entrance into his life, does preside over the poet's greatest work, where nostalgic desire mingles with a forward-looking longing for "new life." The Shelleyan *nostos*, as played out in *Prometheus Unbound*, involves, first of all, a return to previous springs such

as those that introduced him to Intellectual Beauty and, later on, to his own
"Sweet Maie," and, second, a journey back to his original sorority at Field
Place, site of his earliest experiments in electro-sympathetic mingling (*JMS*,
I, 55, Percy's entry).

Yet these "scene[s] of earlie[r] hopes and joys" had become obscured
and "bitter," haunted by such demons as loss, disillusionment, estrangement,
and death (*CW*, III, 127: "Dear Home"). As Shelley restlessly roamed through
Italy while *Prometheus Unbound* was taking shape, Field Place and its
beloved feminine occupants were only accessible via memory and imagination. Moreover, the young man who had so fervently vowed to "fear himself,
and love all humankind" now seemed a kind of beautiful phantom, the children engendered by his and Mary's once-unassailable love died in tragic succession, and Mary herself retreated into "Sorrow's most obscure abode"
("Hymn to Intellectual Beauty," l. 84; *CW*, III, 297: "To Mary Shelley"
[1819]). A "new life" was definitely needed during this time of crisis and
grief, and the birth of Percy Florence Shelley in November 1819 did much to
lift Mary from her depression and to regenerate the Shelleys' union. The
poet's own attempt to give birth to new life was *Prometheus Unbound* itself.
While it powerfully expresses his "passion for reforming the world" and his
hope that "everlasting love" will spawn a universal political, social, and spiritual revolution, his lyrical drama remains nonetheless a deeply personal
work,[13] one that emerged from one of the darkest periods of Shelley's life
(Preface to *PU* 135; *PU*, III. iii. 166).

Shelley siphoned off much of the despair and misery that engulfed him
during this time into a number of works that cluster around *Prometheus
Unbound*, works such as "Lines written among the Euganean Hills," "Stanzas
written in Dejection . . . Near Naples," *Julian and Maddalo*, and *The Cenci*.
But *Prometheus* itself contains its share of imagined and "remembered agonies," many of them involving destructive, diseased forms of sexual desire
("Lines . . . Euganean Hills," l. 330). As early as Prometheus' opening monologue, we see that brutal sexual domination rather than harmonious mingled
being provides the chief erotic paradigm during the Jupiterean age. Immobile,
vulnerable, and alarmingly penetrable, Prometheus tells how "crawling glaciers pierce [him] with the spears / Of their moon-freezing chrystals," while
"bright chains / Eat with their burning cold into [his] bones" and Jupiter's vulture, infected with its master's own (venereal) poison, "tears up / [His] heart"
(*PU*, I. 31–32, 32–33, 35–36).[14] In this initial speech and, again, during his
horrific encounter with the Furies, the Titan suffers as feminized victim of the
hyper-masculine "God of rape," who has enlisted a number of natural and
supernatural surrogates to carry out his campaign of psycho-sexual assault
(Ulmer 82). One of the most powerful and problematic weapons in Jupiter's
arsenal is the "White fire" that pulsates through the tyrant's infamous thun-

derbolts (I. 431). When generated and controlled by "Heaven's fell King," electricity—"the paragon of elements" in Adam Walker's phrase—becomes a purely baneful and *invasive* force, one that can cleave huge trees, "parch" and poison spring water, and torment with its "quick flames" the object of "the great Father's" lust, Thetis (*PU*, I. 140; Walker, *System of Familiar Philosophy*, II, 74; *PU*, I. 78; III. 38; I. 354).[15]

Part of Prometheus' mission, then, is to convert the "Insufferable might" of Jupiterean electricity into the purifying, vivifying fire of Promethean, or, rather, *Asian* love (III. i. 37).[16] But first he has to free himself from what Jessica Benjamin calls the cycle of "erotic domination and submission"—and the death-tending form of sexuality that accompanies it—that he and his dark double Jupiter have created (50). In *The Bonds of Love*, Benjamin examines "how domination is anchored in the hearts of the dominated" and how the master-slave relationship involves a "reversible complementarity" that precludes the healthy "reciprocal attunement" of intersubjective exchange (5, 220, 27).[17] Within the poem's first sixty lines, Shelley's protagonist plays out the "drama of reversible violator and victim" at the heart of Benjamin's study (*The Bonds of Love* 71). Deeply involved in his role as tragic martyr—"Ah me, alas, pain, pain ever, forever!"—Prometheus suddenly can step into the part of his tormentor, who now becomes "the reluctant victim" in the Titan's own sadistic fantasy (I. 23, 49).[18] Though he quickly repudiates this particular vengeful fantasy/prophesy, Prometheus has a much harder time recanting an even more Jupiterean utterance: the vicious curse that has in fact wed him to the "Foul Tyrant" for "Three thousand years of sleep-unsheltered hours" (I. 264, 12).

Prometheus' curse serves as a kind of perverse marriage vow,[19] spoken first by the Titan and ultimately repeated by the Phantasm of his dreadful paramour, that not only binds the drama's central antagonists but also unleashes the forces of that "evil and injurious Love" that Pausanias and Eryximachus describe in the Platonic dialogue Shelley translated shortly before he started work on his lyrical drama (Notopoulos 428). Malevolent, death-dealing, and Self-generated, Pandemian Eros literally plagues the fallen world that we enter in Act I, glimpse again in Asia's colloquy with Demogorgon in Act II, and finally see transformed at the close of Act III. Eryximachus' edifying discourse on Pandemian love in *The Banquet* becomes horrific reportage in *Prometheus Unbound* and in *The Sensitive-Plant*, where the death of a Uranian Venus-like Lady exposes a lovingly interpenetrating garden to the ravages wrought by her Pandemian counterpart. "When the evil and injurious Love assumes the dominion of the seasons of the year," says Eryximachus,

> destruction is spread widely abroad. Then pestilence is accustomed to arise, and many other blights and diseases fall upon animals and plants:

and hoar frosts, and hails, and mildew on the corn, are produced from that excessive and disorderly love, with which each season of the year is impelled towards the other. (Notopoulos 428)

All of these scourges (and then some) issue from the Prometheus-Jupiter union and from the curse itself, which the blighted Earth masochistically cherishes as "a treasured spell" (*PU*, I. 184).[20] At the climax of Prometheus' malediction, victim and victimizer, now indistinguishable, violently consummate their marriage and thus establish rape as the officially sanctioned mode of sexual intercourse:

> I curse thee! let a sufferer's curse
> Clasp thee, his torturer, like remorse,
> Till thine Infinity shall be
> A robe of envenomed agony;
> And thine Omnipotence a crown of pain
> To cling like burning gold round thy dissolving brain.
>
> (I. 286–91)

In this fierce outburst, the "sufferer's curse" metonymically represents Prometheus himself, lustfully/murderously embracing his dark double, who will in turn direct his own "quick flames" and sexual "poison" toward the terrified Thetis (III. i. 38, 41).[21] With Prometheus' cruel "clasp," we are back in the Gothic world of *Zastrozzi*, where no one escapes the deadly sexual roundelay. Prometheus truly has "empower[ed]" Jupiter, as William Ulmer and others point out (*Shelleyan Eros* 81), but he also has mingled with him, solidifying a Self-fueled, violently erotic, and masculinist partnership that infects Earth and her "pining sons" (and daughters) for three millennia (*PU*, I. 159).

Ulmer's analysis of *Prometheus Unbound*'s "Oedipal subplot" helps us see how deeply involved in patriarchal warfare and sexual dynamics Shelley's protagonist is when the drama opens (81). In his compelling reading, Ulmer takes us back to "the crucial opposition of Saturn and Prometheus . . . [and] its extension in the warfare of Saturn and Jupiter":

The crimes of Jupiter represent the acts of Prometheus at one symbolic remove. To understand why Prometheus empowers Jupiter, then, we need only to consider what the tyrant of Olympus actually does: Jupiter overthrows the patriarch. Mediated through Jupiter's symbolic murder of Saturn, Prometheus' displaced parricide asserts the rights of the son in the face of patriarchal tyranny . . . As Asia's cosmological narrative shows, the Titanic viewpoint insists on Saturn as father, no less so for

his defeat and absence . . . Prometheus and Saturn fight for sexual pre-
eminence. Freud's remark that "the shape and movements of a flame
suggest a phallus in activity" glosses Prometheus' theft of fire as sexual
revolt, a wresting of phallic prerogatives from father to son. (81, 82)

Particularly when he pronounces his potent curse, Prometheus commits himself to the oedipal violence and cycles of recrimination Ulmer describes here.
But, paradoxically, the fire theft that Ulmer, following Freud, links with
"phallic prerogatives" ultimately leads Prometheus out of the arena of masculine combat and (back) to the realm of maternal/sisterly sympathy. We
recall that in Adam Walker's mythic/scientific account of the great triumvirate
of electricity, light, and fire, these "vital fluid[s]" originally emanate from the
sun—virile and paternal—and then enter the maternal "reservoir" of the
Earth's atmosphere (*System of Familiar Philosophy*, II, 50, 14). In stealing
fire from the Heavens and from their divine patriarch, Prometheus is facilitat-
ing the sublime journey that Walker recounts and thus enabling the great
Mother to collect and convert to her own feminine nature the seminal flame.

While Jupiter holds sway over the world, however, fire, and its more
subtle affiliate, electricity, remains an ambiguous substance. In the "cosmological narrative" that Ulmer mentions, Asia tells how Jove used "alternating
shafts of frost and fire" to attack and control primitive man (II. iv. 53). Moreover, even the fire that Prometheus bestows upon humanity contains a
Jupiterean spark, as does its new steward:

> And [Prometheus] tamed fire, which like some beast of prey
> Most terrible, but lovely, played beneath
> The frown of man, and tortured to his will
> Iron and gold, the slaves and signs of power.
>
> (II. iv. 66–69)

As "his will" here could be either that of man or of Prometheus, Asia's history lesson subtly implicates the Titan himself in two Self-serving systems:
exploitative science and "all-enslaving" commerce, which in Shelley's earlier
attempt to transform dystopia into Paradise "set[s] the mark of selfishness . . .
Upon a shining ore" (*QM*, V. 54, 53, 55). Perhaps the best gloss on this passage is the crucial section from the *Defence* in which Shelley eloquently condemns the principle of Self that had haunted him since "early youth," to borrow one of his own favorite phrases:

> The cultivation of those sciences which have enlarged the limits of the
> empire of man over the external world, has, for want of the poetical fac-
> ulty, proportionally circumscribed those of the internal world; and man,

having enslaved the elements, remains himself a slave . . . From what other cause has it arisen that the discoveries which should have lightened, have added a weight to the curse imposed on Adam? Poetry, and the principle of Self, of which money is the visible incarnation, are the God and the Mammon of the world. (502–3)

As particularly the final act of his lyrical drama reveals, Shelley's vision of utopia in 1819 does embrace the notion of man's empire over the external world: "All things confess his strength," "The Lightning is his slave," sings the Earth in its ecstatic paean to the wonders of science (*PU*, IV. 412, 418). But presumably Love and the poetical faculty, gifts of Asia and Prometheus, will help regenerated humanity protect (reformed) Promethean science from the "venal interchange" of commerce and other offshoots of vile Selfhood (*QM*, V. 38).[22]

However, Prometheus himself needs regeneration, and disentanglement from his Jupiterean marriage, before he can ensure that "all things," including man and the elements themselves, "put their evil nature off" (III. iv. 77). Unlike many of Shelley's readers, I believe that it is impossible to pinpoint the moment of Prometheus' conversion; I find the process-oriented reading that Stuart Sperry and others offer most convincing.[23] Prometheus' divorce from Heaven's cruel king involves a long and agonizing struggle on the Titan's part, one that requires him to move from hate and disdain to pity and, finally, to love *and* from (Self-)identification with his masculine *Doppelgänger* to spiritual and sensual merger with his feminine second self. It is the crucial process of self-feminization that ultimately allows Prometheus and his sister-spouse to reclaim, purify, and diffuse the vital spark of life and love that Jupiter, with the Titan's aid, had tranformed into electric poison.

Marlon Ross illuminates how Prometheus, in the poem's opening lines, gradually moves out of the isolated confines of monologue into "the dialogic community" ("Shelley's Wayward Dream-Poem" 118). Shifting from the linguistic domain that Ross examines to the realm of gender, I want to emphasize that, as conversation replaces self-communion, Prometheus turns from the virile "Monarch of Gods and Daemons" to Earth, the "Venerable mother" (I. 1, 186). By invoking this maternal figure, Prometheus is taking his first tentative steps (back) to the feminine Paradise that he once shared with Asia and that he now recollects:

> —Mother, thy sons and thou
> Scorn him, without whose all-enduring will
> Beneath the fierce ominipotence of Jove
> Both they and thou had vanished like thin mist
> Unrolled on the morning wind!—
> . . . .

O rock-embosomed lawns and snow-fed streams
Now seen athwart frore vapours deep below,
Through whose o'er-shadowing woods I wandered once
With Asia, drinking life from her loved eyes;
Why scorns the spirit which informs ye, now
To commune with me?

(I. 113–17, 120–25)

The precious elixir that Prometheus was wont to imbibe is the same "liquid light" that the Spirit of the Earth drank from Asia's eyes in the golden era of Saturnian rule (III. iv. 17).[24] For both the Titan and the Spirit, Asia's vibrant "Life of Life," her feminine "ether" or electromagnetic energy, is essential nutriment that they and all living beings long to absorb and interchange, but cannot during the dessicated Jupiterean age (II. v. 48; I. 831).[25] As the drama's first act progresses, Prometheus finds himself yearning more and more for "the ether / Of [Asia's] transforming presence," which, as Panthea reminds him, "would fade / If it were mingled not with thine" (I. 831–33).[26] Though he laments, near the close of the Act, that "thou art far, / Asia," his conversation and communion with feminine figures such as the Earth, Panthea, and Ione are bringing him closer to his ideal sister-spirit, to his own induction into her erotically charged circle, and thus to his own self-feminization.[27] As the act concludes, Prometheus, in John Rieder's words, "is cured of the perverse cathexes which bind him to Jupiter" (782); he is ready to experience the unreserve of mingled being with his sister-spirit(s) and to generate and "circumfuse" the "gravitating fire" of sympathy and (Uranian) sexuality (Darwin, *Botanic Garden, Economy of Vegetation*, I. vii. 338).

Not surprisingly, for dreams (and nightmares) remain at center stage in *Prometheus Unbound*, the Titan's stunning (trans)sexual transfiguration takes place in a remarkable erotic dream, one that redefines sexual love for the soon-to-be inaugurated Promethean-Asian epoch. Though the dream that Panthea recounts in the opening scene of Act II is ostensibly her own, the insights into "communal dreaming" within the poem that Ross offers help us see this crucial dream as Prometheus' and Asia's as well ("Shelley's Wayward Dream-Poem" 112). "Images of sleeping, dreaming, and waking proliferate in the poem," Ross writes, "so much so that the boundary between dreaming and waking, between the ideal and the actual is subverted" (123). Ross also demonstrates how Shelley, in his lyrical drama, blurs boundaries between self and other and between reader and text, with "text" being in many cases "dream." Commenting on Act II, scene i's central episode Ross points out:

It is not enough that Panthea describe her dream to Asia; in order for the dream to have its effect, Asia must herself become a dreamer and inter-

preter; she must apprehend, read, and interpret the dream for herself . . .
It is not enough for each individual to sustain her or his individual
dream; each must become a part of the other's dream and in so doing
sustain a communal dream. (123)

In this scene, an "involving and involved" dream becomes communal property, as it were, or a collaborative project that is created, sustained, and altered
by Panthea, Asia, Ione, and even the Titan himself, who exerts his literally
magnetic influence from *within* the dream (IV. 241).

Though Shelley sets up Asia and Prometheus' reunion as his drama's
climactic moment, the sisterly reunion that opens Act II carries its own emotional and erotic charge, and in fact enables the Titan and his bride to commune and (sexually) mingle before the Spirit of the Hour actually carries Asia
to the unbound Prometheus. Apologizing for her rather tardy arrival in Asia's
vale, Panthea explains that her "wings were faint / With the delight of a
remembered dream" (II. ii. 35–36). Yet, as at least two critics have noted,
Panthea could not have dreamed during the first act, at least not in the usual
sense of the word.[28] Both she and Ione remain awake with "the sacred Titan,"
tenderly solacing him until Panthea sees that "the Eastern star," emblem of
Asia as Venus Urania, "looks white" and departs for "that far Indian Vale" (I.
825, 826). Panthea's dream, it seems, was a reverie or waking dream such as
Shelley describes in his essay "On Life":[29]

Let us recollect our sensations as children. What a distinct and intense
apprehension had we of the world and of ourselves . . . We less habitually distinguished all that we saw and felt from ourselves. They seemed
as it were to constitute one mass. There are some people who in this
respect are always children. Those who are subject to the state called
reverie feel as if their nature were dissolved into the surrounding universe, or as if the surrounding universe were absorbed into their being.
They are conscious of no distinction. And these are states which precede
or accompany or follow an unusually intense and vivid apprehension of
life. (477)

If we choose to take Panthea at her word and attempt to locate her
dream/reverie within the narrative that Shelley gives us,[30] the gorgeous
masque presented by the "subtle and fair spirits" at the close of Act I—when
Panthea claims the dream occured—would be a likely textual and temporal
"space" (I. 658).[31] A dramatic mode that attempts to dissolve the borders
between performers and viewers, the Renaissance masque, as adapted by
Shelley both in Act I and Act IV, serves as the generic equivalent of reverie:
within its fluid boundaries, masquers and audience interpenetrate each other,

"conscious of no distinction."[32] In the Act I masque, the spectators/partici-
pants are Panthea, Ione, and Prometheus, the three mingling figures of the
dream recounted to Asia in the next act. And just as the Spirits' pageantry
prophesies the Titan's triumph over Jupiterean Selfhood and its offspring—
particularly "hollow Ruin," which stalks and destroys Love—the shared
reverie that this masque inspires in its audience involves a vision of the liberated, transfigured Prometheus, radiant with Christlike and *feminine* glory (I.
768).

   Before Panthea communicates the dream to her sister in Act II, Asia urges
her, "Lift up thine eyes / And let me read thy dream" (II. i. 55–56). Panthea's
words and the "soul-enwoven labyrinths" of her "deep and intricate eyes" can
now draw Asia into the reverie, where she can at last mingle her immaculate
ether with the "vaporous fire" that the Titan exudes (Notopoulos 488: *Discourse*; *PU*, II. i. 75). Panthea has mesmerized or "magnetized" her sister, but
she does so with Prometheus' help. Within the reverie that Asia witnesses and
enters, Prometheus becomes the powerful, radiantly erotic mesmerist, envelop-
ing and dissolving his sister-spirits in his own "warm ether" (II. i. 77):

> . . . the overpowering light
> Of that immortal shape was shadowed o'er
> By love, which, from his soft and flowing limbs
> And passion-parted lips, and keen faint eyes
> Steam'd forth like vaporous fire; an atmosphere
> Which wrapt me in its all-dissolving power
> As the warm ether of the morning sun
> Wraps ere it drinks some cloud of wandering dew.
> I saw not—heard not—moved not—only felt
> His presence flow and mingle through my blood
> Till it became his life and his grew mine
> And I was thus absorbed—until it past
> And like the vapours when the sun sinks down,
> Gathering again in drops upon the pines
> And tremulous as they, in the deep night
> My being was condensed.

(II. i. 71–86)

Barbara Gelpi, in her detailed explication of this passage, points out the
"peculiar reversal" of roles here: we would ordinarily expect the suffering
Titan to be the "magnetized/patient" and the lovingly attentive Panthea to act
as the "magnetizer/healer" (*Shelley's Goddess* 183). Furthermore, Gelpi
reminds us, "The direction of the magnetic energy also contradicts Shelley's
own experience, since he himself seemed to get the most benefit from being

magnetized by women," as his 1822 poem "The Magnetic Lady to her Patient" illustrates (*Shelley's Goddess* 231n11). But Shelleyan alchemy as well as mesmerism is at work in this elaborate reverie. The dream itself, as it originates in Act I's enchanting masque and continues in the Oceanides' colloquy, is "an alchemic bath of swirling Dionysian liquidity," Camille Paglia's rich metaphor for Coleridge's daemonic poetry (318).[33] Within the alembic, or retort, of the Titanic-Oceanidean reverie, Prometheus undergoes a radical transmutation: he becomes a radiantly feminine figure, able at last to exude and interchange the "kindling ether" of passionate sympathy (Darwin, *Botanic Garden, Economy of Vegetation*, I. 105). Thus where Gelpi sees a male mesmerist and a female patient, I see Prometheus as a female magnetizer, much like Queen Mab, "pouring the magic of her gaze / Upon the maiden's sleep" (*QM*, I. 77–78).

Like the fledgling scientist who tried to wire himself into the sisterly circle at Field Place, Prometheus joins the electric circuit formed by his "Fair sister nymphs," Panthea, Asia, and even Ione, whose spirit, and senses, mingles with those of the other dreamers during this shared reverie (III. iii. 8). Communing/coalescing with the Oceanides, the Titan's hardened masculinity, as well as his "pale, wound-worn limbs," falls from him (II. i. 62). Shelley emphasizes Prometheus' newly achieved feminine softness throughout the dream episode. His Jupiterean grimace disappears, replaced by "the soft light of his own smiles which spread / Like radiance from the cloud-surrounded moon," that most feminine member of the heavenly pantheon (II. i. 121–22). His limbs are now "soft and flowing,"[34] evidence perhaps of the poet's pure anticipated cognition of "the soft and flowing proportions" that graced the lovely Venus Anadyomene he saw in Florence the following year (II. i. 73; Clark 350).

But it was recollection rather than anticipation that helped Shelley paint his Titan as transfigured Christ. In the autumn of 1818, as he and Mary visited a Bolognese gallery, Shelley found himself transfixed, or, rather, *mesmerized* by a piece entitled *The Saviour*, the work of the northern Italian master Correggio.[35] The similarity between Shelley's description of this beautiful painting and his own portrait of the dreamed and dreaming Prometheus is striking, and has largely escaped critical notice:[36]

There was one painting indeed by this master, *Christ beatified*, inexpressively fine. It is a half figure rising from a mass of clouds tinged with an ethereal rose-like lustre, the arms expanded, the whole figure seems dilated with expression, the countenance is heavy as it were with the weight of the rapture of the spirit, the lips parted but scarcely parted with the breath of intense but regulated passion, the eyes are calm and benignant, the whole features harmonized in majesty & sweetness. The

FIGURE 5.1

Copy of *The Saviour* by Correggio.
Courtesy of the Vatican.

hair is parted on the forehead, and falls in heavy locks on each side. It is motionless, but seems as if the faintest breath would move it. The colouring, I suppose must be very good if I can remark & understand it. The sky is a pale and aerial orange like the tints of latest sunset; it does not seem painted around & beyond the figure, but every thing seems to have absorbed, & to have been penetrated by its hues. I do not think we saw any other of Correggio's [besides *The Saviour* and *Four Saints*], but this specimen gives me a very exalted conception of his powers. (*L*, II, 49–50: to Thomas Love Peacock)

As Correggio's painting enters the text of *Prometheus Unbound*, Christ's lips, "parted but scarcely parted with the breath of . . . passion" become Prometheus' "passion-parted lips" (II. i. 74). The "rapture of the spirit" that Correggio's Savior expresses evolves into the sexualized "intoxication of keen joy" which the Titan imparts to Panthea, Asia, and Ione and, presumably, experiences himself (II. i. 67). Moreover, turning from Shelley's prose description of the painting to the painting itself, we confront an extremely feminine-looking Christ, one whose pleasingly rounded arms and torso easily could have inspired the "soft and flowing limbs" of the transfigured/transsexualized Prometheus.

Another crucial parallel between Correggio's painting and Shelley's dream-episode involves the vapory effect of *sfumato*, with its hazy, dissolving boundaries, that each achieves. In each work, it is the central figure—Christ or, in Shelley's text, Prometheus as Christ—whose radiance produces the blurred contours that suggest the world itself is becoming the "mazy volume of commingling things" that the young Shelley contemplated in his "Epithalamium" (*PS*, I, 119). In Correggio's piece, the beatified Christ seems to create and mingle with the sky itself, which in Shelley's account glows with "the tints of latest sunset; it does not seem painted around & beyond the figure, but every thing seems to have absorbed & to have been penetrated by its hues." The final pronoun could refer to the sky or to the "figure," Christ, and this ambiguity captures and contributes to the *sfumato* that visually conveys a sense of spiritual intermingling. In Shelley's text, though, the mingling is overtly sexual, and the "aerial" sunset and "ethereal rose-like" clouds that Correggio paints metamorphose into Prometheus, "the morning sun" that ultimately "sinks down," and Panthea, "the cloud of wandering dew," who together erotically enact the cycle of evaporation and condensation within their shared dream (II. i. 78, 77, 83). By correlating Panthea and Prometheus' intercourse with this natural process, Shelley opens the dream out, reminding us that, ideally, mingled being (inter)connects us with the world rather than hermetically seals us within the prison of Self.

In fact, though it occurs rather early in the play, this reverie ultimately gives birth to the joyous cosmic mingling that we witness in Act IV. Together, Prometheus, Panthea, Ione, and, most crucially, Asia, discover the unreserve of mingled being, which the reborn Earth and Moon will imitate/enact on the cosmic stage. The dream that drifts from Act I to Act II, enfolding the Titan and the Oceanides within its humid bower, is the closest thing we have to a glimpse of the erotic activity inside the Promethean Cave, lush site of the Titan's sororal Eden. This reverie reunites the Titan and his sister-bride(s), both within its own blurry borders and, with the help of its companion dream which leads Asia and Panthea to Demogorgon, in the waking world.

This brings me to the last correlation between the Correggio painting and the Shelleyan dream-text. In her compelling analysis of Act II's first scene, Barbara Gelpi provocatively suggests that "Prometheus does not desire Asia as an object, nor does he even desire to be with Asia; he desires to *be* Asia" (*Shelley's Goddess* 174). While I would amend this supposition to read "Prometheus both desires to be with *and* to be Asia," Gelpi rightly emphasizes the Titan's desire and need to become the goddess. When we turn back to Correggio's *The Saviour* (and Shelley's epistolary tribute to it) and ahead to the conclusion of *Prometheus Unbound*'s second act, we can see that Prometheus *does* become Asia: Asia as Venus, rising from her "veined shell" (II. v. 23).

As Shelley writes in his letter to Peacock, Correggio's Christ "is a half figure rising from a mass of clouds" (*L*, I, 49). He also seems to be rising from the large sheet of cloth that both swathes his legs and lower torso and serves as a kind of seat, its folds creating an odd, shell-shaped throne. Huddled just below him are four infant angels, chubby Cupids who seem awestruck by the effulgence emitted by the beautiful Christ-as-Aphrodite. I believe that Correggio's painting helped Shelley envision his Titan both as "beatified" Christ and as that other "Child of Light," love-enkindling Venus, with whom Panthea identifies Asia in Act II's climactic episode (II. v. 54):[37]

> How thou art changed! I dare not look on thee;
> I feel, but see thee not. I scarce endure
> The radiance of thy beauty. Some good change
> Is working in the elements which suffer
> Thy presence thus unveiled.—The Nereids tell
> That on the day when the clear hyaline
> Was cloven at thy uprise, and thou didst stand
> Within a veined shell, which floated on
> Over the calm floor of the chrystal sea,
> Among the Aegean isles, and by the shores
> Which bear thy name, love, like the atmosphere
> Of the sun's fire filling the living world,

> Burst from thee, and illumined Earth and Heaven
> And the deep ocean and the sunless caves,
> And all that dwells within them; till grief cast
> Eclipse upon the soul from which it came:
> Such art thou now, nor is it I alone,
> Thy sister, thy companion, thine own chosen one,
> But the whole world which seeks thy sympathy.
>
> (II. v. 16–34)

Commenting on the dream of "purification and transformation" that Shelley presents at the beginning of Act II, John Rieder writes that Prometheus' "cured sexual desire reemerges in all its potency and is finally directed toward Asia. The end product of this dream and the accomplishment of this wish is Asia's transformation in II.v" (783). But the Titan, with the help of the Oceanides themselves, can only "dream" the incandescent Asia into being by first imitating/becoming the brilliant sea-born(e) beauty whose love illuminated the entire world; and this is precisely what he does within the shared reverie that we witness in II.i.[38]

Just as Asia is present, in several ways, at Prometheus' transfiguration, so too is Prometheus in attendance when his sister-spouse becomes a burning fountain of love and sympathy, that fluid fire which interpenetrates all living beings. After listening to Panthea's wondrous account of her sister's birth and rebirth, Asia tells her, "Thy words are sweeter than aught else but his / Whose echoes they are" (II. v. 38–39). As Echo to Prometheus' redeemed Narcissus, Panthea once again mediates between the divine lovers, allowing "the ether / Of [Asia's] transforming presence" to mingle with that of the purified, feminized Titan (I. 831–32). In the next scene, when Jupiter confronts his "fatal Child," Demogorgon orders the tyrant, "Lift thy lightnings not" (III. i. 19, 56).[39] As he sinks to the abyss with Demogorgon, Jupiter discovers, much to his horror, that "The elements obey [him] not" (III. i. 80). As Panthea has already seen, the elements—most important the lightning which Jove wielded with murderous intent—have undergone a "good change": Prometheus and Asia have (re)claimed them, and the fire of poison and destruction has at last become the flame of consentaneous love (II. v. 18).

Just as Panthea, Asia's "shadow," companion, and "chosen one," sexually, spiritually, and sympathetically links Prometheus and his bride, she also connects the fertile dream of II.i with the explosive masque of birth and mingled being we witness in Act IV (II. i. 70; II. v. 33). Gazing into her sister's hypnotic eyes, eyes that both reflect Asia's own image and reveal the "shape" of the transfigured Titan, Asia tells Panthea, "Thine eyes are like the deep blue, boundless Heaven / Contracted to two circles underneath / Their long, fine lashes—dark, far, measureless,—/ Orb within orb, and line through line inwoven" (II. i. 120, 114–17). This last image prefigures the sublime vision of "Ten thousand orbs involving and involved" that Panthea and Ione behold in the drama's finale (IV. 241). These "intertranspicuous" spheres, Shelley's most brilliant and elaborate image of mingled being, represent the purified electromagnetic energy of the Promethean-Asian era,[40] but they also emblematize Panthea's own efficacious eyes, site/sight of Asia's and Prometheus' dream intercourse (IV. 246).

Fittingly, within the great womb-Orb of Act IV, the infant Spirit of the Earth, the Cupid-like progeny of the newly enthroned power of Venus,[41] awaits (re)birth and its own opportunity to experience the unreserve of mingled being with its luminous sister-spirit, the Moon. Panthea describes for us the child *in utero* who will soon burst into full erotic life:

> Within the Orb itself,
> Pillowed upon its alabastor arms
> Like to a child o'erwearied with sweet toil,
> On its own folded wings and wavy hair
> The Spirit of the Earth is laid asleep,
> And you can see its little lips are moving
> Amid the changing light of their own smiles
> Like one who talks of what he loves in dream.
>
> (IV. 261–68)

"'Tis only mocking the Orb's harmony," interjects the pragmatic and perhaps uneasy Ione (IV. 269).[42] Both Panthea's breathless narrative and Ione's ironic remark emphasize the sympathetic attunement between Orb and child, a communion that takes us back to the intimate interchange of Ianthe and the "Queen of spells" in Canto VI of *Queen Mab* (VI. 63). Just as the vibrant Fairy and the dreaming Ianthe engage in "amodal" mirroring, answering each other in a variety of sensory modes, the sublime Orb and the dreaming Earth Spirit "harmonize" visually, aurally, and kinetically. The most striking parallel between the two communions involves the way the child—Ianthe in *Queen Mab* and the Spirit in *Prometheus*—is literally colored by intersubjective experience. As Ianthe listens to, or, rather, *feels* "the Fairy's burning speech," the "varying periods paint[. . .] changing glows" over her frame (*QM*, VI. 2, 4). And Panthea notes how the Earth Spirit's "little lips are moving / Amid the changing light of their own smiles," smiles which are themselves responses to "the Orb's harmony" and changing light: "Purple and azure, white and green and golden" (*PU*, IV. 266–67, 269, 242).

As he did in *Queen Mab*, Shelley is again establishing what Jessica Benjamin calls "the intersubjective foundation of erotic life" (29); but, unlike his earlier utopian poem, *Prometheus Unbound* moves beyond incipient eroti-

cism into the realm of full-fledged sexuality. The gently erotic mirroring we
observe within "the multidinous Orb" becomes passionately sexual when the
Spirit of the Earth and his "chrystal paramour" erupt into mature desire (IV.
253, 463):

> Brother, wheresoe'r thou soarest
> I must hurry, whirl and follow
> Through the Heavens wide and hollow,
> Sheltered by the warm embrace
> Of thy soul, from hungry space,
> Drinking, from thy sense and sight
> Beauty, majesty, and might,
> As a lover or chameleon
> Grows like what it looks upon,
> As a violet's gentle eye
> Gazes on the azure sky
> Until its hue grows like what it beholds.
>
> (IV. 476–87)

Before Shelley allows these sibling lovers their ecstatic consummation, however, he must expose and destroy "the melancholy ruins / Of cancelled
cycles," the horrific work of evolution (IV. 288–89). As Sperry points out, the
passage wherein the great Orb, with the aid of the Earth Spirit's piercing electric beams, "makes bare the secrets of the Earth's deep heart," reveals Shelley's own "peculiar loathing of evolution" (IV. 279; *Shelley's Major Verse*
122). "Well before the methodical investigations and conclusions of Charles
Darwin," Sperry writes, "Shelley had already grasped . . . the horror of an
earthly evolution that, operating through the principles of competition, rapine,
and survival, has left a history that was the very antithesis of his ideal of love"
(*Shelley's Major Verse* 122). The relentless sphere, fittingly piloted by the
Earth Spirit as "Child of Apocalypse," creates a vast trash heap, monument to
the very principle of Self, of which the military debris, urban refuse, and
grotesque remains of "monarch beasts" that the Orb unearths are emblematic
(Hughes, "Potentiality in *Prometheus Unbound*," 608; *PU*, IV. 311).

While Asia's "enchanted Boat" floats smoothly backward "Through
Death and Birth to a diviner day," the vision of regenerative regression that
Panthea witnesses involves abrupt and violent annihilation (II. v. 72, 103).
Earth's abhorrent progeny

> Increased and multiplied like summer worms
> On an abandoned corpse, till the blue globe
> Wrapt Deluge round it like a cloak, and they

Yelled, gaspt and were abolished; or some God
Whose throne was in a Comet, past, and cried—
"Be not!"—and like my words they were no more.[43]

(IV. 313–18)

As Shelleyan apocalypse becomes in the very next line Shelleyan sex, we are again back in the world of *Zastrozzi*, where "the universal wreck of nature" provides the ideal romantic backdrop for Verezzi's passionate union with his beloved Julia (*CW*, V, 52). The postapocalyptic mingling that the Earth and Moon enjoy reminds us just how radically Shelley had to re-envision earth, and heaven, before he could imagine the elaborate erotic masque which his cosmic lovers perform.

Postapocalyptic and planetary, these lovers nevertheless hold out the promise of human rapture as they dissolve in each other's fiery yet fertile atmospheres. The power that "clothes with unexpected birth" the Moon's "cold bare bosom," that "interpenetrates" the "granite mass" of the Earth, and that keeps these bodies spinning within each other's orbits is the "love which is as fire," conspicuously present in Act IV as gravitation, electricity, and magnetism (IV. 360, 361, 370; III. iii. 151).[44] Although the Moon tells her lover, "All suns and constellations shower / On thee a light, a life, a power / Which doth array thy sphere," Shelley's second and third acts encourage us to see the Titan and his bride as the most crucial sources of this primal fire (IV. 440–42). Asia's and Prometheus' mingled ether, permeating the world as the power of sex and of sympathy, thus provides to newly unselfed man the "atmosphere of light" and (erotic) love that envelops Act IV's heavenly paramours (IV. 323). Moreover, Shelley constantly "humanizes" his cosmic siblings, attributing to them strikingly human emotions, assigning the Earth a long hymn to "Man, one harmonious Soul of many a soul," and integrating into their duet specific references to the impassioned lovers who inhabit the Moon's "newly-woven bowers" and Earth's romantic vales (IV. 400, 427).[45]

But Shelley devised an even more effective strategy for ensuring that his cosmic masque did not "discard[. . .] human interest and passion," Mary Shelley's complaint about both *The Witch of Atlas* and *The Triumph of Life* (*CW*, IV, 78: Mary Shelley's Note on *The Witch of Atlas*). He identified Ione and Panthea, our mythic yet touchingly human surrogate readers, with each of the whirling Orbs: Ione with the explicitly feminine Moon, and Panthea with the ambiguously gendered Earth, whose intimate connections with Mother Earth, Asia/Venus, and Panthea herself make him seem more sister than brother to the gorgeous Moon. (The Moon's reference to herself as a Maenad further feminizes her lover by linking the Earth with the woman-identified Dionysus [IV. 467–75].) The Oceanides' commentary on and (direct and indirect) participation in the Act IV masque draw *us* into the text and, ideally,

allow us to enter into the unreserve of mingled being that the planets themselves experience and celebrate.[46]

If Panthea and Ione provide the "human interest" from within the text
itself, the poet and his own sister-spouse hover over the great nuptial masque
as phantoms whose young passion helped inspire this ecstatic vision, and who
now seek a draught of "the liquid light" that suffuses the entire fourth act (III.
iv. 17). Stuart Sperry notes how the poet's astronomical imagery "suggests the
extent to which Shelley had idealized his relationship with Mary," and, I
would add, it also suggests just how much he *needed* to idealize it at this point
(*Shelley's Major Verse* 124). Mary the Moon achieves her brilliant apotheosis
in *Prometheus Unbound*'s fourth act; in *Epipsychidion* she will become the
"cold chaste Moon," whose "soft yet icy flame . . . warms not but illumines"
(ll. 281, 283, 285). In the meantime, Percy the Earth will continue to burst into
green life, aided by the "magnetic might" of two "bright regents," Mary herself and his splendid new love, Teresa Viviani (ll. 348, 360). Like all masques,
Prometheus Unbound IV is written in the optative mode, but the promise of
"new life" that it held out for the Shelleys' own love ultimately went unful-
filled (Preface to *PU* 133).

After *Prometheus Unbound*, Shelleyan mingled being never again
found such joyous artistic expression. The poet's fundamental distrust of sexual love seeps into many of his later works and even infiltrates the utopia he
creates in his lyrical drama. As Demogorgon offers his final admonition, the
serpent of Selfhood, a highly sexualized creature, threatens to "clasp" Eternity
and penetrate the newly born Paradise (IV. 568). The principle of Self also
casts its shadow over the island Eden that Shelley creates for his "vestal sister" Emily in *Epipsychidion*, his 1821 excursion into the realm of sex and
sympathy (l. 390). The speaker's narcissistic relationship with his lover,
whom he calls "Not mine but me," protects him from the (sexual) contagion
with which genuine difference might threaten him; yet it also ensures that
Emily, her "band of sister-spirits," and the "delicious isle" itself remain
trapped within the little world of the speaker's Self (*Epip.*, l. 392; *CW*, II, 382:
"Fragments Connected with *Epipsychidion*"; *Epip.*, l. 477). In *Epipsychidion*'s climactic passage, as the lovers' breath intermixes, their bosoms fuse,
and their "veins beat together," Shelleyan mingled being reaches—or falls
into—the abyss that yawns in even his earliest Gothics (ll. 565, 566). Hoping
that he has at last discovered "passion's golden purity" and the pristine flame
that would truly allow him to "pierce / Into the height of love's rare Universe,"
the speaker instead sinks with the weight of his own ego into death's alluring
embrace (ll. 571, 588). The "one annihilation" that the speaker finally envisions for himself (and his mirroring lover) proves to be the only escape from
the despotic word that forms "chains of lead" around his soul's "flight of fire"

(l. 590). "I" is the insistent monosyllable that tolls its own death as the poem comes to its Self-elegizing close: "I pant, I sink, I tremble, I expire!" (l. 591).

Epipsychidion, like many of Shelley's earliest works, looks to the world "beyond the grave" as a fitting arena for sympathetic-erotic mingling (l. 598). In a cancelled passage whose spirit nonetheless pervades both poem and coda, Shelley writes:

> If day should part us night will mend division
> And if sleep parts us—we will meet in vision
> And if life parts us—we will mix in death
> Yielding our mite [?] of unreluctant breath
> Death cannot part us—we must meet again
> In all in nothing in delight in pain.[47]
>
> (*CW*, II, 382: "Fragments Connected
> with *Epipsychidion*," ll. 175–80)

Whatever gleams of romantic idealism illuminate the notion of *liebestod* in *Episychidion* completely vanish in the brutal world that Shelley presents in *The Triumph of Life*. Sex and death violently intersect within the obscene dance the captives of Life perform on the dusty public road. Sacred Shelleyan watchwords such as *mix*, *mingle*, and *kindle* mutate into indexes of horror as we witness "the agonizing pleasure" of the "ribald crowd" (ll. 141, 156, 152, 143, 136). Surrounded as it is with the "clouds of cold mortality" and selfish desire, carnal love becomes in Shelley's final, unforgettable vision, sheer carnage (*Adonais*, l. 486). The savagely dancing maidens and youths who attempt to outrun the Chariot of Life "mix with each other in tempestuous measure" (l. 141). They finally experience mutual "desolation" beneath the wheels of the Chariot, which mingle them even more promiscuously into an indistinguishable pulp, like "foam [which] after the Ocean's wrath / Is spent upon the desert shore" (ll. 160, 163–64).

In *The Triumph of Life*, the unreserve of mingled being offers no promise of transformative love, no respite from the world of mortal Selfhood. As the frantic lovers, "bending within each other's atmosphere / Kindle invisibly," electric poison rather than electric life supplies the crucial spark (ll. 151–52). Yet Shelley's own yearning for the vital fire of sex and sympathy makes itself felt between the lines of what is perhaps his darkest work. From time to time the poet would turn away from the "sad pageantry" (l. 176) and fierce passions of his visionary epic and contemplate a beautiful "presence" who could make "weak and tame all passions" ("Lines written in the Bay of Lerici," ll. 28, 29). Interleaved among the pages of *The Triumph of Life* are two of Shelley's most lovely lyrics, "To Jane" ("The keen stars were twinkling") and "Lines written in the Bay of Lerici," both addressed to the last avatar of the Shelleyan sister-spirit, Jane Williams.[48] These lyrics, which celebrate the "soft vibrations" of his beloved's voice and touch, provide a gentle counterpoint to the *Triumph*'s "fierce song" ("Lines," l. 22; *TL*, l. 110). Together, Shelley's final poetic works create a rich and oddly beautiful symphony, one that keeps this most Love-devoted and most Self-imprisoned of poets precariously poised between Love's transforming presence and the Self's gruesome nightmare.

NOTES

Introduction: The Principle of Self and Love's Transforming Presence

1. See, for example, Barbara A. Schapiro, *The Romantic Mother*, William Veeder, *Mary Shelley and "Frankenstein,"* Anne K. Mellor, *Mary Shelley* and review of Nathaniel Brown's *Sexuality and Feminism in Shelley*, Alan Richardson, "Romanticism and the Colonization of the Feminine," and Diane Long Hoeveler, *Romantic Androgyny*.

2. Timothy Clark and Jerrold E. Hogle, editors of *Evaluating Shelley*, sum up this debate: "One side (à la Nathaniel Brown) finds Shelley consistently proto-feminist, while the other (à la Anne Mellor) finds him belying his own statements on women's equality by making woman the 'other' created to fulfill the male imagination in his poems and his life" (6).

3. Roy R. Male, Jr.'s "Shelley and the Doctrine of Sympathy" remains the best introduction to the poet's place within the philosophical tradition that sees sympathy rather than self-love as the stronger "passion," to use a key term favored especially by Francis Hutcheson and his student Adam Smith.

4. Although in the *Defence* Shelley call poetry (rather than love) and the principle of Self the "God and the Mammon of the world" (503), love and poetry sustain a definite kinship in Shelley's thought, especially in terms of their "daemonic" roles as intermediaries between the divine and the mortal and between self and other. In Plato's *Symposium*, which Shelley translated in 1818, Diotima depicts Love as "A great Daemon" who "bind[s] together, by his own power, the whole universe of things," much in the same way that the romantic imagination and its incarnation in visionary verse strove to do. Shelley's version of the *Symposium* (*The Banquet*) can be found in James A. Notopoulos' *The Platonism of Shelley*, pp. 414–61 (quotation from pp. 441–42). Notopoulos' book will be my source for Shelley's *A Discourse on the Manners of the Antient Greeks Relative to the Subject of Love*, as well as for all of the poet's translations from Plato.

5. Following Shelley's own practice, I will use the term *Self* as a kind of shorthand for those vices that I have just catalogued, as well as for various other "hateful consequences of selfishness" that the poet examines (*L*, I, 69). Unlike Shelley, however, I will always capitalize this word when referring to its negative denotations and connotations, and will use the lower-case version when discussing its relatively neutral meanings, as in the phrases *self and other* and *self-identity* (keeping in mind that even the latter phrase is problematic when dealing with the Shelleyan self—or Self).

6. Holmes sees two of the books under review as "microbiographical" in nature. These are Desmond Hawkins's *Shelley's First Love* and Barbara Charlesworth Gelpi's *Shelley's Goddess: Maternity, Language, Subjectivity*, both of which have helped me appreciate and understand what Holmes aptly calls the "continuing mystery of Shelley's affective life" ("He Doth Not Sleep" 23).

7. See *LMWS*, I, p. 245, and Holmes, *Pursuit*, p. 727 for accounts of Shelley's murderous double.

8. Chodorow's groundbreaking *The Reproduction of Mothering* offers a revisionary, recuperative account of infantile fusion with the mother—and with the world ("Cognitive narcissism does not entail the infant's loving only itself" [62–63]). For Freud's largely dismissive explanation of the breakdown of boundary lines between ego and object, termed the "oceanic feeling," see chapter 1 of *Civilization and Its Discontents*. Contrary to Freud, such feminist theorists as Chodorow, Jean Baker Miller, and Carol Gilligan do not view the experience of self-other merger as immature, "threatening," or connate with the desire for "the restoration of limitless narcissism" (Freud, *Civilization*, 15, 19), but rather as a key to empathy and to what Gilligan calls an "ethic of care" (63). Kohut, too, sees (modulated) merger experiences, remnants of the child's primary narcissism, in a largely positive light. For Kohut such experiences are central to the development and preservation of a cohesive self.

9. See *PU*, I. 451 for the phrase "loathsome sympathy."

10. See especially Mellor, Introduction to *Romanticism and Feminism*, pp. 7–8 and *Romanticism and Gender*, pp. 25–26; Richardson, "Romanticism and the Colonization of the Feminine," p. 20; and Hoeveler, *Romantic Androgyny*, pp. 97–107, 139–55.

1. Shelley, Christ, and Narcissus

1. Clark's statement regarding the Note to *Queen Mab*, "I will beget a son" (VII. 135) is typical: "Shelley's profound and lifelong admiration of the character and teachings of Jesus and his even profounder conviction that organized Christianity has betrayed the moral leadership of its founder is a fact that cannot be overstressed" (103). David Fuller's valuable survey of Jesus' appearances in Shelley's work follows this tack as well, emphasizing "admiration of Jesus the man; separation of the man from aspects of Judaic myth and history which Shelley deplored; and separation from the Church, which for much of its history . . . was antithetical to its nominal founder" ("Shelley and Jesus" 211). Stephen Behrendt also suggests too rigid a dichotomy— "Despite his rejection of the institution of orthodox Christianity, Shelley admired Christ"—though he rightly points out that Shelley venerated Christ "as political reformer, as visionary prophet, and as the ideal of humanitarian self-sacrifice—and often linked himself, both implicitly and explicitly, with him" (Introduction to *Zastrozzi and St. Irvyne* xviii). This "linkage," however, entails something more problematic than enthusiasm for an extraordinary historical figure, which is how Shelley is generally purported to regard Jesus.

2. In Schapiro's book, Shelley reigns as the arch-narcissist among such lesser lights as Keats, Coleridge, and Wordsworth, all of whom according to Schapiro, "exert more of an effort" to resist narcissistic tendencies, including the "regressive desire for refusion with the mother" and unmediated rage at that mother for her elusiveness, for her separateness (xiv–xv). Actually, Schapiro's "grid"—her book is organized so as to begin with the most extreme narcissist of the group, Shelley, and to conclude with the most "adjusted," Wordsworth—is not wholly inaccurate. However, in taking *Alastor* as a "representative" poem by Shelley and as her "prototype for the Romantic poem of wounded narcissism" (xiii), she oversimplifies—most egregiously, by conflating Shelley, the Poet, and the Narrator (see especially p. 2, where she assigns the Narrator's invocation of Nature to the Poet)—and never seeks to explain the narcissistic patterns she points out in the poem. See also Peter L. Thorslev's seminal essay, "Incest as Romantic Symbol," where Shelley figures prominently in the argument that "brother-sister incestuous love . . . symbolizes perfectly the Romantic hero's narcissistic sensibility" as well as evinces his "intellectual solipsism" (54). (Thorslev focuses only on the writings, not the lives of those authors he discusses.) Analyses by Margaret Homans ("Bearing Demons: Frankenstein's Circumvention or the Maternal," chap. 5 of *Bearing the Word*) and Anne K. Mellor (*Mary Shelley*), which approach both Mary and Percy via biography, come closer to illuminating the latter's narcissistic propensities than does Schapiro's account of the archetypal Mother in Shelley's verse (Mellor pays heed to Percy's actual mother [18–19, 73–74]) or Thorslev's thematic study. Finally, Barbara Charlesworth Gelpi's study of Shelley and the maternal helps us see how the poet's initial boyhood closeness with his own mother allowed him to envision the kind of positive narcissism associated with mother-infant bonding and intersubjective "mirroring."

3. Kenneth Neill Cameron was among the first to recognize the depth of Shelley's "attachment" to Harriet Grove (*Esdaile* 214). See, for example, his commentary on Shelley's 1811 poem "Death-spurning rocks!" in his edition of *The Esdaile Notebook*, pp. 211–14. However, Frederick L. Jones asserts that "It is a mistake to think . . . that losing Harriet had deep and permanent effects on Shelley," but his next statement, with its rather startling lack of psychological acuity, robs his contention of any real credibility: "As Harriet had already found someone to console her before she renounced Shelley, so Shelley had already met *another Harriet* who was soon to make his first love easy to forgo" (*SC*, II, 489: Introduction to *The Diary of Harriet Grove*; emphasis mine). Jones's italicized words echo those of Hellen Shelley, the second youngest of Percy's sisters, whose evaluation of her brother's youthful engagement and disappointment Peacock enlists in support of his own contention that Shelley's passion for his "first" Harriet was superficial and short-lived: "time healed the wound by means of another Harriet, whose name and similar complexion perhaps attracted the attention of my brother" (Peacock, *Memoirs*, 318). Yet Hellen also asserts, "His disappointment in losing the lady of his love had a great effect upon him . . . It was not put an end to by mutual consent" (*Memoirs* 318). Moreover, the skeptical Peacock cites two badly tampered-with letters from Shelley to Hogg which the latter "revised" in order that remarks about his own bizarre passion for Elizabeth Shelley, whom he had never even seen, appeared to refer to the Percy–Harriet Grove crisis. See Peacock,

Memoirs, p. 318, for Hogg's versions of the 23 and 26 December 1810 letters, the former of which is printed accurately from manuscript in *L*, I, pp. 29–30. While the original manuscript of the latter has not been found, as Jones points out, the letter obviously pertains not to Percy and Harriet but to Thomas and Elizabeth (*L*, I, 31–32). Furthermore, Peacock downplays Shelley's love for Harriet Grove in part because he had an emotional stake in preserving the memory of the "second" Harriet, with whom he shared a warm friendship and always preferred to Mary Shelley. Thus Harriet Westbrook Shelley, not Harriet Grove, whom Peacock never met, and not Mary Godwin Shelley, whom he never seemed to forgive, emerges from the *Memoirs* as the most appealing of the poet's loves. Finally, Desmond Hawkins, who traces the trajectory of Shelley's first love affair, finds it a relatively minor episode in the poet's life, despite the young man's extreme grief, even hysteria, upon its demise.

4. Even Jones, who greatly underestimates Harriet Grove's effect on Shelley, affirms: "The loss of Harriet . . . made his reactions against religion far more violent than they otherwise had been" (*SC*, II, 488: Harriet Grove's *Diary*, Introduction).

5. A young officer, Captain Kennedy, who was present during Shelley's penultimate visit to Field Place in June 1814 observed, "His resemblance to his sister, Elizabeth, was as striking as if they had been twins" (Hogg, II, 153). Of Harriet and Percy, Holmes observes, "The curious thing was that the cousins looked very much alike, and Shelley seemed to revel in this sense of twinship" (*Pursuit* 29). Cf. "Fiordispina," lines 11–13: "They were two cousins, almost like to twins, / Except that from the catalogue of sins / Nature had rased their love" (*CW*, IV, 72). Holmes also points out the "striking resemblance" between Aemilia Curran's 1819 portrait of Shelley and the portrait of "La Cenci" that Shelley lingered over at the Colonna Palace and lovingly described in his preface to *The Cenci* (*Pursuit* 517).

6. See *Shelley's Goddess*, chap. 3 *passim*. The poet's only mention of his mother outside his correspondence, the 1822(?) fragment "An Essay on Friendship," confirms a lifelong sense of abandonment on Shelley's part: "I remember in my simplicity writing to my mother a long account of [a Syon House friend's] admirable qualities and my own devoted attachment. I suppose she thought me out of my wits, for she returned no answer to my letter" (Clark 338).

7. See *Shelley's Ambivalence*, esp. chap. 2.

8. See "On Narcissism: An Introduction," in *SE*, XIV, 73–102 (esp. p. 88).

9. Commenting on this first attempt by the elder Groves and Shelleys to discourage their children's romance, Cameron reasonably infers that the outspoken Shelley's religious skepticism lay at the bottom of both this early crisis and the final breakup: "Both *Zastrozzi* and 'Henry and Louisa' show that Shelley's anti-religious views had developed in 1809; and Shelley was hardly one not to discuss them" (*Esdaile* 241).

10. Harriet and Percy first met in 1804, and their romance probably began in the summer of 1808 (see Cameron, *Esdaile*, 306). Although the couple's parents broke off

the engagement in late 1810 and Harriet shortly thereafter became engaged to a local gentleman, Percy retained some hopes for a reconciliation until about mid-January, 1811. See Cameron's "Commentaries" in his edition of *The Esdaile Notebook*, pp. 213–14, 237, 240–41, 248–49, 305–9, for the most convincing chronology to date of the Grove-Shelley romance, which is difficult to trace due to the loss of their letters to each other. For divergent chronologies of the cousins' engagement, see Cameron, *The Young Shelley*, pp. 13–16, 296–97, Jones, Introduction to *The Diary of Harriet Grove* (*SC*, II, 475–90), and Hawkins passim.

11. Writings such as *Henry and Louisa* and *Zastrozzi*—both composed in 1809—predate the crucial shift from Shelley's nascent anticlericalism to his violent denunciations of Christ himself that took place during his nineteenth year; but even in these texts his identification with Christ never resembled a kind of untroubled "hero-worship." Yet his cousin's and sister's defection, their "re-conversion" to Christianity, helped ensure that Shelley's ambivalent love for Christ mutated into something infinitely more powerful—and damaging—in determining his own conception and experience of Selfhood and of Love.

12. Reiman (*NCE* 97n3), among others, locates "The hour which burst / [his] spirit's sleep" and that revealed to Shelley his divine mission within the poet's years at Eton (*CW*, I, 251: *LC*, Dedication, ll. 21–22). However, Holmes (*Pursuit* 15), perhaps following Ingpen and Peck's suggestion (*CW*, I, 424), more convincingly links these autobiographical passages to Syon House, where Shelley first felt the shock of being away from home and found himself surrounded by "tyrants" and "foes" (CW, I, 251: *LC*, Dedication, l. 27).

13. "The idea that I need another person in order to become a self" is Rubin's succinct way of linking (not identifying) the Kohutian selfobject and Kierkegaardian paradigm ("Kohut and Kierkegaard" 142). The essential distinction between these concepts lies in the paradigm's more "objective" status: it exists apart from as well as within its "imitator's" consciousness; whereas, in Kohut's words, selfobjects are "objects which are themselves experienced as part of the self" (*Analysis of the Self* xiv). For Kierkegaard's concept of the 'paradigm,' or 'pattern,' see his *Training in Christianity*, pp. 109–11 and 232–36. Though I do not claim that Kierkegaard's Christian existentialism can be reconciled with Kohut's secular humanism, both of these theoreticians of the self can help illuminate Shelley's self-fashioning and efforts at self-abnegation.

14. While the notion of fusion is encoded in the Kohutian term, the word *merge* may seem a bit strong for the potential self's connection to its Kierkegaard paradigm. Rubin, when she asserts that "the relationship between an individual and her paradigm is an indirect one" (142), is scrupulously true to much of Kierkegaard's own terminology, which stresses "likeness," "resemblance," "correspondence"; yet she neglects the nuance with which Kierkegaard, engaged in his own impassioned *imitatio Christi*, invests his remarks on the paradigm, or, as he calls it later in the text, the "pattern." Regarding the individual's relationship to Christ as "the Pattern," he writes, "A follower is or strives to be what he admires," and, in a more startling passage that has par-

ticular relevance to Shelley as an "absorber" of Christ, he shifts to the first person: "[the Pattern] is taken up into me . . . I swallow him—but, be it observed, since he is 'a claim,' this all is for the purpose of giving him out again as a reflection—and it is I that become greater and greater by coming more and more to resemble him" (*Training in Christianity* 243, 236).

15. Cf. John 12:32.

16. For a lucid, concise account of Kohut's psychology of the self and its relevance to reader-response approaches to literature, see J. Brooks Bouson, *Empathic Reader*, pp. 11–29. Lynne Layton and Barbara A. Schapiro's Introduction to *Narcissism and the Text* is also helpful (see esp. pp. 2–7) The term *selfobject* remains somewhat controversial within the psychoanalytic community, and Kohut himself used it in a variety of ways. These include: someone with whom the developing self fuses as it gropes toward a sense of individuality (though never, for Kohut, separation per se; the self is created and preserved within a matrix of relationships), an other with whom the fragmenting self psychically unites in order to "restore" cohesiveness and wholeness, and the "interpersonal process" that connects self and other (Corbett 28). Unless otherwise indicated, I will be focusing on the first two meanings.

17. For Kohut's remarks on how healthy self-esteem retains remnants of "the old, limitless narcissism" of the small child, see *The Analysis of the Self*, pp. 107–9; quotation from p. 108. As Kohut sees it, the point of therapy is not to eradicate but to "tame" and "transform" those narcissistic tendencies which we all, to a greater or lesser degree, share, and thus to restore "narcissistic equilibrium" (see "Forms and Transformations" passim and "Narcissism and Narcissistic Rage," esp. pp. 363–65 and 388–89). Regarding the alliance between thwarted omnipotent selfobject-self relations and narcissistic disorders, Kohut writes, "Premature interference with the narcissistic self leads to later narcissistic vulnerability because the grandiose fantasy becomes repressed and inaccessible to modifying influences" ("Forms and Transformations" 250). The "grandiose self" forms one pole, "self-esteem," of Kohut's notion of the "bipolar self," a concept which he developed in his later writings (the other pole is "guiding ideals"): "For children 8 months to 3 years of age, Kohut postulates a normal, intermediate phase of powerful narcissistic cathexis of 'the grandiose self' (a grandiose exhibitionistic image of the self) and the idealized parent imago (the image of an omnipotent selfobject with whom fusion is desired). These psychic formations are gradually internalized and integrated within the psychic structure" (Chessick 157; see Kohut, *Restoration of the Self*, chap. 4). In Kohut's view, the grandiose self ultimately generates our ambitions, which "push" us from within, and the idealized parent imago serves as the source of our ideals and aspirations, which "lead" us and help us become more outward-directed (Kohut, "Forms and Transformations," 251–52).

18. "Forms and Transformations," p. 364. Kohut links the development of self-esteem with "the gradual detachment from the idealized other" (*Seminars* 42). The adolescent Shelley's "detachment" from Christ was anything but gradual—or successful.

19. This religiously tinged term, probably an early version of "Self-esteem" ("Hymn," l. 37) appears several times in Shelley's writings. According to his first

usage, in a letter to Elizabeth Hitchener, to be "self devoted" is to be "self-centered," "self-interested" (*L*, I, 173: ?11 November 1811). However, in his Note to *Queen Mab*, V. 189, his 4 October 1814 letter to Hogg (*L*, I, 403), his 5 October 1814 letter to his estranged wife, Harriet (L, I, 266), and his 8 December 1816 letter to Leigh Hunt (*L*, I, 517), self-devotion signifies not "the sordid lust of self" (*QM*, V. 90) but the kind of self-respect and dedication to an other—be it an ideal, a cause, or a person—that symbiotically co-exists with "generosity," "virtue," and dedication to someone or something outside the sphere of one's own ego (*PS*, I, 373; *L*, I, 403). It is extremely rare to find, as we do in these instances, the word self in any but the pejorative capacity that it permanently acquired in Shelley's 1810–11 letters to Hogg. Mary Shelley's *Frankenstein* includes a curious usage of the term *self-devotion* in what Bloom calls the Creature's "equivocal tribute" to his now lifeless creator (*Ringers* 125): "Oh, Frankenstein! generous and self-devoted being!" (*Frankenstein* 217). It seems that Mary is adopting Percy's phrase and putting on ironic spin on it.

20. Freud's distinction between "anaclitic" and "narcissistic" object-choice is also pertinent:

> The sexual instincts are at the outset attached to the satisfaction of the ego-instincts; only later do they become independent of these, and even then we have an indication of that original attachment in the fact that the persons who are concerned with a child's feeding, care, and protection become his earliest sexual objects: that is to say, in the first instance his mother or a substitute for her. Side by side, however, with this type and source of object-choice, which may be called the 'anaclitic' or 'attachment' type, psychoanalytic research has revealed a second type . . . We have discovered, especially clearly in people whose libidinal development has suffered some disturbance . . . that in their later choice of love-objects they have taken as a model not their mother but their own selves. They are plainly seeking *themselves* as a love-object, and exhibiting a type of object-choice which must be termed 'narcissistic.' ("On Narcissism," *SE*, XIV, 87–88)

It is important to note that "narcissism" has quite different connotations in Freud's writings, in Kohut's work, and in Shelley scholarship. For Freud, (secondary) narcissism suggests regression and a failure to establish proper object relations, whereas Kohut sees narcissism more neutrally as "the libidinal investment of the self" necessary for an individual's sense of cohesion and stability ("Forms and Transformations" 243). The intense self-absorption that we sometimes witness in Shelley's behavior and writings Kohut might call "narcissistic disorder" or "narcissistic personality disturbance" ("Narcissism and Narcissistic Rage" 370). Finally, when a literary critic refers to Shelley's "narcissism," he or she is usually making a value judgement, condemning the poet for his self-concern. (For notable exceptions, see Jerrold E. Hogle, *Shelley's Process*, pp. 96–103 and Gelpi, "The Nursery Cave," p. 57.) I will strive for Kohut's neutrality when using this fraught term, and if I imply a pejorative meaning, I will be echoing Shelley's own harsh self-judgement, not that of his critics.

21. Self-absorption also frequently results from what Kohut calls "narcissistic injuries" or "wounds" which often involve the idealized selfobject and nearly always

involve the "mirroring" selfobject, the prototype of which is the infant's not-yet-differentiated mother whose approving responses to the child confirms its sense of cohesion and well-being. When linked with the term *narcissist* or *narcissism* in my discussion, the term *mirroring* will have as its primary meaning "reflecting" or "imitating"—often in a flattering manner—and secondarily, will connote the normative "approving" and "confirming" of the Kohutian mirroring selfobject. In terms of Shelley's own development, we might say that his apparent lack of adequate mirroring in the Kohutian sense led to an unmodified desire for merger with an other who functions almost exclusively to shore up the poet's fragile self-esteem—and precarious sense of identity. *Other*-as-mirror, in effect, became for Shelley other-as-*mirror*.

22. Kohut's focus on preoedipal rather than oedipal issues certainly does not slight the latter. However, as Layton and Schapiro point out in their Introduction to *Narcissism and the Text*, whereas Freudian psychoanalysis highlights "drive-instinctual Oedipal conflict," self psychologists delve into "more archaic problems" involving the developing self and narcissistic disturbances (1).

23. Cf. his remarks in the *Seminars*:

[S]ince transitional phases shape not only one's capacity for detaching oneself from one set of objects—for example, the parental ones—and reinvesting in new objects—for example, the marriage partner—the step from adolescence into adulthood also shakes up a particular mode in which one sees oneself. It echoes, therefore, old trauma about the self, old modes in which self-esteem is shaken . . . But this must be seen not simply as something which happens at a particular given moment, a particular task of the step from adolescence into adulthood, but also, to some extent, a repetition of some point at which the person failed earlier, when in earlier stages of the forming of the self and being secure there was a failure. (*Seminars* 12)

Contrary to his uncharacteristically harsh locution, "the person failed," Kohut's final phrase—"there was a failure"—is more evocative of his usual emphasis on failed *connections* between the inchoate self and its primary, "archaic" selfobjects.

24. See *Beyond the Pleasure Principle*, *SE*, XVIII, 7–64.

25. *Beyond the Pleasure Principle*, SE, XVIII, 16.

26. Shelley first invokes this term in 1811 when he calls Elizabeth Hitchener his "second self," but this notion may have been flourishing in his imagination and interpersonal relations since boyhood (*L*, I, 189).

27. As his mother correctly surmised, Shelley "want[ed] to make a deistical coterie of all [his] little sisters"; but he had already embarked on his "mission," even attempting to "Deistify" his father, who "silenced [his son] with an equine argument" (*L*, I, 42: 11 January 1811). The rift between Shelley and his mother was widened, if not caused, as with Shelley and his cousin and sister, by their religious differences. In his 28 April 1811 letter to Hogg, Shelley first links and then conflates with an ambiguous pronoun his eldest sister and mother when remarking on their "irretrievability"

from Christianity: "A young female, who only once, only for a short space asserted her claim to an unfettered use of reason, bred up with Xtianity, having before her eyes examples of the consequences of Atheism, or even scepticism [i.e., Shelley's own travails] . . . ; a mother who is mild and tolerant yet a Xtian, how I ask is *she* to be rescued from it's influence" (*L*, I, 72). Percy's greatest successes in his role as a "deistical" Christ, gathering and illuminating his disciples, had been in converting his most precious votaries, Harriet and Elizabeth. By the time he wrote the January 11 letter to T. J. Hogg, Harriet already had fallen away ("she . . . is no longer mine, she abhors me as a Deist, as what *she* was before" [*L*, I, 35: 3 January, 1811]) and Elizabeth would soon follow her cousin into "apostasy" ("she does not any longer permit an *Atheist* to correspond with her. She talks of Duty to her *Father* [*L*, I, 70: 26 April 1811]). As Percy writes to his smitten friend that spring, "I will not deceive you, she [Elizabeth] is lost, lost to every thing, Xtianity has tainted her, she talks of God & Xt" (*L*, I, 72: to Hogg, ?28 April 1811). Behrendt, who rightly emphasizes throughout his study of Shelley and audience "the extent to which he saw himself . . . retracing Christ's steps," finds that the poet's efforts as a "recruiter" began in late 1811, but his complex identification with the martyred Christ probably began as early as 1802 with his feelings of abandonment (by his mother) and persecution (by his Syon House schoolmates). As Behrendt asserts, Shelley strove "to assemble from a variety of audiences a fiercely loyal army of disciples who would become the vanguard of the new order of peace, pacifism, and spiritual and moral brotherhood under his careful tutelage" (*Shelley and His Audiences* 4).

28. Hogle sees a Shelleyan "transference" from one identity to another that resembles both the feminine fluidity of identity posited by contemporary French feminists and the feminine self-in-relation ascertained by so-called Anglo-American feminists. (While Hogle does not link Shelley with, for example, Carol Gilligan or Nancy Chodorow, he does draw explicit parallels between the poet's conception of the self and those offered by the French theorists Hélène Cixous and Julia Kristeva. He also likens Shelleyan transference to Alice Jardine's notion of "gynesis" [18, 22, 347n32].) However, I would "transfer" Hogle's indicative to the optative mode and point out that, despite the poet's powerful desire to experience and represent such a mobile, mutable identity, his own assessments of his success are much less optimistic—and more honest—than Hogle's. By "dethron[ing] the center-at-one-with-itself from the position of impetus in Shelley's work and replac[ing] it with [a] centerless displacement of figural counterparts by one another," Hogle attempts to demonstrate that Shelley merely regarded "'Self' as a fabrication defined only in its own terms" and thus as "an illusion, a willed perversion of its own defining process" (14). Hogle's Shelley emerges as a kind of protodeconstructionist who rather too effortlessly achieves "truly relational thinking," infallibly "seeing the self in terms of others" and thus sloughing off the concept of selfhood—and Selfhood—like so much dead logocentric rubbish (27).

29. In his 8 May 1811 letter to Hogg, Shelley decries "that vile family despotism" and "the viler despotism of religion" (*L*, I, 78). In his letters to Elizabeth Hitchener, Shelley often distinguishes between familial ties and intellectual kinships, invari-

ably scoffing at the former and elevating the latter. See, for example, *L*, I, p. 199, and *L*, I, p. 218, where Shelley tells his correspondent, "I wish I knew your mother. I do not mean your natura[l] but your moral mother."

30. This description of Verezzi, the protagonist of *Zastrozzi* (*CW*, V, 6), is echoed in a poem enclosed in a September 1810 letter to Edward Fergus Graham about a "desolate mourner," a "hapless victim" who "finds torn the soft ties to affection so dear" (*L*, I, 16). Shelley includes this poem, which clearly refers to his own despair over his growing estrangement from his cousin/fiancée, in his 1810 novel *St. Irvyne*, named for the "Old House St. Irvyne" (St. Irving's Hills) that was the site of Percy and Harriet's moonlight walks in April 1810 (*SC*, II, 575: *Diary of Harriet Grove* [17 April 1810]).

31. As Jones points out, this probably refers to an early version of *The Necessity of Atheism* that Hogg had composed (*L*, I, 47n1: 17 January 1811).

32. In the *Seminars*, Kohut speaks of "severe infantile disappointment in an idealed figure of the past" and of "the idealizing transference" that may occur in later life as compensation/healing (77). Elsewhere, Kohut discusses "compensatory structures" that the psyche develops, structures that often involve surrogate mirroring and idealized selfobjects: "If earlier mirroring responses are badly flawed . . . the child will intensify his search for the structuring presence of a selfobject that is experienced as an alter ego or for the uplifting, self-organizing experience that comes from the availability of a selfobject that is idealizable" (See *How Does Analysis Cure?* 44–45, 131–33, 204–6; quotations from p. 205).

33. See especially the series of letters that Shelley fired off to his father in the late summer and fall of 1811, just after the poet eloped with his "second Harriet." In the letters of 16 and 27 September, Percy is particularly intent on exposing Timothy's flimsy Christianity and his own true understanding of and kinship with Christ, whose words he rather belligerently echoes as he harps on "the unforgiving spirit of fathers" (*L*, I, 140–43; quotation p. 142).

34. White observes that the elder Shelley "had slight appreciation of the spiritual values of religion, but in Christianity as an institution, he saw the bulwark of the state and the home" (*Shelley*, I, 12).

35. In "Social Speculation and Revolutionary Upheaval," the first chapter of his excellent study, R. A. Soloway details the problems plaguing the Anglican church during the late eighteenth century. Ellsworth Barnard writes that at the beginning of the nineteenth century, the English church "seemed spiritually extinct" (41). Stephen Prickett's essay on the religious context of British romanticism also gives a good idea of the church's spiritual and moral bankruptcy (*The Romantics* 115–63).

36. Joseph Gibbons Merle's 1841 reminiscence of Shelley, quoted in Cameron, *Young Shelley*, p. 124. (Shelley and Merle, who later became a London newspaper editor, were introduced in the spring of 1810 by their mutual friend Edward Graham.) Merle is commenting on a heated debate on religion between Shelley and himself in

which the former angrily refers to "a painting of that imposter, Christ, hanging up in [his father's] library." I see such works as the now lost *Biblical Extracts* (1812) and the "Essay on Christianity" (1817) in part as Shelley's attempts to bestow "credibility" on this "imposter" by refashioning him into a political reformer à la Thomas Paine— and P. B. Shelley—and thus achieving a kind of "priority" and control over his precursor (and here the Bloomian model is apt).

37. This pattern is evident as late as 1821, when, in *Adonais*, Shelley withholds from the "martyred" Keats the explicit parallel with Christ and instead assigns it to himself.

38. When he rejects or, more typically, ignores the Resurrection—and the Ascension—Shelley is not simply debunking Jesus' divinity within the context of his own exposé of Christian "falshood" (*Esdaile* 44: "Falshood and Vice: A Dialogue"). It seems, rather, that he is curbing the threatening "omnipotence" of his omnipotent self-object as well as ensuring that the Crucifixion remains at center stage, as it literally does in Act I of *Prometheus Unbound*, of Shelley's reenactment of his predecessor's life and death. For a rare reference to the resurrection in Shelley's writings, see *The Wandering Jew* (III. 638–57), where the gore of the Crucifixion nevertheless overwhelms Ahasuerus' vision of the transfigured Christ (*PS*, I, 60–61).

39. As Stuart Curran remarks regarding Shelley's "reject[ion] of action as the customary mode of heroism," "One of [Shelley's] major contributions, not only to English literature but to Romantic psychology, is his continuing analysis of passivity" (*Shelley's Annus Mirabilis* 37).

40. See Frederick Burwick's "The Language of Causality in *Prometheus Unbound*," pp. 136–37, 147–50, for an illuminating discussion of how the Passion of Christ metaphysically and linguistically reconciles the Greek words for "doing" and "suffering" into a sacred paradox of an active, creative "passivity."

41. Such pairings in which passivity is linked with virtue, activity with evil include Cythna/ Othman, Prometheus/Jupiter, and Beatrice Cenci/Count Cenci.

42. The first phrase is Peacock's (*Memoirs* 345) and the second Medwin's (*Life* 333). This is Trelawny's first impression of Shelley, whom he met in early 1822: "Swiftly gliding in, blushing like a girl, a tall, thin stripling held out both his hands; and although I could hardly believe as I looked at his flushed, feminine, and artless face that it could be the poet, I returned his warm pressure" (*Recollections* 172). Although in chapter 3 I will be exploring in much greater detail Shelley's "effeminate" heroes as they relate to his own deliberate—as well as seemingly inherent—swervings from traditional masculinity, I want to suggest here that the notion of a feminized Christ contributed immensely to Shelley's frequent adoptions of feminine subject positions.

43. Echoing Paine's description of Christ as "an amiable man" (*Complete Writings*, II, 467: *The Age of Reason*), Shelley often employs this word in his 1810–1811 letters to connote, as John Freeman points out, generosity and disinterestedness (see

"Shelley's Early Letters," p. 124). See, for example the 26 April 1811 letter to Hogg for this usage of "amiable" (*L*, I, 68–70). ("Amiable" is also a key term for the moral philosophers who influenced the poet. Hutcheson and Hume are especially partial to it.) Yet this word as Shelley employs it also at times suggests the kind of emotional and intellectual malleability that he hoped to find in the various—usually female—disciples he cultivated. For this more problematic definition, see his ?25 April 1811 letter to Hogg, a letter that may pertain to Harriet Grove but more probably refers to Elizabeth Shelley (the intricacies of this web of relationships are notorious). Shelley opens the letter with the assertion, "Believe me that I will not so soon give up for lost a being whom I considered so amiable" and concludes with his "hopes" for "this dear little girl [his sister Hellen], who would be a divine little scion of infidelity if I could get hold of her. I think my lessons here must have taken effect" (*L*, I 75–76). Here Shelley is clearly substituting one backsliding "amiable being," Harriet-Elizabeth, with the more susceptible "young female[s]" he found both in Hellen Shelley and in his new pupil, Harriet Westbrook, to whom this letter also refers (*L*, I, 81, 72).

44. Bloom's masculinist model of poetic influence does offer us the indispensable and resonant term *precursor*, which evokes the struggle for ascendency over Christ, the move toward "absolute absorption of the precursor" that Shelley initiates at least as early as 1809 and that most Shelley scholars have ignored (*Anxiety* 11). Yet Bloom, whom Frank Lentriccia dubs "the historian as aesthete" (*After the New Criticism* 326), generally remains within the realm of aesthetics, insisting on an impossible separation between "*the poet in a poet*, or the aboriginal poetic self" (*Anxiety* 11) and "the person-in-a-poet" (*Map* 28). (To be fair, Shelley himself invokes just such a dichotomy in a letter to the Gisbornes: "The poet & the man are two different natures: though they exist together they may be unconscious of each other, & incapable of deciding upon each other's powers & effects by any reflex act" [*L*, II, 310].) When we recognize the essential kinship between these two beings and then turn from Bloom's theory to "the case of Shelley," to borrow Pottle's famous phrase, we can appreciate how seldom the Bloomian scenario of manly battles accords with this most effeminate—that is not to say *feminist*—of poets. Because Shelley, as a "womanly" man, generally evades Freud's—and Bloom's—oedipal scheme, and as a womanly *man*, cannot be situated in Nancy Chodorow's paradigm of "the reproduction of mothering," I find Kohut's model of the non-gender-specific idealized selfobject most valuable in exploring the dynamic between Shelley and Christ.

45. Stuart Sperry, for example, who recognizes Shelley's "extraordinary ambivalence" toward Christ, locates this ambivalence solely in Shelley's strained relations with his father, whom Sperry in his reading of *Queen Mab* VII therefore identifies with the malevolent Christ (*Shelley's Major Verse* 16).

46. For examples of such imagery, culled from the writings of Anselm of Canterbury and Bernard of Clairvaux, among others, see pp. 113–25. The "showings" or visions of Julian of Norwich also feature a vividly maternal Jesus.

47. See, for instance, "Jesu, Lover of my soul" and "Thou Shepherd of Israel, and mine" in Lawson, pp. 88–89 and 131–32. The "sexual and 'womb-regressive'

imagery" of Wesley's hymns receives rather hostile treatment from E. P. Thompson, as does the Methodist movement itself (350–400, quotation p. 371).

48. From the penultimate line of Wesley's "Thou Shepherd of Israel, and mine" (Lawson 132).

49. This quote and its context exemplifies Shelley's habit of indoctrinating his correspondent while—implicitly and/or overtly—admonishing himself. Shelley, writing to Elizabeth Hitchener, tells her, "[D]ivest yourself of individuality, dare to place *self* at a distance which I know you can, spurn those bug-bears *gratitude, obligation, & modesty*" and continues, "with the sister of my soul I have no obligation, to her I feel no gratitude, I stand not on etiquette, alias insincerity. The ideas excited by these words are varying, frequently unjust, always *selfish*." Finally, with a conspiratorial shift into the first person plural, he declares, "*Love* in the sense which we understand it needs not these succedanea" (*L*, I, 151: 16 October 1811).

50. In *Alastor* and *Epipsychidion*, for example, these two strains of narcissism are united.

51. In *Alastor* Shelley had introduced and criticized the kind of self-projection that he (initially) embraces in *Epipsychidion*.

52. Isomaki argues that Shelley transcended in his later work the "vacant antithesis" of love vs. selfishness that obtains in the early letters, *Queen Mab*, and *Alastor* (659). Of Shelley's supposedly successful integration of "a participating self," as he moved from *Alastor* (1815) to "On Love" (1818), Isomaki writes, "In the poem, a 'self-centred seclusion' dooms the Poet; in the essay, a self-center—the prototype—permits one to love" (661, 662). Because Isomaki focuses on *Prometheus Unbound*, where individual desire and universal love strike a rare harmony in Shelley's *oeuvre*, his assessment of Shelley's development seems accurate. Yet Shelley never lost his fundamental distrust of "the principle of Self," nor did he accept his own "resolution" of his central dichotomy as wholeheartedly as Isomaki does. As the despair that pervades "On Love" reveals, Shelley embraced the prototype/antitype model much less unreservedly than either those who champion (e.g., Brown, Isomaki) or those who condemn (e.g., Mellor, Richardson, Schapiro) this aspect of Shelley's thought acknowledge.

53. We have no hard evidence that the poet read à Kempis, but we can reasonably suppose at least some familiarity with *De Imitatione Christi*. Paul J. Korshin (*Typologies in England* 197–98, 215) discusses its extreme popularity and ready availability during Shelley's time: "Between 1650 and 1800 there were at least a dozen separate fresh English translations, all of which were reprinted from two to twenty times . . . The *Imitatio*, incidentally, which had been quite popular in the Renaissance, would be even more widely printed in nineteenth-century England" (197).

54. Ralph Klein is discussing Kohut's concept of 'transmuting internalization', which Kohut elucidates in *The Analysis of the Self*, esp. chap. 2. In the *Seminars*, Kohut provides a relatively concise explanation of this process, which is prompted by what he calls "optimal frustration":

In the developmental sequence—the increasing selectivity of parental responses, the increasing frustration, the increasing loss of the approving object, not by death and sudden disappearance, but by gradual withholding of approval, which is always part of an object that is lost . . .—all this leads to the gradual taking over by the psyche of functions that were formerly performed by others. In the case of the idealized object there is also a loss. There is a recognition that the ideal is not ideal. But it must be recognized not prematurely and not massively; otherwise it becomes traumatic and indigestible. It becomes useful for the psyche when it occurs at the right moment and at the right speed. Then it leads to the setting up internally of the formerly external ideal, with all the ensuing advantages of having an internal ideal object, namely, one's values, goals, and ideals. (*Seminars* 81)

These remarks, along with Kohut's emphasis on "the intimate relationship between idealization and narcissism" ("Forms and Transformations" 246), illuminate Shelley's retreat into narcissism, due first, it seems, to his mother's and later his cousin's and sisters' sudden "withholding of approval," as well as to his own "premature" and "massive" rejection of Christ.

55. See, for example, his 1810 poem "How swiftly through Heaven's wide expanse," where Shelley, melodramatically anticipating his fate as a bereft lover, calls himself a "wretch" (*L*, I, 8: 22 April 1810). In his 20 December 1810 letter to Hogg, Shelley vows to "stab the wretch [Christ] in secret" (*L*, I, 27). In his early letters, novels, and verse, Shelley generally reserves this term for himself (or his speakers and protagonists) and Christ.

56. See *Young Shelley*, pp. 302–3, where Cameron provides a timetable for the composition of Shelley's two Gothic novels, a chronology that is credible except that it implies that after August of 1809—seven months before the novel's publication in March 1810—Shelley set *Zastrozzi* aside once and for all, undertaking no revisions.

57. Tilottama Rajan, drawing on Julia Kristeva's "The Adolescent Novel," provides an astute comment:

Although these novels [*Zastrozzi* and *St. Irvyne*] are jeux d'esprit whose plots border on the ridiculous, rather than dismissing them as adolescent, we might recall Julia Kristeva's characterization of the novel itself as an adolescent form. Noting that the novel allows for a trying out of roles in which the writer dresses up as his characters, she suggests that it creates a space withdrawn "from reality testing" that the novelist is then free to reorganize "in the time before an ideally postulated maturity." ("Promethean Narrative" 242–43)

58. This is precisely how Stephen Behrendt reads both of Shelley's Gothic novels. I am greatly indebted to Behrendt's Introduction to the World's Classics edition to the novels, which he includes in revised form in *Shelley and His Audiences*, pp. 39–48. See also Jerrold Hogle's illuminating essay on Shelley's fiction, which demonstrates how the collapse of linear psychology and chronology in the fiction anticipates the coalescence of characters and the discovery of "an internal 'Now'" in *Prometheus Unbound* ("Shelley's Fiction" 88).

59. Along with his beloved teacher at Eton, Dr. James Lind, and (briefly) Robert Southey, Godwin obviously served as a father figure for Shelley. Both Shelley's second and third letters to Godwin explicitly invite him to assume that role, not only with remarks about how the older man "materially influenced [Shelley's] character" (*L*, I, 227), but with strategically placed references to Timothy Shelley himself: "The habits of thinking of my Father and myself never coincided"; "My father has ever regarded me as a blot and defilement of his honor"; "I have known no tutor or adviser not excepting my father from whose lessons and suggestions I have not recoiled with disgust . . . [My present habits and feelings] are elevated and disinterested. Such as they are you have principally produced them"; "I never loved my father" (*L*, I, 227, 228, 230). While Godwin's influence on Shelley was undeniably profound, it nevertheless cannot rival that of Christ, a much earlier and more permanent presence. While Shelley could cathect Christ as a selfobject incorporating the "androgynous" quality Shelley himself valued and embodied, he generally maintained much more of a psychic distance between himself and Godwin, his paternalistic literary and political precursor.

60. Although subsequent chapters will address the issues of Zastrozzi's oedipal mission and Verezzi's sexual passivity, I want to point out here the generally overlooked fact that the seducer of Olivia Zastrozzi is both Verezzi's *and* Zastrozzi's father. Thus Zastrozzi commits both patricide ("the false villain . . . sank beneath my dagger" [*CW*, V, 102]) and, indirectly, fratricide ("[Verezzi] destroyed himself; but my machinations, though unseen, effected his destruction" [102]). I think that we would be mistaken to read too much into this familial configuration, but in light of Shelley's later quarrels and break with his father, it seems reasonable to detect in this early novel what Sperry in another context calls "Oedipal strains" (*Shelley's Major Verse* 6). More intriguing in relation to this novel is the relative absence of references to his younger brother, John, in Percy's correspondence and recorded conversations and the possibility that the young novelist envisioned parallels between himself and "the vindictive Zastrozzi" and between John and the miserable Verezzi (*CW*, V, 5). Holmes writes that although John was "not born until 1806, when Shelley was already at Eton, . . . the sense of maternal betrayal may have been emphasized by a transfer of attention from the elder son to the younger" (*Pursuit* 11–12). It would of course be absurd to identify literally the then three-year-old John with Verezzi, who on the whole represents Shelley's own desire to compensate for this perceived "maternal betrayal" by supplying his protagonist with three vastly different but equally devoted women: Julia, Claudia, and Matilda. A poem from the *Victor and Cazire* volume entitled "Revenge" and written in December 1809 resurrects and makes more explicit the oedipal theme of *Zastrozzi*, with a ghostly Conrad in the Zastrozzi role pursuing a Verezzi-like Adolphus:

> Thy father, Adolphus! was false, false as hell,
> And Conrad has cause to remember it well;
> He ruined my Mother, despised me his son,
> I quitted the world ere my vengeance was done.

> (*PS*, I, 28: ll. 45–48)

61. In the winter of 1810 and 1811, following the dissolution of Percy's and Harriet's engagement, Elizabeth was a "great consolation" to her brother and appar-

ently attempted to reconcile her favorite cousin and best-loved brother (*L*, I, 32: 26 December 1810). The despondent lover even credits Elizabeth with preventing his suicide, writing to T. J. Hogg, "I could not come on Monday my sister wd. not part with me . . . had it not been for her, had it not been for a sense of what I owed to her to you I should have bid you a final farewell some time ago" (*L*, I, 36: 3 January 1811). It is at this point in the Shelley-Hogg correspondence that the Harriet/Percy and Elizabeth /Thomas pairings begin to form in the friends' imagination. Many have commented on Shelley's incestuous feelings for his eldest sister, on his "romantic friendship" with Hogg, and on the way that an imagined union of his sister and best friend allowed Shelley indirectly to gratify his forbidden desires (see, for example, Cameron, *Young Shelley*, p. 16; Holmes, *Pursuit*, pp. 91–95; and Mellor, *Mary Shelley*, pp. 29, 74). Suffice it to say here that Elizabeth, perhaps aware on some level of her brother's motivations, pulled away from him and from his religious opinions when Percy began orchestrating this liaison.

62. Susan Fischman, commenting on Shelley's Field Place boyhood, writes, "The desire for listeners, especially perhaps female listeners, was never requited so fully or easily again" ("Gender, Audition, and Echo" 147). Holmes and Gelpi use several of Hellen Shelley's letters (cited in Hogg [I, 21–30]) to reconstruct the Percy-centered atmosphere that reigned at Field Place until he embarked for Syon House in 1802. Cameron remarks of one of Hellen Shelley's letters that "The picture is that of a devoted older brother, worshipped by his sisters, gently shepherding them in their frolics; an idyllic, sheltered existence" (*Young Shelley* 6).

63. Although no letters have survived, Hemans herself partially verifies Medwin's claim by referring in an 1822 letter to a rather one-sided correspondence between herself and Shelley. This letter nicely invokes the youthful Shelley's often irritating zeal: "I believe I mentioned to you the extraordinary letters with which I was once persecuted by (Mr. Shelley); he, with whom 'Queen Mab hath been'" (quoted in Ingpen, *Shelley in England*, 80n1).

64. In his 12 May 1811 letter to Hogg, Shelley tells his friend, "I am now with my uncle [Capt. John Pilfold]; he is a very hearty fellow, and has behaved very nobly to me, in return for which I have illuminated him" (*L*, I, 82–83). Shelley is alluding to the Illuminists, a Jacobinical sect that flourished in the 1790s and that Shelley probably learned about during his first term at Oxford when he acquired Augustin Barruel's *Memoirs, Illustrating the History of Jacobism*, trans. Robert Clifford (1797–98). Although, as Mellor points out, Barruel's book offers a "vitriolic attack" on Illuminism (*Mary Shelley* 73), in keeping with Percy's habit of "moulding" his female companions, during their summer 1814 elopement he introduced Mary to the book and thus to the sect's revolutionary principles which it describes as well as condemns. Earlier, in February of 1812, he had recommended the book to Elizabeth Hitchener, telling her that "Altho it is half filled with vilest and most unsupported falsehoods it is a book worth reading" (*L*, I, 264). For a perceptive account of how Mary Shelley responded to her lover's enthusiasm for the Illuminati, see Mellor's *Mary Shelley*, chap. 4, "Promethean Politics." As Holmes writes, "Their doctrine was one of militant egalitarianism, the destruction of private property, religion and 'superstitious' social forms

such as marriage" (*Pursuit* 52). Shelley's fascination with the Illuminati, reflected in his depiction of a group of primitive, communistic Christians in *The Assassins* (1814), in fact helped him (re)embrace Christ as a radical philosophical and political thinker once he gained some distance on the Harriet Grove crisis.

65. In the same context, Cameron calls Locke's *Essay* "a favorite weapon later used against Elizabeth Hitchener" (*Young Shelley* 296).

66. On March 28, 1810, Harriet records in her diary that "Bysshe has sent C[harles] & me Zastrozzi as it is come out" (*SC*, II, 573: *Diary of Harriet Grove*).

67. Surprisingly, Percy rarely expresses anger at Harriet and Elizabeth themselves, but the intensity of his fury at Christ suggests that whatever animosity he did feel toward them he deflected into his attacks on Christ.

68. See Mellor's *English Romantic Irony* for a fruitful application of Arnold van Gennep's and Victor Turner's concepts of "threshold" experiences, "the liminal rites of passage" that the self must engage in as it *becomes* a self (6). Although Mellor does not include Shelley in her study, the cycles of self-creation and (often simultaneous) self-annihilation that he initiates when he elects to follow in Christ's footsteps correspond in part to the romantic ironic processes of "self-becoming" (13). However, Shelley's intensely earnest *imitatio Christi*—with its odd mix of self-exaltation and self-denial—generally precludes the exuberant playfulness that Mellor emphasizes and that distinguishes the 1820 poem "The Cloud" as well as parts of *Zastrozzi*.

69. See Percy's and Elizabeth's comical letter to Edward Graham (23 April 1810) for a giddy "sending up" of Gothic conventions, including a cryptic warning that "my mother brings a blood stained stiletto whic{h} she purposes to make you bathe in the life blood of her enemy" (*L*, I, 10). It is tempting to see this last bit of invention as an intimation of Shelley's bizarre fantasy the following year of a romantic triangle between Edward, Elizabeth, and Mrs. Shelley (see *L*, I, 85–87, 156, 163, 164).

70. The disclaimer embedded in this last quotation exemplifies the way Shelley "has set up a sort of moral and psychological 'buffer' in the person of the narrator" as the author nonetheless compels the reader "to confront what Zastrozzi has to say" (Behrendt, Introduction to *Zastrozzi and St. Irvyne*, xv). As a member of Shelley's "inner circle," Harriet Grove would have recognized that he "is far more sympathetic to Zastrozzi than he allows his narrator to be," especially since she must have heard her cousin voice similar opinions in conversation and in letters (Behrendt xv).

71. Ingpen reproduces a complete manuscript version of the Preface in *Shelley in England*, pp. 671–74 (quotation from p. 671).

72. Besides the fact that in these letters to Hogg he shares with Christ the title *wretch*, Shelley's oscillation between—and frequent blurring of—his desire to kill Christ and to commit suicide suggests that this self-directed aggression may stem from his at least partial recognition that he himself and not simply his "rival" Christ contributed to his breakup with Harriet.

73. As Holmes points out, "The months before Oxford saw a burst of literary publications," including *Zastrozzi*, *The Wandering Jew*, the *Victor and Cazire* volume (with Elizabeth Shelley), several poems later copied into what is now known as *The Esdaile Notebook*, and *St. Irvyne* (*Pursuit* 31). Clearly, a key facet of the young Shelley's self-fashioning involved creating his identity as "a man of letters."

74. Behrendt points out that "Zastrozzi in many ways prefigures the flawed Satan-Prometheus figure Shelley would later 'redeem' in the perfected, benevolent Prometheus" (*Zastrozzi and St. Irvyne*, Introduction, xvi).

75. In the same context, Behrendt comments, "Like Satan, Zastrozzi has been destroyed from within by an ego grown beyond all bounds of reason; in his role of self-appointed avenger he is not unlike the cruel and retributive God of the Old Testament whom Shelley rejected" (xvii). Actually, Zastrozzi's mother "commands" him to seek revenge and thus implicates her son in the very ideology that "ruined" her, an ideology that is founded on the desires and the sins of the father (*CW*, V, 102). When Shelley himself later emulates the very vengefulness and thus the self-absorption that he had criticized in Zastrozzi, we can gauge the intensity of the young author's (narcissistic) rage at the Christ whom he believed struck "at the root of the dearest the tenderest of [Shelley's] ties": "[H]ere I swear that never will I forgive Christianity! it is the only point on which I allow myself to encourage revenge; every moment shall be devoted to my object which I can spare, & let me hope that it will not be a blow which spends itself & leaves the wretch at rest but lasting long revenge!" (*L*, I, 35: to Hogg, 3 January 1811). This passage typifies the conflation of Christ (the "wretch") and Christianity that the hurt and furious Shelley effects in these 1810–1811 letters and that he never fully rectifies even in his later tributes to Jesus.

76. *Sadak the Wanderer* (1810–1811), *The Assassins* (1814), *Alastor* (1815), and perhaps *Prince Athanase* (1817) also allude to the Wandering Jew legend, while Ahasuerus plays a pivotal role in *Hellas*. (Crook and Guiton see "Prince Athanase (a-thanatos = without death) . . . [as a] quasi-Jew figure" [30]).

77. Cf. Romans 13: 12–14 and Ephesians 6: 11–17.

78. Cf. "England in 1819."

79. Crook and Guiton, intent upon establishing that Shelley was—or thought he was—a syphilitic, see the Wandering Jew as "an emblem of an infinitely prolonged existence of pain and infirmity, linked to an undying tormented body" (29). Wasserman and Curran both provide excellent insights into Shelley's increasingly subtle references to Ahasuerus and Christ, but neglect the poet's personal investment in these competing "alter egos." See Wasserman, *Shelley: A Critical Reading*, pp. 37–38, 291–305, 389–401, and Curran, *Shelley's Annus Mirabilis*, pp. 20–21, 24, 41, 42, 54–59, 170, 211n29, 213n10. Sperry's reading of Ahasuerus and Christ as they appear in *Queen Mab* VII acknowledges the biographical underpinnings of this episode. However, rather than focus on the "mutual recrimination[s]" between Shelley and his father, as Sperry does, I would emphasize that Shelley was more eager to play both the part of Christ and of Ahasuerus in his own psychomachia than he was to assign his scorned father either role (*Shelley's Major Verse* 16).

80. Shelley lifts this episode from Lewis's novel for his own poetic "tale of terror," "Ghasta," where Shelley's Wandering Jew wears the same cross of "glowing flame" that marks Lewis' character (*PS*, I, 37). As many have noted, Lewis exerted the single greatest influence on Shelley's early writings, those Gothic novels and poems such as *Zastrozzi*, *St. Irvyne*, "Ghasta," "The Revenge," and *The Wandering Jew* composed during the "votary of romance" period of 1809–1810 (see Cameron, *Young Shelley*, p. 29). See Zimansky for an account of the latter poem's borrowings from Lewis as well as from Radcliffe. ("Borrowing" often verged on, or, in the case of "Saint Edmond's Eve" from the *Victor and Cazire* volume, actually became plagiarism when it came to the young Shelley's enthusiasm for Monk Lewis.)

81. Sleuth work by a number of scholars, including White (*Shelley*, I, 580–81n21), has done much to illuminate the Shelley-Schubart connection, involving as it did a mysterious fragment which both Medwin (*Life* 42–43, 489–90) and Shelley (*PS*, I, 395: Note to *Queen Mab*, VII. 67) claim to have picked up in Lincoln's-Inn Fields. See also *PS*, I, p. 40, and *Shelley's Goddess*, p. 30. Cameron provides the clearest account of the tortuous textual history of Shelley's three prose versions of the Ahasuerus legend (*SC*, II, 650–59). These include a footnote to *The Wandering Jew*, a fragmentary manuscript he gave to Hogg in early 1811, and a Note to *Queen Mab*.

82. This is the same letter in which Shelley exclaims, "I wish I were the Antichrist," a fitting companion for Ahasuerus (*L*, I, 35).

83. Still, Shelley is loathe to allow Ahasuerus to supersede Christ entirely as his exemplar, insisting that he, like Christ in the Wandering Jew legend, was first "injured" and only afterwards injuring (*L*, I, 35). Moreover, even the poet's Zastrozzi-like posturing in the passages vowing revenge does not entirely obliterate his need to cling to the model of Christ, as his paean to "love, love *infinite in extent*, eternal in duration" and his struggle to transcend self, even through death, reveal (*L*, I, 35).

84. The last quote is taken from the "Wandering Jew" prose fragment that Shelley gave to Hogg (*SC*, II, 650). Cameron (*SC*, II, 658–59) notes another important echo from the fragment in this letter. Exhausted by his futile pursuit of death, Ahasuerus cries, "Awful avenger in Heaven, hast thou in thine armoury of wrath a punishment more dreadful! Then let it Thunder upon me . . . that I . . . may pant writhe & die" (*SC*, II, 650). In the letter to Hogg, Shelley declares that if he ever forgives Christianity, may "Infinity, Eternity blast [him] . . . Has vengeance in its armoury of wrath a punishment more dreadful!" (*L*, I, 35). Here, Shelley is obviously linking himself to the Wandering Jew as well as outdoing even Zastrozzi, and Satan, in his fist-shaking ("may God [if there is a God] blast me," not if Shelley does but if he does *not* "gratify" his "insatiable" appetite for revenge [35]). To further complicate things, the context of his allusion to the prose fragment yokes Shelley's role as an avenger to Jehovah's: the "vengeance" he refers to can be Shelley's own against Christ or God's against Shelley.

85. After quoting the Maniac's claim, "Here I cast away / All human passions, all revenge, all pride" (*JM*, ll. 501–2), Curran points out that the Maniac "well understands his failure to transcend his condition by willed selflessness: no matter how chas-

tened the mind, 'I do but hide / Under these words, like embers, every spark / Of that which has consumed me' (503–5)" (*Shelley's Annus Mirabilis* 139). Even in his earliest letters to Hogg, where Shelley's renunciation of self is its most strident, the poet himself intermittently achieves the kind of self-knowledge that he later allows this persona (briefly) to express: acknowledging that "perhaps vanity has a great share in" his own "αφιλαυτια [lack of self-love]," he scrutinizes his "boasted hatred of self" and finds it "inconsistent" (*L*, I, 77–78: 8 May 1811).

86. John James Stockdale published this volume in September 1810, but quickly withdrew it when he discovered that it contained a plagiarized poem from Lewis's *Tales of Terror*, "St. Edmond's Eve."

87. See *CW*, I, pp. 5–33, or *PS*, I, p. 587 (Appendix B), for the *Victor and Cazire* poems printed (*CW*) or listed (*PS*) in order.

88. Long thought to be a joint composition of Shelley and Medwin and never published during Shelley's lifetime, *The Wandering Jew* is now generally accepted as Shelley's own.

89. In one of his most disingenuous letters, Shelley writes to Stockdale of his inability thus far to find a publisher for the poem: "As to its containing Atheistical principles, I assure you, I was wholly unaware of the fact hinted at. Your good sense will point out to you the impossibility of inculcating pernicious doctrines in a poem, which as you will see is so totally abstract from any circumstances which occur under the possible view of mankind" (*L*, I, 18: 28 September 1810).

90. See Anderson, pp. 13–15, for a fuller account of the "Legend of St. John" and its contribution to the Wandering Jew myth. Shelley also links Paulo to St. John the Divine, with whom St. John of the Gospels is often conflated, by ascribing to his hero the gift of prophesy: "I pierce with intellectual eye / Into each hidden mystery; . . . The past, the present, and to come, / Float in review before my sight" (*PS*, I, 65, 66: *WJ*, III. 800–1, 806–7).

91. See esp. Acts 9: 3–6. As Zimansky points out (608–9), Shelley may have borrowed the name Paulo from Radcliffe's *The Italian*, though it is hard to see Vivaldi's longsuffering but absurdly demonstrative servant as the model for Shelley's grim protagonist.

92. One of those gloomy retrospects involves Harriet Grove, at whose brother's estate Shelley wrote the poem and whose presence hovers throughout its lines. Although it is ostensibly about Shelley's newfound happiness with Harriet Westbrook, his bitter memory of his failed relationship with his cousin—"unrequited love," "broken vows," and "friendless solitude"—dominates this lyric (ll. 49, 65, 85). Looking back on his anguish of only a year or so before, Shelley appropriates the martyrdom of the one whom he continued to blame for his cousin's "barren and cold repulse" (l. 62).

93. While in this early work it is the curse that Christ pronounces which links Ahasuerus, through the epigraph, to the disciple St. John, not even his hero's almost immediate repentance of and sixteen-hundred-year expiation for his crime can free

him from the "exquisitely torturing pain" that both mirrors and surpasses—in duration and intensity—Christ's own (*PS*, I, 60: *WJ*, III. 624).

94. Even at seventeen, when he composed *The Wandering Jew*, Shelley was capable of the kind of irony that invokes both Satan and Jehovah as the "Demon" into whose hands Paulo finally commends his spirit (*PS*, I, 83: *WJ*, IV. 1454).

95. According to Cameron, Shelley composed *St. Irvyne* between September 1809 and April 1810 (*Young Shelley* 303). Reiman (*Percy Bysshe Shelley* 3) confirms this date.

96. David Seed traces some of the same parallels between *The Wandering Jew* and *St. Irvyne* that I am emphasizing, though he underestimates Shelley's condemnation of both Paulo's and Ginotti's essential self-involvement and instead sees them—along with Ahasuerus of *Queen Mab*—as embodiments of heroic or "quasi-heroic resistance to the forces of adversity" (50). What Seed ignores, and what both Hogle ("Shelley's Fiction" 86–88) and Behrendt (Introduction to *Zastrozzi and St. Irvyne*, xvi–xviii) underscore is Shelley's conviction that mere endurance of pain is not enough—there must be a loving impulse behind the martyr-hero's willingness to suffer.

97. Both Hogle ("Shelley's Fiction" 86) and Seed (45–46) note that Shelley portrays these men as *Doppelgänger*.

98. Shelley borrows much of his imagery for Ginotti's dream from *The Wandering Jew*, esp. III, ll. 638–89, which further solidifies the link between Ginotti and Paulo (it appears that Shelley wrote Canto III of *The Wandering Jew* before composing Ginotti's narrative). These two episodes in turn borrow heavily from the evil Victoria's mountaintop dream vision in Charlotte Dacre's *Zofloya* (239–40), one of the young Shelley's beloved books.

99. Hogle provides an astute reading of this scene: "What has occurred is a failure of [Ginotti's] own essential will, for he has denied the love-object in the first image and submitted to the tyranny of self-obsession in the second. Enslaved by all that is '*selfish and self-interested*' (V, 180), he cares only for the immortality of his physical being and so chooses the spirit within him corresponding to that desire, the dark underside of the beauty beyond him that he still sees in fleeting glimpses" ("Shelley's Fiction" 87–88). I would simply add that Shelley's pairing of Ginotti with the Wandering Jew suggests that this "love-object" is Christ.

100. As Shelley had by then learned that his engagement with his cousin was finished and perhaps knew that she was now betrothed to another, this poem finds him in the unappeasable Satanic mood that he embraces in some of the winter 1810–1811 letters to Hogg. (Harriet Grove became engaged to William Helyar, whom Shelley did not know but dubbed "a clod of earth," in December 1810, and she married him in the fall of 1811 [*L*, I, 41]. Since the Shelley-Grove affair had just ended, her speedy betrothal especially angered and hurt her former suitor.)

101. Ever eager to expand his female coterie, Percy invites his estranged wife to join him and his new sisters of the soul in Switzerland. See *L*, I, pp. 391–93.

102. As mentioned earlier, Ahasuerus also plays a role in *Alastor* and perhaps in *Prince Athanase*.

103. "And Enoch walked with God: and he was not; for God took him" (Genesis 5: 24).

104. Cf. Matthew 7: 7.

105. In his Note to line 1090 of *Hellas*, Shelley refers to "the sublime human character of Jesus Christ" (*CW*, III, 57). Here, he was following Paine and Spinoza, among others. See, for example, Spinoza's *Tractatus*, pp. 113 and 203, and Paine's *Age of Reason*, pp. 467 and 469 of the *Complete Writings*, Vol. II. Earl Wasserman's reading of the exchange between Ahasuerus and Mahmud, though different in emphasis, is compatible with mine:

> Not only is there the irony of placing Christ's words in the mouth of the Jew who had mocked him; Shelley means also to deny the supernatural status of both Ahasuerus and Christ. There is neither a kingdom of this world nor a 'kingdom' of heaven. As Christ was for Shelley a man who most fully developed the divine human powers and virtues in himself, so Ahasuerus is a man who has most fully developed his inherent powers of thought, not one supernaturally gifted. (390)

106. Though this lyric, "Worlds on worlds are rolling ever," echoes Milton's "Nativity Ode," Shelley exhibits much less joy than his predecessor does at the departure of the pagan gods.

107. One of Shelley's remarks about Jesus himself, from the essay "On Christianity," seems appropriate here: "like a skilful orator he secures the prejudices of his auditors, and induces them by his professions of sympathy with their feelings, to enter with a willing mind into the exposition of his own" (*Prose* 262).

108. As well as through the route of Ahasuerus' agonized wanderings.

109. From Dublin, Shelley wrote to Elizabeth Hitchener of his plans for this work, which he apparently carried out, but the volume was never published and is now lost: "I have met with no determined Republicans, but I have found some who are DEMOCRATIFIABLE. I have met with some waverers between Xtianity and Deism.—I shall attempt to make them reject all the bad, and take all the good of the Jewish Books.—I have often thought that the moral sayings of Jesus Christ might be very useful if selected from the mystery and immorality which surrounds them—it is a little work I have in contemplation" (*L*, I, 265: 27 February 1812).

110. Again, as in the early pamphlets, Shelley exalts Christ in *Laon and Cythna* and *Prometheus Unbound* while challenging him with his own anti-Christian martyr-heroes. See Wasserman, pp. 291–305, and Curran, *Annus Mirabilis*, pp. 55–60, for detailed accounts of the interplay among Prometheus, Christ, Satan, Jehovah, and Jupiter in the latter poem.

111. James A. W. Heffernan's superb *"Adonais*: Shelley's Consumption of Keats" reminds us just how much the elegist dominates this ostensible tribute to his departed brother poet.

112. Bryan Shelley calls this passage "the theological core" of an essay that, as this scholar notes, contains many allusions to Jesus' teachings (128).

2. Shelleyan Doppelgänger: Loathsome Sympathy/Indomitable Selfhood

1. Although the term *Doppelgänger* came into use only after the late-eighteenth-century author Jean Paul Richter used it in his novel *Siebenkäs*, the notion of a split or duplicated self can be found as early as the Zoroastrian religion of ancient Persia, with its "Fravashis," and the myths of classical Greece, where Ixion embraces not Juno but her "cloud-double" (Tymms 24), two versions of the double that Shelley made striking—and strikingly different—use of (see *PU*, I. 191–301 and *L*, II, 434). Otto Rank's *Der Doppelgänger* (originally published 1914, expanded edition 1925) and Freud's comments on that work in "The Uncanny" (1919) have spawned a number of works of literary criticism devoted to the theme, including Ralph Tymms's *Doubles in Literary Psychology*, Robert Rogers's *A Psychoanalytic Study of the Double in Literature*, and C. F. Keppler's *The Literature of the Second Self*. Rank's book remains the best introduction to this psychological and literary phenomenon, but like the three book-length studies I have mentioned, it tends to rely on mere summary of the works in question. John Irwin's *Doubling and Incest / Repetition and Revenge: A Speculative Reading of Faulkner* offers a much more probing analysis, and Irwin's insights can be applied to Shelley as well as to Faulkner, as William A. Ulmer demonstrates in *Shelleyan Eros*. Because, as Keppler reminds us, "double" is an extremely vague term (220), I will use it only to refer to Shelley's paired characters and to his own and his characters' autoscopic experiences. Contrary to Kelvin Everest ("Shelley's Doubles"), I will not describe as doubles Shelley's personæ and literary surrogates.

2. This phrase, from *The Cenci*, connotes not just introspection and self-analysis, but, more specifically, the tendency to plunge "into the depth of darkest purposes." The diabolical Orsino, himself no stranger to crime, says of the Cenci family,

> 'tis a trick of this same family
> To analyse their own and other minds.
> Such self-anatomy shall teach the will
> Dangerous secrets: for it tempts our powers,
> Knowing what must be thought, and may be done,
> Into the depth of darkest purposes.
>
> (II.ii. 108–14)

3. For example, the martyred revolutionary Laon has his wicked counterpart in the tyrant Othman and his flattering mirror in Cythna.

4. Keppler offers a helpful definition of the term *second self* as having both "external reality . . . independent of the first self" and "inward linkage . . . , a basic psychical identity" with it. Such a description illuminates Shelley's own sense that the double—both as ideal twin and fiendish alter ego—is "an always contradictory being, a paradox of simultaneous outwardness and inwardness, of difference from and identity with the first self," though for Shelley, identity would often outweigh difference (9–10). Moreover, whereas Keppler catalogues a wide spectrum of roles for the second self, such as twin brother, pursuer, tempter, and beloved, I will usually restrict my use of the term to those largely positive connotations that Shelley implies in his 1811 letter to Miss Hitchener, in the 1812 poem addressed to Harriet Shelley ("It is not blasphemy" [*Esdaile* 85–87]), and, later, in *Laon and Cythna* (*CW*, I, 281: *LC*, II. 209). Finally, as Keppler's definition points out, the second self phenomenon blurs the distinction between the subjective and objective, so it would be tempting to invoke Kohut's model of the selfobject while examining particular texts. However, I want to reserve that resonant term for Shelley's own psychic interactions with actual people—including Christ, who was never for Shelley merely a "historical" figure—rather than apply it to his connection with his literary creations (surrogates, heroes and heroines, personæ, etc.) or to those fictive beings' relation to each other.

5. In another letter to Hogg, Shelley again invokes his emotional and psychological investment in his sister—as well as in his other "second self," Hogg: "I wish that vile family despotism [and] the viler despotism of religion did not stand between the happiness of the two beings which (excuse the φιλαυτια [self-love]) would constitute mine" (*L*, I, 78: 8 May 1811).

6. It is important to remember that Shelley's sister(s) and cousin served in part as compensatory selfobjects, in Kohut's terms, who helped fill the void left by the elder Elizabeth Shelley (or at least by her "imago" in Shelley's consciousness). Thus the unusual intensity of Shelley's need for mirroring—thwarted in boyhood by his mother's apparent withdrawal—pre-dated but was inestimably aggravated by the Harriet Grove crisis of 1810 and 1811, with all its reverberations in his perceptions of self and of others. His cousin's and sisters' role in establishing for Percy the "sisterly ideal" as the central paradigm for the feminine beloved cannot be overstressed, though the "older woman" (by one year) Harriet and the protective, attentive Elizabeth who "nursed" her brother's broken heart seemed to embody maternal qualities as well. Finally, in their capacity as students, or rather, disciples, of the young radical, Shelley's female siblings and cousin/fiancée also became in a sense his daughters, his intellectual and spiritual offspring who helped gratify his need to be idealized—and feminized, as I will argue in the following chapter.

7. As many readers have observed, Percy invited comparison between himself and Laon (and between Mary and Cythna) by affixing an autobiographical Dedication to his epic (Sperry, for example, skillfully traces the biographical parallels that enrich this often ignored work [*Shelley's Major Verse* 41–64]). Yet the poet's identification (through the first-person narrative) with his hero is by no means absolute, as Shelley undermines—through exploiting the gap between Laon's own hyperbole and his vari-

ous failures—the grandiose claims of a "first self" who gives birth to his own beloved, as well as to "holy and heroic verse" and a revolutionary movement (*CW*, I, 283: *LC*, II. 268).

8. Rank calls the double "the rival of his prototype in anything and everything, but primarily in the love for woman—a trait which he may partly owe to the identification with the brother" (75). This remark helps illuminate T. J. Hogg's oscillating roles as cherished second self and feared rival as he infiltrates, at Percy's invitation, his friend's relationships with Elizabeth Shelley, Harriet Westbrook Shelley, and Mary Godwin. Hogg's gender also made his position as a second self precarious. Shelley found women much easier to idealize (and identify with) than men, and after Hogg's influence waned, the poet's fictive and actual second selves were almost exclusively feminine.

9. Slightly misquoting the *Essay on Man*, Shelley writes, "I confess that I think Pope's 'all are but parts of one tremendous whole' something more than Poetry, it has ever been my favourite theory" (*L*, I, 35).

10. This latter issue would have been particularly prominent in Shelley's mind, as the letters which precede and follow this 3 January missive allude to a journey to Fern, Wiltshire (domicile of the Groves), which Shelley claimed to have taken on the final two days of December. While Jones, Cameron (*Young Shelley* 334–35), and Hawkins (68–70) surmise—probably correctly—that Shelley did not, in Jones's words, actually launch "this desperate adventure for [Harriet's] love" (*L*, I, 33n1), he had probably played out a number of similar scenarios in his restless, often "delirious" imaginings.

11. These poems would include his sentimental love lyrics gathered in the *Victor and Cazire* volume (1810), the bawdy "Epithalamium" and handful of melancholy lyrics from the *Posthumous Fragments of Margaret Nicholson* (1810), and a few lyrics which he later copied into *The Esdaile Notebook*. Many of these poems are addressed to and most were inspired by Harriet Grove.

12. In his earliest writings, such as *Zastrozzi* (written in 1809, published 1810), Shelley had experimented with *Doppelgänger* configurations. In this work, the constellation of characters revolves around the Shelley surrogate (or first self), Verezzi, whose ideal second self, Julia, is supplanted by her dark double, Matilda, and his own *Doppelgänger*, Zastrozzi.

13. Shelley met Elizabeth Hitchener, ten years his senior, during a June 1811 visit to his uncle, Captain Pilfold, in Cuckfield. The daughter of a one-time smuggler, she served as schoolmistress at nearby Hurstpierpoint, and the captain's daughter was among her pupils. As Holmes writes, she "was an unusual figure in the neighborhood, a girl of working-class background who had educated herself in liberal ideas, and . . . had established an independent intellectual standing and gained considerable respect as the local schoolmistress" (*Pursuit* 71). Her connection with Shelley ultimately would cost her that respect, for many considered her as "Shelley's cast-off mistress" upon her return to the fold (*Pursuit* 175).

14. Miss Hitchener lived with the Shelleys and Eliza Westbrook in Lynmouth and then in Wales from July to early November 1812.

15. Shelley also regarded his young wife as a potential second self and in fact refers to her as such in the 1812 poem "To Harriet" ("It is not blasphemy" [*Esdaile* 86, l. 56]). However, the more intellectual and certainly more voluble (on paper and in person) older woman played this role more skillfully than could the young Harriet Shelley, and for a time she even displaced Hogg as Shelley's most trusted friend (*L*, I, 163). Although the circumstances surrounding their falls from grace differed wildly, Hogg's transformation from ideal second self to hated "apostate" following his attempted seduction of Harriet Shelley prefigures Miss Hitchener's sad fate (*L*, I, 212). Hogg even became to Shelley during this late 1811 crisis a kind of pursuing double (not *quite* a Brown Demon) whom Shelley fled but simultaneously wooed in a series of passionate missives (see, for example, Shelley's letter of 10 November, where he impetuously declares, "Will you come—dearest, best beloved of friends, will *you* come," but then commands "Follow us not" [*L*, I, 172]). Hogg's banishment, however, was less permanent than Miss Hitchener's, and he eventually infiltrated his friend's second marriage—this time with Shelley's blessing. Apparently, Hogg held a stronger attraction, both intellectual and erotic, over Shelley than did the repudiated "tormenter and schoolmistress" (*L*, I, 336).

16. A brief extract from the first of Elizabeth Hitchener's fervent letters to Shelley demonstrates just how susceptible she was to her correspondent's tutelege and how apt, as Holmes points out, to "adopt his own terminology" (*Pursuit* 72): "*Self-love* you see prompts me eagerly to accept the opportunity you offer me of improving my mind by a correspondence with you . . . tho' I presume not to *argue* I love to *discuss*, & I so rarely meet with any one possessing the requisites for intellectual pleasures, that if you can spare the time, mine cannot be more agreeably employ'd.—It seems to me you know me better than I do myself" (*L*, I, 98–99n5: 7–10 June 1811). It was, though, Elizabeth and not Percy who introduced the soul-mate appellations, which spawned a whole genealogy of brothers, mothers, and sisters (though no fathers) of the soul (see *L*, I, 145n2, where she writes, "I long to be introduced to *your Harriet* will she ever permit me to call her so, she shall have a Sister's affection, for are you not the Brother of my soul").

17. See *Bearing the Word*, pp. 107–8. Homans ascribes this view to Mary Shelley herself, though the novelist goes a bit farther and implies—through her brilliant exploitation of the *Doppelgänger* theme—that Frankenstein flees not merely the physicality, the powerful and all too palpable body of his creature, but also the distorted yet still revealing mirror of himself that this "filthy dæmon" embodied (*Frankenstein* 71).

18. The Greek word *alastor*, Curran points out, describes "not only a *kakodaimon*, an avenging deity goading his victims to their strict deserts; . . . [but] also the cursed man who suffers from that divine vengeance" (*Shelley's Annus Mirabilis* 21).

19. In a sense, then, she is a type of Frankenstein's creature, an initially cherished and then despised manifestation of essentially self-directed desire.

20. Holmes sums up Elizabeth Hitchener's life after Shelley spurned her:

In her disappointment and shame, Miss Hitchener rather understandably turned on Shelley, writing letters threatening vengeance . . . [Joseph Gibbons] Merle found her the next year in such a state that he would not have been surprised "had her wanderings led to insanity." In fact Miss Hitchener's whole life showed her toughness and spirit . . . She went abroad, married an Austrian officer, and finally returned to run a successful school at Edmonton, dying in 1822. She looked back at her time with Shelley with fondness and regret, and referred to him as her one inspiration in life in her Poems. (*Pursuit* 175)

21. Shelley, it seems, paid her this £100 sum only once. Elizabeth Hitchener's name disappears entirely from his correspondence after the 4 December 1812 letter to Hogg in which she appears as the Brown Demon (apparently Harriet Shelley, whose jealousy of her husband's sister of the soul helped ensure Miss Hitchener's expulsion, adopted this epithet as well [see Hogg, II, 57]). Besides dehumanizing Elizabeth Hitchener by labeling her a demon and hermaphrodite, Shelley also likens her in this letter to a literary "heroine," thereby completely transforming her into an imaginative construct, which in her capacity of second self she had always been (*L*, I, 336).

22. While Mary Shelley claims that this 1815 work "was addressed in idea to Coleridge" (*CW*, III, 120) and Jerrold Hogle (*Shelley's Process* 40–41) and Harold Bloom (*Visionary Company* 286–87) concur, Holmes, following Rossetti and Hutchinson, makes a convincing case that Shelley is addressing himself, arguing that Mary needed to remove this dark poem from the realm of Shelley's own internal struggles: "She always found it difficult to accept that Shelley suffered from deep personal doubts which inevitably reflected on her own relationship with him" (*Pursuit* 288). I see this poem as referring primarily to Shelley himself; but if indeed Shelley did have Coleridge in mind as well, his relationship here to the older poet corresponds to that between himself and Keats in *Adonais*, where Shelley "in another's fate now wept his own" (300).

23. These would include the Hell Devil who appears in his and Elizabeth's "Gothick" epistle to Edward Graham (*L*, I, 9–10: 23 April 1810), Ghasta the Avenging Demon from *Victor and Cazire*, the Spectral Horseman from the *Margaret Nicholson* volume, and those "ghosts of the dead" whose voices *St. Irvine*'s Megalena hears and whose "fearful steps" the young poet pursued "through many a listening chamber, cave and ruin" (*CW*, V, 123; "Hymn," ll. 51, 50).

24. See *An Enquiry Concerning the Principles of Morals*, Appendix II: "Of Self-Love," pp. 294–302 (quotation from p. 300). While Hume allows for "the combined motives of benevolence and self-enjoyment" (302), Shelley's extreme distrust of (his own) Selfhood obliges him to dichotomize rather than reconcile Love and the self. Hume's account of "the selfish system of morals" (296), which posits self-interest as the root of even the most generous acts and which Hume himself rejects as illogical, sums up Shelley's own deepest suspicions about himself and humankind: "There is [a] principle . . . which has been much insisted on by philosophers . . . that whatever affection one may feel or imagine he feels for others, no passion is, or can be disinterested; that the

most generous friendship, however sincere, is a modification of self-love; and that, even unknown to ourselves, we seek only our own gratification, while we appear the most deeply engaged in schemes for the liberty and happiness of mankind" (295). Shelley himself calls this version of self-love "affected, self-deceptive disinterestedness" (*L*, I, 175). See also Godwin's chapter, "Of Self-Love and Benevolence" (*Enquiry*, I, 421–38) where he declares that "the perfection of mind consists in disinterestedness" (437).

25. Or, in the case of Lucretian *simulacra* or "films" emitted from objects and people, the "masks" of the self *were* continually falling away, and constantly reproducing themselves. The notion of simulacra contributed inestimably to Shelley's development of the *Doppelgänger* theme.

26. These last two are characters from Hogg's novel *Leonora*, which Shelley had been urging him to publish.

27. Ten years later, in a letter to Lord Byron, Shelley was to exclaim over the subtlety of "the principle of self" (*L*, II, 309: 16 July 1821).

28. Richard Isomaki points out that Shelley derived his terms *philautia* (self-love) and *aphilautia* (lack or self-love) from Aristotle (660). Isomaki argues—erroneously, I believe—that the poet's "psyche/epipsyche strategy" allowed him to overcome the split between love and the self that pervades his early writings and that these Greek terms imply (661). Isomaki's essay relies too heavily on the problematic essay "On Love" for evidence of self-acceptance—that is, acceptance of himself and of the notion of selfhood—in Shelley's post-1815 writings.

29. It is perhaps significant that a few days earlier Shelley had angrily labeled Christ "the fiend, the wretch," whose presence he could not escape or entirely absorb (*L*, I, 71: 28 April 1811).

30. That Eliza Westbrook, whom Shelley was learning to tolerate but later hated so venomously, functions in this letter as a kind of synecdoche for flawed humanity seems appropriate.

31. This early expression of the Shelleyan paradigm is from "Fragment: Supposed to be an Epithalamium of Francis Ravaillac and Charlotte Cordé," the *pièce de résistance* of the sensationalistic Hogg-Shelley production of late 1810, *Posthumous Fragments of Margaret Nicholson* (*PS*, I, 119: l. 8). Shelley attended Adam Walker's lectures while at Syon House (1802–1804) and began reading Lucretius, under the guidance of his loved teacher Dr. James Lind, during his last two years at Eton (1808–1810).

32. This phrase may link this poem's "venomed melody" passage to the letter's concern with "breathing," for many see these lines (ll. 256–66) as depicting an encounter with a (perhaps venereally infected) prostitute during Shelley's spring 1811 residence in London. See, for example, Holmes, *Pursuit*, p. 637.

33. In this same letter to Hogg, Shelley, anticipating an upcoming visit to Field Place, cavalierly turns his father into a caricature of the angry patriarch, thus effect-

ing—or, rather, furthering—his own emotional severence from the elder Shelley: "The estate is *entirely* entailed on me, totally out of the power of the enemy, he is yet angry beyond measure; pacification is remote; but I *will* be at peace vi et armis; I will enter his dominions preserving a quaker like carelessness of opposition, I shall manage a l'Amerique & seat myself quietly in his mansion turning a deaf ear to any declamatory objections" (*L*, I, 76–77).

34. Theorists such as Carol Gilligan and Nancy Chodorow associate this paradigm, with its emphasis on "flexible" ego boundaries and on what Gilligan terms an "ethic of care," with women rather than with men. Shelley's own development of such a model and his own tendency—in his writings and behavior—to adopt feminine subject positions, though they may not make him a consistently "feminist" thinker, do indicate his affinity with "the feminine." See Gilligan, chap. 2 and Chodorow, "Family Structure," p. 44 ("Feminine personality comes to identify itself in relation and connection to other people more than masculine personality does. [In psychoanaltyic terms, women are less individuated than men; they have more flexible ego boundaries]") and pp. 55–59.

35. Crook and Guiton have offered persuasive evidence that Shelley contracted, or thought he contracted, a venereal disease during adolescence. While their study helps explain Shelley's lifelong fear of contagion, his horror at prostitution, and his general ambivalence about sexuality itself, it does not address the poet's abiding suspicion of masculine sexuality, which involves his sense of himself not simply as a victim—Crook and Guiton's emphasis—but also as an *agent* of pestilence, either in the form of actual disease or of the violence and oppression that he associated with the male eros.

36. Elizabeth Pilfold Shelley, rather than her husband, seemed to be the "potent" force in the Shelley household. We can probably discern some of her vitality in Shelley's portraits of powerful female characters such as Cythna and Asia. Holmes, following Dowden, writes, "There is a hint of a somewhat masculine character, and it was rumoured that [Lady Shelley] could be domineering and even violent within her marriage, but this is not certain" (*Pursuit* 11). Shelley's fantasy of an affair between his mother and his friend Graham, may, as Mellor (*Mary Shelley* 74) and Gelpi (*Shelley's Goddess* 117–19, 123) suggest, emerge from his own oedipal desire, but it definitely attests to his view of her as a highly sexualized woman. See, for example, *L*, I, p. 163, where he refers to his mother's "depravity." However, before the Harriet Grove crisis—with its sequels in the Oxford expulsion and his "*mésalliance*" with Harriet Westbrook—Shelley's attitude toward his father was, as Cameron writes, "fondly condescending" (*Young Shelley* 3), and afterwards, bitterly condescending.

37. If this is true, and not one of Medwin's embellishments, it indicates that Timothy Shelley embraced the kind of cynicism about human nature that his son struggled to combat, in part, undoubtedly, in reaction to "Il Padre's" philosophical stance (*L*, I, 3). Both La Rochefoucauld and Chesterfield endorsed what their contemporary, David Hume, called "the selfish system of morals" (*Enquiry Concerning the Principles of Morals* 296), a philosophy that La Rochefoucauld neatly invokes in one of his *Maxims*: "Self-interest speaks all sorts of tongues, and plays all sorts of roles, even that of disinterestedness."

38. This conversation obviously took place before Shelley did the unforgivable, though Medwin does not provide a specific date. Timothy Shelley was true to his word, and Percy managed, through a number of belligerent letters, to sabatoge any chance of a reconciliation. According to James Bieri ("Shelley's Older Brother"), it seems that Timothy Shelley himself "got" a natural child, a son somewhat older than Percy, whom the poet may have learned about as an adult, or perhaps earlier.

39. This (self-)distrust proved to be well-founded, as Shelley would grow sexually restless within both of his marriages and may have sired at least one illegitimate child, Elena Adelaide Shelley, in 1818.

40. One glaring exception to this pattern would be Shelley's castigation of his mother for her supposed adultery with Graham. This episode initially allowed the poet to revel in the imagined "cornuting [of] old Killjoy's brow" (*L*, I, 87), but it quickly turned from an amusing fantasy of oedipal revenge on his father to a repository of some of his deepest feelings of resentment toward and desire for both his mother and his favorite sister, Elizabeth, whom he imagines the elder Elizabeth Shelley is foisting onto Graham to cover her own misconduct (see esp. Percy's 22 October 1811 letter to his mother [*L*, I, 155]).

41. Shelley and his cousin probably established no sexual relationship, in part because they rarely saw each other and even more rarely spent time alone together. However, that Shelley's intense efforts to quell his selfish impulses and desire during the breakup include a vigorous fight against "sensation" (*L*, I, 180), or sensual appetite, suggests that sexual longing played a larger role in his disappointment than he openly admits. During this period of late 1810–1811, when Shelley's desire for Harriet Grove arouses, and coalesces with, Hogg's for Elizabeth Shelley, Shelley often admonishes himself by criticizing and advising his friend. See, for example, his 1 January 1811 letter to Hogg in which Shelley chastises his friend for offering him a libertine theory of love that involves "the most thrilling sensualities of Epicurism" as a balm for his wounds: "Oh your Theory has cost me much reflexion, I have not ceased to think of it since your letter came . . . Is it not however founded on that *hateful* principle—Is it *self* which you propose to raise to a state of superiority by your system of eternal perfectibility in love" (*L*, I, 34). Clearly, Shelley is placing sensuality in the same camp with selfishness: both are to be resisted, as both interfere with "Love, love *infinite in extent*, eternal in duration" (*L*, I, 35: 3 January 1811).

42. Among the earliest examples of Shelley's imaginative exploration of feminine subject positions is his creation of Verezzi, physically and emotionally overpowered by the "majestic" Zastrozzi and ravished by the sexually aggressive Matilda.

43. The (sometimes mutual) masturbation that was rampant at Eton, which Shelley must have witnessed and of which he may have partaken, would suggest a more literal spin on this phrase. As Anne K. Mellor argues in her review of Nathaniel Brown's *Sexuality and Feminism in Shelley*, a study that discusses onanism and homoeroticism at Eton, the instances of "spontaneous orgasm," which Brown cites in such poems as *Epipsychidion* and "Ode to the West Wind," may instead represent masturbation (Mellor 179). See Brown, chap. 6, esp. pp. 141–42.

44. After receiving news of his grandfather's impending death, Shelley conveys his ill opinion of Sir Bysshe to Elizabeth Hitchener: "He is a complete Atheist and builds all his hopes on annihilation. He has acted very ill to three [for "two"?] wives. He is a bad man. I never have had respect for him, I always regarded him as a curse on society" (*L*, I, 239: 26 January 1812; bracketed insert mine). This "hardhearted apostate" was not to die for three more years (*L*, I, 239).

45. *Zastrozzi*, *St. Irvyne*, "Revenge" (from *Victor and Cazire*), and Rosa's song in *The Wandering Jew* (Canto II) all involve some version of the woman scorned by her "perjured lover" (*PS*, I, 56: *WJ*, II. 519). Shelley returned to this theme in 1819 when he composed the stark ballad entitled, variously, "A Ballad: Young Parson Richards," "Ballad," and "Ballad of the Starving Mother." This moving, generally overlooked piece brilliantly unites Shelley's anticlericalism with a caustic satire on sexual hypocrisy and inequality. See *CW*, III, pp. 152–55. The abandoned woman was a favorite theme of Charlotte Dacre, one of Shelley's early "poetic foremothers," to use Marlon B. Ross's phrase (*Contours* 156). See, for example, her poem "The Exile" in *Hours of Solitude* (I, 11–16).

46. This letter also contains an early, ecologically tinged assessment of "the contagion of the world's slow stain" (*Adonais*, l. 356). Just prior to the statement quoted, Shelley describes the vicinity in such a way that connects industrial and sexual pollution within a vision of physical and moral corruption: "The manufacturers with their contamination have crept into the peaceful vale and deformed the loveliness of Nature with human taint. The debauched servants of the great families who resort contribute to the total extinction of morality. Keswick seems more like a suburb of London than a village of Cumberland" (*L*, I, 223).

47. The poem "Cold are the blasts," one of his earliest works, evinces the young poet's interest in and empathy for female victims of masculine lust and selfishness. Written in 1808, the melodramatic but quite eloquent lyric also appears in slightly revised form in the *Victor and Cazire* volume, with the date July 1810. Whereas the original poem identifies the "fallen Victim" and her "remorseless betrayer" (now "charmed" by another) as "Louisa" and "Henry," Shelley leaves the names blank in the 1810 version. Cameron's suggestion that Shelley did this to "suggest a contemporary story which might be recognized if names were given" seems accurate in light of the poet's growing sense of his own mission as a social reformer (*Esdaile*, Commentaries, 260). As Brown writes of Shelley's vivid depictions of "seduction, abandonment, and prostitution," this theme was "encouraged by the sentimental and Gothic tradition in which he was working, but recognized as a real-life plague spot in the nation's sexual conduct" (*Sexuality and Feminism* 205, 206).

48. Although Brown concludes that Shelley's antimatrimonialism, his hatred of prostitution and sympathy for prostitutes themselves, and his indictment of the male libertine qualify him as "a champion of women," it is more accurate to call Shelley a "detractor of men" (*Sexuality and Feminism* 198). See the essay *On Marriage* in *Prose*, pp. 274–75:

Women . . . in rude ages and in rude countries have been considered the property of men, because they are the materials of usefulness or pleasure. They were valuable to them in the same manner as their flocks and herds were valuable, and it was as important to their interests that they should retain undisturbed possession. The same dread of insecurity which gave birth to those laws or opinions which defend the security of property suggested also the institution of marriage: that is, a contrivance to prevent others from deriving advantage from that which any individual has succeeded in preoccupying. (274)

Thus "the original spirit of marriage" and the original spirit of capitalism dovetail in Shelley's thought as products of masculine self-interest (274). Shelley derived his notion of prostitution as "the legitimate offspring of marriage" at least in part from James Henry Lawrence's *The Empire of the Nairs; or the Rights of Women*, which Shelley first read in 1812 (*PS*, I, 371: Note to *QM*, V. 189).

49. While Barker-Benfield focuses on the eighteenth-century, the "culture of reform" that he discusses penetrated Shelley's world—and, indeed, beyond, into the Victorian Era. See especially, chap. 2 ("The Reformation of Male Manners") and chap. 5 ("A Culture of Reform"). Carol Christ's essay dealing with this later period, "Victorian Masculinity and the Angel in the House," also illuminates Shelley's retreat from masculinity, especially male sexuality. However, where Christ's writers, Patmore and Tennyson, express ambivalence toward "the world of male energy and action" (161), Shelley utterly repudiates it.

50. See, especially, *Queen Mab*, V. 38–93.

51. That this phrase from *Queen Mab* (V. 90) can be found in his elaborate anti-capitalist tirade, cited above, suggests how closely linked the (masculine) appetites for sex and for money were for Shelley.

52. This "horror" and self-repulsion is undeniably sexual in nature in the two later letters. While not overtly connected with "impurity & vice," the revulsion from (him)self that Shelley communicates to Hogg could also involve a sexual element, as Shelley may have during this time succumbed to the "poisonous embraces of a prostitute," from which "no man can rise pure" (*Prose* 142: "On *Memoirs of Prince Alexy Haimatoff*" [a novel by T. J. Hogg]).

53. In their commentary on the letter to Mary Godwin that I have cited, Crook and Guiton point out that "'the impures' was a common euphemism [for prostitutes] during the years 1780–1820" (34).

54. Hogle's essay provides an insightful analysis of the structural problems that plague Shelley's novels and stories as well as of the interchangeable nature of the self-divided characters within each piece. As Hogle remarks of *Zastrozzi*, "The characters sound unnaturally alike because they are mirrors of each other" ("Shelley's Fiction" 86). Like Behrendt (Introduction to *Zastrozzi and St. Irvyne* xvi–xviii, xxii) and myself, Hogle identifies "the essential schism" that Shelley explores throughout his work as "the war of self-involvement versus self-transcendence," a war that Shelley often stages as a combat between and within antagonistic doubles ("Shelley's Fiction" 89, 91).

55. Arguably, Shelley's first substantial—and convincing—representative of his own ideal of disinterested love is Cythna, a female messiah who was not conceived until early 1817. Cythna's gender may have distinguished her sufficiently in Shelley's mind from her—and Shelley's—precursor, though Shelley regarded femininity as one of Christ's salient qualities.

56. After seducing Olivia Zastrozzi, "the perjured Verezzi" reneges on his promise to marry her, marries someone else—presumably from his own caste—and "when the destitute Olivia begged a pittance to keep her from starving, her proud betrayer bade her exercise her profession" (*CW*, V, 102).

57. Kelvin Everest's perceptive analysis of Shelley's doubles—a term that for Everest encompasses "the distanced self-images that populate [Shelley's] poetry" ("Shelley's Doubles" 68)—illuminates the class conflict that underlies *Zastrozzi*, where each of the central characters except Zastrozzi himself holds an aristocratic title. Emphasizing the *Doppelgänger*'s associations with guilt, Everest explores Shelley's problematic status as an "aristocratic radical": "There is . . . an important sense in which Shelley's assault on the practice and ideology of the English ruling class was directed against himself" (72, 65). Like Everest, I would argue that this conflict, yet another example of the poet's profound self-division, helps generate the figure of the "accusatory and threatening" double within Shelley's imagination (65). Shelley's burgeoning radicalism—which necessarily entailed an element of self-rejection—contributed immensely to Zastrozzi's role as the aristocratic Verezzi's "bitterest enemy" and "triumphant persecutor" (*CW*, V, 12, 7).

58. *The Wandering Jew* is itself "dramatic," even in the generic sense, which suggests that Shelley found the drama most amenable to his variations on the *Doppelgänger* theme (Shelley often sets up speeches in this poem by providing captions labeling the speaker, as in a play). Shelley's wide-ranging sympathies with (though not necessarily approval of) a vast array of figures within his 1819 lyrical drama and revenge tragedy suggests that he regarded the drama not as the "objective" form described by Aristotle but rather as the habitat—á la Keats—of "the camelion Poet," who "has as much delight in conceiving an Iago as an Imogen" (*Keats's Letters*, I, 387: to Woodhouse, 27 October 1818).

59. The paradoxical nature of this obsession would identify it with "loathsome sympathy," versions of which appear in *Laon and Cythna*, X. 53 ("savage sympathy") and X. 195 ("horrid sympathy") (*CW*, I, 377, 381). Although Shelley began developing his notion of loathsome sympathy in *Zastrozzi*, he does not articulate it as such until this 1817 epic, where the kind of contagious "gloom and misanthropy" (*CW*, I, 242: Preface to *LC*) that he tries to eschew in the Preface erupts within the poem itself under the rubric of "dreadful sympathy" (*CW*, I, 264: *LC*, I. 232).

60. As pointed out in the previous chapter, Shelley's ardent attempts at self-conquest began as early as his student days at Syon House (1802–1804), where he most likely experienced the epiphanic moment described in the Dedication to *Laon and Cythna* (ll. 21–36) and the "Hymn to Intellectual Beauty" (ll. 55–60). In the poem "I will kneel at thine altar," probably written in the winter of 1810–1811 but dealing with

an incident from 1809, Shelley (re)dedicates himself to "Dear love" and envisions a battle between selfishness and philanthropy, which concludes with love rising from defeat to topple "the throne / Of selfishness" (*Esdaile* 125, 126; see also *PS*, I, 150, for discussion of the poem's date). Shelley's abrupt shift from personal confession to allegory in line 6 underscores the difficulty he had at that time in imagining Love's victory over the Self in any but abstract terms. The 1809–1810 Gothic novels, which sometimes vaguely gesture in the direction of unselfish love, present similar evidence of the young Shelley's mesmerism by the seemingly omnipotent sway of Selfhood. Shelley's subsequent loss of Harriet Grove and Elizabeth Shelley, coupled with his repudiation of Christ as his model of disinterested love, only augmented the Self's threat to the young poet's ideal of "love" and "concord" (*Esdaile*, 125: "I will kneel").

61. It is possible that Shelley, who read Godwin's *Political Justice* for the first time at Eton in 1809, had read this novel before or during the composition of *Zastrozzi*.

62. As Verezzi's *Doppelgänger*, however, Zastrozzi never becomes merely the protagonist's projected conscience or displaced evil impulses. Whenever he assigns a name to a character's double, Shelley always associates the *Doppelgänger* with a relational dynamic, for the Shelleyan double invariably functions as a troubling presence within the interconnected world that the poet envisions. This is true even in *Prometheus Unbound*, where the dark double comes closest to pure self-projection. As C. F. Keppler writes of the kind of physical and/or psychological duplication often identified with the *Doppelgänger*, "duplication would result in no relationship at all, but merely an inert coexistence," and the same can be said of the double as simply a projected aspect of a divided self (2). Save when they are overtly identified as self-images, Shelleyan *Doppelgänger* invariably retain a degree of separateness from their "first selves."

63. The violent thunderstorm that destroys Verezzi's cavern exposes him to new Promethean torments, such as a devastating hailstorm, and it anticipates the "sudden earthquake" that will crack open Cythna's grotto (*CW*, I, 354: *LC*, VII. 334).

64. In separating Verezzi from his beloved, Zastrozzi is in effect re-creating and inflicting on his double his own momentous loss. Zastrozzi's adoration of his mother is evident not just in his single-minded devotion to her final command but also in his description of her during his confession to the Inquisitors: "Olivia Zastrozzi was . . . a woman in whom every virtue, every amiable and excellent quality, I firmly believe to have been centred . . . by heavens! she acted nobly. A victim to falshood, she sank early to the tomb; and ere her thirtieth year, she died—her spotless soul fled to eternal happiness" (*CW*, V, 101, 102). The extreme youth of Olivia Zastrozzi—she was fifteen or sixteen when she gave birth to her son, who was fourteen when she died—contributes to the oedipal thrust of a relationship that ultimately spawned patricide and, obliquely, fratricide.

65. Although Shelley had employed the language of romantic friendship in earlier letters to Hogg, the traumatic possibility of permanent separation from his "dearest, best beloved of friends" (*L*, I, 172) provoked this much more passionate declaration from Shelley (Hogg had recently tried to seduce Shelley's young bride, yet another black mark against masculine appetite in Shelley's book).

66. See Clark, pp. 338, for the "Essay on Friendship" and pp. 347–48 for the "Note" on the "Bachus and Ampelus," which Shelley saw in Naples during 1819. As Holmes says of the latter composition, "The 'Bacchus and Ampelus' takes him back . . . to his schooldays, with an ironic glance at forbidden friendships" (*Shelley on Love* 17). The disapproving silence with which Lady Shelley greeted her son's long epistolary account of his "devoted attachment" to a young schoolfriend (Clark 338), along with the "dissevering" tyranny of the educational institutions themselves (Clark 347), may have contributed to the "forbidden" quality of these "profound and sentimental attachment[s] to one of the same sex" (Clark 338).

67. Shelley frequently uses the word *irresistible* to describe the powerful magnetic field that governs the novel's characters: as the novel opens, Zastrozzi tells his captive that "Resistance is useless" (*CW*, V, 6); Verezzi is "compelled, by an irresistible fascination" toward a mysterious stranger who turns out to be Zastrozzi (34); Verezzi's soul is "filled with irresistible disgust" when Matilda embraces him, and Matilda herself realizes that he feels nothing but "irresistible antipathy" for her (45). A more famous instance of this word occurs in the Preface to *Alastor*, a poem which, like *Zastrozzi*, deals with narcissism and/as doubling: "The Poet's self-centred seclusion was avenged by the furies of an irresistible passion pursuing him to speedy ruin" (*NCE* 69).

68. Shelley even borrows his sinister triangle of victim and victimizers—with Matilda as middle man-woman—from Lewis. If Zastrozzi corresponds to Ambrosio and Matilda to Matilda-Rosario, Verezzi resembles the maiden in distress, Antonia. Together, Zastrozzi and Matilda perpetrate, at least symbolically, the rape-murder of their prey that Ambrosio commits with the help of *his* Matilda. Finally, just as Lewis's evil monk sexually violates and destroys his own sister, Shelley's villain sexually invades—via Matilda—his effeminate brother and successfully urges him toward suicide.

69. Crook and Guiton (34–35) suggest that the novel's missing chapter 8 could imply that Verezzi has been raped, for chapter 7 opens with Verezzi springing back from Matilda, "as if stung by a scorpion," which Shelley elsewhere associates with venereal disease (*CW*, V, 37).

70. Matilda's homicidal fury could not resemble a rape any more closely, down to the "deadly calm" of her post-coital *triste*:

[T]he ferocious Matilda seized Julia's floating hair, and holding her back with a fiend-like strength, stabbed her in a thousand places; and with exulting pleasure, again and again buried the dagger to the hilt in her body, even after all remains of life were annihilated.

At last the passions of Matilda, exhausted by their own violence, sank into a deadly calm; she threw the dagger violently from her, and contemplated the terrific scene before her with a sullen gaze. (*CW*, V, 89)

71. Camille Paglia would categorize Shelley's villainess as "the virago androgyne, plushly female but mentally masculine" (397).

72. At one point, Matilda sexually assaults her "beloved," who then succumbs to her contagious passion: "[S]he pressed her burning lips to his; most fervent, most voluptuous sensations of ecstacy revelled through her bosom. Verezzi caught the infection . . . a Lethean torpor crept over his senses" (*CW*, V, 86).

73. Again, though Zastrozzi does not directly express the kind of lust that incited his father to seduce the young Olivia Zastrozzi and that governs the ferociously passionate Matilda, he himself acknowledges the sexual element in his insatiable appetite for revenge when he describes his obsessive pursuit of Verezzi as a replacement for "love" (*CW*, V, 47).

74. Narrating the events of his tumultuous life to his spiritual brother, Wolfstein, the villainous Ginotti tells him, "*Love* I cared not for: and wondered why men perversely sought to ally themselves with weakness . . . I thought of death—I shuddered when I reflected, and shrank in horror from the idea, *selfish and self-interested* as I was . . . I cared for nothing but *self*" (*CW*, V, 180–81). Shelley establishes Wolfstein and Ginotti as *Doppelgänger* much more overtly than he likens Verezzi to Zastrozzi, so in a very real sense, Ginotti's story—and the negative traits he ascribes to himself—is Wolfstein's as well. (At one point Wolfstein contemplates "the terrible connexion, dreadful although mysterious, which subsisted between himself and Ginotti": "[Ginotti], thought he, . . . watches my every action, [his] power I feel within myself is resistless, and not to be evaded . . . [Wolfstein] felt that he was no longer independent" [*CW*, V, 141]). That Shelley links the doubles of his second Gothic novel in part by allowing Ginotti to seduce Wolfstein's sister, Eloise, reminds us of the sexual triangle that dominates *Zastrozzi* (and Lewis's *The Monk*), and it strangely anticipates the erotic constellations that Shelley and his friend Hogg would attempt to form, with Shelley's beloved women—Elizabeth Shelley, Harriet Westbrook, and Mary Godwin—as "common treasure[s]" and perhaps conduits for the friends' homoerotic desire (*L*, I, 426: to Hogg, ?26 April 1815).

75. Cythna's "commandments" regarding guilt, atonement, and, implicitly, revenge provide apt commentary on Ahasuerus' masochistic embrace of his role as the "monument of the Eternal's ire" (*PS*, I, 65: *WJ*, III. 797):

> Reproach not thine own soul, but know thyself,
> Nor hate another's crime, nor loathe thine own.
> It is the dark idolatry of self,
> Which, when our thoughts and actions once are gone,
> Demands that man should weep, and bleed, and groan;
> O vacant expiation! be at rest.—
> The past is Death's, the future is thine own.

> (*CW*, I, 362: *LC*, VIII. 190–96)

76. His torments upon a "jagged rock" recall Verezzi's incarceration and anticipate Laon's, Cythna's, and Prometheus' suffering within or upon their rocky prisons (*Esdaile* 104: l. 194).

77. The landsman subdues his victim by piling a rock upon "his feeble breast" (*Esdaile* 103: l. 178).

78. Cameron provides insightful commentary on Eliza's October 1811 entrance into the Shelley circle, which also included Hogg:

> With the coming of Eliza, the marriage was put on a new basis, indeed, one might say under new management. It was transformed from a union of two young people who could learn and grow together into that of two dependents and an overseer. If we ask, as Hogg did, why Shelley did not take a firm stand with Eliza, we have first to consider the possibility that Shelley himself had urged Eliza to join them . . . It is . . . likely that we are faced with the first manifestation of Shelley's penchant for a household containing two or more women, a penchant which perhaps had some psychological basis in an unconscious attempt to reconstruct his childhood home. (*Young Shelley* 104)

When Eliza failed to fit the sisterly ideal Percy cherished and instead began to undermine his relationship both with his wife and with his best friend, Percy reverted to his initial dislike of her, which, after his break with Harriet, became "unbounded abhorrence" (*L*, I, 384: to Hogg, 16 March 1814). Thomas and Eliza disliked each other immediately. Protective of Harriet's interests, Eliza accurately assessed and vehemently disapproved of her new brother-in-law's passionate attachment to his best friend, who gleefully satirizes "the guardian angel" in his *Life* (I, 278).

79. The protagonist loses consciousness within his own dream when he witnesses the landsman's murder of his "sister."

80. I have borrowed this phrase from Marlon B. Ross's essay, "Shelley's Wayward Dream-Poem: The Apprehending Reader in *Prometheus Unbound*," p. 112. As Ross observes, as early as *Queen Mab*, Shelley was exploring the influence of dreams and dreamers on the waking world.

81. Although in August 1812, when Shelley composed *The Voyage*, Eliza Westbrook had not yet become the "blind and loathsome worm, that cannot see to sting," the Tan-yr-allt incident of the following February may have involved another Shelleyan *Doppelgänger* with a score to settle with Eliza (*L*, I, 384: 16 March 1814). While many, including Hogg and Peacock, perceived as a hallucination the "atrocious assassination" that Shelley barely escaped while in Wales (*L*, I, 355: 27 February 1813), Holmes, for example, has argued persuasively that Shelley was in fact attacked by locals incensed by his political activities (*Pursuit* 178–98). In any case, the threats that the fleeing assailant supposedly flung at Shelley sound suspiciously like those of a fictional Gothic villain, an evil alter ego hostile toward both women of the Shelley household: "By God I will be revenged! I will murder your wife. I will ravish your sister. By God. I will be revenged" (*L*, I, 355n2: Harriet Shelley to Thomas Hookham, 12 March 1813). I find no evidence that Shelley ever found his sister-in-law sexually desirable. Like the fantasied murder-by-stabbing of Eliza in the 1812 poem, this threatened rape would be an act of violent male sexuality, which Shelley—via his dark masculine doubles—invariably condemns but in which he imaginatively participates. Shelley's final denunciation of Eliza Westbrook as "a libidinous and vindictive woman" reminds us of the abhorrence and sexual revulsion with which he had recoiled from his once-loved Elizabeth Hitchener several years earlier (*L*, I, 530: 17 January 1817).

82. Although *Queen Mab* would seem to hold that distinction, Shelley had tried to detach himself from this work quite soon after its limited and unsuccessful appearance in 1813, and he now regarded *Laon and Cythna* as his official debut in the role of radical poet-prophet.

83. Throughout this study I will be discussing this work in its unexpurgated form as *Laon and Cythna; or The Revolution of the Golden City: A Vision of the Nineteenth Century*, rather than in its revised version, *The Revolt of Islam*, in which Shelley (grudgingly) transformed Cythna into an orphan adopted by Laon's family.

84. Shelley supplies his hero/surrogate with two "second selves," his younger sister Cythna and a beloved male friend, modeled on T. J. Hogg, "the brother of [his] soul" (*L*, I, 176–77). Laon refers to each of these supporting players as his "shadow" (*CW*, I, 281, 332: *LC*, II. 207 and VI. 131). See *LC*, II. 145–62, and V. 25–47, for the break and reconciliation between Laon and his "own heart's brother," based loosely on the year-long estrangement that divided Shelley and Hogg in 1811 and 1812 (*CW*, I, 279: *LC*, II. 146).

85. Commenting on Shelley's strategy in the poem of "arbitrating between optimism and pessimism, historical progress and mere oscillation, the realm of the imaginative and the ideal and that of human actuality" by presenting the epic events from the perspective of eternity, Stuart Sperry writes, "The framework Shelley establishes for the narrative action of *The Revolt* . . . permits him to anticipate repeated defeats for the Spirit of Good within the world and yet to argue the illogic of despair. The design of the poem and its mythology depict the eternal return and self-perpetuation of the living Spirit and the way its powers are transformed and extended through its repeated conflict with evil" (*Shelley's Major Verse* 44).

86. Donna Richardson fruitfully explores this issue in "'The Dark Idolatry of Self': The Dialectic of Imagination in Shelley's *Revolt of Islam*."

87. Though he does not touch on the persecutor-martyr alliance that so fascinated Shelley, C. F. Keppler briefly discusses the double as an "invited intruder" who represents "not the worker-against the first self, but the worker-with and worker-for" (193, 192). In his chapter on "Malevolent Sympathy," a term he borrows from Spinoza and that Shelley himself might have encountered, Karl F. Morrison examines the way early Christian writers, particularly Augustine, "imagined themselves bonded in need to their rivals, indeed, to those who hated and persecuted them" (80).

88. In a letter to Godwin, Shelley reveals his emotional cathexis with his hero and heroine and with their precursor, Christ when he describes the poem as the child of "'the agony & bloody sweat' of intellectual travail" (*L*, I, 578: 11 December 1817). Cf. Luke 22: 44.

89. Logically, Zastrozzi should have dispatched Verezzi when he abducts him in chapter 1, but he tells his cohorts that "[Verezzi's] life must not be lost . . . I have need of it" (*CW*, V, 10). While the narrator tells us that Zastrozzi "for inexplicable reasons, wished not Verezzi's death," the novel itself reads as a kind of *Bildungsroman* in which Zastrozzi earns his degree in sadism (10).

90. Laon's consistent third-person account of the Stranger's words and actions enhances our sense of the hero's profound self-division. Paradoxically, it also allows us to witness the (re)integration of Laon's fragmented psyche as he merges with his dark double, whose henchman in Canto VI was referred to as "the stranger" (*CW*, I, 328: VI. 21). In glancing back to the crisis of Laon's disloyal friend/second self recounted in Canto II, this episode, moreover, suggests that he has completely absorbed this version of the double as well. Finally, as many readers have noted, Laon's domination of the narrative and his relegation of his sister to the role of "shadow" represents his ongoing absorption of his feminine "second self."

91. The climax the lovers achieve on their "wedding night" amid the ruins anticipates their last embrace on the pyre as well as prefigures the erotic finale of *Epipsychidion*: "I felt the blood that burned / Within her frame, mingle with mine, and fall / Around my heart like fire" (*CW*, I, 337: *LC*, VI. 300–2). By alluding to the lovers' "own cold looks" during this episode and invoking the "inconstant" presence of Intellectual Beauty as the presiding deity of their love, Shelley subtly moves his hero and heroine toward a marriage that will be marred by no shadow of parting (*CW*, I, 337: *LC*, VI. 310; "Hymn," ll. 3, 6).

92. In his compelling reading of the poem, Ulmer recognizes the importance of "Othman's predatory sexuality" in determining the problematic role of eros in this work and emphasizes Shelley's fear that erotic desire and aggression remain inextricably linked:

[T]he reunion of Laon and Cythna is itself a brief phase of a larger progression to willed, violent death. When Laon and Cythna embrace their martyrdom, *The Revolt of Islam* characterizes the body as the site of aggressions that can be redirected (even turned against the body itself) but not outgrown . . . Canto 12 celebrates the body's annihilation as the apotheosis of Shelleyan eros. The climactic position of this celebration demonstrates that desire exhausts its propensity for aggression when it exhausts itself. (59, 65)

93. Examining how the opening of Canto III—where Laon's love for "Cythna's pure and radiant self" suddenly becomes "agony" (*CW*, I, 289: *LC*, III. 25, 27)—suggests "the adolescent boy's experience of facing the full implications of sexual maturity and divergence of the opposite sex," Sperry provides an excellent account of Laon's resistance to his growing passion for his sister (*Shelley's Major Verse* 50). Less convincing is his contention that "Laon passes through the crisis, with its threats of regression, to the recovery of a true ideal of masculinity" (62).

94. The autobiographical subtext of these dreams emerges when we recall Shelley's own encounters with *Doppelgänger*, such as that recounted in the 1815 lyric "O! there are spirits of the air":

> Thine own soul still is true to thee,
> But changed to a foul fiend through misery.
>
> This fiend, whose ghastly presence ever
> Beside thee like thy shadow hangs,

> Dream not to chase;—the mad endeavour
> Would scourge thee to severer pangs.
> Be as thou art. Thy settled fate,
> Dark as it is, all change would aggravate.
>
> (*PS*, I, 450: ll. 29–36)

When Othman's despotism spawns the plague in Canto X, it is fitting that those infected by his deification of the principle of Self encounter similar *simulacra*, which in turn contaminate others:

> It was not thirst but madness! Many saw
> Their own lean image every where, it went
> A ghastlier self beside them, till the awe
> Of that dread sight to self-destruction sent
> Those shrieking victims; some, ere life was spent,
> Sought, with a horrid sympathy, to shed
> Contagion on the sound;
>
> (*CW*, I, 380: *LC*, X. 190–96)

These *simulacra* make their final appearance in the Shelley canon as the "busy phantoms" emitted by the captives of Life (*TL*, l. 534).

95. Sperry illuminates the imagery of Laon's dreams and of his clash with Othman's soldiers in *Shelley's Major Verse*, pp. 49–52. My reading of Canto III is greatly indebted to Sperry's commentary and even more so to Ulmer's, which directly addresses the plethora of doubles within this Canto especially:

> Laon's attack on Othman's soldiers links masculinity and domination integrally . . . When the threatening shapes originating in Laon's psyche abduct Cythna in dream, and then Othman's dusky soldiers abduct her in fact, we confront a psychomachia where Laon plays all the roles. These abducting shapes, as surrogate selves, show Laon's libidinal energies intensifying until they generate the aggressions from which he ironically tries to protect Cythna. His psychosexual violence arises not with his resistance to the soldiers but with their appearance. As tyranny's minions, moreover, the soldiers symbolically link Laon with Othman, signifying his internalization of the patriarch's appropriative sexuality. For Laon, transcendence of erotic violence will require a transcendence of patriarchy. (59–60)

96. Among the best accounts of the complex relationship between *Prometheus Unbound* and *The Cenci* are Curran's (*Shelley's Annus Mirabilis* 120–34), Sperry's (*Shelley's Major Verse* 127–42), and Ulmer's (107–30). Both plays were composed in the shadow of Percy's rapidly deteriorating relationship with Mary. He began *Prometheus Unbound* in the fall of 1818, shortly before the death of his and Mary's daughter, Clara, on September 24. As Holmes (*Pursuit* 443–47) and Mellor (*Mary Shelley* 141–42) have stressed, the self-, Claire-, and Byron-absorbed Percy "distinctly contributed" to the little girl's death by imposing on Mary and the year-old Clara a gru-

eling itinerary from Lucca to Venice during the hot Italian summer (Holmes 447). The
gulf between the Shelleys was widened when their three-year-old son, William died in
June 1819. Although begun somewhat earlier than this devastating loss, *The Cenci*
reflects the despair that we see more directly expressed in the self-disgust of *Julian
and Maddalo*'s Maniac, whose most violent ravings Shelley probably added after
William's tragic death. Many readers have noted that the Maniac emerges from the
poem as a kind of double for Shelley's surrogate, Julian. These figures' relationship
does not correspond to the paradigm of idealized first self and vicious *Doppelgänger*
that I am exploring in this chapter, though the Maniac's gruesome imaginings of self-
castration certainly link the poem with the antimasculinist stance that underlies Shelley's creation of dark doubles.

   97. See Curran, *Shelley's "Cenci,"* pp. 172–73, 176, 177, and Behrendt, *Shelley
and His Audiences*, p. 159, for Gothic elements in the play.

   98. Although, as Stephen Behrendt has demonstrated, Shelley was always
intensely conscious of a real or imagined audience, his consciousness of audience
response soars in the Preface to *The Cenci*, in part because he had real hopes for a
Covent Garden production. See Behrendt, *Shelley and His Audiences*, pp. 144–60, for
a probing account of Shelley's efforts to reach and instruct—via *The Cenci*—a wider
audience than he had heretofore addressed. As Behrendt asserts, "In composing a play
specifically intended for the stage, Shelley was attempting to enter into a significantly
different relationship with an audience based not on the solitary and tranquil act of
reading but on the social and more subjective act of witnessing live theater" (145).
Shelley's Preface to *The Cenci* emphasizes tragedy's "capacity of awakening and sustaining the sympathy of men": "The highest moral purpose aimed at in the highest
species of the drama, is the teaching the human heart . . . the knowledge of itself; in
proportion to the possession of which knowledge, every human being is wise, just, sincere, tolerant and kind" (239, 240). Shelley echoes and expands these remarks in the
Defence, pp. 490–91.

   99. Cythna, however, never sentimentalizes her tormentor in her struggle to supplant his brutal reign with the sovereignty of love. She can see Othman, and the moral
corruption for which he stands, for what he is, and she admonishes her first congrega-
tion, the Mariners who rescue her, to first gaze fearlessly on evil before disarming it
with love. See *LC*, VIII. 24–198, 235–43 (*CW*, I, 356–63) for Cythna's sermon. Her
conviction that "no person can be truly dishonoured by the act of another" is what distinguishes her from Beatrice Cenci (*The Cenci*, Preface, 240), whose inability to articulate her agony—and refusal to name the crime itself—represents her desire to erase
the rape from her memory, to blind herself to the evil which she has suffered (and will
do). Compare Cythna's and Beatrice's immediate responses to their attacks: while
Cythna's "madness was a beam of light, a power / Which dawned thro' the rent soul,"
Beatrice staggers into Act III, crying "My eyes are full of blood . . . / I see but indis-
tinctly" (*CW*, I, 345: *LC*, VII. 55–56; *Cenci*, III. i. 2–3).

   100. Shelley emphasizes the sense of sight throughout Act I, most memorably
in the passage on loathsome sympathy (ll. 444–50). Although Prometheus is initially

"eyeless in hate," he carefully scrutinizes the Phantasm of Jupiter/Prometheus ("I *see* the curse on gestures proud and cold, / And looks of firm defiance and calm hate" [ll. 258–59; emphasis mine]), Jupiter's "hell-hounds," and the scenes of horror that these Furies unveil (l. 408).

101. Rieder's essay traces two plots in the play, one that is individualistic, identifying Prometheus with the "One" of the drama's second line ("Monarch of Gods and Dæmons, and all Spirits / But One, who throng those bright and rolling Worlds"), and one that is necessitarian, with Demogorgon as the "One." Like Sperry's analysis of Prometheus' "halting and unfocused" progress toward redemption (*Shelley's Major Verse* 75–92; quotation from p. 76), Rieder's account addresses the vexed questions, "What causal link binds [Prometheus'] defiance to Jupiter's downfall? Why does he not personally overthrow Jupiter?" (777). While Rieder and Sperry stress the "alliance . . . between Prometheus' moral will and historical necessity" (778), I would add that Shelley's need to dissociate his hero/surrogate from Jupiter's violent overthrow contributed to his decision to assign Demogorgon the (oedipally charged) role of deposer.

102. Wasserman, Bloom, and Abrams have been the most influential spokesmen for this view, identifying Prometheus himself with "the One Mind" (Wasserman) or "Man" (Bloom, Abrams). See Wasserman, *Shelley: A Critical Reading*, chaps. 9–12; Bloom, *Visionary Company*, pp. 306–23; and Abrams, *Natural Supernaturalism*, pp. 299–307.

103. See Sperry, *Shelley's Major Verse*, pp. 92–93, for a sensitive commentary on Prometheus' "quiet resignation" at the end of Act I (93).

104. Stuart Curran provides the fullest account of Zoroastrianism in *Prometheus Unbound*. See *Shelley's Annus Mirabilis*, pp. 67–94 (commentary on the Fravashi on pp. 73–74).

105. Curran's insights into the relationship between the Zoroastrian Fravashi and the phantasm that Prometheus summons are worth quoting at some length:

> The Earth's recollection of Zoroaster's encounter with his double is meant to spur Prometheus to summon his own Fravashi: instead, refusing to allow the curse to pass his lips, he calls upon the Phantasm of Jupiter. But Prometheus' sense of surface niceties conceals a Jungian slip. The being he raises . . . is a just spiritual representative of the figure who began his curse, "Fiend, I defy thee." Gaining access to another world where potentiality is as sharply delineated as actuality, the Titan is allowed to observe the inextricable relationship between himself and Jupiter, between self-regarding good and self-regarding evil. Ultimately, they are the same . . . As Zoroastrian doctrine informs the appearance of the Phantasm, those echoes continue as the enlightened Prometheus reaffirms his disavowal of this silent partnership. In rejecting his curse and the mental kinship with his oppressor, the Titan speaks with a moving formulaic selflessness—"It doth repent me" (I. 303)—strongly recalling the standard Zoroastrian prayer of repentance for evil thoughts, words or actions: "I renounce them by these three words: I repent them." (*Shelley's Annus Mirabilis* 74)

For a deconstructive treatment of the Fravashi/Phantasm connection, see Hogle, *Shelley's Process*, pp. 174–76.

106. For example, Prometheus had invited Jupiter to "Let thy malignant spirit move / Its darkness over those I love: On me and mine I imprecate/ The utmost torture of thy hate" (I. 277–80). For her part, the Earth had become infected with the Titan's masochism and (self-)hate: "[T]he thin air, my breath, was stained / With the contagion of a mother's hate / Breathed on her child's destroyer—aye, I heard / Thy curse, the which [I] . . . Preserve, a treasured spell" (I. 177–80, 184). By the end of the play this pernicious spell has become the liberating "spells" that Demogorgon catalogues in his final admonition (IV. 568).

107. Prometheus' intense questioning of the Furies—"What and who are you?" "Can aught exult in its deformity?" (I. 446, 464)—anticipates Asia's interview with Demogorgon, though the cackling hags are much more forthcoming than the reticent Demogorgon. When the catechism is over, the Furies present to the Titan a series of emblematic images corresponding to the grotesque pageantry of an antimasque—what Jonson would call the "foil or false masque"—which preceeds the idealizing displays of the masque proper. The Furies are themselves archetypal denizens of the world of the antimasque. (In *Prometheus Unbound* I, the pageantry and songs of the "subtle and fair spirits" which arrive as the Furies vanish would comprise the masque itself [I. 658].) Like an exemplary masquer, Prometheus not only watches but also becomes a part of the pageantry, most remarkably when he coalesces with the crucified Christ at the climax of the antimasque. For a succinct account of the way the Renaissance masque involved its audience both psychologically and physically in its spectacle, see Stephen Orgel's introduction to *Ben Jonson: The Complete Masques*, pp. 1–39, or *The Illusion of Power, passim*. See my essay "Entering the Stream of Sound" for an analysis of how Shelley recreated the Renaissance courtly masque (and antimasque) for the cosmic stage of *Prometheus Unbound*.

108. Frederick Burwick offers an astute reading of this episode, demonstrating how and why the Furies "muster horrendous evidence that causality itself is perverse, that good produces evil, that time is the process of decay and ruin, that history is but the resurgent cycle of cataclysm" ("The Language of Causality" 144–54, 154–55; quotation from p. 155). However, because of Prometheus' eagerness to skirmish with the Furies, his initiation of an intense colloquy with them, and his full participation in the antimasque that they present, I cannot agree with Burwick that the Titan's invocation of the term *loathsome sympathy* implies that "he fears sacrificing his identity to his perception" (144).

109. That Shelley strongly identified with Beatrice is quite evident in the eloquent verbal portrait he paints of her near the end of his Preface (242). Holmes has noted the "striking resemblance" between the portrait of Beatrice Cenci (wrongly) ascribed to Guido Reni and Aemilia Curran's portrait of Shelley, which she painted in Rome just as Shelley was beginning work on his tragedy (*Pursuit* 517).

110. In the first scene, Cardinal Camillo in fact invokes the notion of love's transforming presence in connection with the beautiful Beatrice. "Where is your gen-

tle daughter?" he asks the count, "Methinks her sweet looks, which make all things else / Beauteous and glad, might kill the fiend within you" (I, i. 43–45). Beatrice does kill the fiend, but not in the way the cardinal predicts, and loathsome rather than loving sympathy wins the day. Beatrice's young brother, Bernardo, voices similiar sentiments to Camillo's at V. iv. 129–35. As if to re-enthrone the redemptive model of influence, Shelley includes in Act IV of *Prometheus Unbound* a passage that echoes and purifies Camillo's sanguine (in both senses) description of Beatrice's powers. Enraptured with her paramour-brother, the Earth, the Moon sees herself as "a lover or chameleon" who "Grows like what it looks upon," as "a violet's gentle eye" that "Gazes on the azure sky / Until its hue grows like what it beholds," and as "a grey and watery mist" that "Glows like solid amethyst / Athwart the western mountains it enfolds" (*PU*, IV. 483–90).

111. Sperry perceptively analyzes how Shelley prompts his reader/spectator to love Beatrice while at the same time "condemn[ing] her actions unblinkingly" (140):

> The moral and emotional catharsis of the play proceeds out of [our] sympathetic identification [with Beatrice] as well as from our struggle to reconcile the inescapable recognition that she has adopted her father's violence with our abhorrence of the forces driving her to it. Such is the power of the dilemma in which Shelley places the spectator, so traumatic our predicament, that its effect is ultimately to force us to see the necessity of moving beyond a conventional standard of ethical judgement . . . to one that is more difficult and complex but also necessary and humane. It is to urge the transcendence of the moral imperative to love. (139)

Ulmer, on the other hand, offers a more skeptical reading of the play and of its audience(s). Turning to Sperry's argument, he writes, "To develop this viewpoint, Sperry must assume, or mandate, a particular response—here a sympathetic love for Beatrice that many readers and viewers no longer feel by act 5" (129n31).

112. This glue, as the physical emblem of her loathsome sympathy with her father, is also what will adhere Beatrice permanently to him (see, for example, V. iv. 57–72). Shelley's "Ode to Liberty" (1820) also invokes the image of infected semen: "O, that the free would stamp the impious name / Of KING into the dust! . . . / The sound has poison in it, 'tis the sperm / Of what makes life foul, cankerous, and abhorred" (ll. 211–12, 222–23).

113. Cf. *The Cenci* III. i. 95–99.

3. A Band of Sister-Spirits

1. Both Demogorgon and Jupiter himself endorse Thetis' reptilian analogy, though Demogorgon demotes the tyrant to a "trodden worm" (III. ii. 60). Usually linked with the vulture that he sent daily to torture and poison Prometheus, Jupiter seemed pleased enough with Thetis' agonized cries to cast himself as the snake in his

final speech to Demogorgon: "Sink with me then—/ We two will sink in the wide waves of ruin / Even as a vulture and a snake outspent / Drop, twisted in inextricable fight" (III. ii. 70–74). The echo here of *Laon and Cythna*, I. 66—"An Eagle and Serpent wreathed in fight"—reminds us how slippery the Shelleyan snake remains, for in the earlier poem, the serpent represents the Spirit of Good (*CW*, I, 259).

2. Most commentaries on the serpent referred to in Demogorgon's final speech focus on its function as the amphisbæna, the snake with a head at each end who serves to remind us that the progress toward Redemption can easily become the regress toward Fall. See, for example, Bloom, *Shelley's Mythmaking*, pp. 137–38, 146. Bloom, Curran, and Wasserman also link this snake with "the great tail-eating serpent, the Ouroboros," though they disagree as to whether this creature represents eternity or temporality (Curran, *Shelley's Annus Mirabilis*, 52). See Wasserman, pp. 370–73. None of the readings I have mentioned acknowledges Jupiter's presence within that ominous coiled serpent of IV. 565–69, which Wasserman calls "neither good nor evil" and associates with "the [morally indifferent] law of Necessity" (373). Crook and Guiton, on the other hand, do (implicitly) connect Jupiter with this snake when they invoke "the Serpentine Evil," syphilis, associated with the tyrant and perhaps tormenting Shelley himself: "There is an analogy between the serpent's uncoiling [in *PU*, IV. 365–67] and Fracastor's view of the cyclical nature of the Serpentine Evil: 'Once again when the Fates shall will it in the course of years, the time will come when the disease lies hidden, consigned to death and night. Later after long centuries this same malady shall arise'" (200). See *Shelley's Venomed Melody*, pp. 126–27, 160–61, and 187–88, for the rationale behind the name "Serpentine Evil"; see pp. 120–23 for Crook and Guiton's credible evidence that Shelley knew Girolamo Fracastor's sixteenth-century Latin poem, *Syphilis sive Morbus Gallicus* quite well. Finally, William Veeder points out the hermaphroditic quality of the ouroboros: the snake swallowing its own tail suggests that "the male can provide both the phallus and its receptacle" (144).

3. Shelley ultimately earned the nickname "Snake" from Byron, in part because of the homophony between "Bysshe Shelley" and *bishelli*, the Italian word for "small snake." (This sobriquet also reflected what the Calvinistic Byron deemed his friend's "devilish" atheism.) See *L*, II, pp. 368–69; Trelawny, *Recollections*, p. 187; Holmes, *Pursuit*, pp. 670–73; and Robinson, *Shelley and Byron*, passim.

4. Another victim of this castration fantasy could, of course, be Timothy Shelley, but Percy was always more self-mythologizing than father-mythologizing. Although he does not specify when Shelley told him about the Great Snake, Hogg writes that Shelley "spoke often" of its legend(s) (Hogg, I, 22). I imagine that this snake would loom especially large in Shelley's consciousness—and conversations with Hogg—in late 1810 and early 1811, when Shelley elaborately described for his new friend the paradisical Field Place (with its beautiful Eve, the young Elizabeth Shelley) and when the Harriet Grove crisis imperilled his own place in this Eden.

5. This phrase comes from a passage drafted for *Epipsychidion*:

> Werc it not a sweet refuge, Emily,
> For all those exiles from the dull insane

Who vex this pleasant world with pride and pain,
For all that band of sister-spirits known
To one another by a voiceless tone?

(*CW*, II, 382: "Fragments Connected
with *Epipsychidion*," ll. 170–74)

6. Commenting on the Dedication to *Laon and Cythna*, Holmes emphasizes that this opening lyric strongly conveys "the shock that the school experience had on [the poet], and in Shelley's elaborate private myth of his own childhood it forms one of the most decisive parts" (*Pursuit* 15–16). Though Holmes does not address the issue of gender here, Shelley's intense relationship with his sisters thoroughly informs the biographer's astute analysis of "the counterpoint between school and home" (*Pursuit* 23). Shelley's other biographers have also underscored the role of gender in his traumatic relocation from the woman-centered Field Place to the male realm of Syon House. Medwin, for example, writes that Shelley had to exchange "for the caresses of his sisters an association with boys . . . of rude habits and coarse manners, who made a game of his girlishness" (15). See also Edward Dowden, *Life*, I, pp. 13–15; Newman Ivey White, *Shelley*, I, pp. 18–20; and Cameron, *Young Shelley*, pp. 6–9.

7. In *The Assassins* the "monstrous snake" that menaces the impaled Wandering Jew figure metamorphoses into "a small snake," a darling playmate of Albedir's and Khaled's children: "The girl sang to it, and it leaped into her bosom, and she crossed her fair hands over it, as if to cherish it there" (*Prose* 133, 138, 139). In *Laon and Cythna*, the beautiful Woman who in Canto I escorts the narrator to the Temple of the Spirit welcomes the "wounded Serpent" into the "marmoreal depth" of her bosom after his fierce foe, the Eagle, drops him into the sea (*CW*, I, 262: *LC*, I. 154, 178). Moreover, both the visionary Woman in the poem and the children in the story communicate with the snake through a mysterious, melodious, and wonderfully efficacious language whose "accents sweet" suggest the primal, wordless language that flows between mother and infant (*CW*, I, 262: *LC*, I. 167). This rhythmic, extra-linguistic "language" thus resembles the Kristevan "semiotic *chora*," a pre-oedipal, presymbolic "flow of pulsions" that underlies and disrupts symbolic language (Moi 162, 161). For Kristeva's distinction between the semiotic process/realm and the symbolic order, see "From One Identity to an Other" in *Desire in Language*, pp. 124–47. The passage from *Laon and Cythna* describing the (re)union of the Woman and the serpent strikingly resembles an archetypal mother-child dyad:

She spake in language whose strange melody
Might not belong to earth. I heard, alone,
What made its music more melodious be,
The pity and the love of every tone;
But to the Snake those accents sweet were known,
His native tongue and her's:

. . . .
[She] [r]enewed the unintelligible strain
Of her melodious voice and eloquent mien;

And she unveiled her bosom, and the green
And glancing shadows of the sea did play
O'er its marmoreal depth:—one moment seen,
For ere the next, the Serpent did obey
Her voice, and, coiled in rest, in her embrace it lay.

(*CW*, I, 262: *LC*, I. 161–66, 174–80)

For a reading of *Prometheus Unbound* informed by Kristeva's psycholinguistic theories as well as by contemporary developmental psychology, see Gelpi, "The Nursery Cave," esp. pp. 61–62, and *Shelley's Goddess*. In her illuminating discussion of Shelley's essay "On Love," Gelpi suggests that "the voice of one beloved singing to you alone" which Shelley plaintively invokes in this essay is that of the Mother/Shelley's own mother, a reading that my remarks on *Laon and Cythna*, I. 154–80, and the conclusion of *The Assassins* would support (*Shelley's Goddess* 53–54). See "On Love," p. 474. Finally, for commentary on the beneficent snake as a key symbol in Gnosticism, see Grabo, *Magic Plant*, pp.135–36, 169, and 208, and Curran, *Shelley's Annus Mirabilis*, pp. 163, 217–18n35.

8. See William Cowper, *The Task*, III. 108–33, a passage that greatly appealed to the Christ-obsessed Shelley.

9. For example, the (feminized) poet is pierced with an "arrow" of grief, hope, and painful love (l. 24), an arrow whose erectness contrasts sharply with the poet's own "bent" spirit (l. 13). He also laments his "weak heart" and lack of "resolution" (ll. 48, 50), qualities which stereotypically suggest a "womanly" temperament. The biographical matrix surrounding this poem complicates, though does not contradict, my reading of the work as paradigmatic of Shelley's efforts to emulate the feminine. Deeply estranged from Mary at the time (January 1822), Percy addressed the poem to his friend Edward Williams, and, more specifically ("dear *friend*," l. 18) to Edward's common-law wife, Jane, with whom Percy was in love, if not sexually involved. Percy would thus want to downplay his own virility in order to reassure Edward that he longed to enter the "nest" of his "happy friends" (l. 8) not as an invasive, predatory male, but as a recipient of their—especially Jane's—tender friendship and sympathy ("Happy yourself, you feel another's woe," l. 56). For similar reasons, Percy casts himself as the sexless Ariel to Edward and Jane's Ferdinand and Miranda in the lovely and much less self-pitying "With a Guitar. To Jane."

10. Shelley's habit of portraying himself as victimized, symptomatic of his need to believe in his own self-abnegation, pervades "The Serpent Is Shut Out," though in a more insidious way than in the earlier poem. In the 1822 lyric, Percy blames Mary— frigid goddess of his "cold home"—for much of his "woe" (ll. 25, 56).

11. The most well-known of Shelley's deer appears in *Adonais*, where the Shelley figure lags behind the procession of mourners: "[O]f that crew / He came the last, neglected and apart; / A herd-abandoned deer struck by the hunter's dart" (ll. 295–97). For passages that put a uniquely Shelleyan spin on the Actaeon myth, see *PU*, I. 454–57; *Epi.*, ll. 272–74; and *Adonais*, ll. 274–79. Veeder points out that Mary Shelley amplifies "the Shelleyan ring to [Victor's] self-pity" in her 1831 revisions of

Frankenstein (198): "The wounded deer dragging its fainting limbs to some untrodden brake, there to gaze upon the arrow which had pierced it, and to die—was but a type of me" (*Frankenstein* 247). The self-adverting "gaze" of the Shelleyan martyr is a particularly nice touch.

12. In Kohut's terms, the poet desires to merge with his idealized (Christ) and his mirroring (Harriet) selfobjects.

13. See White, *Shelley*, I, p. 326. Gelpi's *Shelley's Goddess* showcases this incident, in which Harriet hired a wet nurse. Her analysis of Shelley's fear that the "nurse's soul would enter the child" (White, I, 326) harmonizes with my own thoughts on Shelley's notions of intersubjectivity and (sometimes dangerous) influence. But while Gelpi focuses on the poet's (ambivalent) desire to be mothered, I would emphasize his desire to be mother, or, as I will demonstrate later, to be *sister*. Gelpi herself devotes several perceptive pages to Shelley's "identification with the feminine maternal" (98). See Gelpi's remarkable opening section, "The Nurse's Soul," pp. 3–134.

14. This, according to Stoller, is "one's sense of being either a male or female" and more specifically "a conviction that the assignment of one's sex was anatomically, and ultimately psychologically, correct" (182, 11).

15. In *Gender Trouble*, Butler seeks to free gender once and for all from sex, arguing that gender is purely "performative": "There is no gender identity behind the expressions of gender" (25). See also Alan Sinfield's *The Wilde Century*, especially pp. 183–85.

16. G. S. Rousseau's essay "Nerves, Spirits, and Fibres: Towards Defining the Origins of Sensibility" is key here.

17. See, in particular, chap. 1 of *The Culture of Sensibility*, "Sensibility and the Nervous System," which discusses issues such as the "gendering of the nerves" and the somatic implications of the term *delicacy* (24, 26).

18. I want to stress here that the discussion that follows, though it echoes the language of sensibility that Shelley and his contemporaries employed, does so in order to describe the poet's own sense of gender categories, not in order to asssign essential qualities to actual men and women, either in Shelley's time or our own.

19. Whereas the "idealized" or "omnipotent" selfobject is a powerful, seemingly perfect other who provides the developing self with a model for its aspirations, ideals, and ideal self-image, the "mirroring-approving" selfobject offers a confirmation and acceptance analogous to the gleam in the mother's eye. According to Kohut, the child's original idealized selfobjects are most often his or her parents in all their strength and wisdom, while one's first and most important mirroring selfobject would be his or her primary caretaker—usually the mother—who responds to the child's needs for acknowledgement and approval. As the child grows up, other figures supplement though never completely replace these original idealized and mirroring selfobjects, and both versions of the selfobject are crucial for the individual's ability to achieve and maintain genuine self-esteem. Kohut's clearest, most succinct comparison

of the mirroring selfobject's function to that of the idealized selfobject can be found on pp. 226–27 of *Self Psychology and the Humanities*. See also "On Narcissism and Narcissistic Rage," esp. pp. 364–65, 370, and 386, as well as *The Analysis of the Self*, pp. 37–56 and 105–32.

20. When, after Harriet rejects him and his "detestable principles," Percy vows to "stab the wretch" (Christ), the poet may be displacing some of his anger toward the women who have hurt him onto his all-too-omnipotent selfobject (*L*, I, 27). Perhaps then the gory bosom in "Song" would be not only Christ's but also his mother's and perhaps Harriet's—though at this point (August 1810), Harriet had not yet completely retreated from him.

21. Because these real or imagined women often became for Shelley or his protagonists, "second selves" (later, the more overtly self-projective "antitypes" or "epipsyches"), the term *other* remains problematic. It is perhaps only their gender that remains genuinely "other" and that thus inspires in Shelley "a going out of [his] own nature" in order to converge with the feminine streams of love that he longed both to augment as a (philanthropic and erotic) lover and to drink in as a beloved (*Defence* 487). As a second self, the Shelleyan wife, lover, or heroine may serve as a kind of poultice for the wounded narcissism discussed in chapter 1, but as a woman she can compel him to move beyond the twin gates of his own gender and obdurate Selfhood. Hogle's reading of *Laon and Cythna* illuminates how the "other" can both liberate and entrap the self, depending on whether or not "genuine intertransference"—Shelleyan Love—occurs (see *Shelley's Process*, pp. 96–103; quotation p. 100).

22. Nearly all contemporary accounts of Shelley mention his strikingly effeminate appearance. While some of his physical traits—his "girlish" slimness, his delicate complexion, and his high-pitched voice—were certainly constitutional, I get the sense that Shelley deliberately heightened these qualities in order to become more feminine. Hellen Shelley, for example, writes of the "eccentric quantity of hair" her brother sported in adolescence. Hogg echoes her view of Shelley's long hair as "eccentric," for cropped hair was in fashion at the time (late 1810). His sister, Elizabeth, Hellen continues, "on one occasion, made him sit down to have it cut, and be made to look like a Christian," when Shelley probably much preferred to look like *her*. This episode, moreover, reveals Elizabeth's maternal attitude toward her brother and his willing submission to it. See Hogg, I, pp. 32, 48.

23. The term *usurps* seems a bit strong here, because Percy certainly does not leave Harriet bereft of femininity. On the contrary, he is eager to establish a dynamic in which both lovers remain predominantly feminine. On occasion, as in *Laon and Cythna*, Shelley will slightly masculinize his heroine in order to emphasize his hero-surrogate's own sexual and emotional "womanliness." Significantly, Shelley creates his only bona fide viragos, *Zastrozzi*'s Matilda and, to a lesser degree, *St. Irvyne*'s Megalena, before his place in his cousin's and sisters' affections was really in jeopardy. As Percy lost Harriet and then his sisters, he had to imaginatively reconstruct and internalize the feminine ideal of love and sympathy that these young women represented to him. (Another, more troubling, aspect of this Shelleyan ideal of feminine

sympathy would be the "Percy-worship" in which the poet basked since boyhood. His dramatic fall from such a height certainly deepened the "narcissistic wounds" that he suffered.) Shelley had to banish from his works such violent, sexually voracious, "manly" women as those who dominate his Gothic novels, because they only sullied and confused the (essentially traditional) feminine ideal that Shelley struggled to embody. After mid-1810, Shelley's most radical experiments with gender involve his own strivings toward the feminine rather than his creation of female characters in the image of men.

24. An equally revealing aspect of this passage's migration and transformation is its new role in Hogg's copy as the conclusion of another "Song" from the *Victor and Cazire* collection, "Cold are the blasts." (The composite poem that Shelley gave Hogg is made up of "Cold are the blasts" in its entirety [though with textual variations that differ both from the *Victor and Cazire* and *Esdaile* (129–30) versions], stanza 1 and part of stanza 2 from "Ah! sweet is the moonbeam" [addressed to Harriet Grove], and fragments from the penultimate and final stanzas of "Stern, stern is the voice.") "Cold are the blasts" tells the tragic tale of a fallen woman driven to madness and death by the perfidy of her "remorseless betrayer" (*PS*, I, 96). Closely linked stylistically, tonally, and linguistically to several melancholy "Songs" addressed to Harriet in *Victor and Cazire*, including "Stern, stern is the voice," this melodramatic lyric achieves real emotional force from Percy's deep sympathies, even identification, with the woman "abandoned to sorrow" by her cruel "ruiner" (*PS*, I, 96). Thus the poem, as reworked for Hogg, neatly melds with the stanza at hand from "Stern, stern is the voice," where Shelley himself is, like the spurned woman, a forlorn "outcast" (*PS*, I, 97, 104). However, if Percy identifies with the woman scorned in "Cold are the blasts," he does not imagine a complete role reversal with Harriet playing masculine libertine. Because he was anxious to preserve his alliance with his female cousin and was not simply accusing her of "perfidy" and then attempting to absorb her femininity, Percy refuses to cast her as the male villain in this piece (*PS*, I, 98). He reserves that role for his own *Doppelgänger*, aptly supplied both in Hogg's and in the *Esdaile* version of the poem with one of Percy's favorite aliases, "Henry." For her part as Percy's target audience, Harriet is invited to shed sympathetic and womanly tears over the the grave of the "fallen victim" (*PS*, I, 96). That Percy wants his sister-spirit to imagine this grave as his own as well as that of the dead woman is apparent in the ominous, almost admonitory fourth line that appears in at least one version of the poem: "And sad is the grave where a loved one lies low" (*CW*, I, 9). See also "To St. Irvyne" (1809–1810), where Percy, with his "poor sorrow-torn breast," plaintively requests of his cousin, "When my mouldering bones lie in the cold, chilling grave, . . . / Then, loved Harriet, bestow one poor thought on me" (*Esdaile* 171, 172). For other *Victor and Cazire* lyrics besides "Stern, stern is the voice" that share imagery, tone, and diction with "Cold are the blasts," see, for example, the overtly autobiographical "Song" ("Come [Harriet]! sweet is the hour"), "Song: Despair" ("Ask not the pallid stranger's woe"), and "Song: Sorrow" ("To me this world's a dreary blank") in *PS*, I, 94–95, 100–1. As much as these poems may seem parodic in their relentless melancholy and self-pity, they reflect Shelley's genuine, and justified, fear that his relationship with his cousin is approaching a final crisis. What they do

not reflect is any self-awareness that he himself generated this crisis by inundating her with his "Deistical Principles" (*L*, I, 26). As Veeder, in another context, comments, "Percy did it all his life—generate dilemmas and then see himself as the one put upon" (*Mary Shelley and "Frankenstein"* 227).

25. Hogg's claim that these verses "have never been published" suggests that he never saw the collection itself, which was printed in the fall of 1810, but not published because of Stockdale's discovery of plagiarisms from Monk Lewis (I, 124). At any rate, even if Thomas had seen the volume, Percy could easily have convinced him that Elizabeth-Cazire wrote these verses, as none of the poems therein was identified by author. See Cameron's commentary on this hybrid poem's complex textual history in *Esdaile*, pp. 258–60. Hogg's account confirms that he did believe in Elizabeth's authorship of these lines and also reveals his awareness of the poem's role in Percy's matchmaking: "[These verses] were the composition of his sister, Elizabeth, and he valued them highly as well as their author . . . I was to undertake to fall in love with her; if I did not I had no business to go to Field Place, and he would never forgive me. I promised to do my best" (I, 126–27). Hogg does not, however, divulge just how well Shelley's plot succeeded. See *L*, I, pp. 29–33, 34, 36–37, 41, 43, 72, 92–93, 95, 103–4, 106, 111, 124, 128–29, where Shelley alternately—and sometimes simultaneously—fans and attempts to extinguish the flames of Hogg's extravagant passion. That Hogg only saw Elizabeth Shelley once—"the peep at Warnham Church" in June, 1811 (*L*, I, 124)—and only after he had fallen desperately in love with (Percy's representations of) her, highlights her role as a conduit for the homoerotic charge that obviously flowed between the two young men. This triangle is further complicated by Percy's erotic, and narcissistic, desire for his sister-"twin," a desire that he displaced onto his other beloved, Thomas. (Anne K. Mellor sees Shelley's matchmaking as an "attempt to close the sexual circle between himself and his sister" [*Mary Shelley* 74].) This complex dynamic thus allowed Percy to indulge three forbidden passions: for his male friend, for his female sibling, and for his own sexually ambiguous self, now a kind of composite of his masculine and feminine "second selves." (At one point, frustrated with Elizabeth's retreat into orthodoxy and with her new "scorn" for her brother and his "mad friend Hogg," Percy writes to Thomas: "Do I not pursue virtue for virtue's sake—why then do I wander wildly, why do I write madly: why has sleep forsaken me, why are you & my sister forever present to my mind?" [*L*, I, 103, 104: 16 June 1811]).

26. After examining the manuscript containing the revised passage from "Stern, stern is the voice" and the verses to which it was appended, Cameron concludes, "These verses were presumably written down for Hogg shortly after Shelley and he got together again at Oxford after the Christmas vacation in January 1811" (*Esdaile*, Commentaries, 258). See also *SC*, II, pp. 625–27.

27. The two versions of the passage on which I have been focusing in fact record the stages of his momentous loss: in the August 1810 poem, the speaker bids farewell "to the friend of affection," Harriet, while in the winter 1811 revision he-she says goodbye "to the scenery of childhood," the Edenic Field Place and its beautiful and attentive "band of sister-spirits."

28. The ventriloquism at work in this episode anticipates Percy's adoption of the role of "Mary" when he writes the preface to *Frankenstein*, where his empathic merger with his gifted wife coincides uneasily with a troubling condescension toward her as a "humble" neophyte (*Frankenstein*, Preface, 6).

29. White writes of the poet's arrival at Syon House Academy: "The sensitive and slightly-built boy of ten had been poorly prepared by his previous experience for the world he was now entering . . . His girlish looks were alone a sufficient handicap, but his girlish associations were fatal to any chance of happiness with his fellows" (I, 19).

30. While I cannot endorse Brown's rather outlandish contention that "In his own heart [Shelley] knew what it was to be a woman," I do agree with Brown that the "women-centered world" in which the poet grew up, as well as his own "strikingly effeminate morphological structure," greatly contributed to his deep affinity with the feminine gender (*Sexuality and Feminism* 165, 166).

31. See *Sexuality and Feminism*, esp. pp. 164–96. Although Brown offers a veritable catalogue of Shelley's feminist attitudes and statements, he tends to take the poet too much at his word and rarely probes the ways that Shelley (sometimes deliberately) undercuts his own feminist position. For incisive criticisms of Brown's position, see Mellor's review of *Sexuality and Feminism* and Veeder's remarks on Brown's controversial thesis in *Mary Shelley and "Frankenstein,"* pp. 55, 56.

32. Here I use the term *mirror* in the sense of "reflect" or "imitate," rather than in the Kohutian sense of "confirm" or "approve." Alan Richardson would probably call this emulation/identification a "colonization" of the feminine, but I have to disagree with his overly censorious account of romanticism's "insidious . . . appropriation" of traditionally feminine qualities ("Romanticism and the Colonization of the Feminine" 13). By their very nature, the traits and values that the "sensibility" writers and romantic poets "re-claim[ed]" from women—love, sympathy, sensibility—preclude the kind of monopolization and absorption by one person, one group, one gender that Richardson implies (15). Granted, many male writers of these literary periods, including Shelley, betray their own narcissism and desire to "incorporate the feminine," but their valorization of "womanly" traits such as sympathy, maternal tenderness, and humanitarian kindness actually helps counteract, rather than aggravate, the self-involvement and sexism that have become the focus of current attacks on (masculine) romanticism (19). In the case of Shelley himself, the term *colonize* is particularly inappropriate, for it implies that the poet invaded and then assimilated something purely external to himself. First of all, since boyhood Shelley was remarkably feminine in temperament and physiognomy: any "encroachments" he made onto "feminine domain" would only strengthen, not create, his own feminine traits (15, 13). Moreover, because he was anxious to preserve/re-create what the self psychologist Ernest S. Wolf would call the "selfobject milieu" of his childhood, Shelley longed to share with, not wrest from, women their most characteristic—as defined traditionally—qualities, impulses, and behaviors ("On the Developmental Line of Selfobject Relations" 125).

33. By reflecting/imitating his sisters and cousin—and, indirectly, his mother—Percy also could partake of the vibrancy and animation that all of the Shelley women and that Harriet Grove seemed to exemplify for the poet. Their dynamism thus could help vitalize him as well as mobilize/(re)create his flagging Self-esteem.

34. Gelpi argues throughout *Shelley's Goddess* that relations between Percy and his mother remained warm and intimate, but the emotional energy that the young man invested in his sisters and his cousin and the "narcissistic rage" that he exhibited—particularly in the letters and poems of early 1811—after these young women rejected him point to an earlier rupture in the mother-son relationship. Barbara Schapiro, on the other hand, overgeneralizes and argues that all of the major male romantics felt abandoned by their mothers. She thus undermines many of her own valid observations about the ambivalent images of women in romantic poetry. In Shelley's case particularly, I think that Schapiro is right to discern evidence of anger and resentment toward "the mother imago," to use the psychoanalytic term that Schapiro employs (ix); but her readings of *Alastor* and of *The Triumph of Life* would be more convincing had she included biographical evidence demonstrating Shelley's sense of maternal betrayal.

35. Shelley was sent away to school in 1802, at the age of ten.

36. The haircutting episode involving Percy and Elizabeth, referred to in note 22, as well as Elizabeth's protectiveness toward her distraught brother following Harriet's break with him (*L*, I, 32, 36) suggest that she often adopted a maternal stance toward him. Although we have no comparable examples displaying Harriet in a motherly role, she was a year older than her cousin/fiancé, a seemingly slight disparity that nonetheless creates a significant gap in the relative levels of maturity between an adolescent girl and boy. But even if her status as an "older woman" did not link her with the Mother, her close relationship, which included a correspondence, with her "Aunt Shelley" intimately connected her with *the* mother, Percy's own. However, as captive audiences for Percy the poet and novelist and as (temporary) disciples to his "deistical" Christ, Elizabeth and Harriet each played daughter/pupil to their more intellectually sophisticated, if less emotionally mature, preceptor.

37. The letter quoted is the one to Hogg announcing Shelley's intention to marry Harriet Westbrook: "Gratitude & admiration all demand that I should love her *forever*" (3 August 1811). At the height of the "new" Harriet and Elizabeth's ascendancy, the words *forever* and *eternity* pop up constantly in Percy's correspondence with and about these women. "Forever" turned out to be a pretty brief span of time in the case both of wife and of "eternal" friend, and our awareness of their subsequent and precipitous falls from (Shelley's) grace tends to ironize passages in which Shelley asserts, for example, "the eternity of [his] regard" for Elizabeth Hitchener, his "dearest friend ever ever" (*L*, I, 201, 193). However, Shelley becomes obsessed with "*eternal* love" the year following his loss of cousin and sisters not because he intended to dupe or even simply flatter his new loves, Harriet Westbrook and Elizabeth Hitchener, but because he was soliciting reassurance from them that their devotion to him was steadfast, permanent (*L*, I, 152). From Miss Hitchener at least, Shelley apparently got what he

wanted, as this rather typical closing of one of her letters demonstrates: "[M]y friendship can never change, but binds me / Ever yours / My dearest friend, / E. Hitchener" (*L*, I, 171: 12 November 1811).

38. To be precise, in his letter to Elizabeth Hitchener of 8 October 1811, Shelley refers to the "votaries" of virtue as "the brothers & sisters of [his] soul," and in her reply Miss Hitchener applies this epithet specifically to her relationship with Percy and Harriet: "I long to be introduced to *your Harriet* will she ever permit me to call her so, she shall have a Sister's affection, for are you not the Brother of my soul" (*L*, I, 145n2).

39. Shelley calls Elizabeth Hitchener his "second self" in his letter to her of 14 November 1811 (*L*, I, 183). Variations on this epithet as applied to Miss Hitchener include "my better genius" and "my second conscience" (*L*, I, 196, 215). Harriet Shelley is her husband's "second self" in "To Harriet" ("It is not blasphemy") (*Esdaile* 86, l. 56).

40. Compare Cythna's descriptions of her suspected and then confirmed pregnancy: "there seemed a being / Within me," "There was a babe within" (*CW*, I, 348: *LC*, VII. 136–39, 150).

41. See *Zastrozzi* (*CW*, V, 29, 51) and *St. Irvyne* (*CW*, V, 189–92, 194–97).

42. Laon might qualify, then, the most self-involved of Shelley's protagonists, provided both with his martyrdom(s)—on the tower as well as on the pyre—and with his ideal self-image. Although, or rather because, Laon so nakedly embodies Shelley's own dream of glorious martyrdom and realizes the poet's own desire for an adoring twin, the poet constantly punctures this strangely unheroic hero's inflated self-image.

43. See the Song of Solomon 4: 9, 10, 12; 5: 1, 2. The love-sick sister's comparison of her brother to a roe or "young hart" might have contributed to Shelley's attraction to the deer as a resonant self-image (Song of Solomon 2: 9). On pp. 82–88 of *Eros and Vision*, Jean H. Hagstrum discusses the influence on Shelley's poetry of the Song of Songs, where "voluptuous consanguinity" infuses the notion of a sister-spouse (83).

44. Similiarly, Shelley writes, again to Hogg, about his new love Mary Godwin in the fall of 1814: "[S]o intimately are our natures now united, that I feel whilst I describe her excellencies as if I were an egotist expatiating upon his own perfections" (*L*, I, 402). The homoerotic attraction that flowed between the two friends may have exacerbated Percy's tendency to see his beloved women as extensions of himself, surrogates through whom he could express—and, in Mary's case, consummate—his sexual passion for his friend.

45. See Thorslev's discussion of "brother-sister incestuous love" as "symboliz[ing] perfectly the Romantic hero's narcissistic sensibility . . . [and] intellectual solipsism" (54). While Thorslev focuses on the romantic—particularly the Byronic and Shelleyan—idealization of sibling incest, Alan Richardson rightly observes that the brother-sister union in *Laon and Cythna* and *Manfred*, for example, is "an exclusive and *doomed* relationship" ("The Dangers of Sympathy" 754; emphasis mine).

Richardson provides excellent commentary on the death of Shelley's sibling revolutionaries as a "grisly *liebestod*" that "is uncomfortably reminiscent of the ritual deaths described by Frazer in *Totemism and Exogamy*" (750). I would emphasize more than Richardson does, however, that Shelley was as aware as Levi-Strauss—whom Richardson cites—that incest makes for "a radically anti-social union, which divides the couple from the larger community" (751). Despite his imaginative assaults upon it, the incest taboo remained firmly in place within Shelley's consciousness.

46. As Curran observes, "In most genealogies of the Titans, Asia is not Prometheus' wife but his mother," a fact that provides the cornerstone for Gelpi's reading of the play in *Shelley's Goddess* (*Shelley's Annus Mirabilis* 45). But Shelley himself suggests that his protagonists are brother and sister rather than son and mother when he has Asia address the Earth as "mother" just after Prometheus has greeted his "Mother Earth" (*PU*, III. iii. 85, 109).

47. It is important to note that Shelley gave this advice to Miss Hitchener in October 1811, when she was nearing the zenith of her reign. Shelley offered his friends exhortations regarding self-abnegation as tokens of his esteem: they were worthy, he had decided, to fight the good fight against the Self, both in their own hearts and in the world at large. Moreover, if his "second selves" achieved genuine disinterestedness, their self-conquest would be Percy's victory as well. Shelley's correspondence with Hogg is filled with admonitions against selfishness, and the "unformed" Claire Clairmont was doubtless the recipient of many lectures urging her toward the "habitual contempt of self" (*JMS*, I, 36: 14 October 1814).

48. That the selflessness and generosity of the female sex is a time-worn notion does not detract from its power as a persistent cultural myth. For a detailed historical account of this myth's surge of new life in the late eighteenth and early nineteenth centuries, see Davidoff and Hall, esp. pp. 149–92, 335–43, and 429–36. "Reform of Ruin: 'A Revolution in Female Manners,'" Mitzi Myers's excellent essay comparing Mary Wollstonecraft and Hannah More, also emphasizes that an ideal of feminine self-abnegation flourished during this period, a period that saw the birth of the female Evangelist. Shelley himself, as Hogg reports, "spoke with great animation of [women's] purity, disinterestedness, generosity, kindness, and the like" (I, 181). These qualities are less evident in men, Shelley believed, because of "an independence in the male character" that prevents them from seeing themselves as part of what psychologist Carol Gilligan calls "a network of connection, a web of relationships" (Hogg, I, 81; *In a Different Voice* 32). Both Gilligan and Nancy Chodorow have argued that women more commonly perceive themselves in terms of relationship than do men, and thus have more flexible ego boundaries and a greater capacity for empathy. See Gilligan, *In a Different Voice*, esp. chaps. 1 and 2, and Chodorow, "Family Structure and Feminine Personality" and *The Reproduction of Mothering*, esp. chaps. 1–6. While these American feminists and their adherents tend to discuss their paradigms of feminine identity in terms of interpersonal relationships, French feminists such as Luce Irigaray and Hélène Cixous focus not on woman's capacity to identify with others but on her ability to discover and celebrate the many others who dwell within the self. Cixous speaks in "The Laugh of the Medusa" of the feminine "gift of alterability" (260), and in "This

sex which is not one," Irigaray refers to mercurial woman's refusal to become "fixed, immobilized" (103). Both models, the one stressing feminine empathy, the other feminine multiplicity, will be pertinent to my discussion of Shelley's representation and emulation of the feminine. See Mellor's Introduction to *Romanticism and Feminism* for a lucid, concise account of the central distinctions between "Anglo-American" and "French" feminisms (3–9).

49. Cf. Blake's description of Urizen as a "Self-closd, all-repelling" and "self-contemplating shadow," in *The [First] Book of Urizen*, Chap. I, ll. 3, 21.

50. The young Shelley's plan to purchase in order to educate a little girl provides the most extreme example of this appetite for female pupils (Hogg, I, 27). See also Shelley's 28 October 1811 letter to Elizabeth Hitchener, where he asks his friend to "assist [him] to mould a really noble soul," that of Harriet Westbrook Shelley (*L*, I, 163). Almost exactly three years later, we find Shelley launching a campaign to shape his new sister, the rather intractable Jane (Claire) Clairmont. He first notes "Janes insensibility & incapacity for the slightest degree of friendship," but then cheers himself with the thought, "Characters particularly those which are unformed may change" (*JMS*, I, 35: 14 October 1814). That Claire's was an essentially "unformed" character definitely appealed to Percy, for he repeats the word a few lines later, this time linking it with "softness & feeling": "Converse with Jane. Her mind unsettled. her character unformed.—New occasion of hopes from some instances of softness & feeling. She is not entirely insensible to concessions" (36). In a revealing aside, Shelley remarks, "Hear that Eliza and Hellen [Shelley] go to [?Pongnton] [for Poynton?] in 3 weeks" (35–36; first bracket mine). References to his (real) sisters were extremely rare by this time, and this one fairly erupts into his discourse on Claire, reminding us—and him?— that Claire and Mary, like Elizabeth Hitchener and Harriet Shelley before them, could only reprise roles that originally and indelibly belonged to the women of Field Place. Barbara Gelpi compellingly argues that Shelley's "pedagogical passion" reveals his "identification with the feminine maternal," with the mother who educates, influences, and literally "forms" her child (*Shelley's Goddess* 98). As the young Elizabeth Shelley's often motherly stance toward her brother reminds us, the maternal and the sisterly were not incompatible roles, and Shelley not only longed for the attention of his actual and surrogate mothers and sisters, but also yearned to play both roles himself. In a conversation recorded by Hogg, Shelley's compares "maternal tenderness" and "sisterly affection" (I, 81).

51. Byron would have called this trait "*mobilité*," which he defines as "an excessive susceptibility to immediate impressions—at the same time without *losing* the past" (*Don Juan* 491: Note to 16. 97. 4). As Mellor points out, this quality was one that the author of *Don Juan* himself "possessed to a remarkable degree" (*English Romantic Irony* 200n36). (In an 1822 letter to Hunt, Shelley calls Byron "this Proteus in whom such strange extremes are reconciled," and to John Gisborne he wrote, "Lord Byron is so mentally capricious that the least impulse drives him from his anchorage" [*L*, II, 394, 435].) Byron links *mobilité* to the feminine when he ascribes this trait to the mercurial Lady Adeline, with her "vivacious versatility" (*Don Juan* 448: 16. 97. 3). (Jerome McGann's discussion of *mobilité*, identified in Byron's mind with the

"feminine brain" ["'My Brain Is Feminine'" 42], illuminates how this "versatility" slides easily into duplicity and outright ["bold"] lying—of a paradoxically admirable and "redemptive" kind.) Commenting on Byronic *mobilité*, Paglia rightly sees "the mobile male" as "receptive and half-feminine" (354). Whereas Byron's notion of *mobilité* suggests both psychic and somatic receptivity, a comment by Godwin in his *Memoirs* of Mary Wollstonecraft emphasizes the latter: "Women have a frame of body more delicate and susceptible of impression than men, and, in proportion as they receive a less intellectual education, are more unreservedly under the empire of feeling" (276).

52. Cf. Byron's ambivalent description of *mobilité*: "though sometimes apparently useful to the possessor, a most painful and unhappy attribute" (*Don Juan* 491: Note to 16. 97. 4).

53. Shelley shares the conception of vital feminine self-transmutation with some contemporary women scholars, though he tends to evade or spiritualize the female body in which these theorists ground their paradigms. The French feminists Luce Irigaray and Hélène Cixous, for example, link feminine multiplicity with female physiology and libido, while the critic Camille Paglia associates it with the Dionysian flux and melting of borders that characterizes all-inclusive "Mother" Nature, synecdochally represented by the female body. See Cixous's "The Laugh of the Medusa" and "Sorties," Irigaray's "This sex which is not one," and Paglia's *Sexual Personae*, *passim*. Like the tradition of feminine self-sacrifice, the myth of feminine variability has a long but much more checkered history. The celebrations of the feminine "gift of alterality," as Cixous puts it ("Laugh" 260), that we find in Shelley's poetry and in the writings of the two French theorists I have mentioned are much less common than misogynistic diatribes against feminine caprice or "fickleness," such as the one that Pope offers in his catalogue of grotesque female "Chameleons," *Epistle II. To a Lady* (l. 156).

54. See Chodorow, "Family Structure and Feminine Personality," and Gelpi's interview with Rich in Gelpi's Norton Critical Edition of *Adrienne Rich's Poetry*, p. 115.

55. Reed finds in a passage from Kohut's *Restoration of the Self* a resonant metaphor that reconciles the concept of 'empathy' as "male penetration" with the notion of empathy as "female nurturing":

Although Kohut is discussing creative insight generally, rather than clinical insight specifically, the juxtaposition and related subject matter make this quotation relevant to our exploration . . . : "On this basic level of experience . . . there is no clear separation of observer and observed . . . thought and action are still one . . . We seem to witness the parthenogenesis of an idea of enormous power" (p. 301). If we apply this image to empathy, we note that the antithetical meanings discerned in our exploration thus far reappear and are reconciled through a metaphor of parthenogenesis in which insight is the result of a union within the individual of the male who penetrates and the female who conceives. (18)

56. James A. W. Heffernan's *"Adonais*: Shelley's Consumption of Keats" provides perhaps the best account of how and why "Shelley himself invented the strange story of Keats's death" (295).

57. Crook and Guiton's comment on what Hogg terms Shelley's "monstrous delusion" gets right to the point (II, 40): "There is no other single anecdote that is more embarrassing to those wishing to take Shelley seriously" (86). They devote an entire, illuminating chapter to this episode, pointing out that both Peacock and a daughter of Shelley's friend John Newton basically confirm Hogg's account. Crook and Guiton's interpretation of this incident hinges on the fact that *Elephantiasis Graecorum,* or leprosy, was thought to be among the last, horrific stages of syphilis, from which Shelley may have suffered (89). Their argument is basically compatible with my emphasis on Shelley's sense of psychic and perhaps physical vulnerability to devastating contamination.

58. Hogg states that "this strange fancy continued to afflict [Shelley] for some weeks" (II, 40).

59. Medwin, who claimed to have introduced Shelley to the theories and practices of Franz Anton Mesmer (1733–1815), is using the term *magnetic* in the sense of "susceptible to animal magnetism," the influence that one person, such as a hypnotist or "magnetist," exerts over another via the "electro-nervous fluids" that supposedly exist within and exude from the human body. Robert Peel gleans from J. P. F. Deleuze's *Practical Instruction in Animal Magnetism* (1825) a succinct definition of animal magnetism or "mesmerism," as it was often called:

> Its practitioners for the most part assumed the existence of a magnetic fluid by which one living organism could influence or control another . . . Deleuze postulated "a substance [which] emanates from him who magnetizes, and is conveyed to the person magnetized, in the direction given by the will." He explained that although the magnetic fluid escaped from all the body and the will sufficed to give it direction, "the external organs, by which we act, are the most proper to throw it off," and therefore "we make use of our hands and eyes to magnetize." (151)

Medwin tells us that he magnetized Shelley during his stay with him in Pisa in late 1820 and early 1821 and that Mary Shelley and later another woman (Jane Williams) practiced this form of psycho-physiotherapy upon the poet (269–70). See Percy's poem "The Magnetic Lady to her Patient" (1822), where Jane is the soothing physician.

60. Many readers have noted the feminine and erotic implications of this favorite romantic image. See, for example, Paglia, p. 378, and Mellor, Introduction to *Romanticism and Feminism,* p. 7. For other instances of Shelleyan lyres, see *Alastor,* ll. 42 and 667, and "Ode to the West Wind," l. 57. Paglia is one of the few critics who have discerned just how "woman-identified" Shelley and his protagonists really are. She comes up with an appropriately voluptuous image for the relationship of feminized poet and inseminating wind, a relationship implicit in the Shelleyan metaphors of Aeolian lyre and fading coal: "The poet waits like an odalisque, a Giorgione nude asleep in a meadow" (378).

61. Paglia is particularly good on the troubling aspects of Coleridge's "longing for erotic and creative passivity," and her comments throw light on Shelley's cultivation of his own "thrilling receptivity" (319). See *Sexual Personae*, pp. 317–46.

62. Offering a virtual catalogue of sensibility buzzwords, Mary Shelley, in her Note on *Alastor*, comments on her husband's high-strung nature: "His nerves, which nature had formed sensitive to an unexampled degree, were rendered still more susceptible by the state of his health" (*CW*, I, 198).

63. See *L*, I, pp. 407–21; White, *Shelley*, I, pp. 378–83; and Holmes, *Pursuit*, pp. 265–69.

64. The elephantiasis episode of late 1813 similarly exposes Shelley's horror of contamination. As Crook and Guiton point out, this incident occurred during the period when Percy's marriage to Harriet was collapsing and the poet felt vulnerable to the (sexual) contagion that awaited him outside the once-protective confines of domesticity. (See *Shelley's Venomed Melody*, pp. 89 and 99–100.) Once Percy's "second self" who "breathe[d] magnetic sweetness thro' the frame / Of [his] corporeal nature," Harriet is now gone—at least from her husband's heart—and something more dangerous, more depraved threatens to replace the "soft communion" he shared with her (*Esdaile* 86, 85: "To Harriet" ["It is not blasphemy"], ll. 56, 15–16, 46). Crook and Guiton, who speculate that Shelley contracted a venereal disease as early as 1808 or 1809 (when he was at Eton), suggest that the poet was already "tainted" by the "immedicable plague" of syphilis when he encounters the woman inflicted with elephantiasis (*Shelley's Venomed Melody* 101; *PU*, II. iv. 101). Thus, in their view, the old "leprous" woman—perhaps a prostitute—would have presented him with a preview of his own degenerate(d) condition, rather than infected him in the way that Shelley claimed to believe she did. As Crook and Guiton argue throughout their provocative study, syphilis, whether or not Shelley actually had it, provides a potent metaphor for all kinds of evil in Shelley's writings, and I would stress that when Shelley, in Hogg's account, discovers "symptoms of the fearful contagion" of elephantiasis "in his own person," he obviously feels deeply implicated in a network of (often dangerous) influence, both as donor and recipient (Hogg, II, 39).

65. Among the most noxious of "the taints [London's] wretched walls contain" is the promiscuous, loveless, and mercenary sexuality that seemed both to tempt and to repulse the poet whenever he found himself alone in this city (*Esdaile* 53: "On leaving London for Wales," l. 6). Infection and impurity were much on Percy's mind during the miserable fortnight in 1814, and the letters he wrote Mary reveal that he sometimes sees his ideal second self in the traditional feminine role of the virtuous, pure woman who saves her mate from his own, and others,' worst propensities. In his letter of 27 October, for example, he writes, "Know you my best Mary that I feel myself in your absence almost degraded to the level of the vulgar & impure. I feel their vacant stiff eyeballs fixed upon me—until I seem to have been infected with the loathsome meaning—to inhale a sickness that subdues me to languor. Oh! those redeeming eyes of Mary that they might beam upon me before I sleep!" (*L*, I, 412). In one of the elegant and gallant missives that he wrote to Byron's mistress, the Countess Guicccioli in

1821, Shelley even more explicitly invokes the stereotypical ideal of redemptive womanhood: "I am certain that [Lord Byron's] happiness, no less than yours, depends on the nearness of her who has been his good Angel, of her who has led him from darkness to light, and who deserves not only his gratitude, but that of everyone who loves him" (*L*, II, 340).

66. Mary also represents here a vitalizing force that "waken[s]" the "dead & cold" mind of her lover, who exists in a kind of limbo of potentiality when separated from his beatific moon, not yet the "cold chaste" planet of 1821's *Epipsychidion* (1. 281). Like his original sister-spirits at Field Place, Mary in 1814 embodied for Shelley the spirited, animated, and *animating* female who would appear eventually in his poems as the vibrant Cythna and Asia.

67. Earlier in October, for example, Shelley informs Hogg of his new liaison: "Above all, most sensibly do I perceive the truth of my entire worthlessness but as depending on another. And I am deeply persuaded that thus ennobled, {I shall} become a more true & constant friend, a more useful lover of mankind, a more ardent asserter of truth & virtue—above all more consistent, more intelligible, more true" (*L*, I, 265: to Hogg, 4 October 1814). Partly the poet's high-minded self-justification for abandoning his first wife, this passage nonetheless reveals a salient truth about his psychological make-up. Refusing to acknowledge or cultivate his own self-worth, Shelley instead exalts his various second selves—his sister(s), his cousin, Thomas Hogg, Elizabeth Hitchener, Harriet Shelley, Mary Godwin, and, later, Teresa Viviani and Jane Williams—in order to bask in some of their reflected glory and, with the exception of Hogg, their reflected femininity. As we shall see, he explores both the rewards and the pitfalls of this aspect of the first-self/second-self dynamic in works such as *Laon and Cythna*, *Prometheus Unbound*, and *Epipsychidion*.

68. See *L*, I, 161, 186, 196, 214, 215, 245, 270, and 292, for examples of Shelley's absurd elevation of Miss Hitchener. Carlos Baker mentions without delving into "Shelley's peculiar submissiveness to what he regarded as female superiority" (63). As critics such as Veeder, Mellor (*Mary Shelley*), and Hoeveler have emphasized, this erotic, and erratic, subjection to archetypal Woman or individual women did not prevent Shelley from asserting his own (masculine) will when it suited him. Shelley's attitude toward the mother as prototype of female power and love has inspired two very different interpretations. Schapiro (*The Romantic Mother*) sees Shelley's attitude toward the maternal as profoundly ambivalent, while Gelpi (*Shelley's Goddess*, "The Nursery Cave") argues, more convincingly, that Shelley "was (in an admittedly complicated way) a worshipper in the ancient cult of the Great Mother" ("The Nursery Cave" 45). The Shelleyan sister-spirit, on whom I am focusing, is in part a displaced and less threatening version of the/his mother, who generally remains a shadowy presence in the works that I will analyze. In an 1820 letter to Hunt, Shelley pokes fun at his own penchant for maternal figures:

We see no one but an Irish lady and her husband [Lady Mountcashell and George William Tighe], who are settled here [Pisa]. She is everything that is amiable and wise, and he is very agreeable. You will think it my fate either to find or imagine some lady of 45, very unprejudiced and philosophical, who has entered deeply into the best and selectest spirit of the age, with enchanting manners, and a disposition rather to like me, in every town that I inhabit. But certainly such this lady is. (*L*, II, 180)

Harriet Collins de Boinville, at whose Bracknell home Shelley often stayed in 1813 and 1814, and Maria Gisborne, whom Shelley met in 1818, are among the other "amiable," "wise," and attentive older women to whom he became attached.

69. Crook and Guiton, who come at this Hogg set-piece from a much different angle than mine, make this point on p. 57 of *Shelley's Venomed Melody*. Richard Holmes reminds us that during this period Shelley was busy convincing Hogg "that he ought to fall in love with his sister Elizabeth" (*Pursuit* 44). Hogg neglects to mention this scheme or his own eager compliance with it, but this exciting intrigue may have made Shelley's fervent tribute to the sisterly ideal especially memorable and thus his own account more credible.

70. Hogg claims that "we were now in the very heart of winter," but Crook and Guiton offer credible evidence that the episode actually occurred in early November and that Hogg exaggerated the severity of the cold and the bleakness of the garden they discovered for dramatic effect (I, 78). See *Shelley's Venomed Melody*, pp. 57–58.

71. While it is impossible to know whether Shelley himself applied the phrase *magic circle* to the garden, Hogg's inclusion of this Shelleyan image nicely captures the erotic, communal, and spiritual aura of this sororal paradise.

72. See *Esdaile*, pp. 260–70, for Cameron's excellent commentary on the poem's sources, both biographical and literary, and on its prefigurement of later Shelleyan texts.

73. See, for example, "Song: Despair," "Song: Sorrow," and "Song: To [Harriet]" ("Ah! sweet is the moonbeam"), all of which were written in the summer of 1810; see also "Melody to a Scene of Former Times," a fall 1810 composition (*PS*, I, 94–95, 100–1, 102–3, 127–28).

74. The first quote is from *Henry and Louisa* (*Esdaile* 135: I. 99) and the last two from Richard Crashaw's "The Flaming Heart" (l. 35) and "A Hymn to the Name and Honor of the Admirable Saint Teresa" (l. 108), taken from pp. 929 and 928 of Witherspoon and Warnke, *Seventeenth-Century Prose and Poetry*.

75. This relic dates from the same period that, as Carolyn Bynum has shown, the trope of the mother Jesus emerged in devotional literature. See *Jesus as Mother*, especially pp. 110–69. Marie Delcourt discusses the Lucca crucifix in "Female Saints in Masculine Clothing," the fascinating appendix to her groundbreaking study, *Hermaphrodite*. The Lucca Christ, according to the legends that it helped generate, was not simply feminine but actually female, a "bearded female saint," whose hermaphroditism reflects and enhances Jesus' own ambiguous gender (91). Shelley would soon discover representations of Christ with a more pleasingly feminine face when he views in Bologna, Rome, and Florence those "soft, curled, hermaphroditical Italian pictures"

by Correggio, Titian, and Raphael that Melville so despised (*Moby Dick* 361). But the Volto Santo certainly, and strikingly, verified Shelley's image of his "paradigm," and thus of himself, as a feminine male with nurturant, sensitive, and penetrable breasts.

76. Cf. the "veiled maid" in Alastor (l. 151) and the veiled "female Shape" of Cythna/Laone (*CW*, I, 320: *LC*, V. 387).

77. See *The Faerie Queene* IV. x, especially stanza 41. There also seems to be an allusion to the Sacred Heart of Jesus.

78. As early as the fall of 1814, Shelley realized that the constantly bickering Mary Godwin and Claire Clairmont would be unable to re-create for him the Field Place milieu wherein sister-spirits loved him *and* each other. What he never seemed to realize, however, is that he was unfairly imposing an impossible task on these young women, just as he had with Harriet Westbrook Shelley and Elizabeth Hitchener. The gracious Bracknell home of Mrs. Boinville and her daughter Cornelia Boinville Turner, where Shelley spent a great deal of time in 1813 and early 1814, probably provided the closest approximation of Shelley's ideal boyhood Eden. However, interred within his crumbling marriage to Harriet, the poet always felt himself the Boinvilles' guest, a guest who was fussed over and even loved but who inevitably had to return to his own "desolated hearth" ("Stanzas.—April, 1814," l. 10). (The early lyric that I have just cited, where the poet laments his "sad and silent home" and yearns to join a more sympathetic household, strikingly anticipates "The Serpent Is Shut Out from Paradise," in which Shelley contrasts his own "cold home" with that of his "happy friends" ["Stanzas," l. 9; "Serpent," ll. 25, 8].)

79. Cameron suggests some apt connections between Lionel and the *Alastor* Poet, though his brief commentary on *Rosalind and Helen* does not acknowledge any parallels between Helen and the veiled maid. See *Shelley: The Golden Years*, pp. 253–54. During the ecstatic ritual that the lovers enact in the temple, Lionel's sister-spirit merges with his first great female love when she takes up his mother's harp.

80. This child is as full of "feminine" sensibility as his sensitive father: when we first meet the boy, in the poem's opening section, he is sobbing over his mother's tearful reunion with her childhood friend, Rosalind.

81. See *The Culture of Sensibility*, pp. 104–53.

82. See, especially, his discussion of Byron's rejection of sentiment, softness, and other sorts of ummanliness (*Contours of Masculine Desire* 28–49). Sinfield discusses Charles Kingsley's "Thoughts on Shelley and Byron" (1853), which champions the virile Byron over, as Kingsley puts it, the "womanish" Shelley (87).

83. As Cameron points out in his commentary on *Henry and Louisa*, "Shelley had a special interest in the name Henry, even some sense of identification with it. Henry is the lover of Ianthe in *Queen Mab*. Shelley also used the name in 'Cold are the blasts,' for an unfaithful lover, and in the sixth song in *St. Irvyne*, for a lover who is drowned" (*Esdaile* 263n9). Another of Shelley's Henrys is a victimized sailor harassed by a press gang in *The Voyage*, perhaps the same sailor named Henry who is

mentioned in "Mary to the Sea-Wind." As we trace his journey through these works, we see that Henry is gradually redeemed, and increasingly more Shelleyan—a process that *Henry and Louisa* reflects in miniature. Henry makes his penultimate appearance at the close of *Queen Mab*, where he hovers over his Ianthe and awaits the "Light, life, and rapture from [her] smile," emblem of the "sweet and sacred love" that the mother-figure Mab has sanctioned (IX. 211, 208). His final incarnation is as the young son of Helen in the eclogue *Rosalind and Helen* (1817–1818). Mary Shelley recognizes Percy's investment in this name when she calls the idealized Shelley figure in *Frankenstein* Henry Clerval. Matthews and Everest propose a number of sources, personal and literary, for the name (*PS*, I, 13). To the latter category I would add Henry Brooke's sentimental novel *The Fool of Quality* (1766–1770), whose hero is a generous man of feeling, Henry Earl of Moreland. (I owe this suggestion to Mitzi Myers.) On a more personal level there is young Henry Tredcroft, a Horsham boy whom White believes may have been the angelic schoolmate of the "Essay on Friendship" (White, I, 28).

84. See Cameron, *Shelley: The Golden Years*, pp. 253–55, for a succinct account of the poem's background.

85. Isabella, married to a conservative, "illtempered" brewer then, would be Rosalind, though her (unconsummated) sibling incest, her religious skepticism, and her loss of her children's custody qualify her as yet another Shelleyan self-projection (*LMWS*, I, 41).

86. See *Rosalind and Helen*, lines 146–66 and 276–312 (*CW*, II, 11–12, 15–16).

87. See Cameron, *Shelley: The Golden Years*, pp. 253–54. Ulmer makes a similar observation on p. 45 of *Shelleyan Eros*.

88. Ulmer provides the best account of the Arab maiden's kinship with the veiled maid, who acts as "the visionary afterimage" of the human girl, "the belated duplication of a potentially erotic object" (30).

89. See Ulmer, p. 45.

90. Here the Kohutian sense of mirroring as confirming/approving would work in tandem with the more common definition, reflecting.

91. The mother-child dynamic was implicit already in Helen's and Lionel's relationship. When government authorities seize Lionel and drag him to prison, Helen tells Rosalind, "I stilled the tingling of my blood, / And followed him in their despite, / As a widow follows, pale and wild, / The murderers and corse of her only child" (*CW*, II, 32: *RH*, ll. 874–77).

92. For the interaction of narcissism and oedipal desire in the poetry of the male romantics, see Schapiro, *The Romantic Mother*, *passim*, and Hoeveler, *Romantic Androgyny*, pp. 1–23 and 25–76.

93. See *Rosalind and Helen*, lines 79–81 (*CW*, II, 9).

94. See Brown, *Sexuality and Feminism in Shelley*, esp. pp. 215–18; Mellor's review of Brown's book; Veeder, *Mary Shelley and "Frankenstein,"* pp. 42, 43–44, 55–56, 112–13; Gutschera, "Women in Romantic Epic," pp. 99–102, and "Reenactment in *The Revolt of Islam*," pp. 117–18, 124–25; Sperry, "The Sexual Theme in Shelley's *Revolt of Islam*" and *Shelley's Major Verse*, pp. 40–64; Ross, *The Contours of Masculine Desire*, pp. 128–37; Hoeveler, *Romantic Androgyny*, pp. 97–107; and Ulmer, *Shelleyan Eros*, pp. 50–77.

95. The first quote is from *Shelley's Major Verse*, p. 213n42, where Sperry assails Brown's "argument for 'mono- or unisexuality'" as the Shelleyan ideal, and the second is an excerpt from Brown's lengthy harangue against Sperry in his review of this book (p. 241). The Shelley phrase that Brown cites is from a November 1811 letter to Elizabeth Hitchener: "I almost wish that Southey had not made the glendoveer [from *The Curse of Kehama*] a male—these detestable distinctions will surely be abolished in a future state of being" (*L*, I, 195).

96. Gelpi argues in her illuminating essay "The Politics of Androgyny" that the term *androgyny* usually connotes "the masculine personality fulfilled and completed by the feminine" and only rarely describes "the feminine fulfilled and completed by the masculine" (151).

97. Mellor (review of *Sexuality and Feminism in Shelley*), Hoeveler (107), and Gelpi ("The Nursery Cave" 45–46 and 249–50n2) all strongly refute Brown's view of Shelley as a protofeminist. Annette Wheeler Cafarelli offers a particularly fair-minded assessment: "I think we should regard Shelley's views, like Godwin's, as well intentioned, but as nevertheless sharing the blindness to gender-based issues that bedeviled the sexual ideology of the men of that era" (96).

98. I derive this term from Paglia's accounts of "transsexual self-transformations" in Western literature (342). See, especially, her provocative chapter on Coleridge, pp. 317–46. While the term *androgyny* denotes a fusion of gender attributes and roles, *transsexualism*, as I am employing it, signifies a crossing over from one distinctly defined gender to the other. Because it implies a polar model of sexual differentiation, one that Shelley himself inherited and with which he grappled, transsexualism best describes the poet's strategic moves from the "negative" or masculine pole to the "positive" or feminine pole of gender identity.

99. In *Sexual Personae*, Camille Paglia illuminates how bowers function symbolically as "female zones" (187). Whereas lush bowers are anathema to the Spenserian knight, for the Shelleyan quester, they almost always prove salvific.

100. See, for example, Shelley's letter to Godwin of 8 March 1812, written from Dublin, which opens "Your letter affords me much food for thought;—guide thou and direct me" (*L*, I, 266). The young "disciple" of course continued right along with his own revolutionary mission.

101. See *Prose*, pp. 276–79, for this review, which appeared on 28 December 1817.

102. Sperry's biographically informed reading of *Laon and Cythna*, in its revised version as *The Revolt of Islam*, points out, "Throughout the poem . . . Shelley appears to be looking not so much forward to the millennial future as backward on his own past. Much of the poem's narrative power derives from recollections of the poet's childhood and adolescence, recollections often tinged by a strong element of fantasy" (*Shelley's Major Verse* 44).

103. Paglia probably would file the Hermit under her category of "Teiresias androgyne," the "nurturant male" (465). As Mary Shelley tells us, the Hermit's immediate model was the eccentric, kindly teacher Shelley met at Eton, Dr. James Lind, whom the poet rather self-consciously and melodramatically embraced as an idealized successor to the despised Timothy Shelley. See Mary Shelley's note on *The Revolt of Islam* (*CW*, I, 409); Hogg, I, pp. 35–36, 92–93; Holmes, *The Pursuit*, pp. 25–28. *Prince Athanase* contains another portrait of Dr. Lind, the "divine old man" Zonoras (*CW*, III, 142: "Fragments of a Continuation of *Prince Athanase*," 3. 51).

104. Sperry discusses the "monstrous dreams" (*CW*, I, 290: *LC*, III. 45) that Laon has just prior to the soldier's attack in terms of "the adolescent boy's experience of facing the full implications of sexual maturity and divergence from the opposite sex and his guilt at feelings such as lust" (*Shelley's Major Verse* 50). While I concur with Sperry's reading of this episode, I cannot agree that by poem's end Laon has accepted his sexual identity as a man, a point that Sperry argues on pp. 54, 62, and 64. He has, rather, cleverly discovered a way to preserve his twinship with his second self by adopting her gender as his own.

105. When the narrator first glimpses Cythna at the close of Canto I, he sees her as "One / Who sate beside [Laon] like his shadow," while Laon calls her "mine own shadow . . . / A second self, far dearer and more fair (*CW*, I, 274, 281: *LC*, I. 533–34; II. 208–9). That Cythna verbally "seconds" her brother-lover's estimation of their hierarchy yet in her actions, eloquence, and independent spirit radically subverts the masculine first-self/feminine second-self paradigm attests to the poet's extreme ambivalence toward his hero's quintessentially Shelleyan desire for a feminine mirror/disciple. See *Laon and Cythna*, Canto II, *passim* and IX. 173–81, for passages in which Cythna obediently plays Echo to Laon's Narcissus (*CW*, I, 274–88, 370).

106. As the young mariner in Canto VIII does when he calls himself "but the shade / Of her" whom he loves (*CW*, I, 363: *LC*, VIII. 224–25).

107. Laon's, and the multitude's, veneration of Cythna as a kind of presiding deity over the Festival of Equality connects this passage to the goddess worship that Gelpi unearths in *Prometheus Unbound*.

108. See *Shelleyan Eros*, pp. 59–60.

109. Although she credits Laon with inspiring her to take up the feminist cause, her fervent denunciation of patriarchal tyranny (II. 319–418) implicitly condemns the "brother of [her] soul" as well, a troubling fact that Laon's nightmare visions of his own "foul and ghastly" genitals certainly reflect (*CW*, I, 287, 290: *LC*, II. 417; III. 42).

110. See Matthew 26: 51–52, where a disciple, identified as Peter in John 18: 26, cuts off the ear of one of the high priests who seize Jesus at Gethsemane.

111. Sperry's comment on "the foul, hanging shapes that pluck at Cythna" is perceptive: "Overtones of certain images . . . particularly suggest a boy's growing but partly unconscious awareness that he has heen hung with genitals" (*Shelley's Major Verse* 50). Ulmer sees this dream as an "emission fantasy" (59).

112. This masculine identity seems pretty fragile even in Laon's most virile moment, his attack on Othman's men. Note how Shelley undermines at the same time he displays his hero's kinship with these exemplars of masculine aggression: Laon first sees them as he emerges from "the impotence / Of sleep"; his own weapon is a "small knife," while the soldiers hold "glittering swords"; and he remains "all unaware," as if still in sleep, when he impulsively slays the three men. Shelley makes sure in this poem, as in *Alastor, Rosalind and Helen, Prometheus Unbound*, and *Epipsychidion*, that the sex-crossing voyages his male protagonists make will not be too arduous.

113. This column also ironically recalls the mighty tower to which Laon had compared himself earlier. Boasting of his (supposed) powers as a charismatic revolutionary, Laon had declared, "I will arise and waken / The multitude . . . and who shall stand / Amid the rocking earthquake stedfast still, / But Laon? on high Freedom's desert land / A tower whose marble walls the leagued storms withstand!" (*CW*, I, 278: *LC*, II. 118–19, 123–26).

114. As E. B. Murray explains Cythna's role in this morbid vision, "The principle of revenge is an outgrowth of the principle of self, a perversion of the law of love, which, incarnate in Cythna, had admonished Laon against violence. The fact that the fourth corpse is Cythna suggests that the misconceiving principle of self in Laon had, in effect, murdered her by murdering them" ("'Elective Affinity' in *The Revolt of Islam*" 573).

115. That Shelley embraces this cannibalistic metaphor says a good deal, most of it disturbing, about his strategy for incorporating the feminine. However, I would argue that this passage reveals not a devaluation of women or of femininity but instead enacts, in a twisted way, his worship of the feminine and his desperate desire to embody it. It is significant that when Cythna has a similar fantasy while in her cave-prison—she imagines an eagle bearing Laon's "mangled limbs for food"—we do not see her partaking of this gruesome repast (*CW*, I, 348: *LC*, VII. 133). The Shelleyan recipe for spiritual and sexual health does not call for even a morsel of masculinity.

116. Again, as in Percy's gloomy 28 October 1814 letter longing for Mary's vivifying presence, the feminine second self incarnates a powerful life force that the emotionally and psychically moribund male needs to incorporate, make his own—not as sole possessor but as co-custodian with his sister-twin.

117. "The Hermit of Marlow" is the pseudonym with which Shelley signed the two political pamphlets he wrote during this period: *A Proposal for Putting Reform to the Vote* (February 1817) and *An Address . . . on the Death of the Princess Charlotte*

(November 1817). Composed just before (*A Proposal*) and shortly after (*Princess Charlotte*) Shelley wrote *Laon and Cythna*, these practical-minded essays provide a kind of sturdy, utilitarian frame around his visionary epic and accentuate the poet's identification with the charitable Hermit, who actually alleviates and not simply pities Laon's suffering. Mary Shelley's Note on the poem confirms that her husband's "minute and active sympathy with his fellow creatures gives a thousand-fold interest to his speculations," for while living at Albion House, the poet often visited his impoverished neighbors, offering, as Mary writes, "what alleviation he could" and contracting ophthalmia in the bargain (*CW*, I, 410).

118. See *The Contours of Masculine Desire*, esp. pp. 10–11.

119. Barbara Gelpi, in a brilliant, detailed explication of the Fourth Spirit's song in *Prometheus Unbound*, demonstrates how Shelley uses ivy as a sexually ambiguous symbol, apropos of its connection with the woman-identified Dionysus. See "The Nursery Cave," p. 59 and, for an expanded version of this essay's commentary on the ivy-bloom's significance, pp. 161–62 of *Shelley's Goddess*. The ivy that envelops the Hermit's doorway will reappear in the ruin-bower in which the sibling revolutionaries finally consummate their love (VI. 235–43).

120. In her otherwise insightful reading of *Laon and Cythna*, Diane Long Hoeveler mistakenly concludes that during her separation from her brother, Cythna "has mirrored and mimicked his actions, for just as he was imprisoned in a phallic tower, so was she held captive in a womblike cave" (104). If anything, Laon is the one doing the mirroring and mimicking, both of Cythna's gender and of her stature as a Christlike "prophetess of love" (*CW*, I, 370: *LC*, IX. 174).

121. William Veeder, who greatly illuminates how and why Shelley defuses the oedipal connection between Laon and the Hermit, ignores the old man's (and the poet's) tacit denunciation of the masculine will when he glosses the military-surgical metaphor the Hermit adopts in line 153: "Likening Laon's tongue to 'a lance' . . . the Hermit confirms the son's phallic manhood by crediting him with that transition from language to action which the father could never make" (130). It is true that the Hermit alludes here to Laon's "phallic manhood," but only in order to condemn, not endorse, the impulsive youth's move from (bloody) words to (violent) action, as his warning against needless bloodshed and his celebration of a "quiet" and "meek" feminine leader demonstrates.

122. Cythna and Asia, in their roles as catalysts or conductors "through which the harmony of love can pass" (*Witch*, l. 324), resemble Shelleyan Eros, which the poet in his "Note on the Banquet of Plato" glosses as "the cause of Love in others" (Notopoulos 461). Richard Isomaki makes excellent use of this latter quote, though he does not comment on the fact that Shelley, in the lyrical drama and elsewhere, genders this cohesive power as feminine by identifying it with Asia as well as with Cythna and, in *Epipsychidion*, with Teresa Viviani.

123. For the Shelleyan spin on the terms *prototype* and *antitype*, see the essay "On Love." Although Shelley did not compose this essay until the summer of 1818, its

erotic paradigm is in play even in his earliest writings. As Brown points out, Shelley employs the term *antitype* "in its root sense of 'a corresponding form,' responding 'as an impression to the die,' and thus 'the person or thing represented or foreshadowed by an earlier type or symbol'" (*Sexuality and Feminism* 36).

124. "Laone was the name her love had chosen, / For she was nameless, and her birth none knew" (*CW*, I, 313: *LC*, V. 163–64).

125. See, for example, Veeder, *Mary Shelley and "Frankenstein,"* pp. 55–56; Mellor, Introduction to *Romanticism and Feminism*, p. 8; and Richardson, "Romanticism and the Colonization of the Feminine," p. 20.

126. There is no "Cythno" in the poem, as Veeder implies there should be (56), because the epic enacts a systematic purgation of the masculine, even from its nomenclature.

127. As Marlon Ross asserts, "Those double quotation marks that surround Cythna's narration remind us of how her desire is still contained within [Laon's]" (*Contours of Masculine Desire* 137).

128. Ulmer observes that "[t]his genealogy privileges spirit over body, allowing Laon to assume the role of father while avoiding sexual intercourse" (64n39).

129. In *St. Irvyne*, the villainous Nemphere/Ginotti is the biological father of Eloise St. Irvyne's child. The antipathy to his own masculine generative capacities that Shelley reveals as early as 1809, when he composed *Zastrozzi* and began *St. Irvyne*, may have contributed to his later failures as a parent, failures that scholars such as Holmes and Mellor have rightly refused to gloss over. See Holmes's *The Pursuit*, pp. 444–47, and Mellor's *Mary Shelley*, pp. 32, 141–42.

130. A distorted mirror of the poem's many idealized bowers, the "secret bower" in which Othman attacks Cythna subtly suggests that Laon, too, despite his efforts to purge himself of masculinity, will always be an alien invader of feminine territory (*CW*, I, 345: *LC*, VII. 40).

131. At the end of Canto VI, Laon had gone in search of food and met with a fiendlike woman who called herself "Pestilence." Although she "glued her burning lips" to Laon's, he avoids infection by the "Plague's blue kisses" through shielding himself with Cythna's protective spirit (*CW*, I, 341: *LC*. VI. 429, 432). This strange episode underscores the role of the "second self" as a kind of prophylactic that defeats the "contagion of the world's slow stain": "but that she / Who loved me, did with absent looks defeat / Despair, I might have raved in sympathy" (*Adonais*, l. 356; *CW*, I, 342: *LC*, VI. 465–67).

132. Ulmer's comment is much more accurate than Shelley's own claim in a letter to a prospective publisher: "The authors of [*Laon and Cythna*] are supposed to be my hero & heroine whose names appear in the title" (*L*, I, 564).

133. See, too, *The Witch of Atlas*, where the Witch observes "two sister-twins in infancy" curled together in sleep (l. 531).

134. In an October 1814 entry into the joint journal he kept with Mary, Percy writes, "Jane states her conception of the subterraneous community of women," probably derived from or inspired by her recent reading of Ludvig's Holberg's *A Journey to the World Under-Ground (JMS*, I, 32). That Claire herself fails to note this topic of conversation in her journal entry for the same day suggests that what may have been a passing remark on her part held a particular fascination for Percy. See *The Journals of Claire Clairmont*, p. 48. Feldman and Scott-Kilvert note that Mary read Holberg's novel, "which describes an underground province of Cocklecu, where the women assume the dominant role in society," in January 1817, not long before Percy began work on his epic (*JMS*, I, 48n1). It is likely that she discussed the book with her husband, who may have perused it himself during this time.

135. Mary's first child, Clara, was born prematurely on 22 February 1815 (she died 6 March); her son William was born 24 January 1816; and her third child, Clara Everina, was born 2 September 1817, the month that Percy completed *Laon and Cythna*. Mellor is particularly good on Mary Shelley's deep desire for a stable nuclear family and greatly illuminates Mary's own anxieties about motherhood. See, for example, *Mary Shelley*, pp. 31–33, where Mellor analyzes Mary's reaction to her first baby's death and emphasizes Percy's failure not only to comfort his bereaved lover but also to reassure her "of his primary commitment to her, to their love, and to the family unit she represented" (32).

136. That another of his sister-spirits, Claire Clairmont, was preoccupied at this time not with Percy but with her baby daughter Alba (born 12 January 1817) may have contributed to the hints of masculine resentment, or at least envy, that subtly disrupt the poem's otherwise idealized depiction of mother-child communion. A not-so-subtle disruption, and one that may have been inspired by the poet's repressed anger, is the abrupt and tragic termination of the idyll in the underwater cave. Just as Cythna and her daughter have become "like sister-twins," Othman's minions abduct the baby, whom Cythna never sees until their reunion in the afterlife (*CW*, I, 350: *LC*, VII. 192). Before the child's birth, Cythna had dreamed that she and her baby "should soon be all to one another," making her beloved brother superfluous and provoking him—via his dark double—to steal the child that has replaced Laon in Cythna's affections (*CW*, I, 348: *LC*, VII. 147).

137. This phrase comes from a wonderful letter to Peacock in which Shelley, in Geneva at the time, conveys his intentions to "domesticate" himself, as he puts it elsewhere (*L*, I, 502). After asking his friend to procure a house for his ménage, Shelley vividly describes the "shrines" and "hymns" of the Roman household gods, the Penates: "good wood fires," "the hissing of kettles," "the laugh of children" (*L*, I, 490). This delightful passage ends on a note of self-irony and self-knowledge: "In talking of the Penates, will you not liken me to Julius Caesar dedicating a temple to Liberty?" (*L*, I, 490).

138. In the Dedication, too, an "inchanted dome" is both point of departure and final destination, this time for the poet himself (*CW*, I, 251: *LC*, Dedication, l. 4).

139. This radiant, "aërial" version of Coleridge's pleasure-dome reflects not only Shelley's desire to (re)engender—and re-gender—himself in a magnificent spiri-

tual womb, but also his ambivalence toward the hidden world of female reproduction, imaged in the epic as Cythna's murky underwater cavern (*CW*, I, 271: *LC*, I. 455). The "ivory dome" in which Lionel fulfills his sex-crossing dream and the domed temple dedicated to the woman-identified Prometheus are versions of the epic's highly aestheticized womb-dome (*CW*, II, 38: *RH*, l. 1094). (See *PU*, III. iii. 152–75 and III. iv. 111–18).

140. As Gutschera points out in "The Drama of Reenactment in Shelley's *The Revolt of Islam*," "Donald Reiman . . . establishes that Shelley left Canto I uncompleted until he had written the rest of the poem; the last half of Canto I was written at about the same time as Canto XII" (119n8). See *SC*, V, pp. 150–51, the source Gutschera cites for Reiman's chronology. Thus Laon's remarkably feminized appearance in Canto I and Cythna's role as his shadow result from a teleological process that has steadily worked its way through twelve cantos.

141. Cf. Mellor, Introduction to *Romanticism and Feminism*, p. 8.

142. Carolyn Heilbrun and Camille Paglia, among others, have adopted this useful and witty term. See *Sexual Personae*, pp. 321–28, for example, where Paglia offers a provocative reading of *The Rime of the Ancient Mariner* as "a rhapsody of the male heroine," an archetypal romantic figure "who luxuriates in passive suffering" (323). Paglia calls Christ "the ultimate male heroine, the passive public sufferer" (569).

143. When Prometheus tells Panthea at the close of Act I that "all hope [is] vain but love—thou lovest," he is recognizing her (here a surrogate for Asia herself) as an exemplar of the "long suffering love" that he himself is now beginning to embody (*PU*, I. 824; III. iii. 2). See Ross, *The Contours of Masculine Desire*, pp. 137–44, for a concise, lucid account of Prometheus' progress toward "the feminine principle" that "brings love—as sexual play, as social sympathy, as moral compassion—through the axis of power and into the province of shared desire" (144). I cannot agree, however, with Ross's conclusion that Asia "serves as an extension" of her mate (144), for Prometheus' separation from Asia's "transforming presence" is much more devastating for him than it is for her (*PU*, I. 832).

144. See "The Planet-Tempest Passage in *Epipsychidion*," Cameron's biographical account of the poem that matches its astral bodies to their human counterparts.

145. In fact, Shelley's description of Emily as "this soul out of my soul" subtly maternalizes the poet by suggesting that he has given birth to his sister-daughter (l. 238). His conception of the ideal prototype in the essay "On Love" also casts the speaker in a maternal role, carrying within his womb-mind "a miniature as it were of [his] entire self," a "soul within [his] soul" that yearns for its antitype, the pure, childlike being that dwells within the "intellectual nature" of the beloved (473, 474).

146. At times, Shelley slightly masculinizes Emily, his "eternal Sun," but only to accentuate his own emasculate condition (l. 280). His need to preserve Emily's

essential femininity prompted him, I believe, to cancel his sex-crossing portrait of her in the Preface as "an effeminate looking youth," as well as to excise the passage in the poem that likens her to a hermaphrodite, "that sweet marble monster of both sexes" (*CW*, II, 376, 378: "Fragments Connected with *Epipsychidion*," Preface II; l. 58).

147. Throughout his monumental study of the poet, Hogle links Shelleyan transference—of which the protean adoption of various roles is one aspect—with the feminine gender. See, for example, his discussion of *The Triumph of Life*'s "shape all light," which Hogle identifies as "transference embodied," the "becoming-other in . . . movement from thought to thought that has long been gendered feminine in mythographic renderings of it" (*Shelley's Process* 319–42; quotations from pp. 323, 324).

148. In this "multivoiced lyrical drama," Ross points out, the characters themselves represent the "playful deferral of identity" that I think the poet himself enacts: "Multiple spirits leap up from unitary minds and every figure has at least one double reflecting its desire back to itself . . . Not only does [Shelley] bifurcate the hero; he also triples the heroine . . . The poem is a sphere of see-through mirrors reflecting the inside to the outside and the outside in, reflecting every character in every other" (*Contours of Masculine Desire* 138).

149. Two of the most recent discussions of the Promethean cave are among the best: Hogle's reading of the cave as the site and source of primal transference (*Shelley's Process* 202–4) and Gelpi's analysis of this haven as the hive of Venus, where all "actions and interactions . . . are performed under the sign of the mother" (*Shelley's Goddess* 505–34; quotation from p. 511). But where Gelpi sees a mother-son paradise in the Promethean cave, I would argue that Shelley's deliberate feminization of the Titan—with his "soft and flowing limbs" and remarkable affinity with his "Fair sister nymphs"—casts Prometheus in the role of sister or daughter to the Mother Goddess whom Gelpi illuminates so brilliantly (*PU*, I. 73; III. iii. 9).

4. Sex, Sympathy, and Science

1. Though the fourteen-year-old Mary Godwin was not among this group at the time, she had had plenty of opportunity to cultivate her own interest in Percy Shelley, whose steady stream of letters began arriving at the Godwins' in January 1812, six months before her current visit to the Baxter family in Scotland began in early June. Godwin's letter of 14 March 1812 confirms that Mary shared her step-mother's, step-sister's, and half-sister's fascination with the young poet: "You cannot imagine how much all the females of my family, Mrs. G. and three daughters, are interested in your letters and your history" (*L*, I, 174n6).

2. An ideal largely inspired, as Barbara Charlesworth Gelpi has shown recently, by the late-eighteenth and early-nineteenth-century notion of an erotic Mother Goddess. As his marriage to Harriet was crumbling, Percy sought refuge at the home of Mrs. Boinville, whom the Shelleys had met through their vegetarian friend John Frank Newton. As Gelpi points out, Mrs. Boinville became for Percy a "mother surrogate . . .

with whom Shelley had a relationship at once filial and implicitly erotic while at the same time engaging in a 'brotherly' erotic dalliance with her daughter" (*Shelley's Goddess* 125). In his 16 March 1814 letter to Hogg, Shelley praises "the delightful tranquillity of this happy home" (*L*, I, 383), where two beautiful, intelligent, and attentive embodiments of "female excellence" (*L*, I, 401) "revived in [his] heart the expiring flame of life" (*L*, I, 383).

3. "When passion's trance is overpast" is the first line of an 1821 lyric that laments the death both of "tenderness" and of "wild feelings" in the Shelleys' marriage. See *NCE*, p. 442.

4. In her detailed analysis of this and other letters written by Hellen Shelley, Gelpi makes only passing reference to these episodes (*Shelley's Goddess* 99–100), but her recognition of "something dictatorial, overbearing, and frightening in the character of [Percy's] games and stories" is relevant here (99).

5. In a different context, Gelpi sees Percy's "special Latin lessons," his first taste of schooling outside the home, as "a sign of his male privilege over female speakers of the mother tongue" (*Shelley's Goddess* 93). Whether Shelley at six years old was capable of perceiving the power relations Gelpi rightly discerns is doubtful (and Gelpi herself does not claim for the boy such precosity); but the more mature Percy who (resentfully) put in his time at Syon House conceivably could theorize his new passion for science in terms of gender hierachies.

6. Several excellent studies investigate the relationship between gender and science, exploring how and why the scientific enterprise has traditionally been a masculine one. See, for example, Caroline Merchant, *The Death of Nature: Women, Ecology and the Scientific Revolution*; Evelyn Fox Keller, *Reflections on Gender and Science*; and Sandra Harding, *The Feminist Question in Science*. For a fine discussion of the gendered character of scientific discovery and practice in the romantic period, see Anne K. Mellor, *Mary Shelley*, chap. 5 ("A Feminist Critique of Science"). By the time he wrote *Alastor*, Shelley himself consciously recognized, if not endorsed, the paradigm of a male scientist (here an "inspired and desperate alchymist" [l. 71]) penetrating the mysteries of Mother Earth.

7. Carl Grabo's classic study, *A Newton Among Poets*, provides the best starting place for those interested in Shelley's scholarly and imaginative excursions into the world of "natural philosophy."

8. Shelley actually began attending Syon House in 1802, but Adam Walker, who inspired the Field House experiments as well as the poet's lifelong enthusiasm for natural philosophy, did not deliver his lectures there until Shelley's second (and final) year at the academy. (Medwin claims Walker visited Syon House "the second or third year of Shelley's domicile" there [28], but White notes Medwin's error in the number of years Shelley attended Syon House and reasonably places Walker at the school in 1803–1804. See *Shelley*, I, 22, and 565n14.) Thus the electrifications in the nursery probably occurred during Shelley's second Christmas break from the boarding school (winter 1803–1804) and/or during the summer of 1804. Shelley also had the opportu-

nity to hear Walker at Eton, as well as to read the published edition of his lectures, collected under the title *A System of Familiar Philosophy* (1802). See W. H. Merle's letter to the *Athenaeum* (4 March 1848), included in Appendix III of White's *Shelley* (II, 489–93), for remarks on "Old Walker's" Eton lectures and their dramatic impact on Shelley and his schoolmates (492). See also Andrew Amos's letter to that same publication (15 April 1848) in White, II, 494–96.

9. Walker's closing remarks on electricity, the focus of Lectures VII and VIII, achieve a kind of poetic, even religious, quality as they marvel at electricity's "relationship or affinity to the *living principle*" (*System*, II, 74). In "A Feminist Critique of Science," Mellor traces how this Walker passage traveled a circuit from Percy to Mary and finally made its way, at least in spirit, into the laboratory of Victor Frankenstein (*Mary Shelley* 103–4). In *Overtures to Biology*, Philip C. Ritterbush guides his reader through the rich body of scientific literature that extolled electricity as "the soul of the universe" (15).

10. This category would include not only animals (human and nonhuman), but also at least one species of plant: the *Mimosa pudica*, protagonist of Shelley's lyrical fable *The Sensitive-Plant* (1820).

11. I should note here that Walker, as he acknowledges in his Preface (I, x), did not originate the ideas I am summing up, though he did modify, test, and, most crucially, communicate in "plain and simple" language the complex theories and systems developed by his predessessors (Preface x). It was, for example, Luigi Galvani who in 1791 introduced the notion of animal electricity, or "nerveo-electrical fluid," which he saw as a product of the brain (Heilbron 491). See Mellor's helpful discussion of Galvani's *Commentary on the Effects of Electricity on Muscular Motion* in *Mary Shelley*, pp. 104–5.

12. These last two quotes come from a subsection of Lecture IV ("On Chemistry") entitled "Affinitive Attraction," a concept which the following passages best illuminate:

> I think the grand basis of chemistry is *attraction* and *repulsion*. By attraction, I mean not only that of cohesion and gravitation . . . , but the affinities of matter; the elective attraction, or local affections of it, that is, the tendency which the constituent parts of bodies have to unite readily with some substances, in preference, as it were, to all other parts of matter. Water and spirits are said to have an affinity, because they unite with the utmost readiness and affection. Water and oil have no affinity, because they will not unite . . . Acids and alkalis have so strong an affinity, that they rush into union with effervescence and ebullition . . . Affinities are not confined to the grosser bodies of the chemists; they exist through all nature. Electricity, light, fire, air, water, &c. have all a tendency to unite with some bodies in preference to others. (*System*, I, 153–54, 159)

This segment of the lecture must have struck a powerful chord in the young Shelley, who would later incorporate strikingly similar ideas into his own theories of interpersonal attraction. Shelley's version(s) of "affinitive attraction," however, would supplement the scientist's emphasis on the physical ("grosser" and subtler forms of matter) with the poet's—and the lover's—attentiveness to the intellectual, emotional, and spiritual realms. "Elective affinity," another term for the principle Walker describes, receives its most famous literary treatment in Goethe's 1809 novel, *Die Wahlverwandtschaften*. Like Shelley, who may or may not have read this work, Goethe uses the doctrine of elective affinity to explore the intersection of chemical law and human desire. See Jeremy Adler, "Goethe's Use of Chemical Theory in his *Elective Affinities*," a lucid essay that helpfully situates this science-saturated novel within eighteenth-century "affinity studies," led by figures such as E. F. Geoffroy, P. J. Macquer, and Torbern Bergman (265). However, E. B. Murray's "'Elective Affinity' in *The Revolt of Islam*" almost completely ignores the scientific matrix of this doctrine, arguing that both Goethe's novel and Shelley's epic "replace an *elective chemical* with an *elective spiritual affinity*" (571). Although "combine" or "supplement" would be more accurate than "replace," Murray's essay does demonstrate how elective affinity powerfully binds Shelley's hero and heroine, even during their traumatic physical separations.

13. Male's essay, "Shelley and the Doctrine of Sympathy," provides a wonderful introduction to the ethical and scientific connotations of the term *sympathy* in the late-eighteenth and early-nineteenth centuries. Crook and Guiton, who also discuss the sympathy-electricity nexus, add to Male's explication: "'Sympathy,' which of course is originally a medical term, was the point at which Romantic medicine touched on physics, chemistry, philanthropy and literature; 'sympathy' related man to nature and man to man" (70).

14. Walker may in fact have served as a compensatory father figure who replaced or challenged the less-than-dynamic Timothy Shelley. In this respect, the Syon House lecturer paved the way for Dr. James Lind, Shelley's beloved teacher-scientist-physician at Eton.

15. Gelpi has argued rightly that Shelley's lifelong passion for pedagogy implies his identification with the "mother educator" who was his own first tutor (*Shelley's Goddess* 98–99; quotation 93). However, despite possible forays into "beginners' botany and zoology" by the maternal preceptor and her young pupil (*Shelley's Goddess* 71), the realm of science, or, rather, of the "hard" sciences, remained in the late-eighteenth and early-nineteenth centuries a man's world.

16. See *System*, II, 46 for descriptions of scientific demonstrations involving voltaic piles, Leyden jars, and "a circuit of several people," demonstrations that look suspiciously like Percy's Field Place experiments. Whether or not Walker, in his Syon House lectures, actually presented the "many-person discharge train" he described remains a mystery. If he did not, his pupil is going him one better. (*Discharge train* is eighteenth-century scientist Jean Antoine Nollet's colorful term for the human circuits the young Shelley was inspired to create. See Heilbron, pp. 318–20.)

17. It is a power that in its capacity to "make transparent . . . opaque bodies" also exposes to the scientist's gaze the secrets of Mother/Sister Nature, as Panthea learns when, in *Prometheus Unbound* IV, she witnesses electricity's ability to "[m]ake bare the secrets of the Earth's deep heart" (l. 278).

18. See, for example, *System*, I, 67–68; II, 73–74.

19. "Magnetic and electric attraction probably are the same," Walker asserts at one point (*System*, I, 148). A subtle fluid like electricity, Walker's "magnetic effluvium" shares its cousin's flexible gender identity, at one moment "impregnat[ing]" iron (I, 57, 60) and at another providing a maternal "holding environment" for the earth.

20. It is just this kind of electro-sympathetic "contagion" that alarms William Godwin when he learns of his young disciple's political activism in Dublin during the spring of 1812:

> Do you not . . . exhort persons, who you say "are of scarcely greater elevation in the scale of intellectual being than the oyster . . ." to take the redress of griev-ances into their own hands[?]
>   But if it were exactly the contrary, if you exhorted them to meet, having their hands carefully tied behind them before they came together, what would that avail? Would not the first strong sympathetic impulse, which shot through the circle, like the electric fluid, cause them "to break their cords, as a thread of tow is broken when it toucheth the fire"? (*L*, I, 269n6)

Erasmus Darwin's couplet capturing the spark of the American Revolution offers a more celebratory take on the phenomenon that the cautious Godwin decries: "The patriot-flame with quick contagion ran, / Hill lighted hill, and man electrised man" (*The Botanic Garden* 35: *Economy of Vegetation*, II. 367–68).

21. See, for example, Mark 5:30, where Christ's virtue goes out of him to heal one of his followers, and *Prometheus Unbound* III.iii.10–63, where Prometheus describes the "virtue" of the cave he will share with Asia, Panthea, and Ione. Walker's remarks on "medical electricity," which no doubt inspired his pupil's attempt to cure Hellen's chilblains with electro-therapy, would also be relevant here (see *System*, II, 48–51, 73–74).

22. *Hawkins' Electrical Dictionary* defines induction as follows: "The influence exerted by the interference of fields upon fields or fields upon conductors, such that an electric or magnetic state may be induced in a body by the proximity, without contact, of an electrified or magnetized body" (214). This phenomenon, studied by early-eigh-teenth-century scientists such as Stephen Gray and Francis Hauksbee, was central to the experiments and discoveries of their more celebrated heirs: Benjamin Franklin and Alessandro Volta. See Meyer, pp. 27–28, and Heilbron, pp. 373–402. In his *History of Electricity* (47–50), Park Benjamin points out that Lucretius, to whom Shelley was intro-duced by Eton's Dr. James Lind, was among the first to recognize magnetic induction, which the Roman poet calls a "permeative power" (*De Rerum* [Latham], Book 6, 245). An even earlier allusion to induction appears in Plato's *Ion*, which Shelley translated in 1821. At a crucial point in his dialogue with Ion, Socrates likens the divinely inspired poet to an iron ring that receives through induction the magnetic virtue of a lodestone:

> [I]t is a divine influence which moves you, like that which resides in the stone called Magnet by Euripedes and Heraclea by the people. For not only does this

stone possess the power of attracting iron rings but it can communicate to them the power of attracting other rings; so that you may see sometimes a long chain of rings and other iron substances attached and suspended one to the other by this influence. And as the power of the stone circulates through all the links of this series and attaches each to each, so the Muse communicating through those whom she has first inspired to all others capable of sharing in the inspiration the influence of that first enthusiasm, creates a chain and a succession. For the authors of those great poems which we admire do not attain to excellence through the rules of any art but they utter their beautiful melodies . . . in a state of inspiration and, as it were, *possessed* by a spirit not their own . . . Know then that the spectator represents the last of the rings which derive a mutual and successive power from that Heracleotic stone of which I spoke. (Notopolous 472, 474)

Park Benjamin discusses the scientific implications of this passage on pp. 23–25. Socrates' vision of a chain of influence, with the highly susceptible poet as key link, hints at the joys and the dangers that are in store for each recipient/agent "in this universal and reciprocal attraction" (Notopolous 475; cf. Preface to *LC* [*CW*, I, 244] and, esp., *Defence* 493). From *The Voyage* (1812) through the *Defence* (1821), Shelley's own commentaries on the role of the poet recognize, with mingled dread and delight, the responsibility, privilege, *and* psychic vulnerability that the artist-as-medium is subject to.

23. Crook and Guiton (50–51) discuss the nexus of sexual and erotic electricity in relation to the Hogg and Walker passages at hand. (Though in this instance and elsewhere, our emphases differ, Crook and Guiton's examination of the poet's sexual-medical history has aided greatly my own investigation of Shelley's erotic experiences and imaginings.)

24. Desmond King-Hele notes echoes of *The Economy of Vegetation* and of *The Loves of the Plants* in *Henry and Louisa*, which Shelley wrote in the fall of 1809 (192–94).

25. As mentioned in chapters 2 and 3, Chodorow and Gilligan have developed influential feminist readings of this concept. Jessica Benjamin, in her excellent study *The Bonds of Love*, illuminates the dangers inherent in embracing and embodying radical, "feminine" empathy. See especially pp. 194–95, where she points out that even the most famous theorist of the "self-in-relation" model of identity, Carol Gilligan, offers a "critique of feminine self-sacrifice," an ethos grounded in traditionally feminine qualities such as sympathy, compassion, and passive receptivity (194).

26. I concur with Medwin (16) and Ingpen and Peck (*CW*, I, 424) that Shelley's conversion experience, alluded to in "Hymn to Intellectual Beauty" as well (ll. 55–60), occured at Syon House, rather than at Eton, where, as Ingpen and Peck point out, there was no "glittering grass," nor any grass at all (*CW*, I, 251: *LC*, Dedication, 23).

27. Heilbron (327–28, 340–420) and Park Benjamin (541–42) discuss "the power of points," Franklin's term for "the wonderful effect of pointed bodies both in

drawing off and throwing off the electrical fire" (Franklin, quoted in Benjamin, 541). Shelley may have first learned of electric points from Darwin's *Economy of Vegetation* (I. vii. 339 and Note XIII [p. 84]).

28. Reiman notes "the impassioned, poetic prose" of the essay, which, he adds, "embodies the rhetorical tone of the speeches in *The Symposium*" (*SC*, VI, 642).

29. Pity is what the speaker offers his own spirit, which he sees here as a separate, feminized entity. This dramatic self-division thus allows the speaker to demonstrate or model for his reader part of the process of sympathetic interaction which the essay as a whole celebrates.

30. In "On Love," the references to the understanding, or reason, the imagination, and the "frame" (474) recall a correlative passage in the Preface to *Alastor*: "The intellectual faculties, the imagination, the functions of sense, have their respective requisitions on the sympathy of corresponding powers in other human beings" (69). The "requisitions" of this passage become in "On Love" the even more peremptory "demands" made by "the type within," the "soul within our soul" that comprises our ideal self-image (474).

31. To be more precise, the "antitype" is not the person herself but rather the "soul within [her] soul," the inmost point of that "internal constitution" which Shelley is so eager to discern. Like the lover, the essay's questing speaker, the beloved would look within herself to "dimly see" this so-called antitype as her own "ideal prototype," the inner portrait to which she "eagerly refer[s] all sensations" as she in turn searches for the corresponding antitype (473, 474).

32. As usual, Shelley anticipates any charges of narcissism that his readers might level. Commentators who have detected "egocentrism" (Ulmer's word) in "On Love" include Reiman (*SC*, VI, 644–45), Mellor (review of Brown, 179), Hogle ("Shelley's Poetics" 188), and Ulmer (4–8; quotation 5n8).

33. As Reiman (*SC*, IV, 639, 641–42) and Ulmer (4–8), following Mary Shelley's and James Notopolous' leads, also observe.

34. Steven Jones's illuminating textual study of the 1818 fragment "Love, the Universe," a lyric that is intimately connected with Shelley's translation of *The Banquet*, emphasizes Shelley's concern that "Passion's privacy might always, inevitably oppose the social power of universal love" (9).

35. For Plato and his dialogists this "person of virtue" inevitably would be male—as would the divinely inspired lover. As Pausanias puts it, "Those who are inspired by this divinity [Uranian Love] seek the affections of that sex which is endowed by nature with greater excellence and vigour both of body and mind" (Notopoulos 422). Shelley, who rejects the "exclusively homosexual" component of Uranian Love (Crook and Guiton 167), devotes a good portion of his *Discourse on Love* to the issue of homosexual love in ancient Greece, examining its causes and speculating on its expression.

36. Shelley's initial meditations on what Plato calls "Uranian and Pandemian Love" may have preceded his actual reading of the *Symposium*, which thus would have enriched rather than directly inspired the passionate theorizing we see throughout his earliest extant letters. It is possible that Shelley first read Plato's *Symposium* with Dr. Lind at Eton; at least this is the impression one gets from a passage in *Prince Athanase* that finds the hero and his beloved teacher Zonoros reading "the story of the Feast" (*CW*, III, 142: *Athanase*, Fragment 3, l. 64). Notopoulos discusses, with his usual thoroughness and reasonableness, each of Shelley's possible encounters with this Platonic text before the summer of 1818 (381–82).

37. Both the last-quoted phrase and the reference to "selfdevoted self-interested" love, cited a bit earlier, come from the frantic series of letters Shelley fired off in response to Thomas Hogg's attempted seduction of Harriet Westbrook Shelley in the fall of 1811 (see *L*, I, 166–203 *passim* [letters to Hogg and Elizabeth Hitchener only]). In witnessing Hogg's "soul appalling fall," Shelley saw a noble being, Plato's "person of virtue" who inspires Uranian Love, succumb to "the grovelling passions of the Earth," the progeny of Pandemian Love (*L*, I, 185, 208). A striking passage in a letter to Elizabeth Hitchener reveals that Hogg did in fact enkindle in Shelley the kind of Uranian devotion, complete with its homoerotic element, that Pausanias describes:

> You know . . . the exalted thoughts I entertained of his excellence . . . never could you conceive never having experienced it that resistless & pathetic eloquence of his, never the illumination of that countenance on which I have sometimes gazed till I fancied the world could be reformed by gazing too . . . Virtue has lost one of its defenders. (*L*, I, 168–69)

38. Crook and Guiton emphasize this point in their helpful remarks on Pandemian and Uranian Love (167–69), which they discuss in relation to *Prince Athanase*, an unfinished poem that Shelley conceived in late 1817 and sporadically composed until mid-1819. According to Mary Shelley's note on this fragment, Percy first called it *Pandemos and Urania* and planned to depict the hero's devastating encounter with the former, "the earthly and unworthy Venus," as well as his deathbed communion with his genuine soul mate, presumably the Uranian goddess (*CW*, III, 146).

39. Loeb, p. 111, and Bollingen, 181c (trans. Michael Joyce).

40. The "reproach of libertinism" is another of Shelley's interpolations, this one inserted into Aristophanes' discourse (Notopoulos 431).

41. Brown devotes an entire chapter of *Sexuality and Femininism in Shelley* to the poet's many denunciations of libertinism (78–90), and though he offers some astute analysis, he fails to discern the gnawing self-suspicion that helped fuel these vehement attacks. Brown makes his position clear when he states, "In both thought and practice [Shelley] was the exact opposite of the voluptuary or the libertine" (77).

42. In his fragmentary "Essay on Friendship" Shelley disdainfully dismisses "the smallest alloy of sensual intermixture" from "the sacred sentiments of friendship" he is celebrating (Clark 338). Most scholars assign a late date [ca. 1822] to this frag-

ment, but Barbara Gelpi, among others, reasonably dissents, pointing out that "the subject matter"—and, as Brown points out, the language itself—"suggests that Shelley wrote it around the time that he translated the *Symposium* and also wrote 'A Discourse on the Manners of the Ancient Greeks Relative to the Subject of Love'" (*Shelley's Goddess* 102). See also Notopoulos, "Dating of Shelley's Prose," p. 492, and Brown, *Sexuality and Feminism*, pp. 143–46, 267n82, 268n89.

43. Venereal disease appears twice in the *Discourse*, where Shelley characteristically connects it with prostitution, obscenity, and libertinage (Notopoulos 412).

44. In his helpful reconstruction of Hogg's lost letter, Cameron writes: "By 'perfectibility,' Hogg, using the word in the accepted Godwinian sense, did not mean being 'perfect,' but advancing towards perfection—through a series of love affairs" (*SC*, II, 681).

45. Other highlights of this debate include the letters (to Hogg and Miss Hitchener) chronicling Shelley's agonized reaction to Hogg's "depraved" love for Harriet Shelley (*L*, I, 168; see *L*, I, 166–203, and *SC*, III, 56). This crisis helped cement for Shelley the link between selfishness and "sensation" (*SC*, III, 48: 13 November 1811). Shelley's November 1814 review of Hogg's novel *Memoirs of Alexy Haimatoff* reveals that the poet was still defining himself in opposition to his more worldly friend. "The author appears to deem the loveless intercourse of brutal appetite a venial offense against delicacy and virtue!" Shelley exclaims, but commends Hogg for "afford[ing] a most impressive and tremendous allegory of the cold-blooded and malignant selfishness of sensuality" (*Prose* 142).

46. Nathaniel Brown, in his study *Sexuality and Feminism in Shelley*, has done much to dispel the myth of the sexless, angelic poet, though the figure who, in Brown's words, "joyously celebrated the pleasures of the senses" is in its own way a mythological construct (2). Nora Crook, Derek Guiton and William Ulmer are among those recent critics who recognize, and even emphasize, the darker currents of Shelleyan eros. (Brown himself acknowledges certain ambivalences toward sex in Shelley's writings—involving, for example, the clash between sexual and disinterested love [134–37, 145]—though he remains intent on presenting the poet as an enthusiastic celebrant of sexual love.)

47. As Crook and Guiton remind us, Shelley recalls his first ecstatic communion with Intellectual Beauty as an intensely erotic as well as a religious or "mystical" experience (134). Shelley's "Hymn" holds out a promise that few of his later works realize: that the more voluptuous aspects of "love's delight" need not interfere with one's vow to "fear himself" (ll. 66, 84).

48. Though the cousins met in February 1804, their romance probably did not begin until the summer of 1808, after which Harriet corresponded regularly not just with Percy, but with her "Aunt Shelley" and young Elizabeth Shelley as well. See Cameron (*Esdaile*, Commentaries, pp. 306–9) and Desmond Hawkins (3–5).

49. In "To St. Irvyne" (*Esdaile* 171–72) and "Melody to a Scene of Former Times" (*PS*, I, 127–28) both Harriet and the cousins' time together appear as vivid but fleeting dreams.

50. Over-stimulation rather than disillusionment best describes Percy's response to his beautiful cousin when he encountered her in person. Harriet, who according to Tom Medwin was "like one of Shakespeare's women—like some Madonna of Raphael," largely escaped the poet's (vicious) cycle of idealization and repudiation, though her break with him certainly helped solidify this essentially defensive pattern (47). (Medwin is echoing Shelley's own description of Maddalo's daughter, grown into a gracious woman by poem's end [*JM*, l. 592]).

51. See Brown, *Sexuality and Feminism*, pp. 123–33, for a perceptive, wide-ranging discussion of the Shelleyan erotic dream.

52. It seems that Matilda first has her way with the habitually unconscious Verezzi in the missing chapter 7 (see Crook and Guiton 34–35), but he does not become a willing sexual partner until unlucky chapter 13.

53. The biographical parallels are obvious, the Gothic lovers' ordeal serving as a sensationalized version of the long separations that Percy and Harriet endured. Yet the psychological pattern at work here is evident in Shelley's relationship with his second great love as well. In the previous chapter, I brought up the bleak period in the fall of 1814, when financial woes compelled Percy and Mary to remain apart. In the letter cited, Percy tells his absent love, "It seems as if you alone could shield me fr{om} impurity & vice," while in another note he writes, "I did not forget to kiss your εἰδῶλον κὲνου [unsubstantial image] before I slept. And I slept last night thanks to your sweet goodnight" (*L*, I, 414, 420). In this last passage the simulacral Mary acts as a kind of talisman to protect Percy both from the external world's and his own "impurity & vice." As he declares in the earlier letter, "If I were absent from you long I should shudder with horror at myself" (*L*, I, 414).

54. Matilda employs similar language in an earlier outburst against her rival—"Thy cursed image, revelling in [Verezzi's] heart, has blasted my happiness forever" (56)—as well as in the tirade just preceeding Julia's murder (89).

55. Like the Poet of *Alastor*, the protagonist of Shelley's Gothic novel embarks on a somewhat protracted journey toward this ultimate self-transcendence; the "strange symphony" that helps propel Verezzi toward his death has many movements, the most crucial involving his Pandemian affair with Matilda (*Alastor*, l. 167).

56. One of the poet's more unsavory references to the body occurs in an early letter to Elizabeth Hitchener, the "Sister of [his] soul": "I will dare say I *love*, . . . nor do I risk the supposition that the lump of organised matter which enshrines *thy* soul excites the love which that soul alone *dare* claim" (*L*, I, 149). As Frederick Jones dryly observes, "Miss Hitchener probably did not relish this compliment" (*L*, I, 149n2). Shelley's attitude toward the flesh, first confronted head-on by Edward E. Bostetter in his seminal "Shelley and the Mutinous Flesh" (1959), has received attention more recently in diverse works such as Wasserman's philosophically oriented study (see esp. 417–61), Ulmer's linguistic and historical analysis, and Gelpi's feminist reading of *Prometheus Unbound*. I am most concerned with how Shelley's ideal of selflessness influenced his view of the body, especially the sexual body, an issue that Brown

addresses in *Sexuality and Feminism* (134–37). Both Shelley's earliest diatribe against the principle of Self and his more famous reference to this concept emphasize the Self's mortal, corporeal roots. See *L*, I, 34, where "that *hateful* principle" of Self and the "sensualities of Epicurism" go hand in hand, and the *Defence*, in which the principle of Self ("the Mammon of the world") and the mortal "curse imposed upon Adam" buttress one another (503).

57. In terms of the author's own rather morbid sexual imagination, the fair/foul dichotomy would be a false one. For Shelley, the spectre of decaying flesh lurked just beneath—or even hovered over—the surface of physical beauty, particularly female beauty. A case in point is the poem "To Harriet" ("Oh Harriet, love like mine that glows"), probably written in the summer of 1811 and addressed to his bride-to-be, Harriet Westbrook. It seems a bit premature to be discussing "the charms of [a] form / Which decay with the swift rolling years," when that form belongs to a blooming sixteen-year-old-girl (*PS*, I, 185). (A few years later, as Shelley narrates his version of the demise of his first marriage, this image of Harriet's bodily corruption returns in a more ghastly, and more famous, form: "I felt as if a dead & living body had been linked together in loathsome and horrible communion" [*L*, I, 402].) A number of factors no doubt contributed to Shelley's preoccupation with decaying (female) flesh (see also *L*, I, 95; *Zeinab and Kathema* [ll. 130–56]; "Sonnet: To Harriet on her birth day"; *LC*, III. 226–34 and VI. 424–41; *The Sensitive-Plant*, III. 11–12, 17–21; "On the Medusa of Leonardo"; *The Triumph of Life*, ll. 87–92); but the poem at hand, "Oh Harriet," hints at one crucial reason. In this lyric, Shelley is trying to reassure both his beloved and himself that he is no selfish libertine, lusting only after Harriet's beauteous form: "I'll tell not of Rapture and Joy / Which swells through the Libertine's frame; / That breast must feel bliss with alloy / That is scorched by so selfish a flame" (*PS*, I, 185). But in order to evade the trap of libertine—or Pandemian—love, the poet must deface the very beauty that tempts him and (re)direct his libido towards Harriet's "enchantingly fair" *mind* (*PS*, I, 185). As so often in Shelley's love poetry, though, a more radical route to self-transcendence—and mingled being—beckons: "It were pleasure to die for my love, / It were rapture to sink in the grave" (*PS*, I, 185). Ostensibly a poem urging both himself and Harriet away from "death's darkened portals," this odd love lyric ends up celebrating a romantic paradise just beyond those doors: "Heaven expands to my sight, / For Elysium with Harriet must be. / Adieu, my love, good night" (*PS*, I, 185).

58. Just as she had earlier exploited Verezzi's desire for "sympathy and congeniality of sentiment," Matilda, just before Verezzi finally catches "the infection" of her Pandemian malady, turns to another crucial facet of Shelleyan sentimental love: sacrifice of self (*CW*, V, 86). Acting on the advice of Zastrozzi, who plays a central part in Matilda's charade, the desperate seductress thrusts her arm before a dagger headed for Verezzi's heart (69–70). Faced with this striking evidence of Matilda's "noble contempt of danger," and of Self, the credulous Verezzi finds his "breast [filled] with a tenderness towards her," and by the next chapter he has replaced his "idolised Julia" with the now "angelic" Matilda (70, 52, 75). This last epithet displays the young author's own remarkable shrewdness as a fledgling anatomist of sentimental love;

even as his protagonist falls into the abyss of libertinism, he still hangs onto to "his high sentiments" (73). From chapter 13 until his horrific death, Verezzi is truly Self-deceived.

59. Elsewhere, Julia is "an uncertain vision, which floated before [Verezzi's] fancy more as an ideal being of another world, whom he might hereafter adore there, than an enchanting and congenial female, to whom his oaths of eternal fidelity had been given" (*CW*, V, 86). Moreover, Matilda herself has appropriated Julia's theory of celestial marriage, which in the villainess' heated imagination becomes just another version of Pandemian love, though in a finer tone: "Shall I then call him mine for ever? . . . will the passion which now consumes me, possess my soul to all eternity? Ah, well I know it will; and when emancipated from this terrestrial form, my soul departs; still its fervent energies unrepressed, will remain; and in the union of soul to soul, it will taste celestial transports" (49). If Matilda, caught up in her "delirium of guilty love," taints Julia's—and Shelley's—ideal of spiritual interfusion, the more terrible delirium of another daughter of Shelley's dark imaginings spawns a truly horrific version of postmortal mingling (49). When Beatrice Cenci is informed of her death sentence, she envisions her "father's spirit" *and* form "wind[ing] [her] in his hellish arms" and dragging her "down, down, down, down!" (V. iv. 60, 66, 67). In Beatrice's frantic outburst, Selfhood—her own and her father's—is grossly physical and impossible to escape; and the mingled being which so many of Shelley's characters anticipate or enjoy in superterrestrial settings is for her an endless replay of her own rape, this time "in the void world" (V. iv. 58). Matilda's prurient fantasy and Beatrice's nightmare vision reveal, then, that one of Shelley's earliest strategies for expunging Selfhood from the realm of Eros posed its own problems, problems that the poet himself chose to confront rather than to evade.

60. Cameron is one of the few critics who treats the *Margaret Nicholson* volume with real seriousness, examining it within the context of Shelley's "republican phase" at Oxford. As Cameron points out, during this period the poet discovered writers such as Condorcet, Volney, Paine, Franklin, and perhaps Wollstonecraft, all of whom helped Shelley establish and refine his own antimonarchical, antiwar stance (*Young Shelley* 53).

61. We must wonder, too, whether the poem's (and volume's) supposed author, mad Peg Nicholson, would-be assassin of George III, found her own postmortal paradise—and her own Francis. As she says in the "Epithalamium," "Congenial minds will seek their kindred soul, / E'en though the tide of time has rolled between; / They mock weak matter's impotent control" (*PS*, I, 120: ll. 42–44).

62. *Zeinab and Kathema* (late 1810 or 1811) explicitly sets up the paradigmatic Shelleyan dichotomy of flesh and spirit when its hero contemplates his dead lover's decaying flesh and his own plunge into "the life to come": "My love! I will be like to thee, / A mouldering carcase or a spirit blest, / With thee corruption's prey, or Heaven's happy guest" (ll. 158, 154–56). Here the mingled being that the lovers will experience *may* be joyously spiritual, but Shelley compels his protagonist to confront the more gruesome and equally possible alternative.

63. Parallels between the "Epithalamium" and the volume's final, explicitly autobiographical poem, "Melody to a Scene of Former Times," invite such a reading. The painful contrast between "visioned slumber" or "heavenly sleep" and the sad reality of waking life is the most obvious thematic link that unites the two texts (*PS*, I, 128: "Melody," l. 39; *PS*, I, 119: "Epithalamium," l. 18).

64. We recall that Shelley was in the habit of hooking himself up to his "electrical apparatus" around the time he composed the *Margaret Nicholson* volume (Hogg, I, 56). Shelley's own sensation of "being filled with the [electric] fluid" may thus have influenced Francis's climactic cry, particularly his outburst "I glow, I glow!" (Hogg, I, 56). Shelley also might have drawn on Darwin's description of the electric kiss and the "circling band" of electrified youths and damsels (*The Botanic Garden: Economy of Vegetation* I. vii. 335–66). Finally, Socrates' allegory of the tripartite soul in Plato's *Phaedrus* could have influenced Shelley's suggestion of spiritual orgasm: "Endless kisses drown my soul." In a passage that Shelley will invoke in the *Discourse* (Notopoulos 411), Socrates presents the soul as comprised of two steeds, one honorable and one wanton, and a charioteer. The temperate horse experiences a "flood of passion" in the beloved's presence and "drenches the whole soul with sweat" (Bollingen 251C, 254C). (In an earlier passage from the *Phaedrus*, the soul of the Uranian lover "lets the flood pour in upon her, releasing the imprisoned waters . . . and at that moment tastes a pleasure that is sweet beyond compare" [Bollingen 251E].) Brown looks closely at these passages in his illuminating discussion of the Shelleyan "erotic reverie" and "spontaneous or involuntary orgasm" (*Sexuality and Feminism* 123–26; quotations p. 125).

65. Gelpi comments on the "possibly high-minded but certainly erotic—and aesthetic—intermingling of body and soul" that characterizes Francis's opening salvo (*Shelley's Goddess* 108). While Cameron believes these lines refer to fellatio (*Shelley: The Golden Years* 223, 610n6), Brown more reasonably argues that Francis and Charlotte are engaged in passionate kissing (*Sexuality and Feminism* 248). Crook and Guiton, though, offer the most precise gloss on these heated lines, one with which Gelpi's reading harmonizes: "We have discovered that they are, in fact, a free borrowing from an eighteenth-century translation of 'Lydia, bella puella candida', an erotic lyric then attributed to the Renaissance poet Cornelius Gallus. It belongs to a genre where the theme of 'kisses' provides an opportunity to describe the sensations preceding sexual climax" (42–43).

66. As the editors of *The Poems of Shelley* point out (*PS*, I, 120, 121), Shelley's lines 37–38, involving "flowers of bliss that never fade away" (l. 38), allude to Pope's lines 317–18, while lines 83–84 of the "Epithalamium" ("Oh! you suck my soul away; / Suck on, suck on, I glow, I glow!") echo Eloisa's petition to Abelard: "Suck my last breath, and catch my flying soul!" (l. 324). Moreover, Shelley's "chain of clay" (l. 49) parallels Pope's "lasting chain" (l. 173), and Charlotte's desire to "clasp [Francis's] form" resembles Eloise's longing to "glue [her] clasping arms" around Abelard's "phantom" (l. 234). This last line is part of Eloise's recollection of her erotic dreams (ll. 223–48), a passage that surely influenced Shelley's depiction of the *Alastor* Poet's climactic vision. The Poet's link with Eloise further feminizes this Shelleyan male heroine.

67. This last quote is from the second of two letters Shelley wrote the following spring (April and May 1811) which invoke Eloisa as one "who sacrificed all *self* for another" (*L*, I, 81). See also *L*, I, 70.

68. The Shelleyan version of feminine desire would certainly not please many modern feminists, for the poet bought into, and celebrated, the myth that femininity and the ability to rise above the body's urges go hand in hand. (Although, as emphasized in the previous chapter, Shelley did not see "femininity" and "femaleness" as synonymous, he did view women as the exemplary "vessels" of the feminine principle which men must work hard to cultivate.) The feminist with whom Shelley has most in common when it comes to sexual matters is perhaps Mary Wollstonecraft, who saw sensuality as ruinous to both sexes, though like Shelley, she maintained that "Men are certainly more under the influence of their appetites than women" (*Vindication* 137). Mary Poovey examines Wollstonecraft's complex attitude toward female sexuality in *The Proper Lady and the Woman Writer*, pp. 69–81 (rpt. in the Norton edition of the *Vindication*, 343–55).

69. The purported authorship of the "Epithalamium," as well as its echoes of Eloisa's impassioned epistle, helps establish its feminine voice and perspective. Shelley ascribes the poem and the volume itself to Margaret Nicholson, a "poor maniac laundress" who had attempted to stab George III in 1786 (Hogg, I, 161). (Her republican credentials, like those of Charlotte and Francis, are thus impeccable.) More intriguing, though, is Shelley's teasing comment to his friend Graham, "The part of the Epithalamium which you mention, (i.e. from the end of Satan's triumph[)] is the production of a friends *mistress*" (*L*, I, 23). The editors of *The Poems of Shelley* reasonably suggest that Hogg was the friend and Elizabeth Shelley the mistress, "but it is most unlikely that this attribution was anything but an invention to titillate the interest of either Hogg or Graham or both" (*PS*, I, 118). I would add that Shelley himself would have been stimulated—and perhaps "titilated"—by the notion that his beloved sister would have dreamt up such an intoxicating climax for his poem. Moreover, like his claim that Elizabeth had penned an earlier lyric ("Cold, cold is the blast"), this bit of play-acting allowed Percy to imaginatively merge with his original sister-spirit and "kindred soul" (*PS*, I, 120: "Epithalamium," l. 42). See Hogg, I, pp. 125–26, for the texts that Percy convinced his friend were Elizabeth's.

70. 1812 alone saw the Shelleys' Irish campaign, their involvement in the Tremadoc embankment project (see White, I, 254–58), and, with disastrous results, their efforts to establish in their own home an association of philanthropists, with Elizabeth Hitchener as a charter member.

71. Lyrics such as "A Winter's Day," "A Sabbath Walk," "Written on a Beautiful Day in Spring," and "Mary to the Sea-Wind" reveal that the poet was (re)discovering his sympathetic connection not just with his fellow humans, but with the natural world as well (*PS*, I, 191–92, 199–200, 217, 228–29).

72. *PS*, I, 228: "To Harriet" ("Never, O never"). See also *PS*, I, 184–85, 245, 262–65, 429–30. "To Harriet" ("It is not blasphemy"), composed in 1812, when the poet was at work on *Queen Mab*, offers the most elaborate portrait of Harriet as

Percy's physician/saviour. She is also his "second self" whose eyes beam "with mildest radiance on [his] heart / To purify its purity" (*PS*, I, 264). In the lyric's most striking passage, Harriet augments the magic of her "spirit-beaming eyes" with a more tangible medicine: "will not thy glowing cheek, / Glowing with soft suffusion, rest on mine / And breathe magnetic sweetness through the frame / Of my corporeal nature, through the soul / Now knit with these fine fibres?" (*PS*, I, 262). As Crook and Guiton observe, Percy "is appealing to [Harriet] to transmit her health to him through the electric current that flows through her body" (74). Though most critics, with the exception of Gelpi (*Shelley's Goddess* 179–81), accept Medwin's claim that Shelley had never heard of mesmerism, or animal magetism, until late 1820 (*Life* 270), Shelley had in fact run across this radical healing method long before: on the pages of Darwin's *The Loves of the Plants* (*Botanic Garden* 15: III. note to line 7) and in his beloved *History of Jacobism*, where the Abbé Barruel vilifies "the *Somnambules*," who built their revolutionary platform on the psuedo-scientific ideas of Mesmer and of his chief disciple, Nicholas Bergasse (II. 452; see also Darnton, *Mesmerism*, 73). For Shelley, mesmerism, in this early lyric as in the 1822 poem, "The Magnetic Lady to her Patient," proves most effective when the healer's "magnetic sweetness" is also "woman sweetness" (*PS*, I, 263).

    73. Another version of the Dedication, intended to introduce the "early wilding flowers" that comprise *The Esdaile Notebook*, reads instead "purer soul" (*PS*, I, 435). In his often incisive commentary on *Queen Mab*, Marlon Ross complains that in the Dedication and in the poem proper, Percy's and not Harriet's "claims and desires" remain central: "Percy needs a woman to represent the ideal he moves toward, the object-goal he desires; Harriet with her 'purer mind,' becomes that ideal, that object-goal in her own poem" (*Contours* 127). Ross's terminology here—Harriet as Percy's "object-goal"—chimes with his thesis that "the drive for masculine self-possession and conquest" had Percy in its thrall, just as it did his fellow male romantics (125). However, where Ross sees Percy as striving to have or *gain* Harriet, I am emphasizing the poet's need to *be* her, an important distinction that reveals Shelley's contours of desire as less conventional, and conventionally masculinist, than Ross believes. That, in either case, the "real" Harriet vanishes from the Dedication and the dream vision itself is not surprising, given that the entire universe is transformed, idealized beyond recognition by poem's end.

    74. This last phrase comes from one of the many letters to Elizabeth Hitchener in which the poet agonized over T. J. Hogg's attempt in the fall of 1811 to seduce Harriet while Percy was away. As the letter at hand reveals, Hogg's "soul appalling fall" dramatically confirmed Shelley's sense that sexual passion and Selfhood were inextricably linked (*L*, I, 141):

> Hogg at length has declared himself to be one of those mad votaries of selfishness who are cool to destroy the peace of others, and revengeful when their schemes are foiled even to idiotism . . . This passion of animal love which has seized him, . . . has intoxicated him, and rendered him incapable of being influenced by any but the consideration of self love. How much worthier of a rational being is *friendship* which tho it wants none of the impassionateness which some have

characterized as the inseparable of the other, yet retains judgement, which is not blind tho it may chance to see something like perfections in its object, which retains it's sensibility but whose sensibility is celestial & intellectual unallied to the grovelling passions of the Earth. (*L*, I, 207, 208: December 15, 1811)

As Shelley obsessed over Hogg's betrayal, he also began contemplating the long, philosophical poem which would become *Queen Mab*. About two weeks after composing the letter just cited, Shelley mentioned this ambitious poem to Miss Hitchener: "Some of the leading passions of the human mind will of course have a place in its fabric. I design to exclude the sexual passion & think the keenest satire on its intemperance will be complete silence on the subject" (*L*, I, 218). Clearly, the Hogg crisis and its aftermath pervaded both the conception and the actual "fabric" of Shelley's poem, and in the final, annotated version of *Queen Mab*, the poet certainly did not maintain this promised silence on the subject of sexual intemperance.

75. Since prostitution was for Shelley, at least at this stage of his development, "the legitimate offspring of marriage," this term preserves its literal meaning in the line just quoted (IX. 87), as well as synecdocally refers to love's imprisonment within and defilement by moral codes and socio-economic systems fueled by selfishness (*PS*, I, 371: Note to "Even love is sold" [*QM*, V. 189]). Commerce, sex, and selfishness form a sinister trio in the devastating fifth canto. Commenting on a key passage in this canto—"Even love is sold . . . / And youth's corrupted impulses prepare / A life of horror from the blighting bane / Of commerce" (V. 189, 192–94)—Crook and Guiton observe, "'Commerce,' while possessing the larger meanings 'any sort of venal transaction,' 'intercourse, chiefly immoral, between the sexes,' was also, in the eighteenth century, a synonym for 'prostitution,' and indeed the general and the specific meanings merge here" (143).

76. In Canto IX, Time is a "hoary giant" who has felt the same death blow as that which Necessity has dealt to selfishness (l. 24). Since Crook and Guiton demonstrated how Shelley uses the image of grey hair to signal venereal disease, it is nearly impossible to see Time's hoary locks as simply the result of old age. See *Shelley's Venomed Melody*, pp. 6, 33, 149–50, 156–70, 191, 214.

77. A letter that Shelley wrote just as he was completing *Queen Mab* provides an excellent gloss on this passage. Writing to Hogg, now tentatively reinstated into the poet's good graces, Shelley briefly discusses the progress and prosody of his long poem, then turns to some of its central themes:

The species of Pride which you love to encourage appears to me incapable of bearing the test of Reason. Now do not tell me that Reason is a cold & insensible arbiter. Reason is only an assemblage of our better feelings, passion considered under a peculiar mode of its operation.—This chivalric Pride altho of excellent use in an age of vandalism & brutality is unworthy of the nineteenth century. A more elevated spirit has begun to diffuse itself which without deducting from the warmth of love or the constancy of friendship reconciles all private feelings to public utility, & scarce suffers true Passion & true Reason to continue at war. Pride mistakes a desire of being esteemed to that of being truly estimable. (*L*, I, 352: 7 February 1813)

Although Shelley does not explicitly gender Pride, Reason, Passion, or the "elevated spirit" itself, the date of this letter suggests that *Queen Mab*'s final cantos and the epistle may have cross-fertilized each other; the verb *diffuse*, for example, connects the letter's "elevated spirit" with Canto VIII's vividly maternal earth, whose "virtues" the "balmy breathings of the wind . . . diffuse . . . all abroad" (ll. 113, 112, 113). Moreover, chivalric Pride, the letter's antithesis to the new, regenerative spirit, resembles the poem's prime exemplars of masculine Selfhood—the monarch in Canto III, Canto VII's Ahasuerus, and Time himself, all wretched in their "lonely pride" (IX. 24).

78. Crook and Guiton's brief comment brings out the erotic dimension of the sisterly exchange: "The 'garland of the strangest flowers' (there are hints here of incest and lesbian love) are sexual delights previously considered unlawful" (144). In the Shelleyan Eden, however, this sensuous sister-love is not only lawful, but also among the highest forms of erotic love. We might recall here the loving sisters whom Shelley imagines tending the Oxford garden that he and Hogg discovered, sisters who "by night . . . cherish each other in the same quiet nest" (Hogg, I, 81).

79. Of course, the human body, like everything else on earth, will first have to encounter the recreating and purifying flame of "consentaneous love" (VIII. 108). Shelley is anxious, in his penultimate canto, to present the body (and the mind) as "taintless": free from the horrid diseases and "evil passions" that selfish man's carnal, and carnivorous, habits have helped instill (VIII. 216). (As Crook and Guiton have shown, Shelley connects meat eating and sexual depravity and disease in the conclusion of *Queen Mab* VIII and in the extensive note that accompanies it. See *Shelley's Venomed Melody*, chap. 5, "Love and Vegetables.")

80. Drawing on theorists such as Lacan, Kristeva, and Daniel Stern, Gelpi demonstrates how various psychoanalytic conceptions of intersubjectivity—the interaction and mutual recognition between self and other(s)—relate to Shelley's own central notion of sympathetic interchange. See especially Gelpi's opening chapter, "Infancy Narratives." Jessica Benjamin's *The Bonds of Love* provides a lucid account of what she calls "the intersubjective view" of the human psyche, a view that "maintains that the individual grows in and through relationships to other subjects" (20–21). Benjamin contrasts this perspective to the "intrapsychic" view, which "conceives of the person as a discrete unit with a complex internal structure" (21).

81. See Deleuze, p. 31.

82. Relevant here would be Marlon Ross's distinction, developed in his chapter on the Shelleys, between masculine rivalry and self-possession, on the one hand, and feminine influence, on the other. See *The Contours of Masculine Desire*, pp. 117–21. While I agree with Ross that "Shelley develops a higher consciousness of feminine influence than his male colleagues," I find little evidence of the "conventionally aggressive masculine gestures" which Ross attributes to the poet (121, 120).

83. Barbara Gelpi's commentary on the "lake-reflected sun" of the fourth Spirit's song (*PU*, I. 744) has helped me see how the earlier version of this image in *Queen Mab* VI vividly recapitulates Ianthe and Mab's intersubjective dynamic. In the

song, a Poet, "Dreaming like a love-adept," will "watch from dawn to gloom / The lake-reflected sun"; as Gelpi observes, this last phrase comprises "one of those many reflexive images in Shelley's work that, it is generally agreed, show his fascination with narcissism" (*PU*, I. 738, 743–44; *Shelley's Goddess* 159):

> It is also typically Shelleyan in its Platonism, though it revises Plato in a significant way. Shelley's poet becomes associated . . . with that Platonic enlightened one in the *Republic* who, climbing painfully out of the cave of common opinion and into the light outside, is able, after further accustoming himself to the light, to look upon the sun "and not mere reflections of him [the sun] in the water" (255). In Shelley's poem, however, the poet appears not to strive for some final, sun-identified transcendence of the human mind's limitations. Instead he rests, lake-identified, at Plato's second-to-last stage, with reflected sun his source of illumination. Metaphorically his situation predicates subjectivity as created by a positive form of narcissism or mirroring which cancels the division between subject and object. It does so not by appropriation of all that is not one into a sun-identified subjectivity but by a dual lake-identified recognition: first each subjectivity is formed through introjection of the "not-me," and second, each subjectivity is also an object to other subjects. (*Shelley's Goddess* 159–60)

For a less peaceful image of the Shelleyan marriage/mirroring of fire and flood, see *Julian and Maddalo*, lines 63–85, where, during an apocalyptic sunset, the sea becomes a vast, destructive "lake of fire" (l. 81). Charles J. Rzepka, who points out the Miltonic allusion here, reads this set-piece as an exposé of Julian's solipsism, a quite different form of narcissism than that which Gelpi discusses: "Julian projects his own soul's millenial desires on forms of earth, sea and sky so blended by the sunset over Venice that the city itself, locus of social change, is not so much transformed as encircled and swallowed up by them, 'Dissolved into one lake of fire'" (130). (Though Rzepka's compelling analysis does not dwell on this point, Shelley's criticisms of Julian and his "sublime" and "sentimental" sunset-building serve as deliberate, and harsh, self-reproaches as well [130].)

84. This lake, then—and Ianthe as its human counterpart—is an early version of *Prometheus Unbound*'s "Sea reflecting Love," the Earth's celebratory metaphor for regenerated Man in *Prometheus Unbound* IV (384).

85. This passage, and the lines from Canto I that it echoes (ll. 28–30), highlights the blend of the spiritual (Henry's "sleepless spirit"), the sensual, and the feminine (Henry's receptive "bosom") which characterizes Shelleyan eros. Ross, who sees "Ianthe's 'influence' on Henry as dubious" and conventionally feminine, notes the hybrid nature of this (erotic) influence: "The emphasis on touch (bosom) and sight (smile) indicates how Ianthe's influence is erratically and suddenly reconstituted as physical effect, as subtle sexual allurement even. Conveniently, she functions dually in the poem: as the spiritualized goal and as the physical reward" (*Contours* 127, 128). However, when we recognize that Ianthe's rapport with her earlier "lover," Mab, has both a spiritual and a physical dimension, we can see that the poem does not suddenly

swerve into the realm of sexuality. Nor does the (anticipated) union of Henry and Ianthe serve "the male's [i.e., Henry's or Shelley's] own overriding claims and desires" (*Contours* 127); feminine-identified Henry will certainly not be acting out some conventional male sexual fantasy when his beloved finally awakens. As Shelleyan sister-spirits, Ianthe and Henry *both* will experience the "joys which mingled sense and spirit yield," and thus both will help inaugurate the reign of feminine Passion (IV. 158; cf. IX. 38–56).

86. Though he does not touch on this passage, Stuart M. Sperry, in his reading of *Queen Mab*, explores Shelley's "continuous fascination with the smile," particularly the "original smile" of the mother for her infant (*Shelley's Major Verse* 5). Particularly appropriate here is Sperry's insight, "The smile was all the more fascinating to [Shelley] because it involved that mirroring effect that was for him so close to the essence of love: the way a mother, in smiling at her infant, intuitively teaches it to smile, unconsciously shaping its features, its powers of responsiveness, by the force of her own charm and protectiveness, even as a greater planet attracts and guides a lesser that comes within its orbit" (5).

87. Cf. I. 94–104.

5. The Unreserve of Mingled Being

1. To be precise, apocalypse and immediate rebirth, rather than malignant mortality, generate the sublime Shelleyan sex scene featuring Earth and Moon.

2. Cameron and Holmes, among others, have made this point. Cameron, for example, offers this dryly incisive remark on a passage from "The Retrospect," which celebrates the couple's "ardent friendship": "Professor White regarded this as a 'glowing tribute to Harriet.' It seems to me, however, as with some of Shelley's other tributes to her, rather tame" (*Esdaile*, Commentaries, 282). See also Holmes, *Pursuit*, pp. 85, 93, 228. In explaining, or justifying, to Harriet and to himself his elopement with Mary Godwin, the poet sets up a rather spurious dichotomy between passion and friendship that nonetheless makes explicit earlier hints that Percy and Harriet lacked sexual chemistry: "Our connection was not one of passion & impulse. Friendship was its basis, & on this basis it has enlarged & strengthened. It is no reproach to me that you have never filled my heart with an all-sufficing passion—perhaps, you are even yourself a stranger to these impulses, which one day may be awakened by some nobler & worthier than me" (*L*, I, 389–90: ?14 July 1814). (Shelley's remark in another letter to Harriet that "I am & will be your friend in every sense of the word but that most delicate and exalted one" is more true to his own ideal of passionate friendship, an ideal that crosses gender boundaries and that merges selfless and erotic love [*L*, I, 404: 5 October 1814].)

3. At another point in her invaluable study, Benjamin points out that Laplanche's "idea of the opposition between Eros and sexuality suggests something similar to Winnicott's distinction between having an interaction with the outside other

and relating to the object as one's mental product—a two-person versus a one-person experience" (69–70). The *Alastor* Poet's communion with his veiled maid springs to mind as an apt case study of the "one-person experience."

4. See also the Wordsworthian lyric "Written on a Beautiful Day in Spring" (1812), in which the speaker enjoys the erotic caresses of "the breathing Earth":

> Sensation all its wondrous rapture brings,
> And to itself not once the mind recurs,
>   Is it a foretaste of Heaven?
> So sweet as this the nerves it stirs,
> And mingling in the vital tide
>   With gentle motion driven
> Cheers the sunk spirits, lifts the languid eye,
> And scattering through the frame its influence wide
> Revives the spirits when they droop and die.

> *(PS*, I, 217)

In a later, similarly themed effusion, however, Shelley finds that human sympathy is essential to such ecstatic communions with nature:

> It is sweet to feel the beauties of nature in every pulsation, in every nerve—but it is far sweeter to be able to express this feeling to one who loves you. To feel all that is divine in the green-robed earth and the starry sky is a penetrating yet vivid pleasure which, when it is over, presses like the memory of misfortune; but if you can express those feelings—if, *secure of sympathy* (for without sympathy it is worse that the taste of those apples whose core is as bitter ashes), if thus secure you can pour forth into another's most attentive ear the feelings by which you are entranced, there is an exultation of spirit in the utterance—a glory of happiness which far transcends all human transports, and seems to invest the soul as the saints are with light, with a halo untainted, holy, and undying. (Clark 337; emphasis mine)

Shelley's yearning for Jane Williams—"Radiant Sister of the day"—may have colored this "Fragment on Beauty," tentatively dated 1821 ("To Jane. The Invitation," l. 47).

5. Paglia, *Sexual Personae*, 376.

6. "[M]an never ceases to be a social being," Shelley writes in the *Discourse on Love*, "The sexual impulse, which is only one, and often a small part of these claims, serves, from its obvious and external nature, as a kind of type or expression of the rest, as common basis, an acknowledged and visible link" (Notopoulos 408–9).

7. Worst of all is the recrimination and sexual disgust that erupts in the middle of *Julian and Maddalo* as the Maniac recalls one of his paramour's venomous outbursts:

> "That you had never seen me—never heard
> My voice, and more than all had ne'er endured
> The deep pollution of my loathed embrace—

That your eyes ne'er had lied love in my face—
That, like some maniac monk, I had torn out
The nerves of manhood by their bleeding root
With mine own quivering fingers, so that ne'er
Our hearts had for a moment mingled there
To disunite in horror—these were not
With thee, like some suppressed and hideous thought
. . . .
Thou sealedst them with many a bare broad word."

(ll. 420–29, 432)

As Holmes writes, "The monologue is saturated with ideas of pathological sexual disturbance: sadistic torture, necrophilia, self-castration, suicide, revulsion from familiarity without love" (*Pursuit* 455). Probably written in the summer of 1819, this passage emerges from the profound crisis in the Shelleys' marriage following the deaths of their children Clara in September 1818, and William in June 1819. Holmes (*Pursuit* 443–47) and Mellor (*Mary Shelley* 141–42) provide astute commentary on Percy's role in Clara's death and on Mary's subsequent withdrawal from him. Guilt-ridden and full of self-loathing, the Maniac may embody Shelley's need to atone for the grief he had caused his "spirit's mate" over the years: "Those who inflict must suffer, for they see / The work of their own hearts and this must be / Our chastisement or recompense" (ll. 337, 482–84).

8. William Ulmer's psychoanalytically influenced reading of *Alastor* offers the best account to date of how the poem, which presents "the sensuous languor of death as consummation," reveals/revels in "the deathliness of human desire" (33, 26).

9. The editors of *The Poems of Shelley* point out that "The Sunset" (February 1816), like *Alastor*, reflects the poet's own brush with death in the spring and summer of 1815, when he believed "that he was dying rapidly of a consumption" (see *PS*, I, 510; quotation from *CW*, I, 198: Mary Shelley's Note on *Alastor*). But, as early lyrics addressed to Harriet Grove and late masterpieces such as *Adonais* and *Epipsychidion* remind us, Shelley did not need a fatal diagnosis from "an eminent physician" to help him imagine his own death (*CW*, I, 198: Mary Shelley's Note on *Alastor*). It is significant that in "The Sunset" Shelley's original name for Isabel was Maria. In their headnote to "The Sunset," Matthews and Everest write that the poem "dramatizes the imagined effect of S.'s death on Mary (the cancelled name of the lady in the MS is Maria)" (*PS*, I, 510). However, when we compare "The Sunset" with, for example, *Rosalind and Helen*, where Mary's fictive surrogate Helen lovingly kills/coalesces with her mate, we recognize Isabel-Maria's active role in her lover's death ("That night the youth and lady mingled lay / In love and sleep—but when the morning came / The lady found her lover dead and cold" [*PS*, I, 511]). "The Sunset"—and Mary herself—thus fits into the poet's pattern of self-dissolution and self-feminization through merger with a sister-spirit examined in my third chapter.

10. One brief passage in *Alastor*, central to the crucial verse paragraph that follows the one recounting the Poet's dream, captures the ambiguity of Shelley's lunar

image, and thus his own ambivalence toward Mary herself: "His wan eyes / Gaze on the empty scene as vacantly / As ocean's moon looks on the moon in heaven" (ll. 200–2). Sperry's comment on these lines is superb:

> The imagery of Narcissus that recurs here ironically inverts the customary play of reference. The reflection of the moon within the ocean gazes back unthinkingly at its heavenly begetter, as if it shared the same reality as its source. From one point of view the Visionary Maiden appears the mere projection of the Poet's imagination. Yet we realize from the blank vacancy of his gaze the truth that he owes his identity—his defining quality of pathos—if not to her influence then to her loss. In such a relationship, which is the reality and which the reflection? (*Shelley's Major Verse* 31).

Though he does not note the biographical implications of the passage, Sperry's analysis helps us see how, in the psychological dynamic Percy set up early on in their relationship, Mary—as moon, maiden, and sister-spirit—serves as her mate's "begetter," preserver, and, when she withdraws, destroyer. We can only imagine the resentment and frustration, for both Shelleys, that this dynamic spawned. (In *Epipychidion*, Shelley makes *Alastor*'s image of the two moons—heaven's and ocean's—explicitly autobiographical: "And all my being beams bright or dim / As the Moon's image in a summer sea, / According as she smiled or frowned on me" [ll. 296–98].)

   11. The poem's final lines emphasize the shallop's moonlike properties:

> . . . even like a sphere
> Hung in one hollow sky, did there appear
> The Temple of the Spirit; on the sound
> Which issued thence, drawn nearer and more near,
> Like the swift moon this glorious earth around,
> The charmed boat approached, and there its haven found.

(CW, I, 408: LC, XII. 364–69)

The boat of rare device that in Canto I carries the poem's original narrator, the mysterious Lady, and the Serpent to the Temple seems to be the same vessel, or at least a similar model. See Canto I, lines 142–44, 197–204.

   12. See *Shelley's Major Verse*, pp. 59–61.

   13. Barbara Gelpi, in her monumental re-reading of the poem, is one of the few recent critics who acknowlege this.

   14. Crook and Guiton remark on the sexual nature of these torments and provide compelling evidence that Shelley meant us to see Jupiter not only as a rapist but also as a syphilitic:

> The vulture sent by Jupiter tears at Prometheus' heart rather than the traditional liver, the change suggestive, in Shelleyan terms, of a shift away from the organs of digestion to those of generation. Another detail not found in Aeschylus is that the vulture's beak is polluted by Jupiter's poisonous saliva. Since Jupiter inflicts dis-

ease through his saliva—known to be one of the body fluids which could spread syphilis—he should be viewed as virulently infectious, like those similar figures, Count Cenci and the tyrant in *Queen Mab*. (*Shelley's Venomed Melody* 188)

Crook and Guiton also point out that the Furies, Jupiter's monstrously virile hags, "are essential to the spread of syphilis in Fracastor [*Syphilis sive Morbus Gallicus*]" (187). With its grotesque image of Jupiter's ravenous vulture hovering over the genitals of the splayed Titan, Henry Fuseli's *Prometheus Rescued by Hercules* (reproduced as the frontispiece of Sperry, *Shelley's Major Verse*) graphically conveys the nightmare of sexual torture that Prometheus undergoes in Shelley's play.

15. Jupiterean electricity has much in common with the devastating fire that Ahasuerus describes in Canto III of *The Wandering Jew*. Destructive, but unfortunately for the death-deprived Ahasuerus, not destructive enough, electricity appears in this poem as "red-hot bolt[s] from God's right hand," "bickering fire," and "torrents of electric flame" that both pierce the sky as lightning and ignite "oceans of volcanic fire" within "Etna's womb" (*PS*, I, 65, 64: *WJ*, III. 793, 785, 767, 770, 765). G. M. Matthews' classic essay, "A Volcano's Voice in Shelley," reminds us that not every "outbreak of 'fire' in Shelley's poetry" is electricity and may in fact be some kind of volcanic activity; but, as the final two quotes from *The Wandering Jew* demonstrate, the poet sometimes fuses electric and volcanic fire. That said, Matthews' essay, which discerns in *Prometheus* more infernal flames than those discovered by Carl Grabo, provides a valuable counterpoint to the earlier critic's rather sunny portrait of Shelleyan electricity. As Matthews states near the end of his piece, "Even [Shelley's] purest flame is apt to have some relish of damnation in it" (129).

16. In *A Newton Among Poets*, Carl Grabo briefly discusses "Shelley's symbolical association of electrical power both with love and with hate," with good and with evil (185, 188).

17. "In the intersubjective interaction," Benjamin writes, "both partners are active; it is not a reversible union of opposites (a doer and a done-to)" (48). Benjamin's analysis of the role of gender within "the dialectic of control" illuminates how Shelley often gets trapped within conventional thinking about passive femininity and active masculinity (53). Eager to distance himself from the aggression and reified identity that he associates with masculinity, he valorizes "feminine" receptivity and selflessness and thus preserves the dangerous oppositional model of (feminine) victim and (masculine) violator.

18. This fantasy has its share of "erotic domination and submission," to borrow Benjamin's phrase. Prometheus envisions Jupiter "kiss[ing] the blood / From these pale feet, which then might trample thee / If they disdained not such a prostrate slave" (I. 50–52). "Pale" is a key adjective in Shelley's erotic vocabulary (see, for example, *Alastor*, line 180; *Laon and Cythna*, VI. 337; *PU*, II. i. 62; *The Sensitive-Plant*, I. 22; and "The Indian Girl's Song," line 20).

19. John Rieder discerns "dark sexual undertones" in Prometheus' and Jupiter's mutual "fixation": "Their emnity is so consuming that it produces a kind of intimacy between them" (779).

20. One passage from the Earth's catalogue of woes closely echoes Eryximachus' account of Pandemian Eros' destructive might:

> ... plague had fallen on man and beast and worm,
> And Famine, and black blight on herb and tree,
> And in the corn and vines and meadow grass
> Teemed ineradicable poisonous weeds
> Draining their growth.

(I. 172–76)

Asia's reference to "the unseasonable seasons" with their "alternating shafts of frost and fire" (II. 52–53), part of Jupiter's pernicious heritage, may derive from Eryximachus' remark that under the dominion of Pandemian love, "each season of the year is impelled towards the other." Cf. the "alternate frost and fire" that Prometheus, in his curse, invites to penetrate him (I. 268).

21. Among recent critics, Crook and Guiton (188–89, 194), Ulmer (80, 82), and Gelpi (*Shelley's Goddess* 150–51, 239–42) provide excellent commentary on these brutally sexual passages, though none of them comments on Prometheus' self-appointed role as venomous rapist who sets the standard for Jupiter's own ravishment/infection of Thetis.

22. In Act IV, Shelley has the Spirits of the human mind link through juxtaposition "Poesy" and Science:

> We come from the mind
> Of human kind
> Which was late so dusk and obscene and blind;
> . . . .
> From the temples high
> Of man's ear and eye,
> Roofed over Sculpture and Poesy;
> From the murmurings
> Of the unsealed springs,
> Where Science bedews his Daedel wings.

(IV. 93–95, 111–16)

23. Rieder provides a succinct summary of the prevailing critical views on pp. 777–78 of his perceptive essay. Sperry locates a number of turning points in the drama's first act and notes that the "mood of the hero as we leave him, far from anticipatory exhilaration, is quiet resignation" (*Shelley's Major Verse* 93). See, *passim*, the chapter that Sperry devotes exclusively to Act I of *Prometheus Unbound* (65–92).

24. Cf. III. iii. 148–52. Carl Grabo was the first to identify the Spirit of the Earth as atmospheric electricity, "which is constantly renewed by a return to its parent—Venus, nature—here personified as Asia" ("Electricity, the Spirit of the Earth" 143).

25. Shelley's references to "ether" in *Prometheus Unbound* draw, for example, on Gilbert's theory of an "incorporeal aether" emanating from the earth's pure mag-

netic core, Newton's notion of an "electric and elastic Spirit" that interpenetrates and vitalizes all bodies, and Berkeley's "pure invisible fire" that "seems to pervade and expand itself throughout the whole universe" (Heilbron 172; Newton cited in Grabo, *A Newton Among Poets*, 98; Berkeley's *Siris* quoted in Curran, *Shelley's Annus Mirabilis*, 107). As Stuart Curran observes, "ether . . . was considered the basic fluid of the universe by Shelley's most ancient as well as most contemporary sources of philosophy" (106). In *Overtures to Biology*, Philip C. Ritterbush examines "the etherial hypothesis" in detail, pointing out that Newton and his followers speculated "that the ether might mediate between soul and body," and resolve "the difference between matter and spirit" (7). This subtle fluid, then, would have appealed to Shelley as he tried to reconcile and even blend spirit and body within his key erotic paradigm of mingled being.

26. Though it does not address this passage, Richard Isomaki's analysis of the "necessary reciprocity of love" in *Prometheus Unbound* illuminates why even Asia's potent "love which is as fire" needs to blend with the flame emitted by her (purified) spouse ("Love as Cause in *Prometheus Unbound*" 669; *PU*, III. iii. 151).

27. The Furies, who darkly parody the lovely Oceanides, are ostensibly feminine, but as emphasized in chapter 2, they in fact play the role of masculine rapists who invade the Titan and "work[. . .] like fire within" (I. 476). The lesson in "loathsome sympathy" and "foul desire" that Prometheus learns from this encounter reminds him that he must wisely choose his "mirroring selfobjects," in Heinz Kohut's terminology (I. 451, 489). The joyous erotic mutuality that the Moon describes in Act IV—"a lover or chameleon / Grows like what it looks upon"—can too easily flip over into the horrific mirroring that Prometheus experiences with Jupiter's hags: "Whilst I behold such execrable shapes, / Methinks I grow like what I contemplate / And laugh and stare in loathsome sympathy" (IV. 483–84; I. 449–51). Gelpi, in her analysis of the maternal in Shelley, links these "two sets of tripartite female figures" with "the Terrible and the Good Mother" (*Shelley's Goddess* 174). Her reading of Act II demonstrates how "Promethean subjectivity . . . , having turned from the Furies, now reflects the Oceanides" (174).

28. See Isomaki, pp. 669–70, and Rieder, pp. 783–84.

29. For Gelpi, modifying and refining William Hildebrand's argument in "Naming Day in Asia's Vale," this dream, and even Act II as a whole, is the Titan's own: "Prometheus is experiencing the waking dream of reverie," writes Gelpi (*Shelley's Goddess* 173). Gelpi's insights into Act II, scene i, have helped me tremendously, but her reading tends to subsume the Oceanides into "the Promethean subjectivity" (177). I want to emphasize not only Prometheus' but also Panthea's and Asia's roles as efficacious, literally influential dreamers.

30. Because he defines "dream" in a limited way, Richard Isomaki believes that since "Panthea hasn't slept in the first act, . . . there is no time during the narrative in which the dream could have happened" ("Love as Cause in *Prometheus Unbound*" 669). Isomaki explains the seemingly fractured time scheme of the first two acts by

suggesting that Shelley "freezes time in the play for the purpose of accomplishing the necessary parallelism of love: that the first two acts may happen, in a sense, simultaneously" (669).

31. If the Furies enact the antimasque, or grotesque prelude to the revels, the Spirits of human thought present the delightful pageantry of the masque proper.

32. Discussing linguistic rather than generic recreations/stimulations of reverie, Gelpi illuminates how, in the opening lines of Act II, Shelley uses "slippages" in language in order "to create reverie, the state that they desribe" (*Shelley's Goddess* 172). "Shelley does not insist on the clear, clean line," writes Gelpi, for he believed "that the mergings and dissolution of reverie serve as legitimate, even privileged loci of moral intuitions" (172).

33. The orgasmic, alchemic liquidity of the dream reflects the liquid imagery of the Act I masque. The Spirits themselves, who inhabit a "liquid lair," enter the stage, or mental theatre, "Like fountain-vapours" (I. 687, 668). Of the "twin nurslings," the fifth and sixth Spirits, Ione exclaims, "their sweet, sad voices! 'tis despair / Mingled with love, and then dissolved in sound," to which Panthea replies "Canst thou speak, sister? all my words are drowned" (I. 756–57). Finally, Prometheus, in the aftermath of the masque/reverie, invokes his beloved Asia, "who when [his] being overflowed / Wert like a golden chalice to bright wine / Which else had sunk into the thirsty dust" (I. 809–11). While the Titan could be recalling a distant memory, he may also be describing how his being overflowed within the passionate dream he just helped create. (In the Act IV masque, all of this vital fluid becomes "Love's sweet rain," purifying and refreshing all life [IV. 179].)

34. Gelpi links this image to the mesmeric "rapport" that Prometheus and Panthea achieve:

> There emanates from Prometheus' body the fluid metonymically ascribed to his "soft and flowing limbs" (II. i. 73). The "vaprous fire" (II. i. 75) issuing from those limbs as well as from his "passion-parted lips, and keen faint eyes" (II. i. 74) renders Panthea at once unconscious and united to the consciousness of her magnetizer . . . (*Shelley's Goddess* 181).

35. I am indebted to an excellent article by Frederic S. Colwell, "Shelley and Italian Painting," which identifies the painting by its correct title.

36. Richard Cronin (145) mentions in passing the connection between the painting and the tranfigured Titan, as does Alan M. Weinberg (128).

37. Stuart Curran (*Shelley's Annus Mirabilis* 39, 46–47, 60), Barbara Gelpi (*Shelley's Goddess, passim*), and Jerrold Hogle (*Shelley's Process* 183–85) provide the most detailed and illuminating accounts of Asia's kinship with the goddess of love and beauty.

38. Shelley also may have based his image of Prometheus as Venus on his own portrait of another Venus figure, Cythna, whom Gelpi calls "avatar of the 'foam-born'"

(*Shelley's Goddess* 129). The poet borrowed much of the imagery and even the language of the Promethean-Oceanidean dream narrative (II. i. 55–131) from the opening stanzas of *Laon and Cythna*, Canto XI (i–vii). One example from this passage, wherein Laon beholds the apotheosized Cythna, will have to suffice:

> Her lips were parted, and the measured breath
> Was now heard there;—her dark and inticate eyes
> Orb within orb, deeper than sleep or death,
> Absorbed the glories of the burning skies,
> Which, mingling with her heart's deep ecstacies,
> Burst from her looks and gestures;—and a light
> Of liquid tenderness like love, did rise
> From her whole frame, an atmosphere which quite
> Arrayed her in its beams, tremulous and soft and bright.

> (*CW*, I, 390: *LC*, XI, 37–45)

As embodiments of the radiant (Uranian) Venus, Cythna and Prometheus each can become a glorious "prophetess of love" (*CW*, I, 370: *LC*, IX, 174).

39. Anxious to preserve Prometheus' Christlike, Asia-like identity, so arduously won, Shelley must assign the role of vindictive revolutionary to Demogorgon, whom Ulmer sees as "a figure of death," Freud's Thanatos (104). Rieder examines in great detail how and why Demogorgon "enact[s] Prometheus' original, 'evil wish'": violently to defeat Jupiter (787).

40. Carl Grabo was the first to see these rolling orbs as electrically charged particles of matter. See "Electricity: The Spirit of the Earth" (145–49) and *A Newton Among Poets* (140–50), where he reveals striking parallels between *Prometheus Unbound* IV. 236–79 and various passages from, for example, Beccaria, (Erasmus) Darwin, and Davy.

41. Anne K. Mellor calls the Spirit "a Cupid-figure linked to his mother Asia/Venus" (*Mary Shelley* 104).

42. Bloom calls this "a very great line indeed," one that introduces "humanistic irony" into the vision of "geometric eternity" that the Oceanides encounter (*Shelley's Mythmaking* 145). As D. J. Hughes observes, Bloom and G. Wilson Knight emphasize "the necessity for the human to intrude itself at this point lest the orb turn into something like the crushing chariot of *The Triumph of Life*" (609). That is a real danger, as both whirling Orb and fierce chariot knead into one mass, be it "aerial" (*Prometheus*) or bloody (*Triumph*), everything in its path (*PU*, IV. 260).

43. Sperry provides a compelling reading of this passage:

> The lines reveal Shelley's knowledge of the geological theories of catastrophic change advanced by Sir Humphry Davy, Erasmus Darwin, Cuvier, and others, in which the earth was seen as having evolved through upheavals or floods caused by planets that periodically destroyed its life . . . Shelley grasped the

evolutionary pattern that the more farsighted of his scientific brethren had begun to perceive, but he put no faith in the "progress" it represented. Nor is there anything perverse in Panthea's breaking off with the specter of cataclysm. The point of the passage is that true worldly rehabilitation can come about only when the earth, and the principles of strife and competition that have brought it to its present pass, have been eradicated. (*Shelley's Major Verse* 123)

In "A Spirit in Search of Itself," Joanna E. Rapf discusses the "awesome account of the birth of the Earth, the *reverse* birth process described by Asia at the end of Act II" (41). At the end of the passage, writes Rapf, "the imperative, 'Be not!' is not annihilation in a negative sense, but . . . the annihilation of the material world and a *rebirth* into a 'diviner day'" (41).

44. Commenting on *Prometheus Unbound*, IV. 440–43, Grabo writes, "The moon is now the bride of the earth and beneath the influence of the earth's 'love'—for which, physically, read electricity, magnetism, gravity, and heat—is blossoming into new life" (*A Newton Among Poets* 160). Richard Isomaki illuminates how Shelley employs the notion of gravitation in the play to represent "love as simultaneous reciprocity" (664). Like Grabo, Isomaki reminds us that "Shelley's assumption of one Power beneath magnetism and gravity was good physics in his day" (666).

45. For example, the Earth compares himself to "a youth lulled in love-dreams, faintly sighing, / Under the shadow of his beauty lying," to which the Moon replies:

> As in the soft and sweet eclipse
> When soul meets soul on lovers' lips,
> High hearts are calm and brightest eyes are dull;
> So when thy shadow falls on me
> Then I am mute and still,—by thee
> Covered; of thy love, Orb most beautiful,
> Full, oh, too full!

(IV. 447–48, 450–56)

46. In "Entering the Stream of Sound" I explain in more detail how Shelley, following his Renaissance predecessors, involves his audience in this masque. Fittingly, it is Panthea, the crucial mediator between Asia and Prometheus in Act II, who most actively participates in the Act IV masque, literally immersing herself in "the stream of sound," and who thus mediates for Shelley's readers, helping us imaginatively enter the pageantry (IV. 505).

47. Another discarded passage reads, "may we meet / In one Elysium or one winding-sheet!" (*CW*, II, 379: "Fragments Connected with *Epipsychidion*"). As presented, both choices seem equally appealing.

48. See *Bodleian I*, pp. 194–95, 200–7, 214–15, 290–91.

WORKS CITED

Abrams, M. H. *Natural Supernaturalism: Tradition and Revolution in Romantic Literature*. New York: W. W. Norton, 1971.

à Kempis, Thomas. *The Imitation of Christ*. Trans. Leo Sherley-Price. London: Penguin, 1952.

Allott, Miriam. *Essays on Shelley*. Liverpool: Liverpool University Press, 1982.

Anderson, G. K. *The Legend of the Wandering Jew*. Providence: Brown University Press, 1965.

Andrews, S. G. "Shelley, Medwin, and *The Wandering Jew*." *Keats-Shelley Journal* 20 (1971): 78–86.

Baker, Carlos. "The Necessity of Love: *Alastor* and the Epipsyche." In Ridenour, *Shelley: A Collection of Critical Essays*. 51–68. Reprinted from *Shelley's Major Poetry: The Fabric of a Vision*. Princeton: Princeton University Press, 1948.

Balint, Michael. "Primary Narcissism and Primary Love." *Psychoanalytic Quarterly* 29 (1960): 6–43.

Barker-Benfield, G. J. *The Culture of Sensibility: Sex and Society in Eighteenth-Century Britain*. Chicago: University of Chicago Press, 1992.

Barnard, Ellsworth. *Shelley's Religion*. New York: Russell & Russell Inc., 1964.

Barruel, L'Abbé Augustin de. *Memoirs, Illustrating the History of Jacobism*. Trans. Robert Clifford. London: T. Burton, 1798.

Barthes, Roland. *A Lover's Discourse: Fragments*. Trans. Richard Howard. New York: Hill and Wang, 1978.

Behrendt, Stephen C. *Shelley and His Audiences*. Lincoln and London: University of Nebraska Press, 1989.

———, ed. *Zastrozzi and St. Irvyne*. By P. B. Shelley. Oxford: Oxford University Press, 1986.

Benjamin, Jessica. *The Bonds of Love: Psychoanalysis, Feminism, and the Problem of Domination*. New York: Pantheon, 1988.

Benjamin, Park. *A History of Electricity from Antiquity to the Days of Benjamin Franklin*. New York: Arno Press, 1975. Reprinted from New York: John Wiley and Sons, 1898.

Bennett, Betty T., and Stuart Curran, eds. *Shelley: Poet and Legislator of the World.* Baltimore and London: The Johns Hopkins University Press, 1996.

Bergmann, Martin S. *The Anatomy of Loving.* New York: Columbia University Press, 1987.

Bieri, James. "Shelley's Older Brother." *Keats-Shelley Journal* 39 (1990): 29–33.

Blake, William. *The Poetry and Prose of William Blake.* Ed. David Erdman. With commentary by Harold Bloom. Garden City, N.Y.: Doubleday, 1965.

Blank, G. Kim, ed. *The New Shelley: Later Twentieth-Century Views.* London: Macmillan, 1991.

Bloom, Harold. *The Anxiety of Influence: A Theory of Poetry.* Oxford: Oxford University Press, 1973.

———. *A Map of Misreading.* Oxford: Oxford University Press, 1975.

———. *The Ringers in the Tower: Studies in Romantic Tradition.* Chicago: University of Chicago Press, 1971.

———. *Shelley's Mythmaking.* Ithaca: Cornell University Press, 1969. Reprinted from Yale University Press, 1959.

Bouson, J. Brooks. *The Empathic Reader: A Study of the Narcissistic Character and the Drama of the Self.* Amherst: University of Massachusetts Press, 1989.

Brown, Nathaniel. *Sexuality and Feminism in Shelley.* Cambridge: Harvard University Press, 1979.

———. Review of *Shelley's Major Verse: The Narrative and Dramatic Poetry.* By Stuart M. Sperry. *Nineteenth-Century Literature* 2 (1989): 240–43.

Burwick, Frederick. "The Language of Causality in *Prometheus Unbound.*" *Keats-Shelley Journal* 31 (1981): 136–58.

Butler, Judith. *Gender Trouble: Feminism and the Subversion of Identity.* New York: Routledge, 1990.

Bynum, Caroline Walker. *Jesus as Mother: Studies in the Spirituality of the High Middle Ages.* Berkeley and Los Angeles: University of California Press, 1982.

Byron, George Gordon, Lord. *Byron's Letters and Journals.* 12 vols. Ed. Leslie A. Marchand. Cambridge: Harvard University Press, 1973–1982.

———. *Don Juan.* Ed. Leslie A. Marchand. Boston: Houghton Mifflin, 1958.

Cafarelli, Annette Wheeler. "The Transgressive Double Standard: Shelleyan Utopianism and Feminist Social History." In Bennett and Curran, *Shelley: Poet and Legislator of the World.* 88–104.

Cameron, Kenneth Neill. "The Planet-Tempest Passage in *Epipsychidion*." In the Norton Critical Edition of *Shelley's Poetry and Prose*. 637–58. Reprinted from *PMLA* 63 (1948): 950–72.

———. *Shelley: The Golden Years*. Cambridge: Harvard University Press, 1974.

———. *The Young Shelley: Genesis of a Radical*. New York: Macmillan, 1950.

Chessick, Richard D. *Psychology of the Self and the Treatment of Narcissism*. Northvale, N.J.: Jason Aronson, 1985.

Chichester, Teddi Lynn. "Entering the Stream of Sound: The Reader and the Masque in Shelley's *Prometheus Unbound*." *Colby Quarterly* 30 (1994): 85–97.

Chodorow, Nancy J. "Family Structure and Feminine Personality." In Rosaldo and Lamphere, *Woman, Culture, and Society*. 43–65.

———. *Feminism and Psychoanalytic Theory*. New Haven: Yale University Press, 1989.

———. *The Reproduction of Mothering: Psychoanalysis and the Sociology of Gender*. Berkeley: University of California Press, 1978.

Christ, Carol. "Victorian Masculinity and the Angel in the House." In Vicinus, *A Widening Sphere*. 146–62.

Cixous, Hélène. "The Laugh of the Medusa." In Marks and de Courtivron, *New French Feminisms*. 245–64.

———. "Sorties." In Marks and de Courtivron. 90–98.

Clark, Timothy, and Jerrold E. Hogle, eds. *Evaluating Shelley*. Edinburgh: Edinburgh University Press, 1996.

Coleridge, Samuel Taylor. *Poetical Works*. Ed. Ernest Hartley Coleridge. Oxford: Oxford University Press, 1912.

Colwell, Frederic S. "Shelley and Italian Painting." *Keats-Shelley Journal* 29 (1980): 43–66.

Corbett, Lionel. "Kohut and Jung: A Comparison of Theory and Therapy." In Detrick and Detrick, *Self Psychology*. 23–47.

Cowper, William. *The Poetical Works*. Ed. H. S. Milford. London: Oxford University Press, 1934.

Cronin, Richard. *Shelley's Poetic Thoughts*. London: Macmillan, 1981.

Crook, Nora, and Derek Guiton. *Shelley's Venomed Melody*. Cambridge: Cambridge University Press, 1986.

Cunningham, Andrew, and Nicholas Jardine, eds. *Romanticism and the Sciences*. Cambridge: Cambridge University Press, 1990.

Curran, Stuart. *Shelley's Annus Mirabilis: The Maturing of an Epic Vision*. San Marino, CA: Huntington Library, 1975.

————. *Shelley's "Cenci": Scorpions Ringed with Fire*. Princeton: Princeton University Press, 1970.

Dacre, Charlotte (Rosa Matilda). *Hours of Solitude* (1805). Two vols. in one. Introduction by Donald H. Reiman. New York: Garland, 1978.

————. *Zofloya; or the Moor* (1806). London: The Fortune Press, 1928.

Darnton, Robert. *Mesmerism and the End of the Enlightenment in France*. Cambridge: Harvard University Press, 1968.

Darwin, Erasmus. *The Botanic Garden, A Poem in Two Parts; Containing The Economy of Vegetation and The Loves of the Plants*. London: Jones & Company, 1824.

Davidoff, Leonore, and Catherine Hall. *Family Fortunes*. London: Hutchinson, 1987.

Delcourt, Marie. *Hermaphrodite: Myths and Rites of the Bisexual Figure in Classical Antiquity*. Trans. Jennifer Nicholson. London: Studio Books, 1961.

Deleuze, J. P. F. *Practical Instruction in Animal Magnetism*. Trans. Thomas C. Hartshorn. New York: Da Capo Press, 1982.

Detrick, Douglas W., and Susan P. Detrick, eds. *Self Psychology: Comparisons and Contrasts*. Hillsdale, N.J.: The Analytic Press, 1989.

Everest, Kelvin, ed. *Shelley Revalued: Essays from the Gregynog Conference*. Leicester: Leicester University Press, 1983.

————. "Shelley's Doubles: An Approach to *Julian and Maddalo*." In *Shelley Revalued*. 63–88.

Fischman, Susan. "'Like the Sound of His Own Voice': Gender, Audition, and Echo in *Alastor*." *Keats-Shelley Journal* 43 (1994): 141–69.

Fitzgerald, F. Scott. *The Great Gatsby*. New York: Scribner's, 1925.

Freeman, John. "Shelley's Early Letters." In Everest, *Shelley Revalued*. 109–28.

Freud, Sigmund. *Civilization and Its Discontents*. Trans. and ed. James Strachey. New York, Norton, 1961.

————. *The Standard Edition of the Complete Works of Freud (SE)*. Trans. and ed. James Strachey et. al. 24 vols. London: Hogarth, 1957.

Fuller, David. "Shelley and Jesus." *Durham University Journal* 85, no. 2 (1993): 211–23.

Gallant, Christine. *Shelley's Ambivalence*. London: Macmillan, 1989.

Gay, Peter. *Freud: A Life for Our Time*. New York and London: Doubleday, 1989.

Gelpi, Barbara Charlesworth. "The Nursery Cave: Shelley and the Maternal." In Blank, *The New Shelley*. 42–63, 249–51.

———. "The Politics of Androgyny." *Women's Studies* 2 (1974): 151–60.

———. *Shelley's Goddess: Maternity, Language, Subjectivity*. New York and Oxford: Oxford University Press, 1992.

Gilbert, Sandra M., and Susan Gubar. *The Madwoman in the Attic: The Woman Writer and the Nineteenth-Century Imagination*. New Haven: Yale University Press, 1979.

Gilligan, Carol. *In a Different Voice: Psychological Theory and Women's Development*. Cambridge: Harvard University Press, 1982.

Godwin, William. *Enquiry Concerning Political Justice and Its Influence on Morals and Happiness*. 3 vols. Ed. F. E. L. Priestley. Toronto: University of Toronto Press, 1946.

———. *Memoirs of the Author of The Rights of Woman*. In Mary Wollstonecraft, *A Short Residence in Sweden, Norway and Denmark*, and William Godwin, *Memoirs of the Author of the Rights of Woman*. Ed. Richard Holmes. Middlesex: Penguin Books, 1987.

Goldberg, Arnold, ed. *Advances in Self Psychology*. New York: International Universities Press, 1980.

Grabo, Carl. "Electricity, the Spirit of the Earth, in Shelley's *Prometheus Unbound*." *Philological Quarterly* 6 (1927): 133–50.

———. *The Magic Plant: The Growth of Shelley's Thought*. Chapel Hill: University of North Carolina Press, 1936.

———. *A Newton Among Poets: Shelley's Use of Science in "Prometheus Unbound."* New York: Gordian, 1968.

Gutschera, Deborah A. "The Drama of Reenactment in Shelley's *The Revolt of Islam*." *Keats-Shelley Journal* 35 (1986): 111–25.

———. "'A Shape of Brightness': The Role of Women in Romantic Epic." *Philological Quarterly* 66 (1987): 87–108.

Harding, Sandra. *The Feminist Question in Science*. Ithaca: Cornell University Press, 1986.

Hawkins, Desmond. *Shelley's First Love*. Great Britain: Kyle Cathie / U.S.A.: Archon Books, 1992.

Hawkins, N., and Associates. *Hawkins' Electrical Dictionary*. New York and London: Theodore Audel & Company, 1910.

Heffernan, James A. W. "*Adonais*: Shelley's Consumption of Keats." *Studies in Romanticism* 23 (1984): 295–315.

Heilbron, J. L. *Electricity in the 17th and 18th Centuries: A Study of Early Modern Physics.* Berkeley and Los Angeles: University of California Press, 1979.

Heilbrun, Carolyn G. *Toward a Recognition of Androgyny.* New York: Harper and Row, 1974. Rpt. from Knopf, 1973.

Hildebrand, William H. "Naming Day in Asia's Vale." *Keats-Shelley Journal* 32 (1983): 190–203.

Hoeveler, Diane Long. *Romantic Androgyny: The Women Within.* University Park and London: Pennsylvania State University Press, 1990.

Hogg, Thomas Jefferson. *The Life of Percy Bysshe Shelley* (1858). In Wolfe. Vols. 1 and 2.

Hogle, Jerrold E. "Shelley's Fiction: The 'Stream of Fate.'" *Keats-Shelley Journal* 30 (1981): 78–99.

———. "Shelley's Poetics: The Power as Metaphor." *Keats-Shelley Journal* 31 (1982): 159–97.

———. *Shelley's Process: Radical Transference and the Development of His Major Works.* Oxford: Oxford University Press, 1988.

Holmes, Richard. "He Doth Not Sleep" (Review of recent Shelley scholarship). *The New York Review of Books* 39 (September 24, 1992): 19–24.

———. *Shelley on Love: An Anthology.* Berkeley: University of California Press, 1980.

———. *Shelley: The Pursuit.* London: Quartet, 1974.

Homans, Margaret. *Bearing the Word: Language and Female Experience in Nineteenth-Century Women's Writing.* Chicago: University of Chicago Press, 1986.

Hughes, A. M. D. *The Nascent Mind of Shelley.* Oxford: Oxford University Press, 1947.

Hughes, D. J. "Potentiality in *Prometheus Unbound*." In Reiman and Powers, *Shelley's Poetry and Prose*, 603–20. Rpt. from *Studies in Romanticism* 2 (1963): 107–26.

Hume, David. *Enquiries Concerning Human Understanding and Concerning the Principles of Morals* (1777). Ed. L. A. Selby-Bigge. 3rd ed. Text revised and notes by P. H. Nidditch. Oxford: Clarendon Press, 1975.

Ingpen, Roger. *Shelley in England: New Facts and Letters from the Shelley-Whitton Papers.* London: Kegan Paul, 1917.

Irigaray, Luce. "This sex which is not one." In Marks and de Courtivron, *New French Feminisms*. 99–106.

Irwin, John T. *Doubling and Incest/Repetition and Revenge: A Speculative Reading of Faulkner.* Baltimore: Johns Hopkins University Press, 1979.

Isomaki, Richard. "Love as Cause in *Prometheus Unbound.*" *Studies in English Literature* 29 (1989): 655–73.

Jones, Steven E. "Shelley's 'Love, the Universe': A Fragment in Context." *Keats-Shelley Journal* 42 (1993): 80–96.

Keats, John. *Complete Poems.* Ed. Jack Stillinger. Cambridge: Belknap Press of Harvard University Press, 1982.

———. *The Letters of John Keats, 1814–1821.* 2 vols. Ed. Hyder Edward Rollins. Cambridge: Harvard University Press, 1958.

Keller, Evelyn Fox. *Reflections on Gender and Science.* New Haven and London: Yale University Press, 1985.

Keppler, C. F. *The Literature of the Second Self.* Tuscon: University of Arizona Press, 1972.

Kierkegaard, Søren. *Training in Christianity.* Trans. Walter Lowrie. Oxford: Oxford University Press, 1941.

King-Hele, Desmond. *Erasmus Darwin and the Romantic Poets.* London: Macmillan, 1986.

Klein, Ralph. "Masterson and Kohut: Comparison and Contrast." In Detrick and Detrick, *Self Psychology.* 311–28.

Kohut, Heinz. *The Analysis of the Self.* New York: International Universities Press, 1971.

———. "Forms and Transformations of Narcissism." *Journal of the American Psychoanalytic Association* 14 (1966): 243–72.

———. *How Does Analysis Cure?* Ed. Arnold Goldberg with the collaboration of Paul Stepansky. Chicago and London: University of Chicago Press, 1984.

———. *The Kohut Seminars.* Ed. Miriam Elson. New York: Norton, 1987.

———. *The Restoration of the Self.* New York: International Universities Press, 1977.

———. "Thoughts on Narcissism and Narcissistic Rage." *The Psychoanalytic Study of the Child* 27 (1972): 360–400.

Korshin, Paul J. *Typologies in England, 1650–1820.* Princeton: Princeton University Press, 1982.

Kristeva, Julia. *Desire in Language: A Semiotic Approach to Literature and Art.* Ed. Léon S. Roudiez. Trans. Alice Jardine, Thomas Gora and Léon Roudiez. New York: Columbia University Press, 1980.

Lawrence, James H. *The Empire of the Nairs; or The Rights of Women: An Utopian Romance* (1811). Delmar, New York: Scholars' Facsimiles & Reprints, 1976.

Lawson, John. *The Wesley Hymns: A Guide to Scriptural Teaching.* Grand Rapids: Francis Asbury Press, 1987.

Layton, Lynne, and Barbara Ann Schapiro, Eds. *Narcissism and the Text: Studies in Literature and the Psychology of the Self.* New York and London: New York University Press, 1986.

Leighton, Angela. "Love, Writing, and Scepticism in *Epipsychidion.*" In Blank, *The New Shelley.* 220–41.

Lentricchia, Frank. *After the New Criticism.* Chicago: University of Chicago Press, 1980.

Lewis, Matthew G. *The Monk.* Oxford: Oxford University Press, 1980.

Lichtenberg, Joseph, Melvin Bornstein, and Donald Silver, eds. *Empathy I.* Hillsdale, N.J.: The Analytic Press, 1984.

Lucretius. *De Rerum Natura.* Trans. W. H. D. Rouse. 2nd ed. Cambridge: Harvard University Press, 1982. (Loeb Classical Library).

———. *(On the Nature of the Universe).* Trans. R. E. Latham. Middlesex, England: Penguin Books, 1985.

Male, Roy R. "Shelley and the Doctrine of Sympathy." *Texas Studies in English* 29 (1950): 183–203.

Marks, Elaine, and Isabelle de Courtivron, eds. *New French Feminisms: An Anthology.* Amherst: University of Massachusetts Press, 1980.

McGann, Jerome J. "'My Brain Is Feminine': Byron and the Poetry of Deception." In *Byron: Augustan and Romantic.* Ed. Andrew Rutherford. London: Macmillan, 1990.

Medwin, Thomas. *The Life of Percy Bysshe Shelley* (1847). Rev. ed. Ed. H. Buxton Forman. London: Oxford University Press, 1913.

Mellor, Anne K. *English Romantic Irony.* Cambridge: Harvard University Press, 1980.

———. *Mary Shelley: Her Life, Her Fiction, Her Monsters.* New York: Methuen, 1988; Routledge, 1989.

———, ed. *Romanticism and Feminism.* Bloomington: Indiana University Press, 1988.

———. *Romanticism and Gender.* New York: Routledge, 1993.

———. Rev. of *Sexuality and Feminism in Shelley.* By Nathaniel Brown. *Criticism* 22 (1980): 178–81.

Merchant, Caroline. *The Death of Nature: Women, Ecology, and the Scientific Revolution*. San Francisco: Harper and Row, 1980.

Meyer, Herbert W. *A History of Electricity and Magnetism*. Norwalk, Conn.: Burndy Library, 1972.

Miller, Jean Baker. *Toward a New Psychology of Women*. 2nd ed. Boston: Beacon Press, 1986.

Milton, John. *The Complete Poems and Major Prose*. Ed. Merritt Y. Hughes. Indianapolis: Bobbs-Merrill, 1957.

Moi, Toril. *Sexual/Textual Politics: Feminist Literary Theory*. London: Methuen, 1985.

Morrison, Karl F. *"I Am You": The Hermeneutics of Empathy in Western Literature, Theology, and Art*. Princeton: Princeton University Press, 1988.

Murray, E. B. "'Elective Affinity' in *The Revolt of Islam*." *Journal of English and Germanic Philology* 67 (1968): 570–85.

Myers, Mitzi. "Reform or Ruin: 'A Revolution in Female Manners.'" *Studies in Eighteenth-Century Culture* 11 (1982): 192–216. Rpt. in the Norton Critical Edition of Mary Wollstonecraft, *A Vindication of the Rights of Woman*. 328–43.

Notopoulos, James A. "The Dating of Shelley's Prose." *PMLA* 58 (1943): 477–98.

Orgel, Stephen, ed. *Ben Jonson: The Complete Masques*. New Haven: Yale University Press, 1969.

———. *The Illusion of Power: Political Theater in the English Renaissance*. Berkeley: University of California Press, 1975.

Paglia, Camille. *Sexual Personae: Art and Decadence from Nefertiti to Emily Dickinson*. New York: Vintage Books, 1991. Rpt. from Yale University Press, 1990.

Paine, Thomas. *The Complete Writings*. 2 vols. Ed. Philip S. Foner. New York: Citadel Press, 1945.

Peacock, Thomas Love. *Memoirs of Shelley* (1858–62). In Wolfe. Vol. 2.

Peel, Robert. *Mary Baker Eddy: The Years of Discovery*. New York: Holt Rinehart and Winston, 1966.

Plato. *The Collected Dialogues*. Ed. Edith Hamilton and Huntington Cairns. Bollingen Series LXXI. Princeton: Princeton University Press, 1961.

Poovey, Mary. *The Proper Lady and the Woman Writer: Ideology as Style in the Works of Mary Wollstonecraft, Mary Shelley, and Jane Austen*. Chicago: University of Chicago Press, 1984.

Pope, Alexander. *The Poems of Alexander Pope*. Ed. John Butt. London: Methuen, 1963.

Prickett, Stephen, ed. *The Romantics*. London: Methuen, 1981.

———. "The Religious Context." In Prickett, *The Romantics*. 115–63.

Rajan, Tilottama. "Promethean Narrative: Overdetermined Form in Shelley's Gothic Fiction." In Bennett and Curran, *Shelley: Poet and Legislator of the World*. 240–52.

Rank, Otto. *The Double*. Trans. and ed. Harry Tucker, Jr. New York: New American Library, 1971.

Rapf, Joanna E. "A Spirit in Search of Itself: Non-Narrative Structure in Act IV of Shelley's *Prometheus Unbound*." *Keats-Shelley Memorial Bulletin* 30 (1979): 36–47.

Reed, Gail S. "The Antithetical Meaning of the Term 'Empathy' in Psychoanalytic Discourse." In Lichtenberg, Bornstein, and Silver, *Empathy I*. 7–24.

Reiman, Donald H. *Percy Bysshe Shelley* (Updated Edition). Boston: Twayne Publishers, 1990.

Rich, Adrienne. *Adrienne Rich's Poetry*. Ed. Barbara Charlesworth Gelpi and Albert Gelpi. New York: Norton, 1975.

Richardson, Alan. "The Dangers of Sympathy: Sibling Incest in English Romantic Poetry." *Studies in English Literature* 25 (1985): 737–54.

———. "Romanticism and the Colonization of the Feminine." In Mellor, *Romanticism and Feminism*. 13–25.

Richardson, Donna. "'The Dark Idolatry of Self': The Dialectic of Imagination in Shelley's *Revolt of Islam*." *Keats-Shelley Journal* 40 (1991): 73–98.

Ridenour, George M., ed. *Shelley: A Collection of Critical Essays*. Englewood Cliffs, N.J.: Prentice-Hall, 1965.

Rieder, John. "The 'One' in *Prometheus Unbound*." *SEL* 25 (1985): 775–800.

Ritterbush, Philip C. *Overtures to Biology: The Speculations of the Eighteenth-Century Naturalists*. New Haven and London: Yale University Press, 1964.

Robinson, Charles E. *Shelley and Byron: The Snake and Eagle Wreathed in Fight*. Baltimore: Johns Hopkins University Press, 1976.

Rogers, Robert. *A Psychoanalytic Study of the Double in Literature*. Detroit: Wayne State University Press, 1970.

Rosaldo, Michelle Zimbalist, and Louise Lamphere, eds. *Woman, Culture, and Society*. Stanford: Stanford University Press, 1974.

Ross, Marlon B. *The Contours of Masculine Desire: Romanticism and the Rise of Women's Poetry*. Oxford: Oxford University Press, 1989.

————. "Shelley's Wayward Dream-Poem: The Apprehending Reader in *Prometheus Unbound*." *Keats-Shelley Journal* 36 (1987): 110–33.

Rousseau, G. S. "Nerves, Spirits, and Fibres: Towards Defining the Origins of Sensibility." *Studies in the Eighteenth Century III: Papers Presented at the Third David Nichol Smith Memorial Seminar.* Ed. R. F. Brissenden and J. C. Eade. Toronto: University of Toronto Press, 1976.

Rubin, Jane. "Narcissism and Nihilism: Kohut and Kierkegaard on the Modern Self." In Detrick and Detrick, *Self Psychology.* 131–50.

Ryan, Robert. *Keats: The Religious Sense.* Princeton: Princeton University Press, 1976.

Rzepka, Charles. "*Julian and Maddalo* as Revisionary Conversation Poem." In Blank, *The New Shelley.* 128–49, 255.

Schapiro, Barbara A. *The Romantic Mother: Narcissistic Patterns in Romantic Poetry.* Baltimore: Johns Hopkins University Press, 1983.

Seed, David. "Shelley's 'Gothick' in *St. Irvyne* and After." In Allott, *Essays on Shelley.* 39–70.

Shakespeare, William. *The Complete Works.* 3rd ed. Ed. David Bevington. Glenview, Ill.: Scott, Foresman and Company, 1980.

Shelley, Mary Wollstonecraft. *Frankenstein, or, The Modern Prometheus* (The 1818 text). Ed. James Rieger. Chicago: University of Chicago Press, 1982.

Sinfield, Alan. *The Wilde Century: Effeminacy, Oscar Wilde and the Queer Moment.* New York: Columbia University Press, 1994.

Soloway, R. A. *Prelates and People: Ecclesiastical Social Thought in England, 1783–1852.* London: Routledge and Kegan Paul, 1969.

Spenser, Edmund. *The Faerie Queene.* Ed. A. C. Hamilton. London: Longman, 1977.

Sperry, Stuart M. "The Sexual Theme in *The Revolt of Islam.*" *JEGP* 82 (1983): 32–49.

————. *Shelley's Major Verse: The Narrative and Dramatic Poetry.* Cambridge: Harvard University Press, 1988.

Spinoza, Baruch. *Tractatus Theologico-Politicus* (1670; Gebhardt Edition, 1925). Trans. Samuel Shirley. Leiden: E. J. Brill, 1989.

Stevens, Wallace. *The Palm at the End of the Mind: Selected Poems and a Play.* Ed. Holly Stevens. New York: Vintage, 1972.

Tennyson, Hallam, Lord. *Alfred, Lord Tennyson; a Memoir by His Son.* 2 vols. bound in one edition. New York: Macmillan, 1905.

Thorslev, Peter L., Jr. "Incest as Romantic Symbol." *Comparative Literature Studies* 2 (1965): 41–58.

Trelawny, Edward John. *Recollections of the Last Days of Shelley and Byron.* In Wolfe. Vol. 2.

Tymms, Ralph. *Doubles in Literary Psychology.* Cambridge: Bowes and Bowes, 1949.

Ulmer, William A. *Shelleyan Eros: The Rhetoric of Romantic Love.* Princeton: Princeton University Press, 1990.

Veeder, William. *Mary Shelley and "Frankenstein": The Fate of Androgyny.* Chicago: University of Chicago Press, 1986.

Vicinus, Martha, ed. *A Widening Sphere: Changing Roles of Victorian Women.* Bloomington: Indiana University Press, 1977.

Walker, Adam. *A System of Familiar Philosophy.* 2 vols. London: T. Davison, 1802.

Wasserman, Earl R. *Shelley: A Critical Reading.* Baltimore: Johns Hopkins University Press, 1971.

Weinberg, Alan M. *Shelley's Italian Experience.* London: Macmillan, 1991.

White, Newman Ivey. *Shelley.* 2 vols. New York: Knopf, 1940.

———, ed. *The Unextinguished Hearth: Shelley and His Contemporary Critics.* Durham, N.C.: Duke University Press, 1938.

Witherspoon, Alexander M., and Frank J. Warnke, eds. *Seventeenth-Century Prose and Poetry.* 2nd ed. New York: Harcourt Brace Jovanovich, 1982.

Wolfe, Ernest. "On the Developmental Line of Selfobject Relations." In Goldberg, *Advances in Self Psychology.* 103–14.

Wolfe, Humbert, ed. *The Life of Percy Bysshe Shelley, as Comprised in "The Life of Shelley" by Thomas Jefferson Hogg, "The Recollections of Shelley & Byron" by Edward John Trelawny, "Memoirs of Shelley" by Thomas Love Peacock.* 2 vols. London: Dent, 1933.

Wollstonecraft, Mary. *A Vindication of the Rights of Woman* (1792 text). 2nd ed. Ed. Carol H. Poston. New York: Norton, 1988.

Yeats, William Butler. *Essays and Introductions.* New York: Collier Books, 1961.

———. *The Poems of W. B. Yeats.* Ed. Richard J. Finneran. New York: Macmillan, 1983.

Zimansky, Curt R. "Shelley's *Wandering Jew*: Some Borrowings from Lewis and Radcliffe." *Studies in English Literature* 18 (1978): 597–609.

INDEX

Abernethy, John, 128
affect attunement, 160–61
affective spirituality, 20
affinitive attraction, 269–70n.12
à Kempis, Thomas: *The Imitation of Christ*, 23, 209n.53
androgyny, 107, 260n.98
antitype, 22, 87, 115, 137–38, 209n.52, 245n.21, 263–64n.123, 273n.31. *See also* prototype
audience, 237n.98

Barker-Benfield, G. J., 20, 55–56, 83, 103
Barthes, Roland, 22
Behrendt, Stephen, 4, 24
Benjamin, Jessica, 169, 191; *The Bonds of Love,* 179
Bloom, Harold, 1, 3–4
Boinville, Harriet, 125
Booth, Isabella Baxter, 104
Brown, Nathaniel, 85, 107
Buber, Martin, 1, 3–4
Bynum, Carol, 20

Cameron, Kenneth Neill, 12, 16, 80, 104
Chodorow, Nancy, 7, 92
Christ, 53; as idealized selfobject, 14–17, 21, 23, 32, 43, 57, 58, 83, 211n.59; correspondences with the Wandering Jew, 34–40, 63; feminized, 8, 19, 20, 82, 101, 186–89, 207n.42, 257–58n.75; Shelley's attempts to mold, 19–20; Shelley's hostility toward, 5, 13–14, 18, 21, 23, 25–26, 28, 30–31, 35–36, 38, 49, 98, 214n.75; Shelley's identification with, 4–5, 16–21, 35–36, 42, 82–83,

198n.1, 205n.27, 213n.68; Shelley's regeneration of, 40–44
Christianity, Shelley's views of, 11–14, 25, 26, 100, 198n.1, 214n.75
Clairmont, Claire, 125
Clark, David Lee, 11
Coleridge, Samuel Taylor, 94
contamination/contagion, 7–8, 65, 66–67, 88, 93–94, 95, 137, 154, 157, 255n.65, 277n.57
Correggio: *The Saviour,* 186–89
corruption. *See* contamination/contagion
Crook, Nora, 143, 171
Curran, Stuart, 238n.105

Darwin, Erasmus, 132, 177
death, 32, 34, 59, 60, 99–100, 105, 112, 115, 121, 148, 155, 169, 170; and sexual union, 175; of Shelley's children, 77, 118, 178, 236–37n.96
deer, Shelley's self-image as, 81–83, 243–44n.11
deism, 13, 25–26, 204–05n.27
Deleuze, J. P. F., 162, 254n.59
Doppelgänger, 6–7, 8, 29, 45–46, 48, 49, 51, 52, 53–54, 56–57, 61, 64, 67, 71, 76, 77, 90, 219n.1, 229n.57, 230n.62, 233n.81, 236–37n.96
doubling. *See* second self and *Doppelgänger*
dreams, 63–66, 111–12, 143, 153, 155, 183–84, 188–89, 190, 191

effeminacy, 19, 103, 207n.42, 208n.44, 245n.22
electricity, 179, 183, 186, 193, 280–81n.72, 289n.15; as sexual energy, 9–10, 129–30, 132, 173, 181;

DATE DUE

FEB 1 9 1999	

UPI 261-2505 G   PRINTED IN U.S.A.